AN INTRODUCTION TO PROGI

THE McGRAW-HILL INTERNATIONAL SERIES IN SOFTWARE ENGINEERING

Consulting Editor

Professor D. Ince
The Open University

Titles in this Series

SSADM: A Practical Approach	Ashworth and Goodland
SSADM Version 4: A User's Guide 2/e	Eva
An Introduction to SSADM Version 4	Ashworth and Slater
Object-Oriented Databases:	
Applications in Software Engineering	Brown
Object-Oriented Software Engineering with C++	Ince
Introduction to Software Project Management and Quality	
Assurance	Ince, Sharp and Woodman
Software System Development: A Gentle Introduction	Britton and Doake
Introduction to VDM	Woodman and Heal
Discrete Event Simulation in C	Watkins
Objects and Databases	Kroha
Object-Oriented Specification and Design with C++	Henderson
Software Engineering Metrics	
Volume 1: Measures and Validation	Shepperd
Software Tools and Techniques for Electronic Engineers	Jobes
Reverse Engineering and Software Maintenance:	
A Practical Approach	Lano and Haughton
Coding in Turbo Pascal	Sargent
A Primer on Formal Specification	Turner and McCluskey
Specification and Design of Concurrent Systems	Mett, Crowe and Strain-Clark
Introducing Specification Using Z	Ratcliff
A Programming Approach to Formal Methods	Casey
An Introduction to Formal Specification with Z and VDM	Sheppard
Provably Correct Systems	He Jifeng
Safer C	Hatton
System Requirements Engineering	Loucopoulos and Karakostas
Developing Object-Oriented Data Structures Using C++	McMonnies and McSporran
People and Project Management for IT	Craig and Jassim
Concurrent Systems: Formal Development in CSP	Hinchey and Jarvis
Standardizing SSADM	Bryant

Further titles in this Series are listed at the back of the book

AN INTRODUCTION TO PROGRAM DESIGN

David Sargent
Senior Lecturer
The Open University

McGRAW-HILL BOOK COMPANY

London · New York · St Louis · San Francisco · Auckland · Bogotá · Caracas
Lisbon · Madrid · Mexico · Milan · Montreal · New Delhi · Panama
Paris · San Juan · São Paulo · Singapore · Sydney · Tokyo · Toronto

Published by
McGRAW-HILL Book Company Europe
SHOPPENHANGERS ROAD · MAIDENHEAD · BERKSHIRE · SL6 2QL · ENGLAND
TELEPHONE 01628 23432   FAX: 01628 770224

British Library Cataloguing in Publication Data
Sargent, David
    An introduction to program design. – (The McGraw-Hill international series in
    software engineering)
    1. Computer systems. Programming
    I. Title
    005.1
    ISBN 0–07–707246–4

Library of Congress Cataloging-in-Publication Data
Sargent, David
    An introduction to program design/David Sargent.
       p.   cm. – (McGraw-Hill international series in software engineering)
    Includes bibliographical references and index.
    ISBN 0–07–707246–4
    1. Electronic digital computers – Programming.   I. Title.
  II. Series.
  QA76.6.S2654   1991
  005.1'2—dc20   90-46882
                                                               CIP

McGraw-Hill

A Division of The McGraw·Hill Companies

56CL96

Typeset by the author

Printed in England by Clays Ltd, St Ives plc

Printed on permanent paper in compliance with ISO Standard 9706

For Jean, Kate and Ian

CONTENTS

PREFACE

This book is aimed at the novice student of Computing Science and the reader is assumed to have had no previous exposure to computer programming or design. The book emphasizes design principles and a methodical approach to problem solving for program design. Thus a major objective is to teach readers how to write good designs from which they can develop good programs.

Audience The audience for this book is expected to be people who have a need to solve problems using a computer programming language. A fundamental skill that is required before any computer program can be written is the ability to design a solution to the posed problem. Designing a solution to some problem specification is recognized as the most time-consuming part of the development of a piece of software. It is therefore quite remarkable that very few texts are exclusively devoted to this design phase. This book aims to rectify this deficiency.

Although the majority of readers will be pursuing a study of computing science and programming, the content of the book is applicable to others, in particular, those who are dealing with commercial software packages, such as spreadsheets and databases. Many of these packages now support some form of programming and so design skills are required by their users if such packages are to be exploited to their full potential.

Organization of the chapters Chapters 1 to 8 comprise the foundations of the design methods in the book. They introduce standard variable types and the design language in which a solution is expressed. Chapter 1 gives some background to an approach to software development and gives a brief account of one model of the software engineering life cycle. This sets into context the design phase of the development of a piece of software and it identifies more precisely the scope of the book. In particular, it emphasizes that we shall not be concerned with programming and hence will not be learning a programming language. In Chapter 2 the process of problem solving is begun by providing a framework on which all solutions will be based. We hope the framework developed in this chapter will enable readers to master the technique of problem solving. It consists of four activities: understand the problem, devise a solution, test the design and document the solution. It is in this chapter that a start is made to introduction of the design language. The approach to design used throughout the book is one of modularization with top down design, each level of design being refined in a stepwise manner. Chapters 3 to 8 then develop and expand on the initial ideas, leading to the technique of breaking down larger problems into related subtasks which are designed as procedures or functions.

Chapter 9 forms a break and gives the reader a chance to practise the skills taught in the context of a more substantial problem than was appropriate up to this stage.

Chapters 10 to 15 are paced much faster than the earlier ones and it is assumed by this stage that readers are quite comfortable with the process of design. These chapters introduce the idea of an abstract data type. Chapter 10 looks at a problem which arose earlier in the book and takes a more sophisticated approach to its solution by defining an abstract data type. Thereafter, structures which are familiar in most introductory texts are encountered. The final chapter is concerned with recursion and several of the designs given earlier are expressed recursively.

Exercises There are many exercises within the text which the reader must tackle. The book is written in a way which encourages the reader to participate in the process of design. Design skills are not learnt by reading designs written by others but by writing designs for yourself. Hence the book is problem-based and you are expected to attempt every exercise. If you get stuck then the solutions are so structured that you can read part of them and then try again. If these hints fail to get you going then you can try reading the top level designs which are contained in the solution to all the early problems. We hope that by breaking down the solutions in this way you will be encouraged to *do* rather than just read. You must always read the solution to an exercise, even if you have every confidence that your own solution is correct. This is because new ideas are sometimes introduced by way of the solution. All but the most trivial exercise will have many valid solutions and it would be impossible to give them all. Your solution may therefore not be the same as that given in the text and may even be preferable to it! What you must do with all designs is to test that they perform as specified. You will find that all solutions contain test data, or suggestions for its generation, against which your design should be validated.

Problems Most chapters have at least one problem section, the purpose of which is to give you the opportunity of getting additional practice at the topics introduced previously. Most of the problems are derived from *real* situations, sometimes simplified for the text, but do bear in mind that only the skills taught up to that problem section will be required in their solution. Often this will mean that the specification of the problem has to be simplified and occasionally you may feel the result is a little unrealistic.

Exercise and problem scenarios As most of the exercises and problems are based on simplified versions of real situations there may be occasions where the setting is unfamiliar to you. For example, many sports now provide complex statistics for use by television companies as captions. Several examples like this are to be found in the book and you may be put off by seeing a problem which involves a sport with which you are not familiar, or a financial problem expressed in an unfamiliar currency. Their inclusion is deliberate because a professional software engineer is most unlikely to be familiar with the details of the system she or he is working on. What is important is that the problem is stated in a clear and unambiguous way so that the software engineer has all the necessary facts and rules which will enable a solution to be developed. The difficulties of formal specification are beyond the scope of this book but we hope that by giving you clear descriptions of what is required you can solve problems in subject areas which are totally alien to you.

Several examples are concerned with currency, of which two types are used. These are pounds and pence or dollars and cents. The notation £1.53 denotes 1 pound and 53 pence and there are 100 pence in a pound. Similarly, $2.75 represents 2 dollars and 75 cents and there are 100 cents in a dollar. The symbols p and ¢ will be used to denote pence and cents respectively. For example, 63p is equivalent to £0.63 and 73¢ is equivalent to $0.73.

Solutions All the problems and exercises in the book have full solutions. It would be impossible to cover all possible approaches but we occasionally give more than one solution, particularly in the early chapters of the book. Only the design constructs that have been taught up to the occurrence of a problem will be used in its solution. This means that there are often better or more elegant solutions, but they tend to require more advanced techniques.

The design language By using its own design language the book avoids problems associated with the detailed syntax knowledge that is required when using a programming language. The design language has close similarities with constructs to be found in Pascal, Modula-2 and ADA and a summary of its main constructs can be found in the Appendix but no attempt has been made to express them formally. This would be inappropriate for an introductory book and would be the subject of a formal methods course in a more advanced text.

Assumed knowledge No previous knowledge of design or programming is assumed. However, it is assumed that the reader is familiar with the major hardware components of a simple computer system. In particular, knowledge that data can be entered via a keyboard is required, as is some experience of what output looks like on the screen. An intuitive idea of a **file** on a floppy disk will also be useful but detailed knowledge of files is neither required nor taught. Certainly readers who have used a word processor or some other similar commercial piece of software in a personal computer should have every confidence to start reading this book.

1

INTRODUCTION

In the first section of this chapter we shall try to put into context the subject matter of this book. Software design is not usually something which is carried out by a single individual working in isolation. It is not uncommon to find computer applications which require thousands of program statements. The implication of this is that the development and continued running of computer programs is a sizable task involving many people. There are many stages to the development cycle of the software production and it is this that we will attempt to describe. Within this description will be found the design phase, which is the subject of this text.

Inevitably the description will contain a large number of technical terms which you are not expected to commit to memory. We would hope that you can read this section very quickly and yet get a flavour for the complexities involved in a large software project. Do not get bogged down in this section; if you find all the terminology too confusing go on to Section 1.2.

1.1 SOFTWARE ENGINEERING

Many large pieces of software are now created using an engineering approach which can be viewed as a multi-stage process in which the output from one stage becomes the input to the next. The process is often referred to as the **software engineering life cycle**. Figure 1.1 shows a very simplified version of the cycle.

The reason that we have called it a simplified version is that the cycle may sometimes be more complex than that given here. However this simple description will serve our purpose. The way in which the cycle is depicted here makes it apparent that there are a number of consecutive phases that are carried out through time: requirements analysis, design, implementation and maintenance. Associated with the beginning of each phase is the introduction of a set of documents: the user requirements document, specification of requirements, design documentation and program documentation. We shall give a very brief account of each of the phases and documents that appear in Figure 1.1.

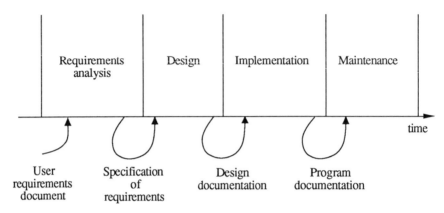

Figure 1.1 The software engineering life cycle

The majority of programs are written for individuals or institutions by computer professionals. For ease of description we shall call the individuals or institutions who use or who are responsible for commissioning a piece of software, **users**.

1.1.1 User requirements document

The cycle commences with the user requirements document. This document should state what is required of the software and is passed to the department or company whose task it will be to create the finished product. Typically such a document will include a number of statements which describe what the software is to do.

For example, a requirement may be that the proposed software should allow the prices of items on sale in a shop to be updated. A statement such as this is called a **functional requirement**. Usually the requirements document will also include some **non-functional requirements**. They take the form of constraints on the system. An example might be that the price update must be done using the bar code on the item whose price is to be updated.

1.1.2 Requirements analysis

The requirements analysis stage is a period when the user is frequently consulted by a computer professional called an **analyst**. The original user requirements are examined by the analyst and are tested for contradictions, ambiguities and internal inconsistencies. In particular the functional and non-functional requirements will have to be identified. The requirements are refined and discussed until the user and the analyst are in agreement as to what the new software should do. There are many techniques for determining the requirements of a system. These include:

- *Interviewing* – Staff who are working with a manual system which is being replaced will need to be interviewed to ascertain what paper work is currently generated and processed.
- *Observation* – This is another technique where the staff are observed so that their current working practices can be analysed.
- *Questionnaires* – Staff may be asked to complete questionnaires related to existing working practices. This may involve details concerning manuals, procedures and rule books.

The outcome after all this consultation will be the **specification of requirements document** which will be the agreed statement between the user and the professional of the software's objectives. It will be from this document that the software will be designed. There is a dichotomy here in that an unambiguous statement of objectives requires the use of specialist language, but at the same time the user has to be able to understand the specification. This is because the specification is effectively a contract between the user and the software developers. Should any problems or disputes arise, it is the specification which should be consulted to resolve them. A satisfactory language for specification has never been found, nor is it likely that one will be, given the fact that it would be trying to satisfy the needs of technical and lay people simultaneously. What must be understood is that the designer must not stray from the specification. The document therefore has a dual role; firstly as a contract between analyst and user and secondly as the starting point for the next phase of the cycle, the design phase. A very simplified version of the specification of requirements document might include sections with the following headings:

1. Introduction
2. Functional requirements
3. Non-functional requirements
4. Quality assurance
5. Maintenance specification

Quality assurance will include a description of the testing procedures whereby the software will be tested and the criteria by which it will be acceptable to the customer. We discuss maintenance below.

In this book we shall treat the statement of the exercises and problems as specifications. By and large they will be written in English. As will become clear this can often lead to some rather long descriptions of what is required since English tends to lack the precision of, say, the language of mathematics and writing unambiguous statements can require a lot of words.

1.1.3 Design

This stage of the cycle involves taking the specification and designing solutions to the problems contained therein. To do this the designer needs to adopt a design **strategy**. It is the design of problems on which we shall concentrate in this book. The outcome of this stage is clearly a design but there should also be some documentation. Typically there is a **systems manual** which is a detailed guide as to how the design was achieved. It is this manual which would be used should changes be required to the system once it is installed. In addition a **user manual** is often written at this stage. This document is intended as a reference for people who will use the system. It may well be that users of the system are not familiar with machines and so this document has to be pitched at the level for the intended users. It may well be accompanied by a tutorial guide which could be text or another piece of software.

1.1.4 Implementation

This is the process of converting a design into a programming language. Beginners and impatient programmers often start the software development process at this point, but the lack of a suitable program structure in the form of a design will inevitably lead to a lot of wasted time and to many unsound programs. A major objective of this book is to encourage good design practice, for only with good designs can reliable and easily maintained software be developed. It is for this reason that we deliberately do not code any of the designs. We want you to concentrate on learning the process of design, not on getting to grips with things like the syntax of some programming language. We shall, however, borrow some of the terminology of programming languages. Thus we shall sometimes refer to designs as programs.

1.1.5 Maintenance

Several topics are covered by this rather vague title. When designs have been coded there is a validation phase which aims to detect and correct any errors in the programs. It must be confirmed that the programs produce the expected output and so match the specification. Program maintenance continues throughout the life of a piece of software. This is not because new errors keep on being discovered but because once the system is installed users tend to ask for modifications and enhancements. This may involve extending the existing software or completely redesigning parts of it. This process of refining and improving is not restricted to purpose-built software but can be witnessed with software packages like word processors, spreadsheets and databases. Successful packages of these types are constantly being updated and improved, each new update being accompanied by a new version number.

That completes this rather brief introduction to the software life cycle, but why is it called a cycle? The reason is that Figure 1.1 makes it look as if the output of one stage becomes the input to the next stage of the cycle. While this is generally the case there is also a substantial amount of **feeding back** from later stages to earlier ones. For example, issues may come to light at the design stage which identify problems arising from requirements analysis. These problems would be fed back and might cause the specification of requirements to be updated or modified. Figure 1.2 reflects this feeding back process, which will often take the form of queries being sent back to an earlier stage.

This more detailed model will not be pursued, but the need for feedback occurs for example when a specification is unclear and this only becomes apparent when detailed design begins.

Finally the model of the software engineering process that we have introduced here is not the only one which is currently practised. Other models exist which may have fewer or more stages than we have shown, but most software developers would be reasonably happy with the model presented here.

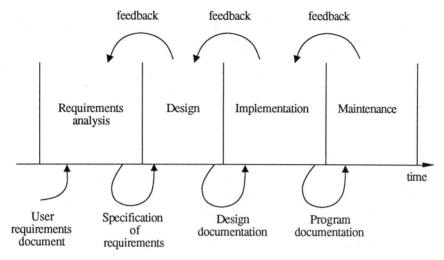

Figure 1.2 Modified life cycle

1.2 THE LANGUAGE OF DESIGN

We believe that designing is not a skill that can be learned by reading about it, rather it must be done. Thus this book contains a large number of design problems which you should attempt to solve. Most designs can be accomplished in a variety of different ways but for all the problems in the book we have provided at least one solution. The book is structured in such a way that design techniques are introduced gradually, as are the data structures which are manipulated within them. It is intended that students new to design read the book sequentially. Experienced designers may use the book as a source of examples, but as the language in which we express our solutions is developed progressively, these details will need to be retrieved from the appropriate chapters or by consulting the appendix.

The language in which solutions to problems are expressed is called **design language** or **pseudocode**. The use of the word pseudocode is supposed to convey that the language is like a programming language but does not have to conform to the strict (syntax) rules of a programming language. In other words design language bridges the gap between normal language and the computer language understood by a particular machine. As we shall see, our design language is a combination of ordinary language and the basic elements of many structured programming languages. It will allow the program designer to concentrate on the problem to be solved and to express that solution in a logical way without having to be concerned with things like syntax, reserved words or individual language restrictions. The style of the statements in designs is such that it would be possible to code them in a variety of languages with minimal effort. Inevitably this has lead to some compromises and therefore some deficiencies, but we hope that its use encourages good design practice and leads to programs which are clear, easily understood and are maintainable. Features of the design language include:

- *Numbering* – Each statement of a design will have a number associated with it. These numbers are not part of the design itself but they have two important purposes. Firstly, they enable individual statements of a design to be identified easily in a discussion of the design. Secondly, they act as a historical record of the development of the design. We shall explain this further in Chapter 2.

- *Indentation* – The design will be presented in a form which helps the reader identify the major structures of the design. This will be achieved by careful use of indentation of paragraphs.

- *Data* – Various qualities will be manipulated and processed by our designs. These qualities will be assigned to variables, whose meaning will be described in Chapter 2. Each variable is referred to by a name or as we shall call it an **identifier**. Designers are free to use identifiers of their choice, but they should be chosen so that they convey to the reader the intent of what quantity they represent. For example, an identifier like *tmp* conveys little meaning, whereas *temperature* clearly has an intent associated with it. Data will normally be assumed to reside in memory but it can be stored permanently on backing store. The data is then said to be stored in a **file**. We shall not be studying files in this book but may occasionally refer to the notion of a file.

- *Logic* – The logic should be kept as simple as possible in order to reduce the probability of errors and to minimize the maintenance effort. Some designers waste an enormous amount of time worrying about the speed of execution of their programs. Most applications are not all that time-critical and attempts at improving execution time can have strong negative effects on the clarity of a design when debugging and maintenance are concerned. We shall not be concerned with designs for which the primary concern is efficiency, that is, with the speed at which it runs on a machine. We shall prefer to concentrate on clarity of design. This is not to say that efficiency of execution is not important. For some applications execution time is of paramount importance, for example operating systems must execute very quickly. However, applications like these these are in a minority and so we can afford to ignore them. Indeed it should be part of the specification process to identify time-critical operations and so the designer should be aware of their existence before designing begins.

Problems will be solved in a top down fashion which means that a top level design is produced, consisting of only a few lines of design that specify the global aims of the solution. Each of these lines is then refined in a stepwise manner until a final solution is reached. This development of the design provides a convenient way for the designer to document the solution and for that solution to be assessed by others, either prior to implementation in a programming language or during maintenance of the resulting program. Since the design language contains a large amount of natural English there is a greater possibility of coordination between members of the development team, management and customer.

The final product of our labours will be a design. Sometimes it will be a complete solution to some problem in which case it will be called a **design** or a **program**. When a user uses the program it will be said to be **executed** or **run**. Although the word *program* usually refers to a piece of code which can be run on a machine it will be necessary to have the notion of running or executing a design. Since we shall not be concerned with implementations, using *design* and *program* synonymously ought not to cause confusion.

On other occasions we may be interested only in some small part of a larger problem. In situations like this we shall refer to **program fragments** or **design fragments**, again the words design and program being used synonymously.

1.3 SUMMARY

In this chapter we have given a brief account of the software engineering life cycle. This consists of four major development stages: requirements analysis, design, implementation and maintenance. This book will be concerned with developing designs none of which will be implemented in a programming language. However, the design language in which they are expressed should enable them to be implemented in many different languages without too much additional effort. The design language will be used to teach new concepts and to express the solutions to the problems. Completed designs will be referred to as designs or programs.

2

A PROBLEM-SOLVING STRATEGY

To the student new to computing science the process of problem-solving can be quite baffling. Typically the student asks 'Where do I begin?'. As with problem-solving in any discipline, one can only give guidelines and strategies for a general approach, together with techniques that can be tried when progress is not being made. In this chapter we try to give some general help to those who are faced with a blank page and who do not know how to get started.

There are four major stages to producing a design solution to a given problem which we now explore.

2.1 UNDERSTAND THE PROBLEM

This may seem to be an obvious statement but subtleties of a specification may not be obvious when expressed in English. Consider the following example:

'Write a design which will enable a user to input between 10 and 20 numbers from the keyboard.'

There are many questions to resolve before designing a solution commences. What does it mean to say the user can input 'between 10 and 20' numbers? It means that the user *must* input at least 10 numbers but should be given the *opportunity* of entering fewer than 20 numbers. However not *more* than 20 numbers may be input. In achieving a solution to this problem the designer should not ask for more data to be input than is strictly necessary. Therefore a solution which asks the user to input 20 numbers and then asks how many of them are really required is totally inadequate.

Another difficulty to be resolved prior to the design stage is what is meant by 'number' in this problem? We shall see that there are different types of numbers that we can use in computing problems. There are whole numbers, like −2, 0, 3, 25 which we shall call **integers** and numbers which have a decimal part, like 3.5, 2.914, 3.0, −2.51 which are called **real numbers**. In other words whole numbers are called **integers**, those with a decimal part are called **reals**. At this stage it may not seem important what kind of numbers are involved but in Chapter 3 we shall see why the types have to be distinguished. In this particular instance the problem is insufficiently well defined for us to make a decision and we would need to go back to the specification stage of the software life cycle for clarification before we could make more progress.

In the exercises which follow we ask you to try to describe what you think might be involved in some specifications. Answers along the lines of the description above are what is expected. You are not expected to discuss the problem of checking that a user has entered a number of the correct type, be it real or integer. Problems associated with checking data input are called **data validation problems** but we shall assume for the time being that users enter data correctly.

Exercise 2.1 Describe what you think is involved in each of the following specifications:
(a) Write a design which will allow a user to enter 15 integers from the keyboard.
(b) Write a design which will allow a user to input up to 100 real numbers.
(c) Write a design which asks the user to specify the number of reals which are to be entered from the keyboard and which then requests the input of that number of reals.

Exercise 2.2 In Exercise 2.1(c) it is decided that the number of reals that a user can enter must lie in the range 0 to 500. How does this change your understanding of the problem?

2.2 DEVISE A SOLUTION

Having understood the problem, a solution to it must be found which is capable of being implemented on a computer. This greatly restricts the number of solutions because a machine is only capable of performing a limited number of simple tasks, but it can do them very fast. The solutions we develop are called **designs** and they must be expressed in a language which uses only these simple tasks. All solutions are constructed from a **top level** design which is a general description of the method of solution and which consists of a sequence of instructions. We shall call the instructions, **statements**. The statements in a top level design will often be sentences in English but as the solution develops the statements take a more precise form which reflect the tasks that a computer can perform.

To illustrate the process of devising a solution, we shall write a design which will enable a user to enter two integers from the keyboard and which will output their sum. The first stage of solving this is to *understand the problem*. A top level design for this problem is:

1 read in the numbers
2 sum the numbers
3 write out the sum

There are several points to note about this design.

(a) Each statement is numbered and we refer to a specific statement as a **step**. For example the second statement would be referred to as step 2.

(b) The design consists of a sequence of statements where step 1 is performed before step 2 which is itself performed before step 3. When a step in a design is performed it is said to be **executed**.

(c) The design gives a general description of what is to be done and provides no detail of how the individual statements are to be carried out. The statements are written in English and it is from them that a solution will be developed by successively refining each of them until a final design is achieved. This method of successive refinement from a top level design is called **top down design** with **stepwise refinement**.

(d) Step 1 includes the words *read in*. We shall take *read in* to mean the act of transferring data from the outside world into the computer. These words are thus part of our design language vocabulary.

(e) The words *write out* in step 3 are the converse of read in and is the act of transferring data from inside the machine to the outside world.

To make progress in refining this design we need to specify what to do with the two numbers that are read in. Each must be stored in memory, which we can think of as consisting of a large number of slates, each capable of having data recorded on it.

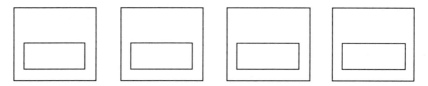

Data can be recorded on a slate by writing on it with chalk. The value on a slate can be changed by writing a new value on it. The fact that the values on a slate can be varied at will gives rise to the slate being called a **variable**.

But how can we distinguish one slate, that is one variable, from another? The answer is that each one can be given a name or more precisely an **identifier**. For the design above, three slates will be required – two will be needed for the data which is read in and one for the value of the resulting sum. The identifiers *FirstNumber* and *SecondNumber* will be used to denote the variables which will hold the input data and *sum* will be used as the identifier for the resulting sum. The identifiers have been chosen so that they convey to the reader what it is that they store.

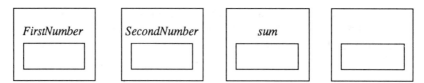

Notice that at this point we do not know what is written on the slates. Until such time as we write on a slate, that is assign a value to the variable, we say it is **undefined**. However after step 1 of the design has been executed, *FirstNumber* and *SecondNumber* will contain the values input by the user. Suppose those input values are 12 and 15 respectively. We then say that the variables have been **initialized** to the values 12 and 15. The situation will then be:

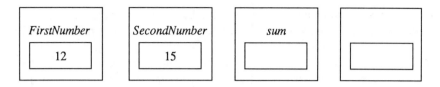

Step 2 now sums the values held in *FirstNumber* and *SecondNumber* and the result is **assigned** to *sum*. We shall see the difference between initializing a variable and assigning it a value as we progress.

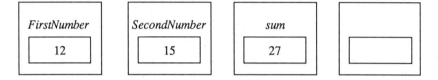

Finally at step 3 the value of the variable *sum* is written out. Notice how, as the sequence of steps was executed, the variables changed from being undefined to having defined values.

Rather than use diagrams to represent variables and their identifiers we shall define them by means of a **data table** which consists of three columns that describe in detail all the variables used in a design. We shall sometimes say that a variable is **declared** in a data table.

Identifier	Description	Type
FirstNumber	First number entered at keyboard	integer variable
SecondNumber	Second number entered at keyboard	integer variable
sum	Sum of entered numbers	integer variable

The first column lists the identifiers. They are printed in italics in order that they may be distinguished easily from ordinary text. Any character other than the space character may be used in an identifier. Should you wish to use more than one word in an identifier then the individual words have to be run together. Making the first character of each word upper case can make the separate words more easily read. This is what we have done with the identifiers *FirstNumber* and *SecondNumber*.

The second column should describe what each variable is going to store. It is not always possible to think of identifiers which accurately reflect what the variable will store. This description column gives the opportunity to make this precise.

The third column specifies the **type** of contents that the variable will hold. The notion of a data type is very important in design and the whole of the next chapter is devoted to its introduction. The problem above is concerned with integers and so the type is specified accordingly. You must take care to define the type of a variable correctly.

Although the statements in the above design can easily be understood by humans it is necessary to refine them further before they could be translated into a programming language. In particular, we need to specify in detail how the variables are to be assigned their values. We begin with a possible refinement of step 1:

1.1   read in *FirstNumber*
1.2   read in *SecondNumber*

Note the numbering system that has been used. Since the step being refined is step 1 the digit 1 is used as the first digit of the refinements, each of which is then numbered sequentially 1.1 and 1.2.

A criticism of this refinement is that it does not include messages to tell the user that input is required. Messages which report information to the user are called **prompts**. All requests for input should be accompanied by a prompt and so this refinement needs to be reconsidered to take account of this. In a trivial way this illustrates a typical design development process; a piece of design is found to be inadequate and so we must back-track to put it right. This means going back to the original step 1 and trying again. Of course the experience gained from the inadequate design should not be ignored, but the new attempt will be a refinement of the original step 1 and in particular will have steps which are numbered accordingly. The next exercise asks you to do this revision.

Exercise 2.3 Using the *write out* command refine step 1 so that it includes prompts for the user. Text that you wish to be output should be enclosed in single quotes.

The refinement of step 2 requires that the variable *sum* be assigned the sum of *FirstNumber* and *SecondNumber*. The design statement which achieves this is:

2.1 $\quad$ *sum* := *FirstNumber* + *SecondNumber*

which is read as '*sum* becomes *FirstNumber* plus *SecondNumber*'. It is called an **assignment statement** and care should be taken not to confuse the := symbol with an equals sign. What happens when this statement is executed is that the values stored in the variables *FirstNumber* and *SecondNumber* are looked up, summed and the result of the summation is then assigned to *sum*. When the value of a variable is looked up the variable is said to be **referenced**. This explains why it is so important that a variable should be initialized before it is referenced. The final statement of the design can be refined as

3.1 $\quad$ write out 'The sum is'
3.2 $\quad$ write out *sum*

Here a prompt is supplied to the user to explain what is being output. The text within quotes will be output as it stands. In step 3.2 it is the value of the variable *sum* which is output. We would normally combine these steps and write the single statement:

3.1 $\quad$ write out 'The sum is ', *sum*

The comma that appears in this statement is to help distinguish the text from the variable identifier. The design at this stage is:

1.1 $\quad$ write out 'Enter the first integer'
1.2 $\quad$ read in *FirstNumber*
1.3 $\quad$ write out 'Enter the second integer'
1.4 $\quad$ read in *SecondNumber*
2.1 $\quad$ *sum* := *FirstNumber* + *SecondNumber*
3.1 $\quad$ write out 'The sum is ', *sum*

We shall not refine this design any further because it is at a point where it could be easily translated into a programming language. One of the difficulties of design is knowing when to stop refining. A general guide is that if a design is at a stage where it can be translated line by line, without major alteration, into the programming language being used, then it is complete. In other words, an experienced programmer could look at the design and the program code and make a direct comparison to see that they correspond. A detailed knowledge of the purpose of the program should not be necessary for this comparison. As this text is not concerned with programming languages we cannot apply this rather unspecific test but we hope that the examples which appear will give you some guidance as to the level of detail to which we shall be refining designs.

The design we have just considered is complete in the sense that it solves a trivial problem. Sometimes we shall want to look at a small part of a design or even a collection of design statements taken in isolation. We remind you that a partial design will be called a **design fragment** or sometimes a **program fragment**.

Exercise 2.4 In the following design fragment all the variables are of type integer. Using the slate analogy above, draw pictures to represent the state of the memory after each statement in turn has been executed. (The symbol * denotes multiplication.)

1   *first* := 5
2   *second* := 12
3   *third* := *second* − *first*
4   *fourth* := *first*∗*third*
5   *third* := 20

In step 3 of Exercise 2.4 what appears to the right of the := sign is an arithmetic expression. This expression is evaluated, by referencing the values of *second* and *first*, before the result is assigned to the variable on the left of the := sign. The fact that the assignment statement operates in this way has two important implications. First, if a variable appears on the right-hand side of an assignment statement then it must first have been initialized. Failure to do so results in an error. Second, there must be an identifier to the left of the := symbol so that the value of the expression can be assigned to a variable. What is not precluded is the rather strange possibility that the same identifier can appear on both sides of an assignment statement. Suppose the integer variable *count* has been initialized with value 3, then consider the statement

count := *count* + 1

The right-hand side is evaluated first, so *count* is referenced and the integer 3 is retrieved. The number 1 is then added to 3 and the result is assigned to the variable *count*. What has happened is that *count* has been **incremented** by 1. The expression on the right-hand side of this assignment statement is very simple but this need not be so – indeed the expression could make many references to *count*. However when, as here, the value of an integer variable is to be incremented by 1 we shall often express this in design terms as

increment *count*

rather than use the assignment above. The two versions are entirely equivalent but the latter can be easier to read in some circumstances. The opposite of increment is **decrement** and so

decrement *count*

would have the same effect as

$count := count - 1$

Increment will be assumed to increase the value of a variable by 1. Should some other incremental value be required it must be stated explicitly. A similar convention applies to the term decrement.

Exercise 2.5 Assuming that *count* is an integer variable what would be the value of *count* after execution of the following design fragment?

1 *count* := 2
2 increment *count*
3 *count* := 2*count
4 decrement *count*

2.3 TEST THE DESIGN

This process involves making sure that the design does what it is supposed to do and that it matches the specification. Usually this means providing some data against which the program can be tested. The results from the test data are computed by hand and compared with the results computed by the design. For this rather straightforward design there is very little to check other than that *sum* is indeed the sum of the input values. In Chapter 4 we shall look at testing of designs in a more systematic way.

2.4 DOCUMENT THE SOLUTION

The final design is clearly one outcome of what has been done so far, but this should not be the only document produced in the design phase. There are other documents which are most appropriately produced concurrently. These might include a *design document* and a *user manual*. The user manual would be a reference for the people who use the system and it would explain to them what the software does and how the user interacts with it. The design document, on the other hand, is aimed at personnel who will be maintaining the program itself. It has to be remembered that designers will not normally be the people who maintain, update and correct programs. Maintenance personnel need to know about the initial design, the final design and the types of data used in the design. For our purposes we shall consider a minimum design document to consist of a statement of the problem, a top level design, a final design and a data table. Additionally, for a complex design, we would include a description of how the final design was obtained from that at the top level. This might mean including some intermediate level design in the documentation. Another helpful device in documenting a solution is to include comments in the design. Comments are not executable statements but are provided to add clarity. In our design language a comment will be text enclosed in braces. To emphasize that comments are not executable they are not given step numbers. Below we give the documentation for the design developed in this chapter.

*   *The problem*

    Write a sequence of statements which will enable a user to enter two integers from the keyboard and which will output their sum.

- *The top level design*

  1 read in the numbers
  2 sum the numbers
  3 write out the sum

- *The final design*

  {A design to input two integers from the keyboard and write out their sum}
  1.1 write out 'Enter the first integer'
  1.2 read in *FirstNumber*
  1.3 write out 'Enter the second integer'
  1.4 read in *SecondNumber*
  2.1 *sum := FirstNumber + SecondNumber*
  3.1 write out 'The sum is ', *sum*

The data table is as follows:

Identifier	Description	Type
FirstNumber	First number entered at keyboard	integer variable
SecondNumber	Second number entered at keyboard	integer variable
sum	Sum of *FirstNumber* and *SecondNumber*	integer variable

In order to avoid printing the same text twice we shall not usually present the documentation altogether but the separate components will be embedded in the text. The solution to the following exercise is typical of the type of documentation that will be provided.

Exercise 2.6 Write a design which enables a user to input three integers and which will produce as output their product. Your documentation should include a top level design, a final design and a data table.

2.5 SELECTION

The design we have just looked at consisted of a sequence of statements which would be executed one after the other. However, the power of a computer is its ability to choose different courses of action dependent upon certain criteria and its ability to carry out statements repeatedly. The former construct is called **selection** and the latter **looping**. We shall study looping in Chapter 4 but here we want to have a brief introduction to the process of selection. Selection is the process of making a decision. Consider the following design fragment:

  1 if it is raining then
  2   I will go to work by car
  3   I will have lunch in the office
  4 else
  5   I will walk to work
  6   I will eat lunch in the park
  7   I will jog after lunch
  8 ifend

If it is raining then I go to work by car and have lunch in the office, otherwise I walk to work, have lunch in the park and jog afterwards. The design illustrates that a selection has to be made between two possible courses of action; which is chosen is determined by whether or not it is raining. The phrase 'it is raining' is an example of what is known as a **condition**. A condition can only have one of the values true or false. Hence the condition 'it is raining' is either true or false; when it is true I go to work by car and have lunch in the office, when it is false I walk, have lunch in the park and jog.

Decision-making is fundamental in design and an **if** statement like that above is one way in which decisions can be handled. The word *if* is followed by a condition which evaluates to either true or false. Following the word **then** are the statements which are to be executed when the condition is true. In this example these statements are numbered 2 and 3 and they are collectively referred to as the **then clause**. Notice how they have been indented in order to give them a collective identity. The word **else** signifies the start of the statements which are executed when the condition is false, these statements being collectively known as the **else clause**. Here the *else* clause consists of the steps numbered 5, 6 and 7. Some *if* statements do not require an *else*, in which case the dummy statement *do nothing* may be used as the *else* clause. Indeed in this situation it is often clearer to leave out the *else* clause altogether. We shall see an example of this in Exercise 2.8. The word **ifend** is most important as this indicates that the *else* statements are now complete. It also indicates that the whole of the *if* statement is concluded.

To see why *ifend* is so important compare the design above with the following:

```
1  if it is raining then
2      I will go to work by car
3      I will have lunch in the office
4  else
5      I will walk to work
6      I will eat lunch in the park
7  ifend
8  I will jog after lunch
```

Here the same statements have been used but they are presented in a slightly different order. In particular, steps 7 and 8 have been interchanged. As a consequence the meaning of this design is quite different from the first one. This is because the *ifend* at step 7 terminates the *if* statement; step 8 is not conditional on whether or not it is raining. In other words this design says that whatever the weather I go for a jog after lunch.

Another point here is that the indentation helps the eye bracket together the statements associated with the *then* and those associated with the *else*. However you should not rely on indentation to determine the logic – it is the location of the *ifend* which does this.

Exercise 2.7 For each of the following *if* statements, identify the condition which determines which selection is executed. Describe what happens if this condition is true. What happens if the condition is false?
(a) if the cheque exceeds £50 then
        a bankers card plus other identification is required
     else
        a bankers card is sufficient
     ifend

(b)   if today is Sunday then
      get up late
      have a bath
      eat brunch
   else
      get up at 7.30
      have a wash
      eat breakfast
   ifend

Exercise 2.8 Write a sequence of statements which will request a user to enter a non-zero integer and then read in a value into the variable *item*. In the event that the user enters zero the message 'Warning the input number is zero' should be output.

The solution to this exercise shows the two ways an *if* statement may be written which has no *else* clause. We shall usually omit the *else* clause when it is not required but occasionally we shall use the *do nothing* statement in an *else* clause for emphasis.

2.6 SUMMARY

In terms of the software engineering life cycle introduced in Chapter 1 we have been considering only the third stage of that cycle, namely design. We have developed a strategy for creating a design to solve a specific problem the main elements of which are as follows:

2.6.1 Understand the problem

The requirements analysis and specification stages of the software engineering life cycle should ensure that a clear and unambiguous statement of the problem to be solved is presented at the design stage. The task of the designer is to ensure that all details of the specification are understood and to convert the specification into a design.

2.6.2 Devise a solution

This is a multi-stage process and may involve going back to previous stages before further forward progress can be made. The major stages are:

Form a top level design Essentially this is a global statement of what the design is to achieve. Another designer reading a top level design should be able to see immediately its purpose. It has very little detail but it does break the problem up into a sequence of subtasks. A difficulty with top level designs is knowing how many subtasks should be included. Too many gives too much detail and therefore makes it hard for another designer to understand. Too few subtasks means that too few subgoals have been identified for the subsequent job of stepwise refinement. There are no hard and fast rules but we shall adopt the fairly arbitrary notion that a top level design should consist of no more than 15 lines of statements. We would hope most top level designs had fewer lines than this.

Another difficulty arises in that there may be more than one approach to a problem and hence a variety of potential top level designs. Sometimes the efficiency of the resulting program, that is the speed at which it runs, may be an important factor in the design and this may determine the adoption of one design as opposed to another. We shall not be concerned with design efficiency because in an introductory text we would rather stress the importance of obtaining correct designs than obtaining efficient ones. But the problem of alternative approaches will still arise. Should a top level design ultimately lead to a clear correct final design then all is well and good. However, the refinement process will often give rise to designs which lack clarity. Then is the time to consider whether an alternative top level design might lead to a better end result. Thus like many other aspects of software, forming a top level design might itself be an iterative process as one design is preferred to another. In reading the text you will not often see this iterative aspect of top level design. When you write your own designs do not get too concerned if you do not get 'the right' top level design at the first attempt.

Refine the design This is the process of taking each step in the top level design and successively refining it. The process gives rise to the name by which it is often known – top down design with stepwise refinement. The refining process is considered complete when each statement in the design can be directly translated into a programming language. In order that we can keep track of the refining process each step in the design is numbered. Integers are used for the steps in a top level design. Numbers like 3.1, 3.2, 3.3 are refinements of step 3 of the top level design. We shall call them second level refinements. Third level refinements of a step numbered 4.2 would be numbered 4.2.1, 4.2.2, 4.2.3 and so on. We shall see explicit examples of this numbering scheme in the next chapter. A design should not normally require more than five levels of refinement although the choice of five is somewhat arbitrary. What we are trying to avoid is having so many levels of refinement that it becomes impossible to follow their development. If it does, then the problem probably needs breaking down into different subtasks at a higher level. We shall see methods for doing this in Chapter 8.

2.6.3 Test the design

In a book at this level it is impossible to 'prove' that a given design is correct. However, what we can do is to use the problem-solving strategy to help minimize the introduction of errors and then to test the final product with test data.

2.6.4 Document the solution

A well-documented solution includes a statement of the problem to be solved, a top level design, a final design and a data table. For complex designs it will also contain intermediate level designs and explanations of how individual top level statements were refined.

The chapter concluded with a brief look at the selection construct which enables one of two possible branches to be followed.

FUNDAMENTAL DATA TYPES

3.1 INTRODUCTION

Chapter 2 has already introduced the idea of a variable of integer type. In this chapter we shall look at type in more detail and examine some basic data types, that is types which we are assuming are part of the design language. These basic data types will be referred to as **built-in** types because they are to be found 'built-in' to most programming languages. Built-in types will also be referred to as **standard** types. We shall require that a variable used in a design must have its type declared in a data table. Most programming languages have an analogous requirement but why should this be so? There are two reasons. Firstly, for each variable declared, the machine must set aside enough memory to hold the data to be stored. Now different types of data have different storage requirements, for example, more space is required to store a real number than is required to store an integer. Hence the type of each variable must be declared in order that memory can be allocated. The second reason is that it helps to avoid, or at worst detect, errors. If we take as an example a variable which has been declared to be of integer type then it is an error to assign to that variable a real value. Programming languages can detect errors of assignment like this and can halt program execution as a result. An error like this which is detected by the machine when the program is running is called a **fatal error** because it stops program execution. You may think that this is rather drastic action but consider the situation where a count was being kept of the number of enquiries into a database (a large electronic repository of information) where each enquiry is subject to a charge. Clearly such a count must have integer values. If by some error of design it was given a real value and this error went undetected and unreported then program execution would not be interrupted. Then subsequent references to the count to work out the cost of the enquiries would be nonsense. That the count was nonsense may not be apparent from the calculated cost and the error may go undetected until an irate customer complained. Thus the typing of variables is a piece of armoury in the attempt to produce error-free programs. What can be assigned to a variable is encompassed in the **assignment compatibility** rule:

> A value may be assigned only to a variable which has the same type as the value or which is compatible with that type.

This rule will be explained in more detail subsequently, but failing to obey it, results in what is known as a **type mismatch**. We shall see an example of a type mismatch shortly.

The purpose of a data type is to enable some data from the real world to be modelled. *Most* such data cannot be modelled by a built-in type. For example, the throws on a roulette wheel can be written down as a sequence of integers which can themselves be represented by a built-in type integer. However, to model the fact that the numbers form a sequence, one after the other, requires a more sophisticated approach which involves defining what is known as an abstract data type (which we shall not be in a position to do until Chapter 10). However, it is crucially important to define operators which act on the data, so as we describe the built-in types, we shall prepare for later by identifying the operators quite clearly.

3.2 THE DATA TYPE INTEGER

Integers are whole numbers such as −10, 0, 215; they do not have decimal points but can be positive, negative or zero. But can numbers like this be modelled on a machine? The answer is a qualified yes. A major difference between integers with which you are familiar and the **data type integer** is that the data type has a smallest and largest value that can be represented. Typically the values lie in the range −32767 and 32767 but some languages have special facilities to enable much longer integers to be used. The size of the smallest and largest integers available may have to be taken into account in some designs. Having identified this difference we shall now ignore it and use *integer* to mean both the integers which you are familiar from the real world and the data type integer.

Integers in the real world can be added together, subtracted and so on. In other words, they can be manipulated and combined using **operators**. The objects upon which they operate are called **operands**. Thus, in the expression 2 + 3, the integers 2 and 3 are the operands and the operator is addition which is denoted by the symbol +.

The operators that are defined on the data type integer include the familiar ones of addition, subtraction and multiplication (denoted by the symbol *). So for example, we can write 5*2, 2 + 17, 25 − 8 and each of the integers in these expressions is referred to as an integer **constant**. Integer expressions can be built up from variables and constants as already illustrated in Exercise 2.5.

The operation of integer division is denoted by **DIV** and does not correspond to division encountered in 'normal' arithmetic and so may be new to you. With integer division the result is an integer, and any fractional part is discarded. The following examples illustrate the notation and the results of integer division.

$$9 \text{ DIV } 2 = 4$$
$$(-9) \text{ DIV } 2 = -4$$

The operator **MOD** (short for modulo) provides the remainder from integer division. So for example, 9 MOD 4 = 1, since 9 leaves remainder 1 when divided by 4. There are difficulties with MOD for expressions like (−9) MOD 4 in that different versions of the same language may give different results. One argument would be that 4 goes into −9 minus two times (to give −8) leaving a remainder of −1. The other argument depends on the mathematical definition of modulo and insists that the remainder must be positive (and so lie between 0 and 3). So, 4 goes into −9 minus three times (to give −12) leaving a remainder of +3. Nearly all languages do not define expressions like 9 MOD −4 where the second operand is negative. We suggest that the use of DIV and MOD is treated with great care when negative operands are involved. For the record we shall define (−9) MOD 4 to have value 3.

These operators are not the only ones that are defined on the integers. There are others which can be applied to integer operands which give rise to what are called **boolean** values. They are called **comparison operators** and as their name suggests they enable integers to be compared to see, for example, if one integer is larger than, or smaller than, another. To see why comparisons are important in computing one has to understand that the route through the program statements being executed by a computer must be able to be varied during the course of the computation. Take as an example a program which is processing the pay-roll of a company. The calculation of income tax illustrates the need for selective action, since the tax rates depend on the gross amount of money earned. Below a certain level one rate of tax applies, above it another applies. To take account of this the program must be written in such a way that different statements will be executed dependent upon the circumstances of the employee whose pay is currently being calculated. Here the program must compare gross earnings against the level at which the tax rate changes and then execute the appropriate instructions. We have already seen that the *if* statement is one way of selecting between two alternative courses of action, the selection being controlled by a condition. We shall encounter many conditions which are expressed using comparison operators.

There are six comparison operators defined on the integers. They are:

=	is equal to
<>	is not equal to
<	is less than
<=	is less than or equal to
>=	is greater than or equal to
>	is greater than

The normal arithmetic rules for comparing signed numbers apply to integers. So, the following integer comparisons $-1 < 5$, $50 > 49$, $2 <> 3$ and $-4 <= -2$ all have the value true. The comparisons $7 < -1$, $4 > 4$ and $-5 > 0$ all have value false. A comparison which involves a variable gives rise to a condition. For example, if *number* is an integer variable then the condition *number* < 5 will be true or false depending upon the value of *number* when the condition is evaluated. Similarly the value of a condition which involves two variables, such as *first* $>=$ *second,* will depend on the values of the variables at the time the condition is evaluated. A more complicated condition is:

first $= 10 *$ *second* $+ 20 *$ *third*

in which the right-hand side is an expression.

Finally there are two operators, generically known as **unary** operators, which require only one operand, that is each acts on a single integer. The negation operator forms the negative of a given number. The same symbol is used as for the subtraction operator. So, for example, we can write −(−5), which of course is just 5. Similarly there is the operator which denotes a positive integer and whose symbol is the same as that used for addition. That completes the description of the operators that are defined on the integers.

Some care is required when writing down integer expressions. For example, does 4 + 2*3 mean 4 + 6 or 6*3? The normal algebraic convention that multiplication and division take priority over addition and subtraction will be adopted in which case 4 + 2*3 means 4 + 6 since the multiplication 2*3 is done before the addition. If this is not what is required then you must use parentheses and write (4 + 2)*3 in order to force the addition to be done first.

Exercise 3.1 Assuming that all variables are of integer type, which of the following are valid assignment statements?
(a) *perimeter := length + breadth + height*
(b) *length + breadth := perimeter*
(c) *height = 10*
(d) *height := 15*length*
(e) *length := area* DIV *breadth*
(f) *ratio := 2.5*4.0*

Exercise 3.1(f) is an example of an assignment which results in a type mismatch error. This is because an attempt is made to assign a real value to an integer variable.

Exercise 3.2 Assuming that all the variables are of type integer which of the following are valid conditions?
(a) *number <= 100*first + 5*
(b) *(first + second) < third*
(c) *5 := 6*
(d) *−1 < number < 10*
(e) *(length*breadth)* MOD 5 >= 100 DIV 7

Exercise 3.3 Assuming that the variable *number* is of type integer, for each of the following conditions, find the range of values for *number* which will make the condition true.
(a) *number >= 5*
(b) *number < 4*
(c) *number = 3*4*

3.3 THE DATA TYPE REAL

Real numbers are numbers like 2.65, 0.0, −23.2849, +2.33, which are written with a decimal point and digits both before and after it. You should note that a number like 3.0 is a real number and not an integer, despite the fact that its decimal part is zero. As was the case for integers there is a difference between a real number stored on a computer and a real number written on a piece of paper. The number of digits of a real number which can be stored in a computer is limited, whereas a number like π has an infinite number of decimal places. (If you are not familiar with the symbol π then please take this statement on trust.) As a consequence, the magnitude of real numbers that can be stored is limited, as is their precision. We shall not be concerned with such problems but certain applications may require extreme precision, in which case that precision should be considered at the design stage.

The operations defined on real numbers are similar to those defined on the integers. Addition, subtraction, multiplication, the six comparison operators and the two unary operators are identical and the same operator symbols are used as for the integer operators. Division, however is different. Division of real numbers is denoted by / and the result of applying it to any two numbers is a real number which is as close as possible to the exact quotient of the two numbers.

There are no other operators defined on the real numbers. You should note that the integer operators DIV and MOD have no meaning in the case of real numbers.

The assignment compatibility rule tells us that only real values can be assigned to real variables. However it *is* legitimate to assign an integer value to a real variable because for any integer value there is a corresponding real value. For example, to the integer 3 there corresponds the real value 3.0. So, if *realnumber* is a real variable then both the following assignment statements are valid and both have the effect of assigning 3.0 to *realnumber*.

> *realnumber* := 3
> *realnumber* := 3.0

Integers are therefore said to be **assignment compatible** with reals, although it is still an error to attempt to assign the real value 3.0 to an integer variable.

Real expressions can be built up using real constants, real variables and the real number operators. So for example, if *decimal1*, *decimal2* and *decimal3* are all real variables then the following are all valid expressions:

> (2.5*decimal1) + decimal2/decimal3
> (decimal1*decimal1 + 5.68/2.44)/(decimal2 − decimal3)

However there is one small difference from the situation for integer expressions. Because integers are assignment compatible with reals, a real expression is permitted to contain integer values and variables.

Programming languages normally have facilities which enable real numbers to be output in a variety of formats. Typically the number of decimal places can be specified but detailed formatting such as this will not be included in the design language. Another complication which will be ignored for the time being is the use of a real variable to represent an amount of money. An amount like $4.65 will be represented by the real number 4.65. Dividing this quantity by 2 would produce 2.325 but there is no coin equivalent to this number. The nearest equivalents are $2 and 32¢ or $2 and 33¢. For the time being we shall allow amounts of money to be expressed to any number of decimal places but we shall consider a more satisfactory representation in Chapter 10.

Exercise 3.4 Assuming that *RealOne* and *RealTwo* are real variables and *IntegerOne*, *IntegerTwo* are integer variables, which of the following are valid expressions?
(a) *RealOne* MOD *RealTwo*
(b) 2*RealOne − 3*RealTwo
(c) 2.0*RealOne − 3.0*IntegerTwo
(d) *RealOne*(IntegerOne DIV IntegerTwo)

Exercise 3.5 Assuming that *RealOne* and *RealTwo* are real variables and *IntegerOne*, *IntegerTwo* are integer variables, which of the following are valid assignment statements?

(a)   *RealOne := RealTwo + IntegerOne* DIV 3
(b)   *RealTwo := 2 + RealTwo*
(c)   *IntegerOne := RealTwo*
(d)   *IntegerOne := IntegerTwo + 3.0*

Exercises 3.5(c) and (d) are examples of type mismatch errors. The assignments attempt to assign a real value to an integer variable. Each would give rise to a fatal error and so would discontinue program execution.

Exercise 3.6 Assuming that *RealOne* and *RealTwo* are real variables and *IntegerOne* is an integer variable, which of the following are valid conditions?

(a)   *RealOne < RealTwo + IntegerOne*
(b)   *RealTwo >= IntegerOne*
(c)   *RealOne = RealTwo*

3.4 THE DATA TYPE CHAR

We now introduce a new data type called character which we shall refer to as data type **char**. Character data is the most common method of communication between people and the computer. Every computer system has an associated set of characters which it uses, but unfortunately different machines have different character sets. We shall use the ASCII character set which includes the 52 letters of the alphabet (lower and upper case), 10 digits, the space character and a variety of punctuation. The characters within the set are ordered; the space character comes before (but not immediately before) the digits, which precede the upper-case letters which are themselves in the order A, B, C, etc., and these in turn precede the lower-case letters. When it is important to 'see' a space character in the text we shall use the symbol ▽ to denote it.

There are six operators defined on data of type char, namely the six comparison operators. A particular value of type char is denoted by enclosing the character in *single apostrophes*. Hence 'A', 'z', ';' are all examples of char constants. The conditions

'A' < 'B',   'Z' < 'a'

are both true whereas the conditions

'A' < '▽',   'a' < '1'

are both false. Variables of type char can be defined in a data table and values can be assigned to them using the usual assignment statement.

Exercise 3.7 Assuming the variables are of type char which of the following are valid conditions? For those that are valid, say whether the condition is true or false.

(a)   '1' >= '▽'
(b)   '9' < '2'
(c)   *ch* = 'A'
(d)   *ch* = 'character'

3.5 THE DATA TYPE STRING

The data type related to type char is the data type **string**. A string is a sequence of characters, so that for example 'A▽short▽string' is a string constant consisting of only letters and space characters. We use apostrophes to delimit the string in just the same way that we did for character constants. Strings can contain non-printing ASCII characters but we shall not go into this here.

Although we are not concerned with programming languages it is the case that many of them have data types integer, real, char and boolean, much as we have defined them above. However the situation for strings is somewhat different; there is much more variation in what, if anything, a particular language supports. Should you wish to implement any design which involves string variables particular attention will have to be paid in translating the design into code.

Like the data type char, the operators defined on the data type string include the six comparison operators. For two strings to be equal their lengths must be the same and each pair of corresponding characters must be equal. Thus 'begin' and 'Begin' are not equal strings because while they have the same length the first characters are not identical. For the inequality operators <, <=, >, >= and <>, string ordering is a generalization of alphabetic ordering. 'Cane' < 'Care' because the first two characters are equal and so the order is determined by the next, that is, the third character. The string 'Can' precedes 'Cane' because it is shorter, but otherwise identical, to it.

There is one other operator defined on strings and that is the **concatenation** operator. This operator 'joins together' two or more strings one after the other. So for example the two strings 'A▽short▽' and 'string' can be concatenated to form 'A▽short▽string' We shall use the symbol + to denote concatenation. The following sequence of statements has the same effect as that just described but it assigns the strings to string variables rather than using string constants.

1 *words* := 'A▽short▽'
2 *word* := 'string'
3 *phrase* := *words* + *word*
4 write out *phrase*

Note that the order in which the variables are concatenated is important. Had we put *phrase* := *word* + *words* then *phrase* would have had the value 'stringA▽short▽'.

String values can only be assigned to variables of type string. A type mismatch will occur if an attempt is made to assign say, a real value to a string variable. However, there is an analogous situation between strings and chars as there was between reals and integers. A variable or value of type char is assignment compatible with a variable of type string. This means that a character variable can be assigned to a string. Thus the following sequence of statements is valid:

achar := 'a'
astring := *achar*

Here, the char variable *achar* is assigned the char value 'a' and then the string variable *astring* is assigned the value of *achar*. It is the assignment compatibility which enables this to be done. However, note that it is not allowed to assign a string to a char variable. This assignment compatibility also allows a char constant or char variable to be used in concatenation. For example, if *schar* is a char variable and *word* a string variable then the statements

> *schar* := 's'
> *word* := 'bottle'
> *word* := *word* + *schar*

would result in *word* having value 'bottles'. This example shows that the number of characters that a string variable contains may vary during program execution. Here *word* started off having six characters and finished having seven. The term **dynamic length** is used to express the number of characters that a string variable has at a particular time. Here are some other string initialization statements:

1 *Null* := ''
2 *Space* := '▽'
3 *TwoSpaces* := '▽▽'

Step 1 initializes a variable to a string which does not contain any characters. Such a string is called a **null** string and it has dynamic length 0. Step 2 gives rise to a string of length 1 but it is not a char variable.

We can picture the variable *phrase* whose value is the string 'A▽short▽string' as follows:

1	2	3	4	5	6	7	8	9	10	11	12	13	14
A	▽	s	h	o	r	t	▽	s	t	r	i	n	g

The character 'h' occupies the fourth position of the string. This idea of position is used for updating and referencing individual characters within a string. The character 'h' could be changed to a 'P' by the assignment

> *phrase*[4] := 'P'

Similarly an individual character of a string can be assigned to a char variable as in the statement

> *letter* := *phrase*[9]

Care needs to be taken to avoid attempting to access a character beyond the end of the string. This string has dynamic length 14 so it is not permitted to attempt to access say, *phrase*[15]. Such an attempt gives rise to what is known as an **out of range error**; such errors are fatal and cause execution to cease.

Sometimes we shall find it useful to define a string variable which is capable of holding only a small number of characters. For example, the post or zip code MK11 1BY is made up of two strings. The first part of this code is a four-character area code. Some area codes have fewer than four characters. The second part of the code is a locality within the area and this is a string having at most three characters. In defining variables to represent data we should try to reflect constraints like this. This is because it helps with program maintenance and also provides a check on values assigned to the variables. For example, if an area code consisting of five characters were to be assigned to an area code variable which had been defined to contain at most four characters, then an out of range error would occur and the fault would be immediately apparent. If the area code had been defined as just a string variable then any number of characters could be assigned to it and the automatic error checking would not pick up this error. The data table below shows how we can define strings which are constrained by the maximum number of characters that may be assigned to them.

Identifier	Description	Type
area	Area post code	string[4] variable
locality	Locality within area	string[3] variable

From this table it can be seen that the variable *area* can hold a maximum of four characters. We say that it has **static length** four. Similarly, *locality* has static length three. If a variable is declared to be of type string, where no static length is specified, then we shall assume that the string can hold up to a maximum of 255 characters. This number is common to many languages, hence its use here.

Exercise 3.8 For the variables *area* and *locality* declared above determine which of the following are valid statements. For those that are valid give the resulting dynamic lengths of the variables.
(a) *area* := 'TN12'; (b) *locality* := ''; (c) *area* := 'MK15'; (d) *locality* := *area*

That completes the list of operations defined on strings but we shall introduce a facility here which will simplify their manipulation. In order to avoid out of range errors when accessing individual characters of a string it is necessary to know its dynamic length. A facility which provides this information is the **length function**. We shall see what a function is in Chapter 8 but until then we shall use *length* in the statements like those below .

> *number* := *length(phrase)* . . .
> if *length(phrase)* < 10 then . . .
> loop while *index* < *length*('computing') . . .

In the first statement *number* is an integer variable and the length of the string stored in *phrase* is assigned to it. We say that *phrase* is an **argument** for the function *length*. In the second statement the length of the string as given by *length(phrase)* is used in a condition. Note the form of its use; the variable whose length is required is enclosed in parentheses. In the third statement a string constant is used as an argument for the function.

Exercise 3.9 Write down the following strings in increasing order of magnitude:
(a)   '▽Dave', 'Dave', 'Da▽ve', 'Dave▽'
(b)   'computing', 'Computing', 'COMPUTING'

Exercise 3.10 Write down the values of each of the string variables *FullName* and *NewName* after the following sequence of statements has been executed.

> *FirstName* := 'John'
> *LastName* := 'Pitt'
> *FullName* := *FirstName* + '▽Edward▽' + *LastName*
> *NewName* := *FullName*
> *NewName*[13] := 'K'

3.6 THE DATA TYPE BOOLEAN

The set of values for the data type **boolean** number only two. The values are true and false and there are three operators defined on these values: **or** (which is referred to as disjunction), **and** (referred to as conjunction) and **not** (referred to as negation).

We shall study these operators later and until then will only need the idea of a boolean variable. Such a variable can only be assigned one of the possible boolean values, true or false. A typical use of a boolean variable is as a **flag**. Flags tend to be used to record a boolean value of an outcome which is not immediately required in the processing sequence. For example, suppose the names in a telephone directory are being searched and all names matching a given name are to be printed out. Then a boolean flag could be used to denote the outcome of the search. If *IsThere* is the identifier of the flag then the value true would indicate that the search was successful and that a match had been found, while the value false would indicate that the search was unsuccessful. At the end of the search a message could be issued to the user dependent upon the value of the flag. Thus we could have:

```
1  if IsThere = true then
2      write out 'All matches have been listed'
3  else
4      write out 'There were no matches'
5  ifend
```

The value of *IsThere* would have to be initialized prior to the search and be updated within the search. Step 1 would normally be abbreviated to:

```
1  if IsThere then
```

because *IsThere* has value true or false and so there is no need to compare it with the value true. Another common use for boolean variables is to record user preferences. For example a response to a prompt such as

Do you wish to continue y/n?

could be assigned to a boolean variable which could be used subsequently as a control condition in a selection statement. A design fragment to achieve this might be:

```
1  write out 'Do you wish to continue y/n?'
2  read in response
3  if response = 'y' then
4      continue := true
4  else
5      continue := false
6  ifend
```

where *response* is a char variable to hold the response and *continue* is a boolean variable. While the meaning of these statements is clear there is another way of achieving the same result which avoids the use of an *if* statement. It has the form:

```
1  write out 'Do you wish to continue y/n?'
2  read in response
3  continue := (response = 'y')
```

To understand Step 3 notice that following the assignment symbol is the condition, (*response* = 'y'). Now this condition is either true or false. It is true if the response is 'y', in which case the value true is assigned to the variable *continue*. Similarly, if the response is not 'y' then the condition (*response* = 'y') has value false and so false is assigned to *continue*.

3.7 PROBLEMS

The problems in this section may involve any of the data types introduced in this chapter. Several of the problems may involve units of measure or currency values with which you are not familiar. You may like to read the appropriate section of the Preface should you be concerned about currency notations. Unless stated otherwise you may assume that amounts of currency can be represented by real variables.

3.1 A quarterly gas bill consists of two parts, a standing charge and a charge for the amount of gas used. The amount of gas used, in cubic feet, is given by the difference between the current meter reading and its previous quarterly value. From these readings the number of British thermal units (BTUs) used is calculated using the fact that one cubic foot of gas has an energy equivalent of 1.016 BTUs. Assuming the standing charge is £8.70 write a design which will enable a user to input the cost, as a decimal number of pence, of a BTU, the current and previous quarter's meter readings and which will produce as output the total amount due expressed in pounds. You may assume that meter readings can be represented by integers.

3.2 There is no data type corresponding to fractions. If a problem involves them it is usual to convert them to a decimal approximation and thereby represent them as real numbers. However we can model a fraction by using two integer variables, one to represent the numerator and another to represent the denominator of the fraction. This problem is concerned with such a representation. Write a design which will enable a user to input two fractions and which will output their product. The output should consist of two integers, one for the numerator of the product the other for its denominator. You may assume that the user does not enter zero for either of the input denominators.

3.3 Boxes of floppy disks are on sale for £5 per box or £45 for 10 boxes. All prices are subject to tax at 15 per cent. Write a design which will enable a user to input a number of boxes and which will produce as output the total cost of the boxes including tax.

3.4 Telephone calls are charged by the number of units used where a unit is a period of time which depends on the distance of the call and the time of day when the call is made. All calls result in a charge which is an integer number of units. As soon as a call has been answered a unit is charged and as soon as the time period of that unit has expired another unit is charged and so on until the call is terminated. For a local cheap rate call a unit is 360 seconds. Write a design which will enable a user to input the duration of a call and which will output its cost. You should assume the duration of a call is a whole number and that a unit costs 4.4p subject to tax at 15 per cent.

3.5 Write a design which will enable a user to input an integer and which will produce as output a message saying whether or not the input was exactly divisible by three.

3.6   This problem is concerned with working out the day of the week on which a given date falls. The rather strange formula below, due to Zeller, calculates the day of the week on which any date after January 1st 1583 will fall or has fallen. The date for which the corresponding day of the week is required must be coded in the following way. The day of the month is the usual day number and so is an integer between 1 and 31 inclusive. The year must be represented by an integer, for example the integer 1989 represents the year 1989. The month must be coded as an integer where March is coded 1, April as 2 and so on until December, which is coded as 10. January and February are coded as 11 and 12 respectively of the *previous* year. So for example, 3rd January 1992 would be represented as day 3, month 11 of year 1991. We shall think of a year as consisting of two parts, a century represented by the first two digits of its integer representation, and a decade represented by the last two digits. (Note we are not using decade with its conventional meaning here. Nor does century have its usual meaning either.) Thus in 1991, century would have value 19 and decade the value 91. With this method of coding the formula for the day of the week is given by

daycode = ((13*month − 1) DIV 5 + decade DIV 4 +century DIV 4 + decade + day − 2*century) MOD 7

The result of this formula is an integer in the range 0 to 6 inclusive. The integer 0 represents Sunday, 1 represents Monday and so on. Write a design which will enable a user to enter a date in three stages: the day, the coded month and the year. The output produced by the design should be the code corresponding to the day of the week on which that date falls.

3.7   Amend the specification of Problem 3.6 so that the user inputs the number of the month in conventional format. That is January is represented by 1, February by 2 and so on. Write a design to match this new specification.

3.8 SUMMARY

In this chapter we first looked at the assignment statement in more detail. We introduced some fundamental data types. A data type consists of a collection of data objects together with a set of operations defined on the objects. Those that we introduced were the data types integer, real, char, string and boolean.

4

FUNDAMENTAL CONTROL STRUCTURES

In Section 4.1 we shall look at a pay-roll problem to calculate the income tax of an employee. Different actions will be required for the calculation of tax dependent upon the earnings of the employee. The statement which enables the different actions to take place is the selection statement introduced in Chapter 2. However, the program would not be of much use if it only calculated the tax of one employee – clearly the calculation needs to be repeated for all the employees. This can be achieved by using a **loop,** which means that certain statements are executed repeatedly. Thus the problem will include both selection and looping in its solution. As the problem is slightly more complex than those we have so far considered we shall take the opportunity of looking at a formal method of testing a design. The method makes use of a **trace table** and the process itself is called **tracing**.

4.1 INTRODUCTORY PROBLEM

We shall consider a very simple tax system in which all employees are liable for a tax of 5 per cent of their gross pay. An employee earning less than £5000 per year is not liable for further taxes but employees earning more than this are taxed additionally at 25 per cent on the earnings in excess of £5000.

The problem is to design a program which will calculate and write out the tax liability of each employee in a certain company. It should also write out the total tax paid by company employees, that is, the sum of all the liabilities of the individual employees. There are 100 employees each of whom is assigned a unique personal identifier number in the range 1 to 100 inclusive.

4.1.1 Understand the problem

What tax liability should be output for an employee earning £9000 per year?
There is a liability of 5 per cent of £9000 plus 25 per cent of those earnings in excess of £5000. So the calculation is

$$0.05*9000 + 0.25(9000 - 5000) = 450 + 1000 = 1450$$

and so the liability is £1450.
The figure of 9000 provides one piece of test data. What sort of value would provide another useful test?
Any value less than 5000 for which the calculation is a straight percentage of the gross earnings.

4.1.2 Devise a solution

We can now write a top level design for the program. Study the design and then read the comments which follow.

```
    {Calculate tax for all employees}
1   initialize variables
2   loop while there are employees to process
3       process employees tax
4   loopend
5   write out total tax paid by employees
```

This top level design can be thought of as a template for many different programs. Essentially it consists of a loop which contains some processing, the beginning of which is at step 2 and the end at step 4. The statement which is repeatedly executed within the loop is step 3. To emphasize this fact, this step is indented. We shall often refer to the repeated steps of a loop as the **body of the loop** or **loop body**. Step 2 has an additional role in that it includes a condition which determines when the loop shall cease execution. The purpose of step 1 will become apparent in due course but we shall ignore it for now.

The next stage is to refine this design. Study the refinement and data table below and then read the commentary which follows:

```
        {Calculate tax for all employees}
1           initialize variables
2.1         loop while pin <= 100
3.1             read in GrossPay
3.2             calculate tax
3.3             write out tax
3.4             update the running total of TotalTax
3.5             increment pin
3.6         loopend
4.1         write out TotalTax
```

Identifier	Description	Type
pin	Personal identifier number	integer variable
TotalTax	Total tax paid by all employees	real variable
GrossPay	Individual yearly earnings	real variable
tax	Tax paid	real variable

Here some detail has been added to the statement within the loop and to the statement controlling the loop. In particular, the loop is to be controlled by using the integer variable *pin*. A variable which is used in this way will be referred to as a **loop condition control variable**, or more simply a **loop control variable**. The abbreviation, loop control variable, may give the misleading impression that the variable is directly controlling the loop – it is not. It is the condition which controls the loop, but of course, the value that the variable takes during execution directly affects the condition. There are two points to note about this design.

1. The value of *pin* is referenced at step 2.1 and so on first execution of this statement *pin* must have been initialized. This will need to be done at step 1 and so its refinement will have to include a statement initializing *pin* to 1. This illustrates a general rule concerning the initialization of variables within loops or within the loop control conditions; they must be initialized prior to the execution of the loop. We shall emphasize this fact by expressing step 1 in the form:

    1 initialize variables referenced in loop

2. There must be some way of updating the loop condition control variable within the loop. Here it is step 3.5. If this step is omitted then the loop will execute for ever! You must always check that the condition controlling the loop (here it is *pin* <= 100) can be satisfied at some stage of execution.

Steps 1, 3.2 and 3.4 can now be refined further:

	{Calculate tax for all employees}
1.1	*pin* := 1
1.2	*TotalTax* := 0
2.1	loop while *pin* <= 100
3.1.1	write out 'Enter gross earnings for employee number ' *pin*
3.1.2	read in *GrossPay*
3.2.1	if *GrossPay* < 5000 then
3.2.2	*tax* := 0.05*GrossPay*
3.2.3	else
3.2.4	*tax* := 0.05*GrossPay* + 0.25*(*GrossPay* – 5000)
3.2.5	ifend
3.3.1	write out 'Employees tax is ' *tax*
3.4.1	*TotalTax* := *TotalTax* + *tax*
3.5	increment *pin*
3.6	loopend
4.1.1	write out 'Employees pay total tax of ' *TotalTax*

The calculation of the tax requires a selection construct, hence the use of the *if then else* statement. Updating the running total *TotalTax* requires a reference to its value and so on the first execution of the loop this value must already exist. This is done at step 1.2. The remaining refinements deal with the output of prompts to aid the user.

4.1.3 Test the solution

There are two major constructs in this design – a *loop* and an *if* statement. To test the design meets its specification we **trace** through it using what is known as a **trace table**. The first task in drawing up a trace table is to identify all the variables and conditions in the design. These then form the heading of the table. Whenever the program asks the user for data, suitable data must be supplied. A trace should be performed with as many different sets of test data as are required to ensure all alternatives in selection statements are tested. To do this here we would need to trace the design using an input value of gross earnings which exceeds £5000 and then with an input value which is less than £5000. To make absolutely sure a trace using an input value of exactly £5000 could be performed. The trace table below corresponds to the first situation. Read it through and then read the commentary below.

Step	pin	TotalTax	GrossPay	tax	pin <= 100	GrossPay < 5000
1.1	1					
1.2		0.00				
2.1					true	
3.1.2			9000.00			
3.2.1						false
3.2.4				1450.00		
3.4.1		1450.00				
3.5	2					
2.1					true	
3.1.2			4000.00			
3.2.1						true
3.2.2				200.00		
3.4.1		1650.00				
3.5	3					

The first row corresponds to the execution of step 1.1. This step initializes *pin* to 1 and so 1 is entered in the appropriate column. Note that this step only creates an entry in one of the columns, none of the other columns are touched. Step 1.2 is then executed and the result is recorded in the appropriate column. So *TotalTax* is set to zero. Next comes step 2.1 in which the condition *pin* <= 100 must be evaluated. To find the value of any variable at a given time go vertically upwards in the appropriate column and the first value you come to is its current value. If no value is encountered the variable is uninitialized. Here we can see that *pin* has value 1 and so the condition, *pin* <= 100, is true and this value is recorded. Since the loop control condition is true the loop *is* executed. The first step within the loop which is of interest to us is step 3.1.2. This requests a value for *GrossPay* and so the test data value is entered. Step 3.2.1 evaluates the condition *GrossPay* < 5000. The condition evaluates to false. This transfers control to the *else* clause of the *if* statement, that is step 3.2.4. This step number is then entered into the table. The result of step 3.2.4 must be calculated by hand before it can be entered into the table. The *if* statement then terminates and *TotalTax* is evaluated and put in the table as the entry for step 3.4.1. This leads to step 3.5 and the incrementation of *pin*.

The first execution of the loop is now complete! Processing returns to step 2.1 and the loop control condition is evaluated to see if the loop should be executed again. It *is* executed again and this time the test data is chosen so that the *then* clause of the *if* statement is executed. The actual value entered for *GrossPay* is 4000.00.

The two values of test data we used checked that both clauses of the *if* statement worked as they should. However, most design errors do not occur for 'normal' data like this. They often occur for unusual or **critical values** of data. The phrase 'critical value' is not a technical term but it is a convenient description for unusual data values. Critical values ought to be identified before any designing is done. In that way the final design can be tested against it. A critical value for this problem is when gross income is 5000, because that is the value at which the selection of the clauses in the *if* statement changes. Good test data should include critical values and the design should be traced with them to check that it performs correctly.

There is another variable which has a critical value. What is it?

The loop control variable *pin* must take values which enable the loop to execute exactly 100 times. Clearly the trace table cannot be continued for all these values and so some more general reasoning is required. The loop must execute for each employee works number from 1 to 100. On the first execution of the loop *pin* has value 1 as required. At the end of this first execution *pin* is incremented to 2, so *pin* has value 2 on the second loop execution. By extension of this reasoning, *pin* will have value 100 on the one hundredth execution. At the end of this execution *pin* is incremented to give 101 and loop execution ceases.

Tracing through a design in this way, using test data, will not prove that a design is correct. What it may do is to throw up an error which you had not identified. Choosing appropriate test data is difficult but you should always try to choose data that will test that loops are executed the correct number of times, that will force all parts of *if* statements to be executed and will test for the critical values related to the problem. We shall see test data for some of the later problems but we shall not always give such a detailed account of its use as we have given here. Indeed we shall rarely use a trace table in later chapters, but they are a useful tool to fall back on when you discover a mistake but cannot identify exactly where the mistake is occurring.

That completes the design for this problem. The loop used in the solution has a format which is typical. It may be expressed as follows:

1	loop while some *condition* holds
2.1	do some processing
2.2	update *loop control variable*
3	loopend

First, at step 1, there is the loop statement itself and this involves a condition which evaluates to true or false. The statements which are to be repeated within the loop are numbered 2.1 and 2.2 here. Usually in a top level design 2.1 and 2.2 would appear as a single statement such as 'process the data'. This general design illustrates explicitly that the loop control variable must be updated within the loop. Its precise positioning will vary according to the problem being solved. Here it has a similar position to that in the problem just solved, that is immediately before the *loopend*. The major point is that the statement must come *somewhere* within the loop. Finally there is a statement which marks the end of the statements to be repeated, that is step 3.

4.2 LOGICAL ERRORS IN DESIGN

Testing a design using a trace table may expose an error in a design. In this section we shall look at some fairly common design errors and explain why they arise and the strategy which should be adopted to put them right. Most of the designs have a similar top level design to that we have just studied – it is in the refinements that things start to go wrong.

The top level design on page 32 can be used as a template for many problems but it has to be used with care and may need modifications. Consider the following problem:

> The value of a micro computer depreciates by 15 per cent compound per year. Write a design which enables a user to input an initial value for the computer and which will produce as output the value of the computer over the next five years. The output generated from an input value of 200 should be:

> After year 1 depreciated value is 170.00
> After year 2 depreciated value is 144.50
> After year 3 depreciated value is 122.83
> After year 4 depreciated value is 104.40
> After year 5 depreciated value is 88.74

4.2.1 Understand the problem

At the end of one year the micro will have depreciated by 15 per cent. What will be its value expressed in terms of its original value?
It will have 85 per cent of its original value. This new value then depreciates by 15 per cent and so on for five years.

4.2.2 Devise a solution

A possible solution would be to input the data and then to work out the depreciated value for each of the five years. This would lead to a solution along the following lines:

1   write out 'Enter initial value of micro'
2   read in *value*
3   *year* := 1
4   *value* := 0.85**value*
5   write out 'After year ' *year,* ' depreciated value is ', *value*
6   *year* := *year* + 1
7   *value* := 0.85**value*
8   write out 'After year ' *year,* ' depreciated value is ', *value*
9   *year* := *year* + 1
10   *value* := 0.85**value*
11   write out 'After year ' *year,* ' depreciated value is ', *value*
12   *year* := *year* + 1

13 *value* := 0.85* *value*
14 write out 'After year ' *year,* ' depreciated value is ', *value*

This solution is poor because much of the code is repeated. The reason why it has to be repeated is because a loop has not been used. Furthermore if the specification was changed so that the values were required over a 15-year period then the design would require major changes. A better approach is to exploit a loop. Can the top level design of page 32 be exploited? The design below is an attempt to modify it.

1 initialize variables
2 loop while there are more years
3   calculate the depreciated values
4 loopend
5 write out results

A moment's thought should convince you that this is not going to lead to an efficient design either. Step 3 can be refined to calculate the depreciated values but these will have to be stored in memory for use at step 5, when they are written out. This will involve five different variables. What is required is that step 3 should write out the value as soon as it is calculated. So, a second attempt at a top level design is:

{Calculate depreciation for each of five years}
1 initialize variables
2 loop while there are more years
3   calculate and write out depreciated value
4 loopend

What would have happened if you had been unable to anticipate this difficulty? Attempts to refine the design would identify the difficulties. This would be a signal that perhaps the top level design could be improved. Do not expect to go straight to a top level design, even the most general designs like that on page 32 may need some modifications before they fit the problem. The process is one of refining and if necessary going back, making changes and so on. If you do need to go back then it is a good idea to start afresh with the new design making sure that all its steps are correctly numbered. A final design and data table corresponding to this follows.

{Calculate depreciation for each of five years}
1.1   write out 'Enter initial value of micro'
1.2   read in *value*
1.3   *year* := 1
2.1   loop while *year* <= 5
3.1   *value* := 0.85* *value*
3.2   write out 'After year ' *year,* ' depreciated value is ', *value*
3.3   increment *year*
4   loopend

Identifier	Description	Type
value	Current value of micro	real variable
year	Number of years passed	integer variable

Note how step 3 has been refined into three different steps. The loop is controlled by the variable *year* and one of these steps updates its value on each loop execution. Step 1 does all the necessary initialization.

4.2.3 Test the design

That the loop executes the correct number of times needs to be checked, that is, output *is* obtained for the next five years. The critical data in this design is the loop control variable. A potential critical value for the user input is 0.00 and the design should be checked with this as input. Note that we do not have to test for negative input values. This is because they are meaningless and we are assuming that unless specified otherwise, all data input is done correctly and does not require validating. A trace table using an input value of 200 is shown in Figure 4.1. Program execution is completed with the final output value being 88.74.

The design below is a modification of this problem. It requires the user to input the depreciation rate and it outputs the number of years it takes for an original value of $100 to have depreciated to $50 or less. The rate of depreciation is a real number in the range 0 to 100. The top level design is:

    {Calculate when depreciation halves value}
1   initialize variables referenced in loop
2   loop while current value > 50
3   calculate new current value
4   loopend
5   write out results

This can be refined to:

    {Calculate when depreciation halves value}
1.1   *year* := 0
1.2   *NewValue* := *OriginalValue*
1.3   write out 'Enter the depreciation rate as a number between 0 and 100'
1.4   read in *rate*
2.1   loop while *NewValue* > 50
3.1   *NewValue* := (100 − *rate*)*NewValue*/100
3.2   increment *year*
4   loopend
5.1   write out 'Original value will have halved by the year ', *year*

Identifier	Description	Type
OriginalValue	Constant value representing $100	real constant value 100.00
year	Elapsed number of years	integer variable
rate	Depreciation rate	real variable
NewValue	Current depreciated value	real variable

Step	value	year	year <= 5
1.2	200.00		
1.3		1	
2.1			true
3.1	170.00		
3.3		2	
2.1			true
3.1	144.50		
3.3		3	
2.1			true
3.1	122.83		
3.3		4	
2.1			true
3.1	104.40		
3.3		5	
2.1			true
3.1	88.74		
3.3		6	
2.1			false

Figure 4.1 Trace table for depreciation design

It would appear that in this design there is an error at step 1.2 because the identifier *OriginalValue* is referenced and yet there is no statement which initializes it. However, if we look at the data table, *OriginalValue* is defined to be a **real constant** with fixed value 100.00. The use of a constant definition like this can simplify program maintenance because the program can be designed to refer to *OriginalValue* rather than the specific number 100.00. Should the number 100.00 be subsequently changed then the only change required in the program is the alteration of the constant value in the data table. All references to *OriginalValue* in the program will then be references to the new value specified in the data table. This is particularly useful for programs which use things like tax rates. These usually remain the same for many years but it is possible that the government may wish to change the rate. If tax has been declared as a constant then an alteration to the rate can be easily accommodated by changing the value in the constant's definition. Contrast this with the situation where every calculation involving tax used the actual rate expressed as a number. A change to the value would mean searching out every occurrence of these calculations and making the appropriate alterations. This is a very time-consuming and error-prone activity. Most programming languages have a facility for defining constants like this and so we provide a similar facility in the design language.

This design still needs testing. The critical values for the rate of depreciation would appear to be 100 and 0. Both of these values should be used as test data. The value of 100 results in *NewValue* being assigned 0.00 at step 3.1 and loop execution ceases after this first pass. The output is therefore year 1 which is what we would expect. The trace table below shows what happens when 0 is used as the rate of depreciation.

Step	year	NewValue	rate	NewValue > 50
1.1	0			
1.2		100.00 †		
1.4			0	
2.1				true
3.1		100.00		
3.2	1			
2.1				true
3.1		100.00		
3.2	2			
2.1				true
3.1		100.00		
3.2	3			
2.1				true
3.1		100.00		
3.2	4			
2.1				true
3.1				
3.2				

The value marked † is obtained from the data table.

Here, *NewValue* always retains its original value of 100.00. A little thought should convince you that this will be the case on every execution of the loop and so the loop will never cease executing! Therefore this design would appear to be in error. The specification of the problem needs to be examined to see if a rate of depreciation of zero is allowed as user input. In this instance the specification is (deliberately) vague. Does the range 0 to 100 mean inclusive? In a real problem this should have been clarified at the outset. The design above is fine if zero is excluded but if it is not, then an alternative design is required. A top level design which produces a message for the user when a zero depreciation rate is input is:

```
    {Depreciation with zero rate as a possibility}
1   read in the rate of depreciation
2   if the rate is zero then
3       write out 'No depreciation ever takes place'
4   else
5       process depreciation for this rate
6   ifend
```

You can complete the design based on this top level design in the next problem section.

Exercise 4.1 Write a top level design which enables a user to input exactly 20 real numbers and which produces as output their average.

The top level design given in the solution to Exercise 4.1 can be refined in many ways. One of them is given below together with the data table.

{Find the average of 20 real numbers input from keyboard}

1.1	*count* := 1
1.2	*sum* := 0
2.1	loop while *count* <= 20
3.1	write out 'Enter number ', *count*, ' now'
3.2	read in *number*
3.3	*sum* := *sum* + *number*
3.4	increment *count*
4	loopend
5.1	*average* := *sum*/20
5.2	write out 'The average is ', *average*

Identifier	Description	Type
count	A count of the number of inputs	integer variable
number	Number entered by user	real variable
sum	Cumulative sum of inputs	real variable
average	Average of 20 numbers	real variable

This design needs to be tested to ensure that the loop executes the correct number of times. A trace table with 20 loop executions is not very realistic. One way of overcoming this is to replace 20 by some more manageable, smaller number and create a complete trace table for the loop stages of the design using this smaller number. In the trace table in Figure 4.2 the value 2 has been used rather than 20 in step 2.1.

Step	*count*	*sum*	*count* <= 2	*number*
1.1	1			
1.2		0		
2.1			true	
3.2				5.5
3.3		5.5		
3.4	2			
2.1			true	
3.2				3.5
3.3		9.0		
3.4	3			
2.1			false	
5.1				

Figure 4.2 Testing the loop using 2 instead of 20

Here it is easier to see that when the loop control variable has the value 3, the loop ceases execution. It is immediately obvious from the table that the user has entered precisely two numbers and that *sum* correctly records their total. Using a modified loop control variable is one way of testing that a loop which would normally execute a large number of times executes the correct number of times. However it should be stressed that modifying the design is for test purposes only and should be done with care.

Exercise 4.2 There are other ways to initialize the variable *count* and to express the condition in step 2.1 of the design above. Write down possible initial values for *count* together with the required loop statement for each value. The places where these occur are marked ?? in the design below. Notice that the design does not inform the user which number is being requested, as was done above. You may also like to modify the prompt so that it does so here.

	{Find the average of 20 real numbers input from keyboard}
1.1	*count* := ??
1.2	*sum* := 0
2.1	loop while *count* ??
3.1	write out 'Enter a number'
3.2	read in *number*
3.3	*sum* := *sum* + *number*
3.4	increment *count*
4	loopend
5.1	*average* := *sum*/20
5.2	write out 'The average is ', *average*

The solution to Exercise 4.2 shows that there are many correct ways in which a design may be refined. In the last alternative the position of the loop control variable was changed, which made it easier to check that the loop executed the correct number of times. However, statements cannot in general be moved without there being a change in their logic. The exercise below gives you the opportunity of trying to find a logical error.

Exercise 4.3 The design below is an erroneous solution to the problem of finding the average of 20 inputs from the keyboard. Identify the errors.

	{This design contains errors}
1.1	*count* := 0
1.2	*sum* := 0
1.3	write out 'Enter a number'
1.4	read in *number*
2.1	loop while *count* <= 20
3.1	*sum* := *sum* + *number*
3.2	write out 'Enter a number'
3.3	read in *number*
4	loopend
5.1	*average* := *sum*/20
5.2	write out 'The average is ', *average*

Exercise 4.4 Write a design which enables a user to input as many non-negative real numbers as desired and which will produce as output the number of reals entered together with their average. Execution of the design should allow a user to not enter any numbers at all

and hence terminate the program immediately. In that event a message that an average does not exist should be output.

The solution to Exercise 4.4 used a **sentinel value** to control the loop. The design below is based on the same top level design and the same identifiers and sentinel value are used. However, the design is in error. Try to identify the errors before reading on.

	{Erroneous design for Exercise 4.4}
1.1	*count* := 0
1.2	*sum* := 0
1.3	*number* := 1
2.1	loop while *number* >= 0
3.1	write out 'Enter a non-negative number as data or a negative to quit'
3.2	read in *number*
3.3	*sum* := *sum* + *number*
3.4	increment *count*
4	loopend
5.1	if *count* = 0 then
5.2	write out 'No data has been input so the average does not exist'
5.3	else
5.4	*average* := *sum/count*
5.5	write out 'The average of your ' *count* ' numbers is ' *average*
5.6	ifend

Since data is entered at the beginning of the loop, at step 3.2, input of the sentinel value would result in it being added to the variable *sum* and in the variable *count* being incremented. This could be rectified by replacing step 5.1 by:

5.1.1	decrement *count*
5.1.2	*sum* := *sum* − *number*
5.1.3	if *count* = 0 then

This effectively removes 1 from the count of the number of data entries and subtracts the sentinel value from *sum* to compensate for the fact that it was added to *sum* within the loop. The design is therefore more complicated than it needs to be and rather than try to rectify the error in the way we have done it would be much better to go back to the top level design and start again.

The fundamental difference between this design and the one in Exercise 4.4 is that in the latter design the variable *number* was initialized by user input and the value entered determined whether or not the loop executed at all. In this design the program statement 1.3 initializes *number* to a value which forces the loop to be executed at least once. In the next chapter we shall see another type of loop construct which is always executed at least once.

The following design is also erroneous. Try to find the errors before reading on.

	{Erroneous design for Exercise 4.4}
1.1	*count* := −1

1.2	*sum* := 0	
1.3	*number* := 1	
2.1	loop while *number* >= 0	
3.1		*sum* := *sum* + *number*
3.2		increment *count*
3.3		write out 'Enter a non-negative number as data or a negative to quit'
3.4		read in *number*
4	loopend	
5.1	if *count* = 0 then	
5.2		write out 'No data has been input so the average does not exist'
5.3	else	
5.4		*average* := *sum*/*count*
5.5		write out 'The average of your ' *count* ' numbers is ' *average*
5.6	ifend	

This design avoids the problem of including the sentinel in the sum of the inputs. By initializing *count* to −1 it also gets the correct value of the count on exit from the loop. Unfortunately the value of *sum* is incorrect because on the first execution of the loop it is assigned the value 1 at step 3.1 (this being the sum of the initial values of *sum* and *number*). This could be put right by initializing *sum* to value −1 but to someone reading this design this would seem a very odd choice of an initial value. You should try to avoid initializing variables to non-natural values in order to rescue what is a design deficiency elsewhere.

By looking at designs which contain errors we hope to alert you to some of the dangers that are lying in wait. Trying to get round a faulty design as we have just been doing is discouraged. It is much better to take note of the difficulty and return to the previous level of design. If the error is still in this design then go back to its predecessor. Once you have got back to a design which avoids the difficulty then it can be refined afresh and with the knowledge gained from hindsight.

4.3 PROBLEMS

4.1 The specification of the depreciation of microcomputers given at the start of Section 4.2 is now to be modified to include some data validation. If the user inputs a non-positive number for the initial value of the micro then a message is to be output saying that the value must be positive and the user is to be prompted to try again. All subsequent input attempts must be validated in the same way.

4.2 Write a design which enables a user to input a string and which will output each character of the string on a separate line. You may assume that the user inputs at least one character and that each occurrence of the *write out* statement produces a new line.

4.3 In Problem 4.2 what difference would it have made if the assumption that the user inputs at least one character had been removed from the specification?

4.4 Complete the design of the amended depreciation problem whose top level design is given on page 40 in which the original value of the article is held as a real constant.

4.5 A fast-food outlet requires its staff to enter the details of a customer order on a till which will produce the customer's bill. For each menu item on the order the unit price is entered, followed by the number of such items required by the customer. The bill produced by the till gives the total cost and the number of items which make up the order. The latter quantity is used as a check by the sales assistant to ensure that each customer gets the correct number of packages of food. Input of an order is terminated by zero being entered as the unit price. Write a design which will enable an order to be entered into the till and which will produce as output a bill having the form given above.

4.6 In Chapter 3 we saw that a type mismatch occurs if an attempt is made to assign a real value to an integer variable. However, situations can arise where it is necessary to assign a real number which has a zero decimal part, for example a real number like 3.0, to an integer variable in order that it can be processed using integer operators. This problem asks you to write a design to achieve this for positive real numbers which have zero decimal part. The output from the design should be the equivalent integer.

4.7 The integer part of a real number is defined to be the largest integer which does not exceed the number. For example, the integer part of 7.91 is 7. What amendments would be required to the design in Problem 4.6 in order to assign to *wholenumber* the integer part of a positive real number input from the keyboard? (The definition of integer part applies to negative real numbers as well but we are considering only positive real numbers here.)

4.8 Word processors often have a utility which counts the number of words in a given document. Some provide more sophisticated utilities which can supply the average word length in a document. Here we consider a simplified version of the latter utility. A line of text is to be processed to find the average length of the words it contains. The text, which is to be entered from the keyboard, must begin with a non-space character and must terminate with a single-space character. For the purposes of this problem a word is defined to be any sequence of non-space characters. Words must be separated from each other by exactly one space and no two-space characters may be placed side by side. You may assume that the user enters data as instructed. The constraints on the input format will be relaxed in Problem 5.22.

4.9 Most word processors give the user the option of right-justifying the text, that is aligning the last character of each line at the right-hand side. One way of doing this is to put extra space characters between the words. In Chapter 9 we shall look at this problem in detail but for now we shall look at a much simplified version. Write a design which will insert one extra space every time a space character is encountered in a string. Your design should enable a user to input a string which should then be copied character by character to a new string containing the extra space characters where appropriate. Finally the new string should be written out. You should assume that the input string does not contain adjacent space characters.

4.4 SUMMARY

In this chapter we have created designs using the fundamental control structures of *if* statements and *while* loops. We have used them in the problem solving strategy of *understanding the problem, devising a solution* and *testing the solution.* We have also seen how we can test a design using a trace table.

5

FURTHER LOOP STRUCTURES

In this chapter we shall introduce two new kinds of loops. The first type will execute a fixed number of times whereas the second will be similar to a *while* loop in that its execution will be determined by a condition. However, unlike the *while* loop, the condition will come after the steps which are to be executed repeatedly. We shall also describe a strategy which will give guidance as to the type of loop which should be used in a particular situation.

5.1 *FOR* LOOPS

In Exercise 4.1, 20 real numbers were to be input by a user in order to find their average. The design for this problem is reproduced below.

	{Find the average of 20 real numbers input from keyboard}
1.1	*count* := 1
1.2	*sum* := 0
2.1	loop while *count* <= 20
3.1	write out 'Enter number ', *count*, ' now'
3.2	read in *number*
3.3	*sum* := *sum* + *number*
3.4	increment *count*
4	loopend
5.1	*average* := sum/20
5.2	write out 'The average is ', *average*

The loop control variable *count* ensures that the loop is executed the correct number of times. This solution uses a *while* loop, but a while loop is most effective when the number of executions of the loop statements is not known at execution time. Here the number is known in advance, it is 20. Contrast this with Exercise 4.4, where the user was allowed any number of inputs. The loop in that example continued until the user entered zero.

In situations where we know in advance how many executions of the loop are required, an alternative loop structure, called a *for* loop, can be used. Below we have reproduced an equivalent design to that on page 47 using a *for* loop instead of a *while* loop.

	{Find the average of 20 real numbers input from keyboard}
1.1	*sum* := 0
2.1	loop for *count* from 1 to 20
3.1	write out 'Enter number ', *count*, ' now'
3.2	read in *number*
3.3	*sum* := *sum* + *number*
4	loopend
5.1	*average* := *sum*/20
5.2	write out 'The average is ', *average*

Note here that the variable *count* forms part of the *for* statement, as does the range of values it can take. The first value of this range that *count* takes is called the initial value and the last value is called the final value. There is no need to initialize *count* at step 1 as there was before. Moreover, step 2.1 implies that *count* will take successive values 1, 2, 3 and so on up to and including 20. This means that there is no equivalent statement to *increment count* of step 3.4. However, notice that there is still a need to initialize *sum*, since it is referenced within the loop. The rules for using a *for* loop can be summarized as:

1. Initialize any variables referenced in the loop prior to the loop. There may not always be any but you should be careful to check.

2. In final designs you must specify the initial and final values over which the index should vary as part of the *for* statement. In the example above the initial value was 1 and the final value was 20. Positive, negative or zero values are all permitted for the initial and final values but if the initial value is greater than the final value then the body of the loop is not executed at all and execution would continue with the statement following the loopend.

3. The loop control variable must not be incremented within the body of the loop or an error will result.

Setting the initial value for the loop control variable in a *for* loop is the same thing as assigning it a value. We shall therefore usually use the assignment symbol instead of the word *from* in this statement. The general structure of a *for* loop can then be seen to have the form:

1	loop for *control variable* := *initial* to *final*
2	process to be repeated this fixed number of times
3	loopend

We shall insist that in *for* loops the automatic updating of the loop control variable be in increments of 1. This is very restrictive, but as many programming languages impose this restriction we shall do so as well. The cost of the restriction is that we shall have to use more complex expressions within the loop should we require other increments. Thus we shall not allow:

```
1  loop for count := 2 to 100 step 2
2      write out count
3  loopend
```

where *step 2* means increment *count* by 2. You could, of course, use this in your designs if your programming language supports it. If *we* want to write out all the even numbers between 1 and 100 we would write.

```
1  loop for count := 1 to 50
2      write out 2*count
3  loopend
```

Should it be required to write out these even numbers in reverse order then the initial and final values cannot simply be exchanged because the loop will then not execute at all. What has to be done is to use a **downto** *for* loop as in:

```
1  loop for count := 50 downto 1
2      write out 2*count
3  loopend
```

The same sort of rules apply to a *downto* loop as before. If the initial value is less than the final value then the loop will not execute at all and execution will continue with the statement following the loopend.

Exercise 5.1 Write down the output resulting from each of the following designs:

```
(a)  1    loop for index := 3 to 7
     2        write out 2*index − 1
     3    loopend
     4    write out 'end'
(b)  1    loop for index := 7 to 3
     2        write out 2*index − 1
     3    loopend
     4    write out 'end'
(c)  1    loop for index := 7 downto 3
     2        write out 2*index − 1
     3    loopend
     4    write out 'end'
(d)  1    loop for index := −1 downto −1
     2        write out 2*index − 1
     3    loopend
     4    write out 'end'
```

5.2 PROBLEMS

5.1 The following design appeared in the solution to Problem 4.2:

{write out input string one character per line}
1.1   write out 'Input your string '
1.2   read in *line*
1.3   *index* := 1
2.1   loop while *index* <= *length(line)*
3.1   write out *line*[*index*]
3.2   increment *index*
4   loopend

Explain why the *while* loop can be replaced by a *for* loop. Write a design, based upon that given, which uses a *for* loop instead of a *while* loop.

5.2 Many problems involving strings require them to be manipulated and split into other strings. Consider the problem of holding a person's address on computer. One way would be to declare a string variable to hold the street name, another to hold the town, a third to hold the county and a fourth for the post code. However, not all addresses have this format; some houses have names, others may be situated in villages whose address includes the name of the nearest town, and so on. One way of overcoming the different address formats is to hold the whole address in a single string variable and to separate the components by a special symbol. For example, the string: 'High Bank*Lucks Farm*Greenwood Lane*Tonbridge*Kent' would represent the address which is more familiarly written:

High Bank
Lucks Farm
Greenwood Lane
Tonbridge
Kent

This method of representing addresses is sometimes called **free format**. To recover the individual components the single string has to be split at each asterisk. This problem is a simplified version of this process. Write a design which will enable a user to input a string similar to that above but consisting of just two words separated by a single asterisk. The design should assign to *firstword* and *secondword* the two words of the input string and neither should contain the asterisk itself. The output should be the two words written out on different lines, together with appropriate prompts. You may assume that the user inputs at least an asterisk and your solution should use a *while* loop and a *for* loop.

5.3 A competition for ice skaters has eight judges who award marks for the performance of each skater. The mark awarded by a judge to an individual skater is a real number, to one decimal place in the range 0 to 6 inclusive. All eight judges present a mark for a skater and the eight marks are collected together. The highest and lowest marks are discarded and the average of the six remaining marks is then the score obtained by that skater. This marking process is supposed to remove any bias an individual judge may have for a particular competitor. Write a design which will allow all eight marks to be entered and which will produce as output the score obtained by this procedure. The eight marks entered should not be assigned to variables and then manipulated; instead appropriate running values should be stored.

5.3 DESIGN AND SCREEN OUTPUT

As we have already stated we shall not be too concerned with the format of output data to the screen. A particular problem arises with the output of real numbers which can be output in a variety of different formats dependent upon their magnitude. Programming languages allow the programmer to specify how many digits and decimal places should be displayed. Detail like this can be added after the major work on the design is complete and so we shall not consider it here.

However, we shall need a mechanism for some control of our hypothetical output. In particular, we shall occasionally require the screen to be cleared. The statement

clear screen

will be taken to mean 'clear the whole of the screen and place the cursor at the left uppermost corner'.

So far, we have only used the term *write out* to send string constants and variable values to the screen. We shall assume that at the completion of execution of this statement that the cursor goes to the leftmost position of the next line. In other words, *write out* also generates a new line. When we do not wish for a new line to be generated we shall use the statement *write*, in which case the next statement that involves screen activity will take place immediately to the right of this output. This is particularly useful for data input when you want the cursor to be positioned just after the prompt in readiness for the user to supply the input. The following design extract illustrates the use of *write* and *write out*.

1 clear screen
2 write 'Enter a string▽'
3 read in *line*
4 write out 'The text you entered is given on the next line'
5 write out *line*
6 write out
7 write out 'Program▽terminated'

The output produced by this sequence of statements when the user enters the string 'This is my line of text' is shown in Figure 5.1.

```
Enter a string ▽This is my line of text
The text you entered is given on the next line
This is my line of text

Program ▽terminated
```

Figure 5.1 Example screen output

Notice how the data entered all appears on the same line as the prompt. This is because the prompt is controlled by a *write* statement which leaves the cursor on the same line as the prompt. Step 6 has the effect of outputting a blank line to the screen. Occasionally the output from a problem will be required in the form of a table, like that in the exercise below. We shall not include in the design language methods by which output can be formatted as a table. Instead space characters will be used to give an approximation to the creation of columns.

Exercise 5.2 The table below is part of a ready reckoner to convert feet and inches into millimetres. Write a design which will create a ready reckoner for measurements from 1 to 36 inches in increments of one inch. You may assume that 1 inch is equivalent to 25.4 millimetres. Note that for measurements of less than one foot a blank appears in the column labelled *Feet*. (There are 12 inches in a foot.)

Feet	Inches	Millimetres
...	...	...
	10	254.0
	11	279.4
1	0	304.8
1	1	330.2
...	...	...

5.4 PROBLEMS

5.4 Write a design which will enable a user to input some text into a string variable and which will produce as output the text with each sentence on a new line. For this problem a sentence is defined to be any sequence of characters terminating with a full stop. You may assume that the user does not enter a null string.

5.5 Write a design which will enable a user to input the day of the week on which a month starts and the number of days in the month and which produces as output a calendar for the month in the format shown below.

Sun	Mon	Tues	Wed	Thurs	Fri	Sat
		1	2	3	4	5
6	7	8	9	10	11	12
13	14	15	16	17	18	19
20	21	22	23	24	25	26
27	28	29	30	31		

The day on which the month starts should be entered as an integer where 1 corresponds to Sunday, 2 to Monday and so on.

5.5 PRE- AND POSTCONDITIONED LOOPS

The two loop structures we have met so far, the *for* loop and the *while* loop, may be classified according to the number of executions of the body of the loop. In the *for* loop the number of executions is specified by the initial and final values of the loop control variable. For the *while* loop the number of executions is not known beforehand and it relies upon an update to the loop control condition to determine when loop execution should cease.

The *while* loop which we have been using is called a **preconditioned** loop because the condition, which is used to determine whether or not the body of the loop is executed, is evaluated *before* the loop is executed. In other words the loop has the form

> loop while *condition*
> statements in loop body
> loopend

In this form of loop, if the condition evaluates to false then loop execution ceases and control passes to the statement following the loopend. A consequence of this is that it is possible for the loop not to execute at all and for control to pass directly to the statement after the loopend. This will happen if the condition evaluates to false on the first (and therefore only) occasion on which the condition is tested.

Now the loop control condition can be placed at the end of the loop, after all the statements within the body of the loop. A loop having this property is called a **postconditioned** loop. We shall consider the following postconditioned loop.

> repeat
> statements in loop body
> until *condition*

In this type of loop construct the statements within the loop body are always executed at least once. At the end of their first execution the condition is evaluated and if it is false the loop executes again. This continues until the condition evaluates to true when loop execution immediately ceases and control passes to the next statement in the sequence. We shall refer to a loop of this type as a **repeat until** loop, or more simply a **repeat** loop.

In order to decide which of the three loop constructs you should use you will first need to determine whether or not the loop is to execute a fixed number of times. If it is, then use a *for* loop. If it is not, then try to ascertain the minimum number of times the loop should execute. If the minimum is zero, a *while* loop must be used. If the minimum is one or more, a *repeat* loop can be used.

In Chapter 4 a design was developed for calculating the number of years it takes for a known sum to halve in value given an input depreciation rate (assumed non-zero). A top level design which uses a postconditioned loop is:

> {Calculate when depreciation halves value using repeat loop}
> 1   initialize variables referenced in loop
> 2   repeat
> 3   calculate depreciated value
> 4   until depreciated value is halved
> 5   write out results

Using the identifiers of Chapter 4 this can be refined to:

> {Calculate when depreciation halves *OriginalValue* using repeat loop}
> 1.1   *year* := 0
> 1.2   *NewValue* := *OriginalValue*
> 1.3   write out 'Enter the depreciation rate as a number between 0 and 100'

1.4   read in *rate*
2   repeat
3.1   *NewValue* := (100 − *rate*)*NewValue*/100
3.2   increment *year*
4.1   until *NewValue* <= 50
5.1   write out 'Original value will have halved by the year ', *year*

There are some points to note about this design. Firstly the variable *year* is referenced within the body of the loop and so it must be initialized before its entry. The loop condition control variable *NewValue* is initialized prior to the first execution of the loop and it then gets updated within the loop itself. The next example will illustrate that unlike *while* loops, postconditioned loops can have their loop condition control variables initialized within the loop rather than prior to it. The context will decide where the initialization should be done. Secondly the inequality on the condition has become less than or equal to rather than the greater than of the *while* loop design. Care needs to be exercised on conditions when you decide to change a design from one type of loop to another.

To emphasize that the loop control variable must be updated within the loop a general description of a repeat loop is as follows:

1   repeat
2   do some processing
3   update *loop control variable*
4   until some *condition* holds

The precise positioning of the updating of the loop control variable will be determined by the details of the design solution but the major point is that it must be somewhere in the loop.

Exercise 5.3 The top level design below is taken from Exercise 4.4. It enables a user to input non-negative real numbers and outputs their average. Redesign the solution using a postconditioned loop.

    {Find average of an arbitrary number of non-negative numbers}
1   initialize variables referenced in loop
2   loop while there are numbers to be input
3   process the data
4   loopend
5   calculate average and write out results

This exercise shows how important it is to initialize variables correctly. It also illustrates that although there are many different ways of solving the same problem, some are easier to understand than others. The preconditioned version has the slight disadvantage that the same statements (the requests for data) appear in two different places. But it is clear that *sum* and *count* have correct values throughout. Version 1 of the postcondition design overcomes the problem of the repeated statements but has the disadvantage that *count* is initialized to a number which does not appear to be natural from the specification of the problem. Version 2 is probably the worst design in that it has the same difficulty as version 1 concerning *count*, but has the added complication that *sum* has the wrong value on loop termination. As we are more concerned with clear designs rather than efficiency, the slight overhead of the repeated statements in the preconditioned design is acceptable because of the clarity of the remainder.

5.6 PROBLEMS

5.6 Write two designs, one of which uses a preconditioned loop, the other a postconditioned loop, which will enable a user to enter characters from the keyboard and which will produce as output the number of occurrences of the lower-case letter 'a'. The characters should not be stored in a string and termination of input should be by using the sentinel value '*'. Which design is to be preferred?

5.7 When economists are discussing inflation they often quote the *rule of 72*, which says that the period in which a fixed sum of money will decline to half its value is 72 DIV *rate* years, where *rate* is the annual rate of inflation. Test the accuracy of this rule by writing a design which will produce a table of the values of *rate*, the precise number of years for the decline and 72 DIV rate for each of the values of *rate* from 1 to 36 per cent.

5.8 A modified version of the 'rule of 72' described in Problem 5.7 uses real division, rounding the result to the nearest whole number, rather than integer division. A fractional part of 0.5 or more is rounded up. All other values are rounded down. Using this modified rule write a design which will output a table of all the rates from 1 to 36 per cent inclusive for which the actual number of years and the estimate differ. The table should include the rate of inflation, the actual number of years for the decline and the estimate of this number of years.

5.7 NESTED CONTROL STRUCTURES

The designs have seen so far have generally consisted of loops and if statements. Often the *if* statement has been inside the loop. We say the *if* statement is nested within the loop. To be more specific the *if* statement is nested to a level one deep. We have constructs which are nested one within another to any depth and in this section we are going to focus on nested constructs in detail. In particular, we shall look at nested *if* statements which provide a method of selection between more than two alternatives.

5.7.1 Nested loops

Consider the problem of finding the average of 20 real numbers that we looked at in Section 5.1. With some extravagant imagination we might picture this as being part of a statistical package. But the user of such a package is likely to need to find the averages of lots of collections of 20 numbers. In other words the user needs to be given the opportunity of repeatedly running the program. A top level design which includes this facility is:

```
    {Averaging program for sets of 20 real numbers}
 1  repeat
 2      find the average of 20 numbers
 3      check if another execution is required
 4  until no more executions are required
```

This design enables the averaging program developed in Section 5.1 to be run repeatedly. By choosing a postconditioned loop we are imposing the restriction on the user that this program must execute at least once. Although this is a new design we are not throwing away the work we did to produce the design for averaging just one set of 20 numbers. That design will constitute most of the refinement of step 2 here. In the refinement below the outer loop is controlled using a character variable which is updated as part of step 3.

{Averaging program for sets of 20 numbers}

1	repeat
2.1	*count* := 1
2.2	*sum* := 0
2.3	loop while *count* <= 20
2.4	write out 'Enter number ', *count*, ' now'
2.5	read in *number*
2.6	*sum* := *sum* + *number*
2.7	increment *count*
2.8	loopend
2.9	*average* := *sum*/20
2.10	write out 'The average of this set of 20 numbers is ' *average*
3.1	write out 'Do you wish to process another 20 numbers? y/n '
3.2	read in *ch*
4.1	until *ch* = 'n'

Identifier	Description	Type
ch	Loop control variable	char variable

Note how this design exploits the earlier one. So although this is a new problem resulting in its own top level design and subsequent numbering, the earlier design has been copied and used in its entirety in steps 2.1–2.9.

If the structure of this design is examined it can be seen that it has an *outer* loop and an *inner* loop nested within it. The outer loop has an *until* statement to match the *repeat* at step 1 and the inner loop has a *loopend* to match the *loop while* at step 2.3. It is most important that the beginnings and ends of loops are matched in this way. A preconditioned loop must have the matching pair of statements *loop while* and *loopend*; a postconditioned loop the pair of statements *repeat* and *until*; and the *for* loop the pair *loop for* and *loopend*. Also an inner loop must terminate before the outer loop in which it is nested. The following sequence is invalid:

repeat {loop A}

  loop while {loop B}

  until {end of loop A}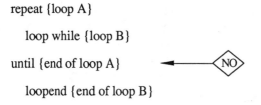

  loopend {end of loop B}

Exercise 5.4 This problem concerns writing a design for a simple guessing game played between two people. The first player inputs an integer and the second player repeatedly guesses what the first player entered. After each unsuccessful guess the program should output a message saying either that the guess is too small or that it is too large. As a result of a successful guess the program should output a suitable message of congratulation followed by a request to repeat the whole game afresh. Your design should use both a pre- and post-conditioned loop.

5.7.2 Nested *if* statements

These are much more complex than nested loops because it is very much easier to make a semantic error, that is to get the logic incorrect. With nested loops you have to be careful to match the start of a loop with its end and to make sure that inner loops are completely contained in the immediate outer loop. The same rules apply to *if* statements, but complications arise because not all *if* statements have an *else* clause and because the logic is generally harder to understand. We begin by reminding you of the structure of an *if* statement.

```
if condition then
      statements          {the then clause}
else
      statements          {the else clause}
ifend
```

Sometimes an *if* statement does not have an *else* clause. When this is the case we remind you that there are two methods of writing it down.

```
if condition then
      statements   {the then clause}
else
      do nothing   {the empty else clause}
ifend
```

```
if condition then
      statements   {the then clause}
ifend
```

Exercise 5.5 What would be output by each of the following design fragments if x had value 15 or 5?

(a) if $x > 10$ then
      write out 'It is bigger than 10'
   else
      write out 'It is not bigger than 10'
      write out 'But it could be equal to 10'
   ifend

(b) if $x > 10$ then
      write out 'It is bigger than 10'
   else
      write out 'It is not bigger than 10'
   ifend
   write out 'But it could be equal to 10'

In Exercise 5.5(b) the *ifend* has been incorrectly positioned and this results in a **semantic** error. Thus positioning of the word *ifend* is crucial and if incorrect can have disastrous consequences on the logic of a design. The same comment applies to the positioning of the *else* statement. The design in (a) can be modified so that it distinguishes between the cases where x is bigger than 10, is equal to 10 and is less than 10. To do so requires the use of nested *if* statements.

```
if x > 10 then                      {start of outer if statement}
    write out 'It is bigger than 10'        {the outer then clause}
else                                {start of outer else clause}
    if x < 10 then                      {start of inner if statement}
        write out 'It is smaller than 10'       {the inner then clause}
    else                                {start of inner else clause}
        write out 'It is equal to 10'           {the inner else clause}
    ifend                           {end of inner if statement}
ifend                           {end of outer if statement}
```

You can see how important good indentation is with this example. Although indentation does not alter the logic it does make it easier to read. Notice how the inner *if* is indented so that it is clear that the whole of this inner *if* is in fact the *else* clause of the outer *if*.

A striking feature of this example is that x could satisfy one, and only one, of three possible outcomes; it could be less than 10, equal to 10 or greater than 10. Notice how this was achieved. The else clause consisted of an *if* statement. This observation can be generalized to the situation where there are four alternatives, only one of which is possible. For example if *compass* is a char variable then the fragment

```
if compass = 'N' then
    write out 'North'
else
    if compass = 'S' then
        write out 'South'
    else
        if compass = 'W' then
            write out 'West'
        else
            write out 'East'
        ifend
    fend
ifend
```

writes out the word corresponding to the symbol for north, south, east or west. Notice how each *else* (except the last) is immediately followed by an *if*. It is this form of nested *if* that is required when only one of many alternatives can take place.

Exercise 5.6 At a particular point in processing a character variable *ch* can have one of the three values 'a', 'b' or 'c'. Write a design fragment that will change the variable to its upper case equivalent.

You may have written the following design as your solution to the last problem.

```
1   if ch = 'a' then
2       ch := 'A'
3   ifend
4   if ch = 'b' then
5       ch := 'B'
6   ifend
7   if ch = 'c' then
8       ch := 'C'
9   ifend
```

This is a sequence of *if* statements. This solution *would* work here but it is extremely inefficient. For, suppose that *ch* actually had value 'a', then this design executes the comparisons at steps 4 and 7. The nested version requires just the one comparison for this value of *ch*. Even if *ch* has value 'c' the nested version requires only two comparisons to this version's three.

The outcome of these two versions was the same, even if their efficiency was not. This may not always be the case, that is, a nested sequence of the type above cannot always be rearranged as a sequence by ignoring the *else* clauses. Suppose instead of changing the lower-case letter to an upper-case one we were required to change 'a' to 'b', 'b' to 'c' and 'c' to 'd'. The nested statements then become:

```
if ch = 'a' then
    ch := 'b'
else
    if ch = 'b' then
        ch := 'c'
    else
        ch := 'd'
    ifend
ifend
```

Attempting to rearrange these as a sequence without *else* clauses would give:

```
1   if ch = 'a' then
2       ch := 'b'
3   ifend
4   if ch = 'b' then
5       ch := 'c'
6   ifend
7   if ch = 'c' then
8       ch := 'd'
9   ifend
```

Now if *ch* starts off with value 'a' this sequence of statements will change its value to 'd' because step 2 changes it to 'b', step 4 evaluates to true and hence its value gets updated by step 5 to 'c'. Then step 7 is true and so step 8 updates the value to 'd'.

Multiple *if* statements can be nested in ways other than that shown above. Consider the following hypothetical car insurance premium table where there are two age categories and two types of car:

	saloon car	sports car
under 25	100	150
25 and over	80	120

The following design fragment determines the premium for these possible categories.

```
if the car is a saloon then
    if person is under 25 then
        premium is 100                  {saloon driver under 25}
    else
        premium is 80                   {saloon driver 25 and over}
    ifend
else
    if person is under 25 then
        premium is 150                  {sports car driver under 25}
    else
        premium is 120                  {saloon driver 25 and over}
    ifend
ifend
```

The structure of the outer *if* is quite different here. Each of the *then* and *else* clauses of the outer *if* is itself an *if* statement.

Exercise 5.7 Rewrite this design so that the outermost *if* tests for the age of the person.

Exercise 5.8 Write a new design for Exercise 5.4 which uses two repeat loops and nested *if* statements.

Finally we look at the situation where an *if* statement has no *else* part and the *then* clause is an *if* statement. An example is given by

```
if x > 1 then
    if x < 10 then
        write out message
    ifend
ifend
```

Under what circumstances will the message be written out? It will be output when x is bigger than 1 and less than 10, in other words when x lies in the range 1 to 10 (excluding 1 and 10 themselves). Another way of writing this fragment is:

```
if x > 1 and x < 10 then
    write out message
ifend
```

This uses the word *and* between the two conditions. We shall be studying this operator in Chapter 7 and so we shall avoid using it until then.

5.8 PROBLEMS

5.9   Problems 3.6 and 3.7 were concerned with working out on which day of the week a given date falls. The output from the solutions was a code representing the day of the week; 0 for Sunday, 1 for Monday and so on. Write a design fragment which takes such a code and outputs the name of the day of the week.

5.10   Write a design which will prompt for and read in a string which may contain multiple space characters between its words but which must terminate with a non-space character. The output from the design should be the input text with all multiple spaces replaced by single spaces.

5.11   We have already seen a problem related to the word processing facility of finding the average word length in a document. Here we shall look at a simplified version of the problem of counting how many occurrences of a particular word there are in a piece of text. Write a design which will enable the user to enter a string from the keyboard and which will output the number of occurrences of the pattern 'an'. You may assume that the user enters at least one character as input. You should not find it necessary to use the boolean operator *and* in your solution.

5.12   The Roman numerals corresponding to the numbers 1 to 9 are I, II, III, IV, V, VI, VII, VIII and IX. Decimal numbers between 5 and 8 have a Roman numeral form of 'V' followed by an appropriate number of 'I's and those between 1 and 3 consist only of 'I's. A design fragment which exploits this division in order to convert a decimal *number* in the range 1 to 9 to a string representing the roman numeral equivalent is:

```
1   initialize variables
2   if number >= 5 then
3       convert number
4   else
5       convert number
6   ifend
```

Complete the details of the design fragment.

5.13   Problem 4.9 introduced a first step towards solving the problem of right-justifying a piece of text by looking at the simpler problem of inserting extra space characters into a string whenever a space character was encountered. The specification is now slightly changed so that the input string is permitted to have adjacent space characters. However, when this occurs only one extra space character is to be inserted into the string which forms the result. You may assume that the input string does not terminate in a space character, nor is it null.

5.14   Exercise 5.2 developed a ready reckoner which converted feet and inches to millimetres. In this problem you are asked to design a ready reckoner that will do the conversion the other way round, that is from millimetres to feet and inches. The output should be a table in which the first column contains measurements of 100 millimetres up to 1000 millimetres in increments of 100. The second and third columns should contain the equivalent measure in feet and inches. So, for example, 600 millimetres should appear in the table with the integer 1 in the foot column and a real number (approximately 11.6) in the inches column. You may find Problem 4.6 helpful in obtaining the correct integer number of feet. (There are 12 inches in a foot, 1 inch = 25.4 millimetres.)

5.9 ADDITIONAL PROBLEMS

The problems in this section may require the use of nested loops and nested *if* statements.

5.15 The process of counting occurrences of 'an' explained in Problem 5.11 could be performed dynamically, that is, as characters are entered from the keyboard. Write a design which performs this dynamic analysis where the user indicates termination of input with an asterisk.

5.16 A program is to be written which will provide a summary of a cricketer's batting performance over a season. As with many problems you do not have to understand the game of cricket in order to get a solution. If you are unfamiliar with the game (or have never even heard of it) treat the problem as a challenge in which the specification tells you all you need to know in order to get to the solution. The output of the program will be of the form:

Innings	Not out	Runs	Average
24	4	1000	50.00

A cricketer who goes into bat is called a batsman and is said to have started an innings. The objective for the batsman is to score *runs* during his innings. The innings may terminate in one of two ways. The batsman may be *out* or his innings may close with him being *not out* (for example, if the weather intervenes and it is impossible to continue with the game). As with all sports, averages are important to the players. A cricketer's batting average is the total number of runs scored divided by the number of completed innings, where the number of completed innings is the number of innings minus the number of times the batsman was *not out*. It is possible for a cricketer to have batted several times and always to have been not out. In this case there are no completed innings, the average does not exist and so the abbreviation 'N/A' for Not Applicable should be output in the average column. It is also possible for a cricketer not to have batted at all, in which case the batting average is inappropriate and the message 'Did not bat' should be output instead of the data given in the example above. Data is to be entered into the machine as follows. The user is first to be prompted for the number of times the cricketer batted, that is for the total number of innings. Then the score obtained for each of these innings should be entered. Should the cricketer have been 'not out' in an innings then the score for that innings should first be coded by having 1000 added to it. The coded value should then be entered as the score for that *not out* innings.

5.17 Easter in the Christian church falls on the first Sunday following the first full moon that occurs on or after March 21st. The algorithm below, due to Gauss, will calculate for a given *year* (>= 1583) a number, which we shall call *day*, representing the day on which Easter falls. We shall not give a derivation of this algorithm. You are asked to take it on trust. Indeed, there is no need for you to understand the details in order to attempt the problem.

If *day* <= 31 then Easter is on March *day*, otherwise it is on April (*day* − 31). The algorithm uses the following intermediate values to calculate day.

(a)   *Century*: this is given by

(*year* DIV 100) + 1;

(b)   *Golden*: this is the 'golden number', the number of the year in the 'Metonic cycle' and is used to determine the position of the calendar moon. Its formula is

(*year* MOD 19) + 1;

(c)   *Gregorian*: this is the 'Gregorian correction' and is the years in which a leap year was not held, for example, 1700, 1800, 1900 etc. The formula for this quantity is

(3**Century*) DIV 4 − 12;

(d)   *Clavian*: this is the 'Clavian correction' for the Metonic cycle and amounts to about eight days every 2500 years. Its formula is

(8**Century* + 5) DIV 25 − 5 − *Gregorian*;

(e)   *factor*: this is a variable used to store an intermediate value. It has no astronomical significance. Its formula is

(5**year*) DIV 4 − *Gregorian* − 10

(f)   *Epact*: this is the epact which is the age of the moon on January 1st and is used to calculate when the full moon occurs. Its value is not given by a simple formula. First evaluate formula

(11**Golden* + 20 + *Clavian*) MOD 30

and assign the result to *Epact*. Then revise the value of *Epact* according to the following table:

Calculated value of *Epact*	Revised value of *Epact*
24	*Epact* + 1
25	*Epact* + 1 provided that *Gregorian* > 11
all other values	*Epact*

A design for calculating the day on which Easter falls is then given by:

{Calculate when Easter falls}
1   initialize variables
2   *day* := 44 − *Epact*
3   if *day* < 21 then
4   *day* := *day* + 30
5   ifend
6   *day* := *day* + 7 − (*day* + *factor*) MOD 7
7   write out Easter using *day*

Use this design in a program which writes out the dates of Easter for all the years from 1900 to 1999.

5.18   A test to help decide whether or not a certain author was responsible for writing a book which has lain undiscovered in an archive is to compare the frequency of occurrence of words of a given length in the book with the frequency of occurrence of words of the same length in an authenticated text. The test requires the book to be analysed to see how many words of various lengths it contains. In this problem we want you to count how many words of length six or more occur in a piece of text. For this problem a word is defined to be any sequence of non-space characters. The text is to be input from the keyboard into a string variable and the output is to be the count.

5.19 Problem 5.4 was concerned with writing out a piece of text, each sentence being put on a new line. In this problem the specification is modified as follows. Each line of output must begin with a non-space character and words must be separated by single space characters. This means that any leading space characters are not output and multiple spaces between words are to be output as a single space character. You may assume that the input string terminates with a full stop. So, if the input line is:

'▽▽New▽sentences▽▽go▽on▽new▽lines.▽▽Leading▽and▽▽multiple▽spaces ▽are▽output▽▽as▽single▽spaces.▽▽▽Input▽must▽▽terminate▽with▽▽a▽ full▽stop.'

then the output should be:

New▽sentences▽go▽on▽new▽lines.
Leading▽and▽multiple▽spaces▽are▽output▽as▽single▽spaces.
Input▽must▽terminate▽with▽a▽full▽stop.

5.20 Generalize Problem 5.11 to the situation where the pattern being searched for is 'the'. You may assume that the user inputs at least two characters.

5.21 The input in Problem 5.13 could well have started with a sequence of space characters. Typically this would happen on the first line of a new paragraph. When this occurs the initial spaces are not normally adjusted when the text is justified. Modify the design from Problem 5.13 so that any initial space characters are left unaltered, whereas subsequent ones are dealt with as before. You may assume that the input contains at least one non-space character.

5.22 The specification of Problem 4.8 is now changed so that a more general input string is permitted. Here the input may have adjacent space characters and may begin with spaces. However, it should terminate with a non-space character. The output is to be as before, namely the average length of the words in the input.

5.23 It is hypothesized that in the English language the letter c precedes the letter k more often than any other letter. Write a design which will enable a user to test this hypothesis against a particular piece of text input as a string. The output of the program should be a message saying whether there were more, an equal number, or fewer occurrences of ck than of k preceded by any other letter.

5.10 SUMMARY

In this chapter we have introduced two new types of loop. A *for* loop is a loop which executes a fixed number of times, that is, the design specifies how many executions are to take place and the processing does not affect this number of executions. By contrast, the number of times a *repeat* loop or a *while* loop execute is determined by the processing. A *repeat* loop is called a postconditioned loop because the condition which determines whether or not the loop continues to execute is at the end of the loop. This means that a *repeat* loop is always executed at least once. The *while* loop is a preconditioned loop because its control condition is at the beginning of the loop. This means that if this condition is not satisfied when first encountered, then the loop will not execute at all. Thus a significant difference between a postconditioned loop and a preconditioned loop is that the former must execute at least once, while the latter may not execute at all.

We also saw in this chapter how we could specify output format in design language. We have not provided many facilities, as we are not too concerned with screen layout. One difficulty is writing out values so that they are in tabular form. Essentially if, say, three variables appear in a *write out* statement they can be thought of as being output in columns. For more detailed output you will have to consult the language in which you intend to implement the designs.

We concluded the chapter by looking at statements which were nested one inside another. The hardest construct to understand is the nesting of *if* statements. A nested sequence of *if* statements can be arranged so that one possibility can be selected from several exclusive cases.

6

FURTHER DATA TYPES

Most of this chapter will be concerned with the study of arrays and the ways in which they are manipulated. We shall look at methods whereby arrays can be searched to find individual items. We shall also introduce records that are data structures capable of storing data of different types.

6.1 THE DATA TYPE ARRAY

In Chapter 5 we looked at the problem of finding the average of 20 numbers input from the keyboard. The solution we developed did not store the individual numbers, but kept a running record of their sum. Had we wanted to store the individual numbers we would have to have declared suitable variables. One way of doing this would have been to use 20 different variable identifiers, all declared to be of type real. Fortunately there is an alternative way. In Figure 6.1 the boxed portion represents a single structure - an **array** called *numbers* which consists of **elements**, each of which holds a real number. This array can hold up to five elements but we could have drawn it to hold any number of them. Each element has a corresponding number called its **index**. Thus for example the element whose index is 1 has value 3.45; 10.5 is the value of the element whose index is 4.

	numbers
1	3.45
2	2.04
3	−100.3
4	10.45
5	0.0

Figure 6.1 An array of five elements

Exercise 6.1 What is the index corresponding to the value 0.0 and what is the value whose index is 1?

To summarize, the structure illustrated in Figure 6.1 is called an array and it has two important properties:

1. It consists of a *fixed* number of elements (five in the illustration).
2. The elements must all be of the same type (here they were of type real).

The first property is reflected by the index numbers. The index numbers do not have to start at 1 but they must be consecutive integers. The values over which they can range is called the **index range** and the notation [1..5] is used to denote the index range for the example above. The smallest number in the range is called the **lower bound** and the largest number the **upper bound** of the range. Arrays are sometimes referred to as **structured types** because they are constructed from other types. The array *numbers* is constructed from the type real. By contrast the type real is called a **simple type**. We have already met one other structured type, string. A string is a sequence of type char and so is a structured type. Each element of an array must have a fixed type, which is called its **base** type. The array, *numbers*, above would be declared in a data table as:

Identifier	Description	Type
numbers	An array of integers	array[1..5] of real variable

Exercise 6.2 What are the lower and upper bounds of the range [−3..1] and what values can this range take?

Exercise 6.3 For each of the following diagrams decide whether or not it represents a valid array and if so declare it in a data table.

	names		*identity*		*list*
1	Dave	0	6579	−3	10
2	Millichamp	1	Herriot	−2	20
3	Lyle	2	4917	−1	30
4	Christopher	3	true	0	40

Array elements may be referenced using the same notation as was used for strings, so that *names*[3] references the element 3 of the array *names*, that is, it references 'Lyle'. This is very similar to the method used to reference individual characters of a string, but here it is a complete element which is referenced. Until an element is initialized its value is undefined, so it is possible for an array to have some of its elements initialized and others not. As usual it is an error to access an element which has not been initialized. It is also an error to attempt to a ˋcess an element whose index is not within the declared range of the array. Such an error is called an **index out of range error**.

Operations that are defined on arrays are the operations of the underlying base type. Thus *names* has underlying base type string so all the string operations can be performed on this array. A design fragment which will enable a user to input the names of four people into the array *names* is:

```
1  loop for index := 1 to 4
2     write out 'Enter the name of person ', index
3     read in names[index]
4  loopend
```

Identifier	Description	Type
names	An array of names	array[1..4] of string variable
index	Loop control variable	integer variable

Since we know in advance the size of the array, a *for* loop is appropriate for the input. Sometimes a *downto for* loop is required to access array elements. For example, the design below would write out the names of *names* in reverse order, that is starting at index 4 and working backwards to index 1.

```
1  loop for index := 4 downto 1
2     write out 'Element ', index, ' has value ', names[index]
3  loopend
```

Exercise 6.4 The results of a survey to determine what proportion of a sample of people were married are stored in array *survey* of base type boolean indexed from 1 to 250. The status of being married is recorded using the value true. Assuming that the array has been initialized, write a design fragment which will output the number of married people in the sample.

Sometimes nested loops are required in order to manipulate an array. Consider the problem of creating a football league fixture list in which each team plays every other team twice, once at home and once away from home. If there were only three teams in the league called Liverpool, Everton and Newcastle, then the complete list of fixtures would be:

```
Liverpool  v  Everton
Everton    v  Liverpool
Liverpool  v  Newcastle
Newcastle  v  Liverpool
Everton    v  Newcastle
Newcastle  v  Everton
```

We shall consider the problem where there are 22 teams in the league, their names being held in an array called *team*. The example above suggests that each team must be paired with all subsequent teams on both a home and away basis. This leads to the following top level design.

```
   {Fixture list}
1  loop for all teams except the last
2     loop for all subsequent teams
3        write out home and away fixtures
4     loopend
5  loopend
```

In order to refine this design, two loop control variables are required. Study the design and data table and then read the comments below.

{Fixture list}
1.1   loop for *firstindex* := 1 to *maxsize* −1
2.1   loop for *secondindex* := *firstindex* + 1 to *maxsize*
3.1   write out *team*[*firstindex*], ' v ', *team*[*secondindex*]
3.2   write out *team*[*secondindex*], ' v ', *team*[*firstindex*]
4   loopend
5   loopend

Identifier	Description	Type
maxsize	Array index upper bound	integer constant value 22
firstindex	Loop control variable	integer variable
secondindex	Loop control variable	integer variable
team	Array of league team names	array[1..maxsize] of string variable

In this design, the **integer constant**, *maxsize*, has been used for the index upper bound rather than the number 22 in the declaration of team. This is a common way of declaring arrays and its advantage lies in program maintenance. If the league changes size, then the array would need to redefined to match the new size. The design makes no reference to the number 22, all references are to *maxsize*. Hence a different-sized league can be accommodated by just redefining *maxsize* – the design itself would not need amending. When this method of defining arrays is used, the data table must define *maxsize* prior to it being used in the declaration of the array. In other words, the entry for an integer constant must precede its use in another declaration. This will be referred to as the **declare before use rule**.

Testing that the design for the fixture list is not as straightforward as before, because it is not just a matter of referencing each array element in turn. The difficulty is to ensure that the loops execute the correct number of times and use the correct index values. The following trace table shows the output for the three teams illustrated above:

Step	*firstindex*	*secondindex*	Output at 3.1	Output at 3.2
1.1	1			
2.1		2		
3.1			Liverpool v Everton	
3.2				Everton v Liverpool
2.1		3		
3.1			Liverpool v Newcastle	
3.2				Newcastle v Liverpool
1.1	2			
2.1		3		
3.1			Everton v Newcastle	
3.2				Newcastle v Everton

Note how the constant *maxsize* is assumed to be available as soon as program execution begins. This design enables the fixture list for one football league to be written out. Most football leagues have more than one division but the basic design can be adapted to cater for this. Suppose there are two divisions each having the same number of teams and that the names of the teams are held in two arrays, *teams1* and *teams2*, one array for each division.

Then the following design would enable fixture lists to be produced for both divisions.

	{Fixture list for two divisions}
1.1	write out 'First division fixtures'
2.1	loop for *firstindex* := 1 to *maxsize* −1
3.1	loop for *secondindex* := *firstindex* + 1 to *maxsize*
4.1	write out *teams1*[*firstindex*], ' v ', *teams1*[*secondindex*]
4.2	write out *teams1*[*secondindex*], ' v ', *teams1*[*firstindex*]
5	loopend
6	loopend
7.1	write out 'Second division fixtures'
8.1	loop for *firstindex* := 1 to *maxsize* −1
9.1	loop for *secondindex* := *firstindex* + 1 to *maxsize*
10.1	write out *teams2*[*firstindex*], ' v ', *teams2*[*secondindex*]
10.2	write out *teams2*[*secondindex*], ' v ', *teams2*[*firstindex*]
11	loopend
12	loopend

Variables used in this design need to be added to the data table. However both *teams1* and *teams2* are arrays of the same type and there is a more convenient way of referring to a collection of variables which share a common type. We use what is known as a **type definition**. A type definition assigns an identifier to a structured type, as shown in the following data table:

Identifier	Description	Type
maxsize	Array index upper bound	integer constant value 22
teamlist	Array type definition	array[1..*maxsize*] of string
firstindex	Loop control variable	integer variable
secondindex	Loop control variable	integer variable
teams1	Array of first division team names	*teamlist* variable
teams2	Array of second division team names	*teamlist* variable

Note how the Description identifies *teamlist* as a type definition, the Type column providing the details of the definition. When the arrays are specified, their Type entry can then be given as *teamlist variable*. Other than enabling several variables of the same type to be declared in this way, a type definition has other advantages. First, it is more secure because all the variables are declared using an identifier which itself only has to be defined once. Hence the phrase *array*[1..*maxsize*] *of string variable* is being written only once rather than for each variable declaration of this type. A second, more important, advantage is that if the structure has to be changed, then as there is only one occurrence of its definition, you can be sure that all variables of its type are correctly updated. Care has to be taken about the order in which type definitions are made, particularly if, like here, they reference another user-defined identifier. In this example the definition of *maxsize* must precede that of the type identifier *teamlist* because the former is used in the definition of the latter. Furthermore the definition of *teamlist* must precede the declaration of *teams1* and *teams2*. These examples are merely an application of the declare before use rule. We shall always organize data tables so that constant definitions precede type definitions, which in turn preceded variable declarations. In this way violations of the declare before use rule can be avoided.

The design above, while being correct, is somewhat inefficient in that it contains a large piece of repeated design. Essentially steps 2 to 6 are the same as steps 8 to 12. The former operate on *teams1* while the latter operate on *teams2*. In Chapter 8 we shall see how such repetition can be avoided.

6.2 PROBLEMS

6.1 In this problem we shall simulate the memory of a computer by an array called *memory*, indexed 1..*maxsize* of base type integer where *maxsize* is an integer constant. We shall not give a specific value to *maxsize* in this problem as we have no need to know its numerical value. Of course if you implemented this design an actual value would be required. A common memory management task is to fill parts of memory with a certain fixed value. The task here is to write a design to do this, subject to the following constraints. The user is to be prompted for the initial and final addresses (in our simulation, index numbers) of the portion of memory to be filled. You may assume that both user inputs *are* integers and *do* lie in the range 1 to *maxsize*, but you should *not* assume that the final address exceeds the initial address. If it does not, an error message should be generated and the program should terminate, otherwise a request for the fixed value with which the locations should be filled should be made. This value should then be assigned to the appropriate locations. If the final address is equal to the initial address then the input is valid.

6.2 This problem is based on the same memory model as that in Problem 6.1. Another memory management task is to move a range of memory contents to another location. Write a design to do this, subject to the following constraints. The user is to be prompted for the initial and final addresses, which are subject to the same validation as described in Problem 6.1 with program termination for invalid inputs. For a valid input range the user should be prompted for the start address of the destination. If there is room for the values between the destination and *maxsize* then the contents should be moved accordingly. Otherwise, a suitable message should be output and the program should terminate.

6.3 Assuming that the array *authors*, indexed 1..*maxsize* of type string has been initialized, write a design which will output the element that precedes all the others in alphanumeric ordering.

6.4 A common operation in computing is the **sorting** of data into a significant order such as numerical or alphabetical. Searching for a particular item of data is quicker when the data is sorted than when it is unsorted, because there are very efficient methods for searching sorted data. However, the overhead for using these methods is that the data has to be sorted first. One step in a sort might be to merge together two data sets which are themselves in order. In this exercise we shall consider the problem of merging two sorted arrays into a single sorted array. You may assume that the initial sorted arrays are indexed 1..6, are initialized with integer elements, and that they are to be merged into an array indexed 1..12.

6.3 THE LINEAR SEARCH

In the previous section we considered an array, *team*, which held the 22 names of teams which made up a football league. Suppose the array was now also to be used to record the position of each team in the league. At index 1 would be stored the team at the top of the league, at index 2 the team in second place, and so on. As the weeks went by so the array elements could be changed to reflect the current league table. In order to find the position of a team in the table we would have to go systematically through the array until the name of the team is found, at which point the index represents the position. This systematic process of looking for a data item is called **searching** and a lot of computing time is devoted to it. In this section we are going to look at just one method of searching called the **linear search** because it involves going through the array looking at adjacent elements until the search item is found, or not. It is important to realize that any array search method must allow for two possible outcomes: either the item is found, or the whole array is searched and the item is not there. The latter must be reported to the user of the search.

It is this latter constraint which complicates searching algorithms. We cannot simply write a design like:

repeat
    search for item
until item is found

because if the item is not present access will be attempted eventually beyond the index upper bound of the array we are searching. This can be overcome by changing the condition under which loop execution finishes to:

repeat
    search for item
until (item is found) or (the end of the array is reached)

This uses the boolean operator **or** which we shall study in Chapter 7. Meanwhile there is a trick we can use that avoids the use of the boolean operator and which, incidentally, leads to a more efficient algorithm. We shall illustrate it for a league of four teams. The trick is to redefine the array holding the names so that it includes an element with index 0 as shown below. (A smaller array has been used for convenience in this illustration.) The element at index zero will be called a **dummy element** or **dummy item**.

team

0	
1	Liverpool
2	Everton
3	Newcastle
4	Sunderland

The element with index 0 is used only for searching. To search the array for a given name we assign that name to *team*[0]. Searching then starts at the *end* of the array, that is, at index 4 and it works back towards the beginning. This search will always be successful. If it ends before index zero, then the team position has been found as given by the value of the index. If the name is not in *team*, then the search ends at index 0, indicating that the search was unsuccessful. These two possibilities are indicated in Figure 6.2, where in (a) the name Everton is searched for, and in (b) Leeds is searched for.

team

0	Everton
1	Liverpool
2	Everton
3	Newcastle
4	Sunderland

(a)

team

0	Leeds
1	Liverpool
2	Everton
3	Newcastle
4	Sunderland

(b)

Figure 6.2 Searching an array

In (a) the search stops at index 2 and in (b) at index 0, indicating Leeds is not in the array. A top level design for this algorithm is:

{Linear search}
1   initialize variables referenced in loop
2   loop while search item is not found
3   search the array
4   loopend
5   write out results

For the original array of 22 elements, this can be refined to:

{Linear search}
1.1   write out 'Enter the name of a team'
1.2   read in *searchitem*
1.3   *team*[0] := *searchitem*
1.4   *index* := *maxsize*
2.1   loop while *team*[*index*] <> *searchitem*
3.1   decrement *index*
4   loopend
5.1   if *index* = 0 then
5.2   write out 'Item is not in the array'
5.3   else
5.4   write out 'Position of ' *searchitem*, ' is ', *index*
5.5   ifend

Identifier	Description	Type
maxsize	Array index upper bound	integer constant value 22
team	Array of team names	array[0..*maxsize*] of string variable
searchitem	Name being sought	string variable
index	Loop control variable	integer variable

It is implicit in this example that a name of a team occurs only once in the array. However, if the array was a list of surnames then it would be quite possible for there to be repeated names. In this instance a search of the array would need to produce all the occurrences of the searched for item and a different strategy would be required. When defining an array which is going to be searched you have to decide what kind of search will be required in order that you can define the index lower bound appropriately. The next exercise will show why an index lower bound of 0 does not help when more than one match is a possibility.

Exercise 6.5 Suppose the array *surnames* indexed 1 to *maxsize* has been initialized with surnames. Write a design which enables a user to input a name and which will output the index of all elements which match the user input. In the event of there being no matches a message to this effect should be output instead.

The output from the search of the last exercise is not very useful on its own unless the indexes were going to be used for further processing. We shall now look at applications of searches and the uses to which the search index can be put. Consider the table below, which gives a list of towns and the number of churches that are to be found within their boundaries.

Town	Churches
Tonbridge	15
Elgin	10
Buxton	15
Chard	8
Harwich	19

An extended version of this table could be used to record the number of churches in a given town. The town column could be searched for a given town and the number of churches it contained could be read off. It looks as if the table should be represented as an array, for then the search techniques we have just developed could be exploited. However, it is not possible to represent each row of the table as an array element because the first column is of type string and the second of type integer and array elements can only be of a single fixed type. We shall see later in this chapter that there is a data structure, called a **record** which can hold mixed types and so each row of the table could be represented by a record. The whole table could then be represented by an array of such records. In fact what we are trying to do here is to represent a piece of data for which there is no standard type available – we are having to 'build up' a representation using the basic building blocks of arrays, records, string and integer. A more sophisticated and less error-prone method of representing data for which there is no built-in data type is to separate the task of representation from the development of the design which uses it. What would be done here is to define an **abstract data type** to represent the table. The abstract data type consists of a method of storing the data, together with the means by which it may be manipulated. The latter would include operations for inserting new entries or deleting old ones. This abstract type can then be used by the designer in much the same way as, say, the data type *real* is used – namely variables can be defined to be of the abstract type and they can be manipulated using the provided operations. Of course the abstract data type itself has to be designed but this can be undertaken as a totally separate task. At this stage we do not have the required design skills to follow this approach of separating data design and program design. We believe that the basic design skills must be mastered before embarking upon abstract data type design and so we shall temporarily ignore the problem and return to it in Chapter 10.

It is possible to represent the table of towns and churches without using records. What we do is to split the table into two separate columns:

Tonbridge		15
Elgin		10
Buxton		15
Chard		8
Harwich		19

Each column can now be represented as a separate array, but before this is done it will have to be decided what the index range is to be. The upper bound is not a problem because a constant *maxsize* can be used whose value can be defined dependent upon how many towns are likely to be listed. But should the lower index be 0 or 1? It really depends upon how the arrays are to be searched. The likelihood is that the *town* array will be searched and as its entries are unique, a linear search using index 0 would be appropriate. In the diagram below the identifiers *town* and *churches* have been used for the arrays.

	town			*churches*
0		0		
1	Tonbridge	1		15
2	Elgin	2		10
3	Buxton	3		15
4	Chard	4		8
5	Harwich	5		19

To use this representation to find the number of churches for, say, Buxton the array *town* would be searched using the index 0 method. This would result in a match at index 3 which would then be used as the index in the *churches* array to retrieve the number 15. The link between the towns and the number of churches is maintained by virtue of the array indexes. Arrays which are used in this way are called **parallel arrays**.

Exercise 6.6 Write a design which will enable a user to carry out repeated searches of the towns and churches table. For each search your program should request the name of a town and should write out the number of churches the town has. If the town is not in the table, a suitable message should be output. You may assume that both arrays have been initialized and so your design should start from the point where the array *town* is about to be searched. A sentinel value will be required to terminate the program.

6.4 PROBLEMS

6.5 Word processors often have a spelling check option so that a document can be scanned and incorrectly spelled words can be identified. A difficulty with spelling checkers is that many documents contain technical terms which could not be expected to be included in the word processor's general purpose dictionary. One way of overcoming this is to allow the user to generate what is often called a user dictionary into which technical and specialized words can be inserted. The user dictionary is created in a file and so contains a permanent record of specialist words. However, the user may not always want to insert a specialist word into the user dictionary because some words, like proper names, may only arise in the current document. To cater for this, on the first encounter with a word which is neither in the main or the user dictionary, the word processor will ask the user to confirm that it is spelled correctly. If so the word is stored dynamically, in main memory, and thereby becomes part of the dictionary available to the word processor for checking the remainder of the document. Thus, even things like names can be checked throughout the remainder of the document without having to ask the user if they are correct on each of their subsequent occurrences. In this problem we are going to model this dynamic part of a spelling checker by assuming that the dynamic dictionary is held in main memory as an array. Your task is to check this array to see if it contains a word. To make the problem more self-contained we shall make the assumption that the word whose spelling is to be checked is input from the keyboard. The result of the search will be a message output to the screen which reports whether or not the word is in the dictionary. You may assume that the array in which the words are stored is called *dictionary*, that it is indexed from 0 and that the elements 1 to *size* contain words (so that index zero represents a dummy element).

6.6 This problem is based on Exercise 6.6. Write a design which will enable a user to enter an integer and which will output the names of all the towns which have that number of churches. If no towns have that number of churches a suitable message should be output.

6.7 This problem is based upon Problem 6.5. A more advanced facility offered by some spelling checkers is to suggest some words when it believes the original word is incorrectly spelled. A spelling checker can never be sure a word *is* incorrect because the dictionaries they contain are relatively small. But when a word is encountered which is not in the dictionary the spelling checker can try to offer alternative suggestions. In this problem we shall consider a very simplistic model of this suggestion process. The specification of this problem is as in Problem 6.5 except that if a word is not in the dictionary then the output should consist of all words whose initial two letters are the same as the first two letters of the searched-for word. This matching process implies that both the input word and all the words in the dictionary consist of at least two characters. Should there not be any words in the dictionary satisfying this constraint then a message should be output saying that no suggestions are possible.

6.5 MULTIDIMENSIONAL ARRAYS

By now you should be confident in handling arrays, using a single identifier to hold a list of values all of the same type and recovering the individual values by means of an index. We shall now look at the situation of an array where two indexes are required in order to recover the individual array elements. Such an array is called a **two-dimensional** array. Figure 6.3 represents a two-dimensional array, called *births*. The figure shows the number of births in a maternity ward in each month for each of the years 1987, 1988, 1989 and 1990.

This array has twelve rows, one for each month, and four columns. So *births*[3, 1987] represents the number of births in March 1987 where the first index, 3, corresponds to the month and the second index 1987 represents the year. More generally, the element *births*[i, j] will be found at the intersection of row i and column j and represents the number of births in month i of the year j.

	1987	1988	1989	1990
1	38	36	39	35
2	31	30	30	32
3	42	40	44	37
4	46	44	47	42
5	28	30	31	32
6	31	30	29	34
7	24	27	26	24
8	29	29	32	27
9	33	31	31	30
10	36	35	36	37
11	27	30	31	27
12	35	31	36	34

Figure 6.3 Birth data from a maternity ward

Exercise 6.7
(a)   Using the array referencing notation just introduced, write down the element whose value is 47.
(b)   What is the value of the element *births*[11, 1990]?

The array above would be declared as follows:

Identifier	Description	Type
births	Array of numbers of births	array[1..12, 1987..1990] of integer variable

In order to manipulate this array two indexes must be declared. Assuming that the variables *month, year* and *total* have been declared of type integer, the following design fragment will count the total number of births in 1988:

```
total := 0
loop for month := 1 to 12
    total := total + births[month, 1988]
loopend
```

Exercise 6.8 Write a program fragment which sums the number of births in May for the years 1987 to 1990.

To sum all the entries in the array, two loops are required, one nested inside the other:

```
        {Total all array entries, scan by row}
1   total := 0
2   loop for month := 1 to 12
3       loop for year := 1987 to 1990
4           total := total + births[month, year]
5       loopend
6   loopend
```

In this design the outer loop is controlled by *month*. This means that for a given month the values for all years are summed so that when *month* has value 1, the total 148 is obtained, this being the number of births in January for the four years concerned. In other words the array is being summed by rows. In other problems the elements may need to be referenced in a different order. We shall use the terms **scan by row** and **scan by column** to denote the two different ways in which elements of a two dimensional array can be referenced. A design which scans the data of Figure 6.3 by column in order to sum all its elements is:

```
     {Total all array entries, scan by column}
1    total := 0
2    loop for year := 1987 to 1990
3        loop for month := 1 to 12
4            total := total + births[month, year]
5        loopend
6    loopend
```

The total births for each year are obtained first and are themselves then summed to give the overall total. It is often useful to check that a two-dimensional array is being scanned in the correct order by drawing up part of a trace table. The partial trace table below corresponds to the scan by rows design:

Step	total	month	year
1	0		
2		1	
3			1987
4	38		
3			1988
4	74		
3			1989
4	113		
3			1990
4	148		
2		2	
3			1987
4	179		
3			1988

Notice how for each month the design loops through all the years. In other words the outer loop selects the month and the inner loop then takes us through each year. So the array is being scanned row-by-row. Two-dimensional arrays can be generalized to three or more dimensions. However, an array of whatever dimension can only have elements of a single type.

Consider the following example. A survey has been carried out to see how much television people of various ages and sex watch on each day of the week. The days of the week are coded so that 1 corresponds to Sunday, 2 to Monday and so on. The ages are integers in the range 5 to 99 and sex was coded with 0 corresponding to female and 1 to male.

All the data is stored in a three dimensional array called *hours* of type, array[1..7, 5..99, 0..1] of real variable, where the first index corresponds to the day code, the second to the age and the last to the gender. The array element

hours[3, 15, 1]

then represents the number of hours of television watched on Tuesday by all the 15-year-old males who were interviewed. The total amount of television watched by these members of the survey is calculated using the design fragment:

loop for *day* := 1 to 7
    total := *total* + *hours*[*day*, 15, 1]
loopend

Similarly, the total hours watched by all 15-year-olds, regardless of gender, is:

loop for *day* := 1 to 7
    loop for *gender* := 0 to 1
        total := *total* + *hours*[*day*, 15, *gender*]
    loopend
loopend

The total hours watched by all interviewees in the survey would require three loops.

loop for *day* := 1 to 7
    loop for *gender* := 0 to 1
        loop for *age* := 5 to 99
            total := *total* + *hours*[*day*, *age*, *gender*]
        loopend
    loopend
loopend

Some care is required when dealing with multidimensional arrays to ensure that the correct index is being used, particularly when a loop is involved.

Exercise 6.9 Write a design which will write out the age of the females who watched the least amount of television in the period Thursday to Saturday inclusive. You may assume that the survey was so large that none of the elements in the array have the same value.

6.6 PROBLEMS

6.8 When printing a book a typesetter has to keep an eye open for the appearance of 'rivers'
  – apparent streaks of white appearing on the page. They are formed by the spaces
  between the words of the text. If two or three lines of text all have a space character in
  roughly the same position then the reader appears to see a white river within the page.
  The text below has several rivers:

We have printed this very
narrow in order to
demonstrate that rivers are
very prone to occur when
using a narrow page.
However rivers can occur
on wider pages but they
are more likely to occur
on narrow margins like
this.

In this problem we are going to develop an automatic system for identifying rivers, but on a much simplified scale. A river will be defined as any sequence of two or more spaces aligned vertically. The page of text will be represented as a two-dimensional array of char in which the first index will be used to denote the number of the line and the second the position of the character within that line. The design is to output the coordinates, that is the line number and character position, of the start and finish of all the rivers on the page. You may assume that the array representing the page is already initialized.

6.9   Dot matrix printers use pins in the print head mechanism which are fired at the printer ribbon, thereby making the imprint of a dot on the page. By arranging these dots in a pattern, letters can be formed. The number of dots used to form each letter varies but as the number increases there is generally an improvement in the quality of letter produced. Typically each letter is formed on a nine row by six column matrix. We have drawn some examples below:

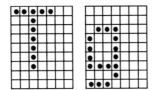

In this representation the last two columns have been reserved and left blank for the space between letters. In this problem we shall simulate the process of producing a *single* character by representing it using a two-dimensional array of boolean. The value true will represent the presence of a dot, and the value false its absence. The output should be a single letter occupying six columns and nine rows of the screen and so will be a magnified version of the character being represented. In fact the output should be similar to the examples above but without the grid lines. Your design need not give details of the initialization of the array.

6.10 Computer printout from a data processing department often has the title of the document printed out using 'big' letters similar to that illustrated below. The reason this method is adopted is because on a very fast line printer only one size of character can be output. Therefore to create document headings which are of a size that they can be easily recognized another trick is required. Using 'big' letters is one such trick.

	A	A	
A			A
A	A	A	A
A			A
A			A

This particular diagram represents a large capital 'A'. It has five rows and four columns but usually more would be used. The symbol which makes up the shape is itself a capital 'A'. In this problem you are to represent this diagram using a two-dimensional array. You are to write a design to initialize the array and then to write out the contents so that a 'big' letter will be formed.

6.7 RECORDS AND TABLES

An array is a very limited data structure for storing data because of the restriction that each element of the array must be of the same type. Much more common in computerized data processing is the need to store data which has entries of different types. Consider a simplified library catalogue entry which holds the name of the author, the book title and the number of copies kept in the library. It might look something like:

Sargent D.R.   Countdown to Mathematics Vol 1   3

Essentially there are three different pieces of information here. First there is the name, which is of type string. Next there is the title, again of type string. Lastly there is the number of copies kept, which is of type integer. Usually there will be many such entries in the catalogue:

Author	Title	Copies
Sargent D.R.	Countdown to Mathematics Vol 1	3
Sargent D.R.	Countdown to Mathematics Vol 2	4
Easteal C.	Software Engineering	1

One way of representing the catalogue would be to define three parallel arrays, one for each of name and author, of type string, and a third for the number of copies held, of type integer.

Fortunately there is a better way using a data structure called a **record**. The three components which form the rows are called **fields** and all three fields taken together form a single record. Each field in a record must be given an identifier whose type is defined in a data table in the usual way. For the example above, the identifier *author* could be used for the first field and it would be declared to be of type string. The second field could be called *title* also of type string. Lastly we could use *copies* to identify the third field and declare it to be of type integer. Notice that the order in which the fields have been specified has been heavily emphasized. This is an important part of the structure of a record and it is represented diagrammatically as:

	author	*title*	*copies*
entry	Sargent D.R.	Countdown to Mathematics Vol 1	3

This record has identifier *entry* and it is declared in a data table as follows:

Identifier	Description	Type

entry	Record
	   author {Name of author}
	   title {Title of book}
	   copies {Number of copies held}
	recordend
		record variable
		string variable
		string variable
		integer variable

This data table defines *entry* to be a record variable. Each of the fields is given an identifier, these being listed in the Description column accompanied by a description of the field contents. Note how the fields in the description column occur between the words **record** and **recordend**. The Type column defines the type of data associated with each field. Thus *author* is defined to be the first field of the record, its type is string and it holds the name of the author of the book. When several records have to be declared, all with the same structure, it is better to define the record structure using a type definition. The data table below illustrates the method:

Identifier	Description	Type

booktype	Record type definition
	   author {Name of author}
	   title {Title of book}
	   copies {Number of copies held}
	recordend
		
		string variable
		string variable
		integer variable

entry1	An individual record	*booktype* variable
entry2	An individual record	*booktype* variable

6.7.1 Operations on records

The two basic operations on records are assignment of values to fields and retrieval of those values. To do either operation we must first select the appropriate field, which we do by using the identifier of the record variable followed by a full stop and the identifier of the required field. Thus, for example,

    entry1.author

would refer to the author field of the record *entry1*. As with all variables, records are undefined until initialized and so their individual fields are uninitialized until values are assigned to them. The statements below illustrate how the record *entry1* could be initialized:

    entry1.author := 'Sargent D.R.'
    entry1.title := 'Countdown to Mathematics Vol 1'
    entry1.copies := 3

Care must be taken to assign only values of the appropriate type to a field. Complete records can be assigned to other record variables of the same type in one go. Thus:

entry1 := *entry2*

would have the effect of assigning all the field values of *entry1* to *entry2*; there is no need to transfer them field-by-field.

The other operations defined on records are those inherited by the individual fields. So, for example, string operations can be performed on the fields *author* and *title* of the records *entry1* and *entry2*. For records with a large number of component fields, the 'dot' notation for accessing them can become quite tedious. The **with** statement provides a shorthand alternative:

with record *entry1* do
    author := 'Sargent D.R.'
    title := 'Countdown to Mathematics Vol 1'
    copies := 3
withend

Note how the word **withend** terminates the use of the *with* statement.

Exercise 6.10 Write down a data table to define a record variable *employee* with the following four fields: the name of the employee, a works number, the age of the employee and the salary of the employee. You should use a type identifier for the record structure as illustrated on page 82. Choose appropriate types for the fields and then write down statements to initialize the record using values of your own choice.

As we have already stated, records are rarely used singly; the library catalogue will have many entries. These entries can be stored using an array of records, one element for each entry in the catalogue. A data table for a representation of the catalogue capable of holding up to 500 entries is:

Identifier	Description	Type

booktype	Record type definition
	    author {Name of author}
	    title {Title of book}
	    copies {Number of copies held}
	    recordend
		
		string variable
		string variable
		integer variable

catalogue	Representation of catalogue	array[1..500] of *booktype* variable

An individual record in the array is accessed using the usual array index method so that *catalogue*[4] represents the fourth element of the array. But this element is a record and so to access an individual field we use the dot notation. So, *catalogue*[4].*copies* would access the *copies* field of the element of *catalogue* whose index is 4.

Exercise 6.11 Define an array indexed 1 to *maxsize* whose elements are records having the fields described in Exercise 6.10. It is anticipated that individual fields of the records will be searched, so the definition of the array should take note of this. Using your definition write a design which will enable a user to initialize all the elements of the array except that reserved for searching.

Everyday life provides many other examples of tables, for example, sporting league tables, stock market share price tables, horse racing cards and form guides, price lists and so on. The holiday car hire table of Figure 6.5 is typical of the format of a table.

Holiday area	Number of people	Type of car	Number of doors	Cost per week
Costa Blanca	1 to 4	VW Polo	3	£73
Costa Blanca	5	Seat Ronda	5	£105
Portugal	1 to 5	Renault 5	3	£73
Portugal	6 to 8	Two Metros	3	£135

Figure 6.5 A car hire table

The body of the table has a number of rows, each of which has a number of columns consisting of data of different types. The table can be represented by defining a record structure to correspond to the rows and using an array of such records to represent the multiplicity of the rows.

6.8 PROBLEMS

In some of the problems in this section we shall use records to model some of the operations undertaken by the **operating system** of a computer. If you want to attempt these problems then read the following description; otherwise go straight to those problems which are based on other ideas.

One of the tasks of an operating system is to manage the permanent storage, on backing store, of data created by users. For example, a document created using a word processor can be stored on a floppy disk. The data recorded is called a **file**, which is given a name by the user so that it can be recalled at some later date. Not all characters may be used in a file name. In particular a space character may not be used. Different operating systems have different restrictions on file naming but in the following description the conventions used are based on the operating system MSDOS. For this operating system a file name can have up to eight characters. Additionally what is known as a file name extension can be entered by the user. File name extensions are of up to three characters and are used to classify files whose contents are related. (Because we are creating a model there will not always be a direct correspondence with this text and MSDOS.) The following are all valid MSDOS file names:

ONE.TXT; LETTER1.DOC; LETTER2.DOC; MEMO; LETTER3.DOC

The operating system records file names on the disk in a special location called a **directory**. The directory holds the names of all the files held on the disk. A directory entry has the following record structure:

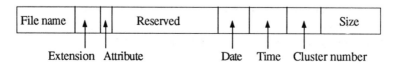

We shall explain the purpose of the attribute and cluster number fields in the next problem section. The date and time fields record the date and time when the file was last updated. The size field records the size of the file in bytes (a byte being eight bits), where a bit is either a 0 or a 1. A root directory of an MSDOS disk can hold a maximum of 112 files. (Do not worry about the word 'root' here.) The data table below defines how we shall model the directory of such an MSDOS disk.

Identifier	Description	Type
entry	Record type definition	
	filename {File name}	string[8] variable
	extension {File extension}	string[3] variable
	attribute {File attribute}	char variable
	time {Time file was saved}	integer variable
	date {Date file was saved}	integer variable
	cluster {First cluster number}	integer variable
	filesize {File size}	integer variable
	recordend	
directory	Array of directory entries	array[0..112] of *entry* variable

6.11 Define an array which will enable the information of Figure 6.5 to be represented. You should use a constant definition for the upper bound of the index range but you need not specify its value. A type definition should be used for the records representing the rows.

6.12 The diagram below shows part of a table of computer systems and their prices. The model number is a unique identifier and the complete table has 100 entries.

Model number	Memory (K)	Floppy disk size (K)	Colour monitor option	Price
PC88C	640	360/720	yes	£775
PC1512D	512	360	no	£495
PC88S	640	360/720	yes	£825
PC1640	640	360	yes	£550

The table is to be represented in such a way that it can be searched for a specific model number input by the user. Write a design which will enable a user to enter a model number and which will produce as output all the details of that model listed in the table. You may assume that the structure holding the data has been initialized appropriately.

6.13 Write a design which will enable the table in Problem 6.12 to be searched on the memory field. The user is to input a memory size and the output of the design should be a list of all models having a memory size greater than or equal to that specified by the user. If no machine has this property then a suitable message should be written out.

6.14 Libraries which have computerized record systems often keep a key word index of the book titles within the library. Indeed, articles in journals are also kept in a key word index. The purpose of such an index is to enable users to find books or articles related to some key word. So, for example, if a user is interested in ornithology a key word search of the index would list all works which included the word ornithology in their titles. We shall illustrate a key word index on the following titles:

> Introduction to Programming and Computer Science
> Software Engineering
> A Science Primer

Words like *to*, *and*, *the* and so on are not included in the index and so these three titles would result in the key words Introduction, Programming, Computer, Science, Software, Engineering and Primer. A query on the word Programming should produce the first title, whereas one on the word Science should output both the first and third titles. (The case of the characters in the key words would be ignored in a search but we shall ignore this difficulty.) The method whereby the title can be obtained by this process is to produce a table of key words and what are called remainders. Essentially the remainder contains all the words of a title other than the key word. The table for the titles above would be as below. Here the entries are ordered on the key word field. Study the table and then read the commentary.

Key word	Remainder
Computer	▽Science/Introduction to Programming and▽
Engineering	/Software▽
Introduction	▽to Programming and Computer Science
Primer	/A Science▽
Programming	▽and Computer Science/Introduction to
Science	/Introduction to Programming and Computer▽
Science	▽Primer/A▽
Software	▽Engineering

The titles are reconstructed by joining together, that is concatenating, the key word and the remainder in a special way. We shall show how the first title can be reconstructed from the key word *Computer*. To this is concatenated all the characters of the remainder up to the slash. This gives 'Computer▽Science'. All characters after the slash are now placed before this string (together with a space character to separate the two parts) to give the required title. Sometimes the remainder does not contain a slash character, as in the entry Software. This is simply because the title is just the concatenation of the keyword and remainder (together with a space). Finally if the remainder begins with a slash character this indicates that the keyword is the last word of the title, which can therefore be constructed by concatenating the remainder followed by the key word.

In this problem we want you to design a solution for searching the table for a key word and if found reconstructing all the titles containing that key word. You may assume that the table above is represented as an array of records given in the data table below, that the table has been initialized and that *keysearch* holds the key word for which titles are required. For simplicity you should search every item in the table.

Identifier	Description	Type
size	Size of key word index	integer constant
indextype	Record type definition	
	keyword {The key word}	string variable
	remainder {Rest of title}	string variable
	recordend	
keyindex	Key word index	array[1..*size*] of *indextype* variable
keysearch	Search item	string variable

6.15   This problem is based on the operating systems model introduced at the beginning of the section. When a file is deleted from a disk its directory entry is not erased but the first character of its filename is changed to a special character to denote that the file is erased. We shall use a space character for this purpose. An entry in the directory which has never been used will have this special character in its file name field. Figure 6.6 shows the state of a directory when the disk on which it resides has been in use for some time. The third and fourth entries of this directory are deleted files because the first character of their file names is a space character and the sixth entry has never been used. For simplicity, not all the directory fields have been given data values. Furthermore the date field has been represented as an integer (whose values would exceed the maximum permitted on most implementations). We shall modify this in a subsequent problem.

Filename	Ext			Date	Time		Size
LETTER1	TXT			230489	1256		1024
MEMOCOPY	TXT			040287	1830		2560
▽ETTER2	DOC			311290	0915		1024
▽ETTER3	TXT			100188	1632		1024
MEMO	TXT			040287	1145		1536
▽							

Figure 6.6 Disk directory

Users can ask the system to list all the (non-deleted) files on a disk. Such a listing is called a **directory listing,** which for the directory above would be:

```
LETTER1      TXT      1024      230489      1256
MEMOCOPY     TXT      2560      040287      1830
MEMO         TXT      1145      040287      1145
```

where the fields are listed in the order file name, file extension, file size, date and time. Assuming that the directory has been represented by the variable *directory*, defined above, and that it is already initialized, write a design to produce such a directory listing.

6.16   In Problem 6.15 the date was represented by an integer which would be impossible to implement on many systems because in this form dates would exceed the maximum allowable value for an integer. This problem asks you to modify the date field used in the model of a directory. You should model the date field using a record having three fields, the first for the day, the second for the month and the last for the year. Each of the three fields should be of integer type. Write a data table to represent the directory with this amendment to the representation of the date.

6.9 SUMMARY

In this section we have studied arrays and records. Arrays can have a single index or they can be multi-dimensional when they have an index for each dimension. An important property of arrays is that they contain a fixed number of elements, all of which must be of the same type. Arrays can be searched and we looked at a linear search method which used the element index 0 for a dummy item.

In contrast to arrays, records can hold data of different types in what are called fields. The order in which the fields are declared determines the structure of a record, and the type of each field must be specified in its declaration. Records are rarely used singly; more often an array of records is declared to represent a table.

7

AIDS TO DESIGN

In this chapter we shall extend the idea of multi-path selection. We have already seen that nesting *if* statements gives rise to multi-path selection but when they are nested more than two deep, following their logic can become a bit awesome. Fortunately there is a better control structure available when the choice of possible paths through the program is large. This new control structure greatly aids the clarity of designs and hence makes them easier to understand and to maintain. Another aid to program design are data types which users can define and we conclude the chapter by examining a variety of such definitions.

7.1 THE CASE STATEMENT

In Section 5.7 we encountered the following design extract which converts certain lower-case characters to their upper-case equivalent:

```
if ch = 'a' then
   ch := 'A'
else
   if ch = 'b' then
      ch := 'B'
   else
      ch := 'C'
   ifend
ifend
```

This was an illustration of a nested sequence of *if* statements, one inside the other. Had we wanted to convert the lower-case characters 'd', 'e' and 'f' as well, then further nesting would have been required, leading to a clumsy design whose purpose might not be obvious to a reader. The construct which will enable a single choice to be made from several possible courses of action is a **select case** statement, or more briefly a **case** statement.

```
select case depending on ch
    'a'   :  ch := 'A'
    'b'   :  ch := 'B'
    'c'   :  ch := 'C'
  default : do nothing
selectend
```

The variable *ch* that controls this case statement is called a **case selector** because it is its value that determines which of the four possible courses of action are undertaken. If the value of *ch* is 'a' then the first choice is selected and its value is reassigned the value 'A'. Similarly, if the value of *ch* is 'b' then the second choice is selected, if it is 'c' the third choice is selected. If *ch* has none of the values 'a', 'b', 'c', then the **default** statement is executed. Once a choice has been made and the associated statements executed, control passes directly to **selectend**, thus terminating the case statement.

The values for the selection, 'a', 'b', 'c', are called **case labels**. Sometimes several case labels may require the same actions. For example, users are often asked whether they wish to continue with an application. The response can be stored in a variable of type char with expected values 'y' or 'n' to denote the user choice. But 'Y' or 'N' ought to be equally valid responses. This can be achieved as follows:

```
select case depending on ch
    'y',  'Y'  :  continue with application
    'n',  'N'  :  quit application
     default   :  do nothing
selectend
```

Here each selection, other than the default, comprises a list of case labels. To see how a case statement is used, consider the problem of writing a design which will enable a user to input a string and which will produce as output the number of occurrences of each vowel and the number of non-vowel characters in the string. What should be produced if the input string is 'The$\triangledown$Price$\triangledown$Of$\triangledown$Bread'? Whether the vowels are upper- or lower-case is of no interest and so the vowel 'a' occurs once, 'e' occurs three times, 'i' and 'o' occur once and 'u' occurs zero times. There are 12 non-vowel characters. A top level design is:

```
1   initialize variables referenced in loop
2   loop for all characters in the input string
3       process character
4   loopend
5   write out results
```

This may be refined to:

```
1.1     write out 'Enter your string '
1.2     read in subject
2.1     loop for i := 1 to length(subject)
```

3.1   select case depending on *subject*[*i*]
3.2   'A','a' : increment *acount*
3.3   'E','e' : increment *ecount*
3.4   'I','i' : increment *icount*
3.5   'O','o' : increment *ocount*
3.6   'U','u' : increment *ucount*
3.7   default : increment *othercount*
3.8   selectend
4   loopend
5.1   write out 'The count of a is ' *acount*
5.2   write out 'The count of e is ' *ecount*
5.3   write out 'The count of i is ' *icount*
5.4   write out 'The count of o is ' *ocount*
5.5   write out 'The count of u is ' *ucount*
5.6   write out 'The count of other characters is ' *othercount*

The data table is as follows:

Identifier	Description	Type
subject	Input string	string variable
acount	Count of occurrences of 'a'	integer variable
ecount	Count of occurrences of 'e'	integer variable
icount	Count of occurrences of 'i'	integer variable
ocount	Count of occurrences of 'o'	integer variable
ucount	Count of occurrences of 'u'	integer variable
othercount	Count of occurrences of non-vowel characters	integer variable

Test data should include the possibility that the user enters a null string so this should give sensible results. For this design all counts are output as zero, which is what would be expected for a null string input. Test data should also include strings consisting of only vowels and some of only non-vowels. A check should be made that space characters are included in the non-vowel count.

In this example the case selector was a character. A selector used in a *case* statement does not have to be of char type, integer case selectors can also be used. We shall see later in the chapter other types that can be used for selectors, but of the types that have so far been defined only integer and char may be used. This means that strings and real numbers may not be used as selectors.

Sometimes there are no actions to be undertaken by the *default* case. This is analogous to the situation where there is no *else* part in an *if* statement. In situations like this, rather than write *do nothing* as the default actions, the whole statement can be omitted. The first problem of the next section provides an example.

7.2 PROBLEMS

7.1 Redesign the solution to step 5.1 of Problem 5.9 using a *case* statement.

7.2 This problem is concerned with validating a date input by a user. The data is to be input as two integers representing the day and the month respectively (in that order). Your task is to verify that the numbers input are consistent with each other in the sense that the date 30 2 is invalid because the 30th February does not exist. You may assume that the user inputs positive integer values and that the year is not a leap year. The output from your program should be a message saying whether or not the input represents a valid date.

7.3 Modify the design in Problem 7.2 so that it caters for the possibility of a leap year. The user will now input three integers corresponding to the day, month and year in that order. For the purposes of this question a leap year is defined to be one which leaves zero remainder when divided by four.

7.3 COMPOUND BOOLEAN EXPRESSIONS

In this section we shall look at boolean variables in more detail and shall consider the operators **and**, **or** and **not** which are defined on them. We already know that a *condition* is an expression which has the value *true* or *false* and that such expressions are often referred to as boolean expressions.

We often wish to construct conditions which involve more than a single comparison. Such conditions arise by connecting simple boolean expressions together using the boolean operators to form what are known as **compound boolean expressions**. For example, our first attempt at writing a linear search design in Chapter 6 used a compound boolean expression:

repeat
    search for item
until (item is found) or (the end of the array is reached)

We had to include the second part of this condition in order to ensure that access beyond the index range of the array holding the data was not attempted. The loop continues execution until either the item is found or the end of the array is reached. In other words, if either of the conditions (item is found), (the end of the array is reached) becomes true then the loop terminates execution. Note that it is possible for both conditions to be true (when the item being searched for is the last item in the array) but loop execution still ceases.

By contrast, two conditions linked by the operator *and* both have to be true in order to make the compound condition true. Thus, the compound expression

$(index > 1)$ and $(index < 6)$

is true if *index* has a value which exceeds 1 and is less than 6. In other words, it is true whenever *index* has one of the values 2, 3, 4 or 5 since then both conditions are true. (We assume here that *index* is an integer variable.)

Exercise 7.1 What is the value of the expression $(count < 20)$ and $(index <= 5)$ if
(a) $count = 15$, $index = 3$
(b) $count = 25$, $index = 5$
(c) $count = 20$, $index = 3$
(d) $count = -3$, $index = 6$

Exercise 7.2 What is the value of the expression (*count* < 20) or (*index* <= 5) if
(a)   *count* = 15, *index* = 3
(b)   *count* = 25, *index* = 5
(c)   *count* = 20, *index* = 3
(d)   *count* = 25, *index* = 6

The last operator defined on boolean variables is the operator *not*. Suppose the boolean variable *found* has value true, then *not found* has the value false. Equally if *found* has value false, then *not found* has value true. In other words the operator not negates the current value of a boolean variable.

Figure 7.1 expresses the results just described in the form of a table known as a **truth table**. In this table *x* and *y* are boolean expressions.

x	*y*	*x* and *y*	*x* or *y*	not *x*
true	true	true	true	false
true	false	false	true	false
false	true	false	true	true
false	false	false	false	true

Figure 7.1 A truth table

In the examples we have given we have used brackets to enclose expressions like (*count* < 20). The reason for this is that the logical operators *and*, *or* and *not* take precedence over the comparison operators like <. We shall not go into detail about boolean operator precedences but will rely on careful use of brackets to ensure expressions are evaluated as we intend. In fact, *not* takes precedence over *and* which takes precedence over *or*. To illustrate some of the difficulties that can arise if brackets are omitted consider the expression

(*count* < 20) and (*index* <= 5)

with its brackets removed, thus:

count < 20 and *index* <= 5

In this expression *and* would take precedence over the comparison operators and so that an attempt would be made to evaluate the expression

20 and *index*

But 20 is not of boolean type and so an error would result.

Exercise 7.3 If *number* and *total* are integer variables and *flag* is a boolean variable, determine the ranges of values that will cause each of the following compound boolean expressions to have value true:
(a)   (*number* > 5) or (*total* < 5)
(b)   (*number* > 5) and (*number* < 15)
(c)   (*number* > 15) and (*number* < 5)
(d)   (*number* > 15) or (*number* < 5)
(e)   (*total* > 5) and not *flag*

Exercise 7.4 For each of the following write down a boolean expression which will yield the value true if:

(a)   the character variable *answer* has the value 'y' or 'Y'.

(b)   the character variable *answer* has one of the values 'y', 'Y', 'n' or 'N'.

(c)   the integer variable *day* has value in the range 1 to 31 inclusive and the integer variable *month* has value in the range 1 to 12 inclusive.

Care has to be exercised with the use of brackets when a compound expression contains both *and* and *or*. Consider the problem of representing the mid-week times of cheap rate telephone calls as a boolean expression. The cheap rate is defined to be the period 6pm to 11pm Monday to Friday and all day Saturday and Sunday. We shall use the real variable *time* to represent time on a 24-hour clock and the boolean variable *weekend* which will be true if the day is a Saturday or a Sunday. With these assumptions the following boolean expression has value true during cheap rate times.

((*time* > 18.00) and (*time* < 23.00)) or *weekend*

Here we have enclosed the expression preceding the word *or* in brackets. Although this is strictly unnecessary because the operator *and* takes precedence over the operator *or*, use of brackets ensures that it is evaluated as intended. Note that this expression is not the same as:

(*time* > 18.00) and ((*time* < 23.00) or *weekend*)

which would represent a cheap rate period of 6pm to 11pm Monday to Friday and any time after 6pm (up until midnight) on Saturday and Sunday.

A final problem that can arise with boolean operators is that the value of a compound expression is often determined by the first condition in the overall expression. For example, if *count* has value 25 then the expression

(*count* < 20) and (*index* <= 5)

must evaluate to false, irrespective of the value of *index*. To make this deduction we are exploiting the fact that, for the boolean expression *x* and *y* to be true, both *x* and *y* must be true and so, if *x* is false it does not matter what the value of *y* is, the overall expression will be false. What would happen if this design was to be implemented would depend upon how boolean expressions like this are evaluated in the programming language being used. Some languages may do as we have just argued and conclude that, since the first part of the condition is false, there is no need to examine the second part of the condition. Evaluations done in this way are called left to right evaluations. Other implementations will evaluate both parts irrespective of this argument and so will evaluate the expression (*index* <= 5). We shall take the view that there is potential danger from relying on left to right evaluation and assume that both expressions will be evaluated. We shall see in Problem 7.8 that where both parts of the boolean expression are evaluated this can lead to difficulties.

Exercise 7.5 In Problem 5.11 we derived a solution to the problem of counting the number of occurrences of the pattern 'an' in an input string. The solution used a nested *if*. Rewrite the solution using a single compound boolean expression instead of this nested *if*.

7.4 PROBLEMS

7.4 This problem concerns validating a user input into an integer variable called *number*. Write a design which prompts a user to input an integer that satisfies the inequality 2 <= *number* <= 5, that is, an integer in the range 2 to 5 inclusive. You may assume that the user enters only integer values but your design should check that the input lies in the required range. If it does not, a message should be output saying that an input error has occurred and the user should be repeatedly asked to try again until such time that valid data is input. The dialogue below illustrates the prompts which should be issued when an input error occurs.

> Enter an integer in the range 2 to 5 inclusive ? 1
> You must enter an integer in the stated range 2 to 5. Try again ? 6
> You must enter an integer in the stated range 2 to 5. Try again ? 3

7.5 Write a design which will remove from a string any text from (and including) an opening brace, up to and including the first closing brace which follows. Should only an opening brace be in the string then remove all text thereafter. If there is no opening brace then the string should be left unaltered. Your design should enable a user to enter a string and should write out the string resulting from the deletion. You may assume that the input string is not null.

7.6 One of the problems that a compiler has to deal with is to check that brackets within expressions are well-formed. A sequence of brackets is well-formed if there are equal numbers of opening and closing brackets and the number of closing brackets never exceeds the number of opening brackets. In this problem you are to ask the user to input a string which should consist of an expression that includes brackets only of the type '[' or ']'. The output from the program should be a message reporting whether or not the expression was well-formed. If at any stage of the processing, the number of closing brackets exceeds the number of opening brackets then the error should be reported immediately, together with the position at which it occurred.

7.7 This problem is concerned with the linear search which was introduced in Section 6.3. An alternative method which avoids the use of a dummy item in the array to be searched requires the use of a boolean operator. This search process has the form

> repeat
>   search for item
> until (item is found) or (the end of the array is reached)

Write a design incorporating these design steps which will search an array *names* indexed 1..*maxsize* of base type string for an item input by a user. You may assume that the array is initialized and the outcome of the search should form the output of your design .

7.8 The design below is an attempt to solve Problem 7.7 using a preconditioned loop rather than a postconditioned loop. The data table is as given in Problem 7.7 but the design is in error. Find the error and correct it.

{An erroneous linear search}
1.1   write 'Enter item to be searched for '
1.2   read in *item*
1.3   *index* := 1
2   loop while *index* <= *maxsize* and (*item* <> *names*[*index*])
3.1   increment *index*
4   loopend
5.1   if *index* <= *maxsize* then
5.2   write out 'Item is at index ', *index*
5.3   else
5.4   write out 'Item is not in list'
5.5   ifend

7.9   The specification of Problem 6.1 is modified in this problem so that the initial and final address values input by the user are checked to be in the range 1 to *maxsize* inclusive. As each value is input it should be tested to see if it lies in this range. If it does not, a message should be output reporting the error and program execution should terminate immediately. The further constraint on the input values described in Problem 6.1 should also be incorporated into this design.

7.10   In Problem 5.20 we looked at the problem of finding the number of occurrences of the pattern 'the' in an input string under the assumption that the user inputs at least two characters. Rewrite the design using a single compound boolean condition instead of the nested *if* statements used in the solution.

7.5 SUBRANGES

The data types we have had at our disposal so far have given us limited opportunity to define variables which closely match the values that can be taken by the variables. For example, we have used integer variables to represent the months of the year. Clearly, when a month is expressed in numerical format then the only possible values for a variable representing it are the integers 1 to 12 inclusive. Similarly we have used integer variables as indexes to array elements when the only valid values for such variables are the integers determined by the declared index range of the array concerned.

In this section we shall see how a variable can be defined so that it can be only assigned values of a **subrange** of the integers. This will then make it possible to define a variable *month* so that it can only be assigned integer values in the range 1 to 12 inclusive. An obvious advantage of this is that it makes the purpose of the variable clearer to the reader. However, much more important is the fact that it would be an error to assign, say, the value 13 to *month*, this being a value outside its declared range. Many systems would identify this as an error at run time and would cease execution. Although, from the design point of view this would be too late, it would avoid the situation where the program continued to run with the error undetected. Results from the run could be used without it being known that something had gone seriously wrong somewhere. The process of defining a variable so that it matches as closely as possible the values it could take is called **strong typing**.

Subranges of the integers are not the only means of achieving strong typing. Character variables can also be restricted in a similar way. The reason is that both integers and characters are examples of what are known as **ordinal types**. An ordinal type is one for which the values can be listed, in order, one after the other. The listing of the integers is:

. . . −2, −1, 0, 1, 2, 3, . . .

The ordering we have adopted for the characters is the ASCII ordering. It may surprise you to know that the boolean variables are of ordinal type. The ordering of the two boolean values is:

true, false

where true precedes false. Later in this chapter we shall see some other ordinal types called **user defined** ordinal types. Subranges can be constructed from any ordinal type; indeed, they can be constructed only from ordinal types. So any data type which is not ordinal cannot have a subrange. Thus, it is not possible to define a subrange of the real numbers because the reals are not of ordinal type; they cannot be listed one after the other. Similarly strings are not ordinal for the same reason and so subranges of strings do not exist.

A variable can be declared to have subrange type in much the same way as an array index is defined. Indeed, a variable used to access an array can be defined to be of the same type as the index range used in the definition of the array. This can add to the security of a design but care has to be taken when doing this because such a variable may legitimately assume a value outside this range. A case in point is in Problem 7.7, where the variable *index* is used to access an array but it can assume a value which exceeds the upper index bound. In the data table below all the variables are of some subrange type:

Identifier	Description	Type
digit	One of the digits 0, 1, 2, 3, 4, 5, 6, 7, 8, 9	0..9 variable
lowercase	Lower case character	'a'..'z' variable
uppercase	Upper case character	'A'..'Z' variable
twodigits	A positive integer having 2 digits	10..99 variable

The format is similar to that used for array index ranges, namely, the first and last values must be specified, in order, and separated by two full stops. It is implicit in the notation 0..9 that the underlying data type is integer. The data table below uses type definitions to define *digit* and *lowercase*.

Identifier	Description	Type
digittype	Subrange type definition	0..9
lowertype	Subrange type definition	'a'..'z'
digit	A digit	*digittype* variable
lowercase	Lower case character	*lowertype* variable

Exercise 7.6 Declare, using a subrange implicit in each description, appropriate variables to represent each of the following. (If you are unsure of what possible values an item can have, read the first part of the solution, which is descriptive, then write a definition.)

(a) The numerical component of a vehicle issued with a new registration plate. The number can have up to three digits.

(b) The years of the 20th century, that is, the nineteen hundreds.
(c) Examination grades which use the first seven upper-case letters of the alphabet.
(d) The number of days in a month.
(e) The number of days in a year.
(f) The hours on a 24-hour digital clock.
(g) The minutes on a 24-hour digital clock.

Subranges can be used as selectors in case statements. In Problem 5.12 we looked at the problem of converting a digit into its Roman numeral equivalent. Essentially the solution there consisted of a number of cases. The design fragment below gives an alternative method of solution. It assumes as before that *number* is initialized to a digit in the range 1..9 inclusive.

```
1   roman := "
2   select case depending on number
3        9    : roman := 'IX'
4        5..8 : roman := 'V'
5               number := number − 5
6               loop while number > 0
7                   roman := roman + 'I'
8                   number := number − 1
9               loopend
10       4    : roman := 'IV'
11       1..3 : loop while number > 0
12                  roman := roman + 'I'
13                  number := number − 1
14              loopend
15  selectend
```

Alternatively, the repetition of the loop statements within the case construct can be avoided as follows:

```
1   roman := "
2   select case depending on number
3        9    : roman := 'IX'
4               number := number − 9
5        5..8 : roman := 'V'
6               number := number − 5
7        4    : roman := 'IV'
8               number := number − 4
9   selectend
10  loop while number > 0
11      roman := roman + 'I'
12      number := number − 1
13  loopend
```

In both solutions note how a subrange has been used as a case label.

7.6 PROBLEMS

7.11   Redefine the array *directory* of Problem 6.16 using appropriate subrange types. You should assume that year is a two digit integer with 0 representing 1980 and that cluster numbers are integers in the range 2 to 355 inclusive. You should redefine the time field as a record of two fields, hours and minutes.

7.7 USER DEFINED ORDINAL TYPES

Subranges cannot always be found which best represent the type of data to be described. For example, if we are trying to record say, the number of hours worked during a week in an array it would be convenient if the index to the array could take values like monday, tuesday etc., instead of having to code Monday as 1, Tuesday as 2 and so on. Most programming languages provide facilities whereby the designer can extend the range of standard data types to include types which are more appropriate to the particular problem. One such facility is the provision of **user defined ordinal types**, which are also known as **enumeration types** or **enumerated types**. A major objective in providing enumerated types is to aid the self-documentation of a design, in other words to make the design more easily understood. As the section develops, try to notice how the use of enumerated types leads to designs which do document themselves. The data table below defines an enumerated type called *weekdays*. A variable of this type can take one of the values *sunday, monday, tuesday, wednesday, thursday, friday, saturday*. The data table also declares an array whose index range is *sunday..saturday*. Notice that this declaration extends our previous understanding of an array. In Chapter 6, an array was assumed to have an index range which consisted of consecutive integers; now the index range can be successive enumerated type values.

Identifier	Description	Type
weekdays	Enumerated type definition	(*sunday, monday, tuesday, wednesday, thursday, friday, saturday*)
day	Day of the week	*weekdays* variable
hoursworked	An array of hours worked	array[*sunday..saturday*] of real variable

The enumerated type values are listed in the Type column of the table. Such a list cannot include the same value more than once and the order in which the list is written determines the order of the values. Hence *sunday* precedes *monday* which precedes *tuesday* and so on. We have used lower-case initial letters in this definition to emphasize the fact that the values used in a user defined ordinal type are not strings. Thus if *day* had been initialized to have value *tuesday* it would be an error to attempt to output the value using the normal write out statement used for outputting strings. In fact, we shall not supply a direct method by which the values listed in a user defined ordinal definition can be output to the screen. We shall see later how this problem can be overcome, but initially we shall concentrate on using user defined ordinal types for their mnemonic significance to aid design clarity.

The array is used to store the number of hours worked on each day of the week by an employee of a certain company. We can picture the array as follows:

	hoursworked
sunday	0.00
monday	7.30
tuesday	8.00
wednesday	8.30
thursday	8.45
friday	7.45
saturday	4.00

Here, 7.30 represents 7 hours 30 minutes.

Exercise 7.7
(a)   How would the entry whose value is 8.45 be referenced?
(b)   What is the value of *hoursworked*[*friday*]?

Exercise 7.8 Write down enumeration type definitions, in the form of a data table, to represent the following data:
(a)   Colours of the rainbow.
(b)   Suits in a pack of cards. (The usual increasing order of the suits is clubs, diamonds, hearts and spades.)
(c)   Months of the year.
(d)   Names of the notes in a musical scale.

Exercise 7.9 Use your answer to Exercise 7.8 to define by means of a data table:
(a)   A variable *paint* of type *rainbow*.
(b)   A variable *summer* whose values can be any of the months *may, jun, jul, aug*.
(c)   An array *hand* indexed by *suit* whose values are the number of cards of each suit in a hand of whist. (A hand of whist consists of 13 cards.)

Variables of an enumerated type can be used in control statements or loops just as would integers or char variables. In particular, a variable of enumerated type can be used as a selector in a case statement. We shall consider some examples using the array *hoursworked*, which we shall assume has been initialized.

The design fragment below works out the earnings of an employee based upon the hours worked each day. The hourly rate for a weekday, that is Monday to Friday is £10.50, the rate for Saturday is £15.30 and that for Sunday £18.90.

```
pay := 0
loop for day := sunday to saturday
    select case depending on day
                sunday                    :  pay := pay + hoursworked[day]*18.90
        monday, tuesday, wednesday,
            thursday, friday              :  pay := pay + hoursworked[day]*10.50
                saturday                  :  pay := pay + hoursworked[day]*15.30
    selectend
loopend
```

Here the enumerated type variable *day* is used to control the loop and is used as a selector in the case statement. The operation of the case statement is straightforward and is analogous to the situation where we used an integer as the selector. The execution of the loop statement needs a little explanation. What it does is to initialize the variable *day* to *sunday*, and at the completion of each loop execution, increments its value. The loop is repeated until it completes the pass of the loop during which *day* has the final value *saturday*. However, it is worth looking in more detail at what we mean by *increments* in this context. It means that the value of *day* is updated from its current value to the next value given in the list which comprises the ordinal type definition. We call such a 'next value' a **successor**. Similarly the value immediately preceding a given ordinal value is called its **predecessor**. The terms successor and predecessor apply to all ordinal types, not just user defined ordinal types. Care has to be exercised when using these terms because not every ordinal value has a successor or predecessor. For example, there is no successor to the value *saturday* in the definition above. This is at variance with our common experience which would dictate that we cycle round to Sunday in this situation. This is not the case here; an attempt to find the successor of *saturday* will result in an error. Similarly an attempt to find the predecessor of *sunday* would also be an error.

The design fragment above can be improved by using the fact that it is permissible to use a subrange as a label in a case statement. So the list *monday*, *tuesday*, ... and so on could be written as a subrange and this subrange could be used in the case statement. The design below does this.

```
pay := 0
loop for day := sunday to saturday
    select case depending on day
            sunday      :  pay := pay + hoursworked[day]*18.90
        monday..friday  :  pay := pay + hoursworked[day]*10.50
           saturday     :  pay := pay + hoursworked[day]*15.30
    selectend
loopend
```

Exercise 7.10 Using the definitions given in the solution to Exercise 7.8 write down the predecessor and successor of each of the following:
(a) *yellow*; (b) *spades*; (c) *sep*; (d) *do*.

Unlike integer variables we cannot obtain the successor of a user defined ordinal type by incrementing its value using the + operator. There is a special function called **succ** which produces the successor to any ordinal value it is given, provided a successor exists. Similarly there is a function **pred** which produces the predecessor value.

We can illustrate the use of the function *succ* by using the variable *day* defined above. Suppose we wished to update the value of this variable to its successor. This is easy except for the case when *day* has value *saturday* and this has to be treated as a special case. A piece of design to achieve the required result is :

```
if day = saturday then
    day := sunday
else
    day := succ(day)
```

Exercise 7.11 In this problem the date will be represented using three variables; *day* for the numerical value of the day, *month* which will be of enumerated type *months* defined on page 278 and *year* which will be a year in the 20th century. You may assume that all three variables have been initialized. Your task is to design a program fragment to update the variables so that they represent the day following their current value. For simplicity you may assume that leap years do not exist.

One problem with user defined ordinal types when implemented in programming languages is that the identifiers used in their definitions cannot be written out to the screen. This is in common with all other identifiers; the value stored by a variable may be written out but the identifier by which that variable is known cannot be written out. So if we have an integer variable called *number* which is initialized to 5 then we can write out the value 5 but we cannot write out the word number. Usually this is of no consequence but it can be a problem when user defined ordinal types are being used. Consider the problem of initializing the array *hoursworked*. A design fragment which achieves this is:

```
loop for day := sunday to saturday
    write 'Enter hours worked '
    read in hoursworked[day]
loopend
```

The difficulty with this design is that the user is not prompted with the day of the day for which input is currently being requested. Surely better prompts would specify the day as in, 'Enter the hours worked on Monday'. What cannot be done is:

```
loop for day := sunday to saturday
    write 'Enter hours worked on ', day     {NOT ALLOWED}
    read in hoursworked[day]
loopend
```

Here we have attempted to do the obvious thing and augment the prompt with the name of the day. This is not allowed because *day* is not a string. There is no easy way out of this dilemma. One way of overcoming the problem here is to define a parallel array of type string as below.

Identifier	Description	Type
nameday	Names of the days of the week	array[*weekdays*] of string variable

```
nameday[sunday] := 'Sunday'
nameday[monday] := 'Monday'
nameday[tuesday] := 'Tuesday'
nameday[wednesday] := 'Wednesday'
nameday[thursday] := 'Thursday'
nameday[friday] := 'Friday'
nameday[saturday] := 'Saturday'
loop for day := sunday to saturday
    write 'Enter hours worked on ', nameday[day]
    read in hoursworked[day]
loopend
```

In this design when the name of the day is required then the appropriate element of the array *nameday* is referenced.

7.8 PROBLEMS

7.12   Define a subrange *weekday* of the user defined ordinal type *weekdays* and hence define an array *weeklywork* of type real and indexed on this subrange.

7.13   A company making machined parts works a three-shift system from Monday to Friday inclusive. The shifts are referred to as the early, late and night shifts, the first shift of the week being the Monday early shift and the last being the Friday night shift. The table below shows the number of parts produced by each shift in a typical week:

	Monday	Tuesday	Wednesday	Thursday	Friday
early	100	132	98	174	211
late	213	169	216	148	196
night	175	221	201	100	75

The company wants to keep a computer record of the number of parts produced each week in a two-dimensional array, indexed by user defined ordinal types representing the shifts and the days of the week. Write a design which will enable a user at a keyboard to input the production for each shift in a given week and which will produce as output a table similar to that above. As data is input the design must provide prompts which tell the user the name of the shift and the day of the week for which input is being requested. You should use suitably defined and initialized parallel arrays for the input and output in the design.

7.9 THE DATA TYPE SET

In Exercise 7.4 we looked at an example where a variable was tested to see if it contained one of the four character values 'y', 'Y', 'n' or 'N'. A compound boolean expression was used to determine whether or not this was so. Testing whether a character variable has a specific value is a quite common activity. Typically it arises in menu-driven systems where the choice input by the user must be tested to see if it corresponds to a valid choice before processing continues. Using compound boolean expressions is not always the most elegant way of testing user input, particularly if there are a large number of possible user choices.

A more efficient way is to use a **set**. For our purposes, a set is best defined as a collection of objects all of the same ordinal type. The individual objects of the set are called **elements**. Thus we could have a set whose elements were of type integer or one whose elements were of type char or one whose elements consisted of a user defined ordinal type. However, we cannot have a set of strings because a string is not of ordinal type. We write a set by listing its elements, in any order, enclosed in brackets. Thus [5, 3, 7] is a set with three elements. It is precisely the same as the set [3, 5, 7]. Furthermore, a set may not contain repeated elements. Variables may be declared to be of set type as illustrated in the following data table.

Identifier	Description	Type
numberset	Set of elements of integers	set of integer variable
weekdays	Enumerated type definition	(*sunday, monday, tuesday, wednesday, thursday, friday, saturday*)
DaysetType	Set type definition	set of *weekdays*
dayset	Set of elements of type *weekdays*	*DaysetType* variable

Here, *numberset* is declared to be a set variable whose elements must be of integer type. The definition of *dayset* is more complex. It is a set variable whose type is *DaysetType*, in other words whose elements must be the user defined ordinal types sunday, monday, etc. Set variables are undefined until initialized. A set may be initialized as follows:

> *numberset* := [3, 5, 7]
> *dayset* := [*monday, sunday, friday*]

Should we wish to update *dayset* so that its elements were the user defined ordinal values monday to friday inclusive, we could either list all the values or we can exploit the fact that ordinals are ordered and write:

> *dayset* := [*monday . . friday*]

Several operations are defined on set data types but we shall only be concerned with one of them – the test for membership. A given value either is, or is not, a member of a particular set. For example, the character 'a' *is* a member of the set ['a', 'e', 'i', 'o', 'u'] but the character 'b' is not. The following design fragment, which loops until a vowel is input by the user, illustrates this construct.

> repeat
>   read in *ch*
> until *ch* in ['a', 'e', 'i', 'o', 'u']

Notice here how a set constant has been used rather than using a variable suitably initialized. Sometimes it is necessary to test whether an object is not in a set. Consider for example, the problem of asking a user to input any character other than a digit. If the input character is a digit then the user must try again. The obvious validation test to use here is to check that the input character is not a member of the [0, 1, 2, 3, 4, 5, 6, 7, 8, 9]. To express this in design requires a little care because there is not an operator 'is not a member of'. The design below shows how to achieve the required result.

> repeat
>   read in *ch*
> until not (*ch* in [0, 1, 2, 3, 4, 5, 6, 7, 8, 9])

The character is tested to see if it *is* an element of the set and then the boolean negation operator is applied to the result.

7.10 PROBLEMS

The problems in this section may draw upon ideas from any part of the chapter.

7.14 Small advertisements in newspapers often abbreviate words in order to save space. Typically this is done by removing the vowels from the words For example, the advertisement '3 bedroomed detached house with garden' would be abbreviated to '3 bdrmd dtchd hs wth grdn'. Write a design which enables a user to input a string and which produces as output the input string with the all the vowels removed. You may assume that each word of the input string consists of at least one character.

7.15 The method by which the abbreviations were obtained in Problem 7.14 means that words beginning with a vowel have it and all the other vowels removed. This can make it difficult to deduce what the original word was. For example, the word *one* would be abbreviated by this method to *n*. A better method of abbreviation does not remove a vowel if it starts a word. So the advertisement '3 bedroomed flat very good condition inspection anytime' would be abbreviated to '3 bdrmd flt vry gd cndtn inspctn anytm', where the words *inspection* and *anytime* do not have their initial vowels removed. Write a design which enables a user to input a string and which produces as output the input string with the vowels removed in the manner just described. You may assume that the words in the input string are separated by single space characters and that the string contains at least one character.

7.16 This problem is concerned with counting the frequencies of pairs of characters in a string. The count is restricted to lower-case letters and within word pairs so that punctuation marks and spaces are not considered. The counts are to be recorded in a two-dimensional array, suitably indexed. Your design should input a string, calculate the pair counts and write out the results in the form of a table. The illustration below shows the type of output required.

```
    a b c d e f g h i j k l m n o p q r s t u v w x y z
a 0 1 0 0 0 0 0 0 0 0 0 0 0 0 1 0 0 0 0 0 0 0 0 0 0 0
b 0 0 0 0 0 0 0 0 0 0 0 0 0 0 1 0 0 0 0 0 0 0 0 0 0 0
```

7.17 In Problem 7.13 parallel arrays were used to handle the difficulty of input and output related to user defined ordinal types. In this problem you are asked to give an alternative design which avoids their use by exploiting case statements to generate the correct prompts.

7.18 This problem is based on Problem 7.13. The company notices that the shift which produces the most items in a week is often followed by one whose production is very low. The suspected cause is that the shift following the high production shift has to spend a lot of its time on emergency maintenance, replacing parts which have worn on the machines during the previous shift. The company therefore wishes to assess its maintenance policy. The current policy is that all routine maintenance is done by the Friday night shift, which means that that shift never produces the best production figures of the week. Write a design which finds and then outputs the shift with the best production for the week. The output should specify the day and the name of the shift, the number of items produced and the number of items produced by the next shift. In the event that the shift producing the largest number of items is not unique, then the last shift of the week producing that largest number of items is deemed to have the best production. An illustration of the output required, based on the data given in Problem 7.13 is:

> The best production was on the Tuesday night shift.
> It produced 221 items.
> The next shift produced 98 items.

7.11 SUMMARY

In this chapter we introduced the case statement which enables a selection to be made from several possibilities. The selector which controls this statement must be of ordinal type. We also considered compound boolean expressions as a means of controlling program flow.

The remainder of the chapter was concerned with introducing new data types to aid program design. The types introduced were subranges, user defined ordinal types and sets.

8

PROCEDURES AND FUNCTIONS

8.1 INTRODUCTION

Large software systems require teams of programmers to work together to produce the overall program. In Chapter 1 we introduced the notion of the software engineering life cycle whose purpose is to aid the creation of large software projects. Large programs are not just scaled up versions of small programs. Sheer length of code is not their only difference. A large program is conceptually more difficult to write, as is the problem of coordinating a team of programmers all of whom have the same goal. This chapter is concerned with a key aspect of software development, particularly development by a team of programmers. It is concerned with **modularization**, that is the breaking down of large programs into more manageable **procedures**. Each of the procedures of the decomposed problem can be designed in the way we have developed so far, that is, in a top down manner with stepwise refinements. By careful design of what the procedures are to do, their detailed design can be left to the different programmers whose designs can then be brought together to form the final product.

To illustrate this modular approach consider a large educational institution which awards course completion certificates based upon two components: assessment results obtained continuously during the course presentation and a final examination result. In Figure 8.1 we show a chart for creating the final course results.

Starting at the top left of this chart, data about individual examinees is entered from a terminal. The data entry software includes a data validation process so that any input errors are reported and data entry for them is repeated. The output from this process is a file of examination scores for each candidate, that is, a permanent record is created on backing store. On the right-hand side we have an equivalent file of continuous assessment results. Of course there would be a considerable amount of processing in order to obtain this file but we have omitted the details for simplicity. The *final results program* takes the data from these two files and produces a result statuses file from which a printed copy of the results can be obtained using the print program.

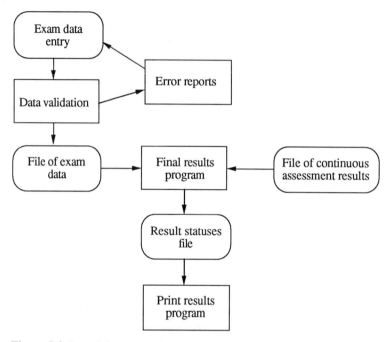

Figure 8.1 A modular approach to exam results

We can identify four major tasks from this diagram: the preparation of the exam results, the preparation of the continuous assessment results, the creation of the result statuses and finally the printing of results. Four different people could be given the task of designing each of these large components. But could they work independently of one another? Some of the tasks must receive information from an earlier process and they all have to revise information and pass it on. For example, the final results program needs continuous assessment data and examination data to produce its result statuses, so it must know the format in which the data is stored on each of these files. In other words the file structure of the examination results must be known to both the person preparing this data and the person writing the final results program. The same is true for the continuous assessment file.

What this example illustrates is how a major task can be broken down into a number of smaller subtasks, each of which may have to communicate with other subtasks in a way that ensures the necessary passage of data between them. This is a fundamental idea of this chapter. Data which a subtask needs to access is called **source data** and that which it computes for onward transmission is called **results**. We shall use the term **procedure** for a design corresponding to a subtask. Specification of procedures will require not only a description of their purpose but also a specification of source data and results.

Top level designs of more complex problems will now take a slightly different form because many of the steps of such a design can refer to some subtask. Each subtask can then be dealt with independently and each will have its own top level design and subsequent refinement. To illustrate this, the design below corresponds to a possible top level design for the final results program of Figure 8.1.

```
1  loop for each student
2      get examination results data
3      get continuous assessment data
4      process data
5      write out results to result statuses file
6  loopend
```

In order to get to this design we have broken the problem down into more manageably sized procedures. This is a basic concept of top down design; decompose into smaller independent procedures, each of which is simpler to solve than the original. Sometimes this will lead to refinements in which certain procedures occur more than once, or to procedures for which standard solutions are available. The advantages of this approach are immediately apparent. Individual procedures can be allocated to different members of the design team, or if only one designer is involved, that designer can concentrate on a single procedure rather than on the overall problem. Furthermore, procedures that exist to do standard tasks can be exploited without having to worry about how they were designed. All this avoids duplication of design elements and leads to clearer and more easily understood designs.

Modularization also alleviates the problems of program maintenance. This usually begins as soon as the system is installed. Maintenance is not only concerned with correcting bugs but is also concerned with meeting new demands from users or updating standard data information held in the system. A typical example of the latter is updating a program which deals with salaries when things like income tax rates are changed by the Government. Modularization of the program minimizes the difficulties of implementing the changes because only those procedures which are directly concerned with income tax rates need to be updated; other procedures not dependent upon the rates can be left alone.

8.2 SOURCE DATA AND RESULTS

In this section we shall begin the process of specification of procedures. These have already been described as subtasks, but another way of looking at a procedure is to think of it as a **black box** which takes source data, transforms it and passes on the results to the next stage. What has to be clearly identified is the source data and results of the procedure. Any data which is required by a procedure in order to perform its task must be specified as source data. We shall assume that a procedure only has access to its specified source data. Any data which the procedure may generate or define within the black box will be called **local** data. The term local will become clear as the chapter unfolds. Data generated by the black box must be specified as results if it is required by processes external to the box. If it is not, then it is not passed out and so is lost when the procedure concludes its execution. There are two consequences of this. First, any local data generated within the black box which is required externally must be specified as results. Second, if a procedure is designed to update a variable then that variable must be specified as *both* source data and results. A variable specified as source data but not results will be unaltered by the procedure execution. Some examples should make this clear.

A small stationery company keeps records of stock levels on cards containing the information illustrated below:

stock number	description	quantity	price
1	Diaries	100	4.50

The entry *stock number* is an integer which uniquely identifies the item of stock, *description* details what the item is, *quantity* records the number of the items in stock and *price* is the retail cost of one item. When a new item of stationery is stocked it is assigned a unique stock number, this being the first unused integer in the stock numbers. It is decided to computerize the stock control system and it is envisaged that there will not be more than 500 separate items to record. An array, called *stock* indexed from 1 to 500, will be used to store records, each of which has three fields, *description*, *quantity* and *price*. The design we shall consider will be much simplified in order that we can concentrate on modularization techniques and the identification of source data and results.

The program is to load in data from backing store (that is permanent storage) and then to present the user with a menu of possible choices. These choices can be executed until such time as the user wishes to quit, at which time the data is to be saved to backing store. Upon executing the program the user will be presented with the following menu:

```
1   Update stock level
2   Create an entry for new stationery item
3   Display the complete stock list
4   Quit
Enter your choice _
```

A design for such a stock keeping program is:

```
 1  load in data from backing store using the procedure load
 2  repeat
 3      display options using procedure menu
 4      read the user's choice using procedure choice
 5      select case depending on user's choice
 6          '1' : update stock level using procedure update
 7.1         '2' : find stock number for a new item using procedure findnext
 7.2               enter new item into stock at appropriate index using newitem
 8          '3' : display all items in stock using procedure display
 9      selectend
10  until user's choice = '4'
11  save data using procedure save
```

Each of the procedures in this design will now be examined and described in more detail.

The procedure *findnext* This procedure finds the next stock number to be used when a new stationery item is stocked by the company. It does so by examining each of the array elements of *stock,* in turn, until the first unused one is encountered. (This implies that *stock* needs initializing in such a way that unused elements can be recognized. A simple way would be to initialize the description field of all elements to 'zzz' on the grounds that no stationery item is likely to have this description.) If the array is full then the procedure returns the stock number zero. What data does *findnext* need access to in order to find the next stock number? Clearly it needs access to *stock* in order that this array can be searched.

What must it produce as results? A new stock number and so this must form the results. Thus this procedure must have source data *stock* and results the next unused stock number. In the next section we shall introduce some notation by which the source data, results and procedure description can be brought together in a more succinct form.

Before analysing the next procedure we shall clarify what constitutes source data and results. In the procedure just discussed the source data was assumed to be in memory and so was immediately available for passing into the procedure. Any data which is not immediately available will not be considered as source data. Hence data that has to be read into memory from a backing store, or from a device such as a keyboard, will not constitute source data. Similarly, for data to constitute results it must be immediately available for use by another process. Now the stock number returned by *findnext* would be available in memory for any process which needed access to it. In contrast, any data written to backing store, or some other device like the screen, will not constitute results because it is not *immediately* available for use by other modules. In the case of backing store the data would have to be retrieved, while data written to the screen is effectively lost to the program because screen contents cannot be directly manipulated by other processes.

The procedure *display* This option should present the user with a screen output of all the items on the stock list. What data must this procedure have access to in order to do this? The array *stock* holds all the details required and so *stock* must be specified as source data. Does the procedure produce any results for immediate onward transmission to another process? It does not – information is transmitted to the screen but screen output does not constitute results. Hence this procedure has source data but no results.

The procedure *menu* This procedure must write out the menu on each loop execution. What is its source data? It has none, it does not need access to any data in order to write out the prompts. Does it have any results? No, its only actions are to send data to the screen and that is not results. This procedure is an example of one which has neither source data nor results.

The procedure *choice* This procedure should read the keyboard and ignore all inputs other than the menu options 1, 2, 3 or 4. What is the source data? There is none because keyboard input is not source data. What are the results? The choice input by the user. This will be used at steps 5 and 10. This procedure has no source data but does have results.

The procedure *newitem* This procedure must prompt the user for the details of the new stock item and must then enter them into the appropriate element of *stock*. What is the source data? The details of the new stock item are all input from the keyboard and so they are *not* source data. The new details are to be stored in *stock* at the index corresponding to the stock number. The procedure *findnext* has found this index but it must be communicated to *newitem*. Hence it must be source data of *newitem*. Is there any other source data? Yes, the array *stock* must be source data because the procedure updates its contents. The array *stock* must also be specified as results, otherwise the updates will not be communicated out of the procedure.

It is worth emphasizing that if *stock* is not specified as results then inside the black box the array would be updated with the new details, but that once the procedure had finished execution the updated version would not be communicated outside the procedure. That would mean that *stock* would contain the same data as it had before *newitem* executed. In other words, no updating would have been done. Some procedures require this facility of receiving a piece of source data, changing its values within the black box but upon ceasing execution to leave the source data with its original value. This is achieved by specifying the data as source data only.

The procedure *save* This procedure must make a permanent copy of *stock* on backing store. It is clear that the procedure must have *stock* as source data. The data on backing store will be held in a file – all data stored on permanent storage devices are held in files. This permanent file is not immediately available to other processes and so is not results. However, files must be given file names so that they can be distinguished. How does the procedure determine what file name should be used? As we shall not be studying files or file transfer in this book, their details will remain a real black box whose mysteries need not concern us. The file name will not be considered as source data to the procedure. If this worries you then you can think of the file name as being data supplied from the keyboard and which is therefore not source data.

The procedure *load* This procedure is to get the data from a file in backing store and place it in *stock* in memory. Clearly *stock* must therefore be results, but does the procedure have any source data? There is nothing in memory to which the procedure needs access and so there is no source data. However, the same difficulty arises as with *save*, namely the procedure needs to know the file name under which the data is held on backing store. Again the black box approach will be taken so that the file name is not source data.

The procedure *update* The user is to be prompted for a stock number which is to be validated to ensure there is an item to which it corresponds. If there is no such item the user is to be given a warning and processing should return to the main menu. If it is valid then the details of the item, description, quantity in stock and unit price should be written out. The user should then be prompted for a new quantity in stock which will be used to update the appropriate field. Processing then returns to the main menu.

Exercise 8.1 What are the source data and results of the procedure *update*?

The following guidelines can be used to determine source data and results of procedures:

- Keyboard input is not source data.
- Screen output is not results.
- Data which is updated by a procedure must be specified as both source data and results. Updates to source data are not communicated outside the procedure unless the source data is also specified as results.
- Data created by a procedure which is to be referenced outside it must be specified as results.
- Data referenced by a procedure must either be specified as source data or must be created by the procedure itself.
- Procedures which communicate with files will not include the file name in their source data.

Some programming languages permit procedures to update data which is not specified as results. A procedure which updates a variable in this way gives rise to what is known as a

side effect. Side effects can be very difficult to spot and generally lead to designs which are difficult to maintain and modify. We take the view that side effects are to be avoided and so insist that data modified by a procedure must be specified as results. By so doing it is quite clear which variables will be updated by a procedure and which will not.

8.3 A PROCEDURE EXAMPLE

In this section we shall introduce some notation which will enable procedures to be specified more succinctly than hitherto and also look at how procedures are used.

It is often necessary to compute the number of days between two dates. For example, when a car is being hired and charged by the day, then the number of days for which the car is on hire must be calculated. One way of doing this is to give each day of the year a numeric value, then elapsed days between two dates can be calculated by subtracting the numerical values. Here we shall develop a procedure to convert a date to a numerical value. We shall assume that the year is not a leap year and that 1st January corresponds to numeric day 1 of the year.

Exercise 8.2 What values do each of the days January 4th and February 3rd have in this method of coding?

Figure 8.2 gives the specification for a procedure which does this conversion process. Study it before reading the commentary below.

numericdate

day	Day of month	integer parameter
month	Month in numeric form	integer parameter
{Convert the date as given by *day* and *month* to a numeric form where 1st January represents day 1, 2nd January represents day 2 and so on. The year is assumed not to be a leap year.}		
daynumber	numeric version of date	integer parameter

Figure 8.2 Specification of the procedure *numericdate*

First note the following points:

- The procedure is given a name - *numericdate*.
- The first boxed section contains the source data, that is the data which is required in order that the procedure can carry out its task. Effectively this box is a data table defining each source data item. We shall explain the word parameter that appears in the type definition shortly. Unlike the procedures that have been considered so far this one has two source data items. Procedures can have zero or more source data items and results.
- The next boxed section contains the description of what the procedure is to do to the source data.
- The final box defines the results. Again it has the form of a data table.
- The three parameters *day*, *month* and *daynumber* are referred to as **formal parameters** of the procedure.

Exercise 8.3 Write a specification in the style of Figure 8.2 for the procedure *newitem* using the description given in Section 8.2. You may assume that the array holding the individual records is of type *stocktype*.

Now we could go on to design the procedure *numericdate* using the methods we have already learned. However, we shall not do so immediately but first look at how the procedure can be used. Delaying the detailed design will enable us to demonstrate two important aspects of procedures; the meaning of the term parameter and the fact that a procedure can be used without knowing about its detailed internal workings.

You will recall that a procedure is a subtask of a larger task. When that larger task uses the procedure, it is said to **call the procedure**. The design statement below is a call to the procedure *numericdate*.

> *numericdate*(3, 2, *number*)

Assuming *number* has already been defined, the effect of this call is to execute the procedure *numericdate* with source data 3 and 2. The result of the call is assigned to the variable *number*. We say that 3, 2 and the variable *number* are **passed** to the procedure for execution. The order in which these data items are passed is crucial. Thus the *first* data item, the integer 3, corresponds to the *first* parameter of the procedure, that is *day*. The *second* item passed, the integer 2, corresponds to the *second* parameter of the procedure, that is *month*. The final item of data passed is the variable *number* and it corresponds to the third parameter, *daynumber*. Note how the first two parameters correspond to the source data and the last to the results. Hence the effect of this call is to convert the date 3rd February to numeric form and to assign to the result to the variable *number*. We shall say that *numericdate* **returns** the variable *number*.

Exercise 8.4 What would be the effect of the call *numericdate*(4, 1, *today*)?

Exercise 8.5 The date 10th March is to be converted to numeric form and the result is to be assigned to the variable *yesterday*. What, if anything, is wrong with the procedure call *numericdate*(3, 10, *yesterday*) to achieve this effect?

These two exercises illustrate an important feature of procedures, namely that they can be called with different source data and can assign the results to different results variables. This is achieved by passing actual data items to the **formal parameters** of the procedure specification. The adjective 'formal' is used because the formal parameters of procedure specifications only assume values when actual values are passed to them as a result of a procedure call. The items of data passed to a procedure are called **actual parameters**.

We can think of formal parameters as *dummy* variables which take on specific values only when the procedure is called. These dummy variables are used in the design of the procedure to express the detail of the processing. We shall see examples of this when we look at procedure design.

In all the calls above, the result was assigned to a variable which was assumed to have been declared of type integer by the calling program. Source data can also be passed in the form of variables, provided that they are of the correct type, have been declared by the calling program and have been initialized. The following design fragment and data table of a program which calls *numericdate* illustrate how this is done:

thisday := 20
thismonth := 3
numericdate(*thisday*, *thismonth*, *thisnumber*)
write out *thisnumber*

Identifier	Description	Type
numericdate	(*day*, *month*, *daynumber*)	procedure(integer, integer, integer)
thisday	Actual parameter corresponding to the formal parameter *day*	integer variable
thismonth	Actual parameter corresponding to the formal parameter *month*	integer variable
thisnumber	Actual parameter corresponding to the formal parameter *daynumber*	integer variable

The variables *thisday* and *thismonth* are the actual parameters corresponding to the source data of the procedure. Their type is declared to be integer *variable* because they are variables in the calling program (as opposed to formal parameters of the procedure). The description column here spells out the correspondence between the actual and formal parameters. In future, descriptions will rarely be so explicit. The variable *thisnumber* is an actual parameter corresponding to the results formal parameter *daynumber*. Actual parameters corresponding to *source data* must be initialized before the procedure call, whereas actual parameters corresponding to *results* do not. This is because the purpose of this procedure is to *assign* values to results. The data table also **declares** the procedure *numericdate* by listing its identifier, listing the formal parameters in the Description column and specifying its type to be *procedure* in the Type column. The formal parameters are enclosed in brackets and the order in which they are listed will be the order in which the corresponding actual parameters must occur when the procedure is called. The type of each of the formal parameters follows the word *procedure* in the type column. The types are enclosed in brackets in the order of their corresponding parameter identifiers. We shall shortly see examples where the parameter types are not all the same. Procedures must obey the declare before use rule and so a design which calls a procedure must first declare it.

Exercise 8.6 Write a design fragment which will assign to the variables *todayno* and *tomorrowno* the numeric equivalents of 20th March and 21st March respectively and then write out their values. Your fragment should make calls to the procedure *numericdate* and should include a data table for all the variables it uses.

In the solution to this exercise, an expression is used as the actual parameter corresponding to the formal parameter *day*. Expressions can be used where a source parameter is expected but a results parameter must be a variable. The solution also illustrates a powerful property of procedures, namely their ability to be called with a variety of different source data and to have results assigned to different variables on each call.

The point that formal parameters are *dummy* variables cannot be put too strongly. The identifiers used for the formal parameters in a procedure specification (or indeed in the description column of a procedure declaration) are unknown to the calling program. In the specification for *numericdate* the identifiers *day*, *month* and *daynumber* were used for the formal parameters. A designer who wishes to use this procedure only has to know the number of formal parameters, their declared order and their type. The formal parameter identifiers are not required to be known. This implies that designers who use *numericdate* are free to choose their own identifiers for actual parameters. That is precisely as it should be to maintain the independence of the modular structure. But it does imply that the identifiers *day*, *month* and *number* could be used as actual parameters in calling programs. The fact that the formal parameters of *numericdate* are *dummy* variables ensures they remain distinct. In the following design fragment and data table, the actual parameter identifiers are identical to the formal parameter identifiers.

1 *day* := 21
2 *month* := 5
3 *numericdate*(*day, month, daynumber*)
4 write out *daynumber*

Identifier	Description	Type
numericdate	(*day, month, daynumber*)	procedure(integer, integer, integer)
day	Day of the month	integer variable
month	Month number	integer variable
daynumber	Numeric equivalent of date	integer variable

In this fragment the formal and actual parameters maintain their own identity. This is because the actual parameters are *passed to* the formal *dummy* parameters. We shall not be concerned with the method of parameter passing but the *dummy* parameters are then processed to create the *dummy* results parameter. This value is then returned to the actual parameter *daynumber*.

For the time being the use of the same identifiers for formal and actual parameters will be avoided. However, bearing in mind that identifiers should reflect the quantity being stored, it is not always possible to think of two different identifiers to represent essentially the same kind of item. The problem of thinking up meaningful identifiers is compounded when the same procedure is to be called with a whole variety of different source data.

Exercise 8.7 Write down a data table for a program which uses the procedure *confirm* below. Your table should include the identifiers of the actual parameters that will be used when the procedure is called.

confirm

prompt	A string prompt	string parameter
{Write out *prompt* and read in a character from the keyboard. If the character is 'y' or 'Y' assign true to *result* otherwise assign it the value false.}		
result	True for 'y' or 'Y'	boolean parameter

Another point about parameters is that, like any variable quantity, their type should be defined to match as closely as possible the data that they will store. So in the procedure *numericdate* above it would have been better to define the parameter *month* to be of integer subrange type, specifically 1..12, because months can only take numeric values in the range 1 to 12. Such a definition would add to the security of the procedure.

Exercise 8.8 How should *day* and *daynumber* have been defined?

The solution to Exercise 8.8 would suggest the specification in Figure 8.3 (in which a new identifier has been used for clarity) is better than that of Figure 8.2 because the parameter types more closely model the variables which will be passed into and out of it.

numericdate2 (interim specification)

day	Day of month	1..31 parameter
month	Month in numeric form	1..12 parameter
{Convert the date as given by *day* and *month* to a numeric form where 1st January represents day 1, 2nd January represents day 2 and so on. The year is assumed to not be a leap year.}		
daynumber	numeric version of date	1..365 parameter

Figure 8.3 An interim specification for *numericdate2*

However, many programming languages only permit real, integer, char, boolean, string and type identifiers to appear in formal parameter definitions. We shall also adopt this convention, which means that the subranges will have to be replaced by suitably defined type identifiers. The following data table of the calling program must make these definitions:

Identifier	Description	Type
daytype	Subrange type definition	1..31
monthtype	Subrange type definition	1..12
yeartype	Subrange type definition	1..365
numericdate2	(*day, month, daynumber*)	procedure(*daytype, monthtype, yeartype*)

The order in which these definitions and declarations have been made takes note of the declare before use rule. Hence the definition of *daytype* precedes that of *numericdate2* because the procedure declares one of its parameters to be of this type. The specification of the procedure then takes the form shown in Figure 8.4.

numericdate2

day	Day of month	*daytype* parameter
month	Month in numeric form	*monthtype* parameter
{Convert the date as given by *day* and *month* to a numeric form where 1st January represents day 1, 2nd January represents day 2 and so on. The year is assumed to not be a leap year.}		
daynumber	numeric version of date	*yeartype* parameter

Figure 8.4 The final specification for *numericdate2*

Exercise 8.9 Decide whether or not the parameter definitions in each of the following procedure specifications are valid. For any invalid ones give reasons why they are invalid.

splitnumber

number	An integer in the range 0 to 9999	integer parameter	◦
{Return the *thousands*, *hundreds*, *tens* and *units* digits of *number*.}			
thousands	Number of thousands in *number*	integer parameter	
hundreds	Number of hundreds in *number*	integer parameter	
tens	Number of tens in *number*	integer parameter	
units	Number of units in *number*	integer parameter	

search

searchitem	Item being searched for	integer parameter
datalist	Array to be searched	*arraytype* parameter
{Search the array *datalist* for *searchitem*. If the item is found then set *isthere* true and assign to *position* the index at which the search item is stored. If the item is not there set *isthere* to false.}		
position	The position of search item	integer parameter
isthere	Flag to denote found	boolean parameter

Below is a data table for a program which calls *search*:

Identifier	Description	Type
search	(*searchitem*, *datalist*, *position*, *isthere*)	procedure(integer, *arraytype*, integer, boolean)
arraytype	Array type definition	array[1..20] of string variable

errormessage

	{No source data}	
{Write out the message 'You have made an error'.}		
	{No results}	

The procedure *errormessage* in Exercise 8.9 has neither source data nor results and hence does not have any parameters. The notation for calls to procedures like this is slightly different in that the call will not include any brackets. The program fragment and its data table below illustrates this:

```
  {A fragment illustrating a call of a procedure which does not have any parameters}
1  if ch = '9' then
2      errormessage
3  ifend
```

Identifier	Description	Type
errormessage	( )	procedure( )
ch	Any character	char variable

In this data table the bracket notation has been retained in order to emphasize that this procedure has neither source data nor results.

8.4 BRINGING IT ALL TOGETHER

We shall now develop a complete program which uses the procedure *numericdate2* in order to solve the following problem.

Write a design, using the procedure *numericdate2* of Section 8.2, which enables a user to input two dates and which will output the number of days (inclusive) between them. In order to input a date the user should first be prompted for the month, which should be input as an integer between 1 and 12 and then for the day, which should be an integer between 1 and 31. It is assumed that the two dates are in the same year and that the first date input precedes the second date input. We shall assume that the year in question is not a leap year and no data input validation is required. A typical dialogue, in which the user responses are underlined, would be:

Enter the month as an integer 4
Enter the day of this month 2
Enter the second month as an integer 4
Enter the day of this month 6
5 days elapsed between 2/4 and 6/4 (day/month)

The main program will be designed first, followed by that for the procedure. A clue to the main program design can be gained by working through the calculations for the example above. The numeric values generated by *numericdate2* for the two dates are 92 and 96. The number of days (inclusive) between these is $96 - 92 + 1$, that is 5. This observation enables the following top level design to be produced:

{Calculate elapsed days between two dates}
1 input the two dates
2 convert the dates using procedure *numericdate2*
3 calculate elapsed days
4 write out results

The final design, together with data table, is given below. Check that you understand its details, examine the data table and then read the commentary which follows it.

	{Calculate elapsed days between two dates}
1.1	write 'Enter the month as an integer '
1.2	read in *month1*
1.3	write 'Enter the day of this month '
1.4	read in *day1*
1.5	write 'Enter the second month as an integer '
1.6	read in *month2*
1.7	write 'Enter the day of this month '
1.8	read in *day2*
2.1	*numericdate2(day1, month1, numeric1)*
2.2	*numericdate2(day2, month2, numeric2)*
3.1	*elapsed := numeric2 − numeric1 + 1*
4.1	write out *elapsed*, ' days elapsed between ', *day1*, ' / ', *month1*, ' and ', *day2*, ' / ', *month2*, ' (day/month)'

Identifier	Description	Type
daytype	Subrange type definition	1..31
monthtype	Subrange type definition	1..12
yeartype	Subrange type definition	1..365
numericdate2	(*day, month, daynumber*)	procedure(*daytype, monthtype, yeartype*)
day1	Day of first date	*daytype* variable
day2	Day of second date	*daytype* variable
month1	Month of first date	*monthtype* variable
month2	Month of second date	*monthtype* variable
numeric1	Numeric version of first date	*yeartype* variable
numeric2	Numeric version of second date	*yeartype* variable
elapsed	Days between dates	*yeartype* variable

We can now turn our attention to the problem of designing *numericdate2*. Its specification is:

numericdate2

day	Day of month	*daytype* parameter
month	Month in numeric form	*monthtype* parameter
{Convert the date as given by *day* and *month* to a numeric form where 1st January represents day 1, 2nd January represents day 2 and so on. The year is assumed to not be a leap year.}		
daynumber	numeric version of date	*yeartype* parameter

Essentially there is nothing new, other than some notation to denote that it is a procedure that is being designed rather than a complete program. A top level design is given below.

numericdate2

day, month

> 1   select case depending on *month*
> 2   process data
> 3   selectend
> 4 process *day* data

number

The box structure of the specification is mirrored in this design in order to maintain the emphasis that the procedure is a separate entity and a piece of design in its own right. The name of the procedure appears first, followed by a list of the source data formal parameters. The top level design then occupies the space previously used by the specification of the process. Finally the results are listed. We shall call the middle design section of this diagram the **procedure body**.

The procedure body now needs refining. The case statement will need to generate, for each possible month, the number of days up to the beginning of that month but excluding the month itself. Step 4 will add to this number, the number of days indicated by the parameter *day*. A final design is:

numericdate2	
day, month	
1	select case depending on *month*
2.1	1 : *dayselapsed* := 0
2.2	2 : *dayselapsed* := 31
2.3	3 : *dayselapsed* := 59
2.4	4 : *dayselapsed* := 90
2.5	5 : *dayselapsed* := 120
2.6	6 : *dayselapsed* := 151
2.7	7 : *dayselapsed* := 181
2.8	8 : *dayselapsed* := 212
2.9	9 : *dayselapsed* := 242
2.10	10 : *dayselapsed* := 273
2.11	11 : *dayselapsed* := 304
2.12	12 : *dayselapsed* := 334
3	selectend
4.1	*dayselapsed* := *dayselapsed* + *day*
4.2	*number* := *dayselapsed*
number	

In this design the variable *dayselapsed* has been used to store the number of days elapsed since the beginning of the year. A variable like this, which is used only within the procedure body is called a **local variable** of *numericdate2*. It is called *local to the procedure* because it has no existence outside the procedure body. In other words, the main program cannot reference *dayselapsed*. An alternative way of saying this is to say that the **scope** of the variable *dayselapsed* is the body of the procedure *numericdate2*. We shall study scope in more detail shortly. All local variables must be declared in a data table for the procedure. Here, *dayselapsed* can assume any value between 1 and 365 and so the most natural way to define it is of type *yeartype*. The data table below does this.

Identifier	Description	Type
dayselapsed	Cumulative days elapsed	*yeartype* variable

The testing of a design which uses procedures needs to ensure that the calls to the procedures have the correct parameters and that the expected results are obtained from the calls. Test data here should include that given in the dialogue above.

Exercise 8.10 Write a design fragment which reads in a number in the range 0 to 9999 and which outputs the thousands, hundreds, tens and units digits on separate lines. Data input validation is not required but your fragment should call the procedure *splitnumber,* described in Exercise 8.9, whose design should be included in your answer.

We have stressed throughout that data types should be chosen which best represent the data which is being manipulated. Choosing types for parameters has again highlighted this process. What we have touched on here is what is known as **data design** which we shall study in more detail in Chapter 10 when we discuss abstract data types. To give you a flavour of what is involved and how procedures can help in data design, consider the problem of maintaining a bank interest account. A procedure to calculate the interest due on an account might be specified as follows:

calcinterest

balance	Amount in account	*moneytype* parameter
rate	Interest rate to apply to account	*ratetype* parameter
{Calculate the amount of interest due on the amount *balance* with an interest rate of *rate*. Return the interest due as *interest*.}		
interest	Interest due on account	*moneytype* parameter

In this specification the way in which money and the interest rate are to be represented has not been stated. Instead type identifiers have been used to define them. If we now want to design a program to calculate the interest due on an account it would appear that we are forced to decide how to represent money. Should it be represented by a real variable, so that an amount of $3.45 would be stored as 3.45? A difficulty with this is that when operations of multiplication and division are applied, the result might have more than two decimal places. An alternative would be to represent money by a pair of integers in which case problems like this can be avoided. Further progress seems impossible without taking a decision. However, study the design and data table below in which the identifiers of the procedures are meant to reflect their purpose:

1   write out a prompt for current balance
2   read in *balance* using procedure *readmoney*
3   write out prompt for interest rate
4   read in *rate* using procedure *readrate*
5   *calcinterest(balance, rate, interest)*
7   write out *interest* using procedure *writemoney*

Identifier	Description	Type
moneytype	Type representing money	See text
ratetype	Type representing interest rate	See text
readmoney	(*money*)	procedure(*moneytype*)
readrate	(*rate*)	procedure(*ratetype*)
calcinterest	(*balance, rate, interest*)	procedure(*moneytype, ratetype, moneytype*)
writemoney	(*money*)	procedure(*moneytype*)
balance	Current balance in account	*moneytype*
rate	Interest rate applicable to account	*ratetype*
interest	Interest due on account	*moneytype*

In this program, whenever an operation has to be carried out on money data, such as reading in a money quantity, an appropriate procedure is called to do the job. This makes the main program independent of the representation chosen for money. This independence is gained by introducing procedures to manipulate money quantities. We shall return to the problem of data design, and in particular abstract data types, in Chapter 10.

8.5 PROBLEMS

This problem section covers Sections 1 to 4 of this chapter.

8.1 Write procedure specifications in the form of Figure 8.2 for each of the procedures *load*, *menu*, *choice*, *update*, *findnext*, *display* and *save* described in Section 8.2. The parameter *stock* should be specified to be of type *stocktype* in these specifications.

8.2 A bank offers varying rates of interest on its deposit accounts dependent upon the amount of money on deposit. A program to maintain the interest on accounts has the following structure:

```
 1  repeat
 2      get account number from user using procedure getaccount
 3      if the account number is valid then
 4          get the balance for the account using procedure getbalance
 5          get the interest rate applicable using procedure getrate
 6          calculate interest due using procedure calcinterest
 7          update balance using procedure addinterest
 8          write out details of interest paid using procedure print
 9          save the new balance on backing store
10      ifend
11  until transactions for the day are completed
```

The purpose of each of the procedures is as follows:

The procedure *getaccount* The user is prompted for an account number. The number is validated against a file of current account numbers held on backing store. If it is an existing account then the procedure returns the number, together with a boolean flag set true. If it does not then the flag is returned with value false.

The procedure *getbalance* This procedure retrieves from backing store the balance corresponding to a given account number.

The procedure *getrate* For a given amount on deposit this procedure returns the interest rate applicable for that amount.

The procedure *calcinterest* This procedure calculates the interest due on a deposit at a given rate of interest. Its detailed specification is given in Section 8.4.

The procedure *addinterest* This procedure adds together the interest and balance and returns the total.

The procedure *print* This procedure writes out the details of a given account namely; the account number, the old balance, the interest paid and the new balance for the account.

The procedure *save* Makes a permanent copy of the balance for an account on backing store.

By identifying the source data and results, write specifications for each of these procedures. You should assume that quantities of money are of type *moneytype*, interest rates are of type *ratetype* and that account numbers are of type *accounttype*.

8.3 Write procedure specifications in the form of Figure 8.2 from each of the following descriptions:

  (a) The procedure *swap*, which has as source data two real parameters and which returns the two parameters with their contents exchanged.

  (b) The procedure *reversecopy*, which has as source data an array indexed 1 to *maxsize* of type string and which produces as results an array whose elements are in reverse order from those of the source array.

  (c) The procedure *reverse*, which has as source data an array indexed 1 to *maxsize* of type string and which produces as results the same array but with its elements reversed.

8.4 A procedure is to be written which takes a year as source data and which has two results: a boolean whose value is to be true if the year is a leap year, false otherwise; the next occurrence of a leap year. You may assume that the source data can be represented by an integer and that a leap year is one in which its integer representation is exactly divisible by four. Write a specification and a design for this procedure. Include in your answer a data table containing the declarations of the actual parameters for a program which calls the procedure .

8.5 Write a procedure design corresponding to the specification:

confirm

prompt	A string prompt	string parameter
{Write out *prompt* and read in a character from the keyboard. If the character is 'y' or 'Y' assign true to *result* otherwise assign it the value false.}		
result	True for 'y' or 'Y'	boolean parameter

8.6 In this problem you may assume that the following type definitions have been made in the main program:

Identifier	Description	Type
maxsize	Array index upper bound	integer constant
vector	Array type definition	array[1..*maxsize*] of integer
compare	(*first, second, result*)	procedure(*vector, vector*, boolean)

Write a design for the following procedure:

compare

first	First array	*vector* parameter
second	Second array	*vector* parameter
{Compare the two arrays element by element. If the arrays have identical corresponding elements assign *result* the value true otherwise assign to it the value false.}		
result	True if arrays identical	boolean parameter

8.7 The following specification is an example of a procedure which has no results. Write a design for it.

blanklines

n	Number of blank lines	integer parameter
{Output *n* blank lines to the screen.}		

8.8　The integer part of a real number is the largest integer which does not exceed the number. For example, the integer part of 23.45 is 23. Negative real numbers are a little more difficult. The integer part of −3.45 is −4 and not −3 as you might at first suppose. This is because −3 exceeds −3.45 (it is nearer to zero than −3.45 is and hence is larger than it). However, −4 does not exceed −3.45 and so must be its integer part. You are to write a procedure to find the integer part of a real number. The specification of the procedure is:

integerpart

x	A real number	real parameter
{Find the integer part of *x*, that is, the largest integer which does not exceed *x*.}		
intx	Integer part of *x*	integer parameter

8.9　A large educational establishment employs a large number of tutors, each of whom marks a number of student scripts. Each marked script contains a form on which the tutor enters the grade obtained on each question and the overall grade for the script, this being the sum of the individual question scores. The forms are passed to the data processing department for recording on computer records. The individual scores and the overall grade are entered into the machine by data processing operatives. Input data is to be validated to check that the overall score is indeed the sum of the individual scores. Write a design for the specification given below of this validation process.

totalvalid

question1	Score on Question 1	integer parameter
question2	Score on Question 2	integer parameter
question3	Score on Question 3	integer parameter
total	Recorded total grade	integer parameter
{If the sum of the three question scores is the same as the recorded total grade then assign true to valid, otherwise assign the value false and write out an error message that the total is not the sum of the individual question scores.}		
valid	True if *total* is correct	boolean parameter

8.10　Automatic change machines must calculate the number of coins of each denomination to issue before delivering the coins to the customer. This problem is concerned with a design for a procedure for doing this calculation. It is assumed that the only coins in the machine are pound coins, fifty pence coins, twenty pence coins, ten pence coins, five pence coins and one pence coins. (There are 100 pence in a pound.) The procedure is to return the minimum number of coins of each denomination which are required to make up any input sum of money. The amount, three pounds 45 pence, is written as £3.45 which will be passed to the procedure as the integer 345. Write a design for this procedure whose detailed specification is:

change

money	An amount of money in pence	integer parameter
{Find the least number of coins of each of the denominations £1, 50p, 20p, 10p, 5p, 2p, 1p to make up the amount represented by *money*.}		
pounds	Number of pound coins	integer parameter
fifties	Number of 50p coins	integer parameter
twenties	Number of 20p coins	integer parameter
tens	Number of 10p coins	integer parameter
fives	Number of 5p coins	integer parameter
twos	Number of 2p coins	integer parameter
ones	Number of 1p coins	integer parameter

8.6 MORE ON PROCEDURE CALLS

In Section 8.2 we gave a design for a program to control the stock level of a small company. It is reproduced below.

```
1        load in data from backing store using the procedure load
2        repeat
3          display options using procedure menu
4          read the user's choice using procedure choice
5          select case depending on user's choice
6            '1' : update stock level using procedure update
7.1          '2' : find stock number for a new item using procedure findnext
7.2              enter new item into stock at appropriate index using newitem
8            '3' : display all items in stock using procedure display
9          selectend
10       until user's choice = '4'
11       save data using procedure save
```

In this design the references to the procedures are very imprecise and do not mention parameters. This is because it is a high level design which has had little refinement and so it still reflects the major design structure. As the design develops, so it will be necessary to convert the calls into precise procedure calls like the ones used in the previous section. However, the jump from the informality expressed in this design to a completely refined statement like

> *newitem(stocklist, stocknumber)*

is sometimes too great for an intermediate design. Something in between the two extremes may make the development clearer.

8.6.1 Informal references to procedures

The following problem illustrates an adaptation to the design language which enables procedures to be referenced in a less formal way than a procedure call but in a way that makes the actual parameters visible.

THE PROBLEM

Write a design which will output the number of leap years between the two input years. Both inputs could themselves be leap years and so both could potentially contribute to the number of leap years. A year for this exercise is any integer value and a leap year is an integer which is exactly divisible by four. The design will use the procedure *leapyear* from Problem 8.4.

UNDERSTAND THE PROBLEM

How many leap years are there between 1987 and 1995?
Two – 1988 and 1992.
How many between 1988 and 1996?
Although these years still represent an eight-year period there are now three leap years – 1988, 1992 and 1996.

DEVISE A SOLUTION

A top level design for this problem is:

1   initialize variables
2   calculate the number of leap years
3   write out results

The refinement of step 2 will involve the procedure *leapyear*. How can this help? It returns the next leap year following the year supplied as source data and so by repeatedly adding four to this value we can calculate how many leap years there are up to and including the second input year. The problem identified above when the first year input is a leap year is also resolved by *leapyear*, because it returns a boolean to tell us whether or not the source data is a leap year. We use the identifiers *nextleapyear, isleapyear* respectively for these two items in the design below:

1.1   input *firstyear* and *secondyear*
2.1   find *isleapyear*, *nextleapyear* using procedure *leapyear* with source data *firstyear*
2.2   if *isleapyear* then
2.3   *leapcount* := 1
2.4   else
2.5   *leapcount* := 0
2.6   ifend
2.7   count the leap years from *nextleapyear* to *secondyear*
3   write out results

Here step 2.1 is a very informal call to the procedure *leapyear*. You may find it useful to use such an approach in intermediate designs because a description like this can convey more meaning than the procedure call *leapyear(firstyear, isleapyear, nextleapyear)*. In the final design such imprecise statements will have to be replaced by procedure calls which specify the actual parameters. The final design and data table for this problem are as follows:

1.1.1   write 'Input the first year '
1.1.2   read in *firstyear*
1.1.3   write 'Input the second year '
1.1.4   read in *secondyear*

2.1.1   *leapyear(firstyear, isleapyear, nextleapyear)*
2.2.1   if *isleapyear* then
2.3   *leapcount* := 1
2.4   else
2.5   *leapcount* := 0
2.6   ifend
2.7.1   loop while *nextleapyear* <= *secondyear*
2.7.2   increment *leapcount*
2.7.3   *nextleapyear* := *nextleapyear* + 4
2.7.4   loopend
3.1   write out 'There are ' *leapcount* ' leap years between the two input years.'

Identifier	Description	Type
leapyear	(*year, currentleap, nextleap*)	procedure(integer, boolean, integer)
firstyear	First input year	integer variable
secondyear	Second input year	integer variable
isleapyear	Flags for leap years	boolean variable
nextleapyear	Next leap year	integer variable
leapcount	Count of leap years	integer variable

TEST THE DESIGN

Critical data here would include the situation where the two input years differ by less than four and when the years entered are themselves leap years. Data having these properties should be used to trace through the design.

8.6.2 Procedures with common source data and results

At the beginning of this section (page 126) it was mentioned that the design statement

7.2   enter new item into *stock* at appropriate index using *newitem*

could be refined into the procedure call

7.2.1   *newitem(stocklist, stocknumber)*

where *stocklist* and *stocknumber* are the actual parameters corresponding to the formal parameters of the specification. This may have surprised you if you were sufficiently aware to check back on the specification of *newitem*. This is because *newitem* has two source data parameters and one results parameter:

newitem

stock	Array holding stock records	*stocktype* parameter
partnumber	Index to array and stock number	integer parameter
{Prompt and read in the description, quantity and price of the new stock item and assign the details to the record at index *partnumber* of the array *stock*}		
stock	Updated array	*stocktype* parameter

From this specification we might expect a call to *newitem* to have the form

        newitem(stocklist, stocknumber, stocklist)

where three actual parameters are supplied, the first two for the source data and the last for the results. In fact, parameters which are both source data and results are listed only once in a call, the second occurrence being omitted. Note that the order of the parameters still matches that of the specification although the number of parameters has to take account of those which are both source data and results. The data table below shows how the procedure *newitem* is declared. It includes details of the individual records and the array holding them.

Identifier	Description	Type
entry	Record type definition	
	description {Item description}	string variable
	quantity {Number in stock}	integer variable
	price {Unit price of item}	real variable
	recordend	
stocktype	Array type definition	array[1..500] of *entry*
newitem	(*stock, partnumber*)	procedure(*stocktype*, integer)
stocklist	List of stock items	*stocktype* variable
stocknumber	Stock number of new item	integer variable

Exercise 8.11 For each of the procedures in the solution to Problem 8.3 write a data table for a calling program. The data table should declare the procedure and define actual parameters which could be used in a call to the procedure.

8.6.3 Functions – procedures with a single result

A special kind of procedure is one where there is only one results parameter. Many procedures which have this property can be designed as a **function procedure**, or **function** for short. The term function will be used rather than function procedure and the word **routine** will be used to mean either a procedure or a function.

We have already seen many examples of functions. The first function we came across was in Chapter 3 when the string function *length* was introduced. You will recall that if *name* is some initialized string then *length(name)* is the dynamic length of the string, that is, the number of characters it has. The function was used in design statements like

loop for $i := 1$ to *length(name)*

In this context it is being used as an expression because it is evaluated and the value is used immediately (here the value determines whether the loop executes another time). Contrast this with a procedure call, where the computed value is returned to a variable (the actual parameter) which must then be referenced in order to determine its value. Here are some other examples of the use of the function *length*:

if *length(name)* > 10 then . . .
number := length(name)
write out *length(name)*
sum := sum + length(name)
ch := name[length(name)]
blanklines(length(name))

In each case the function has a numeric value which is used immediately in the statement. In the first example *length(name)* is evaluated and the result is compared with the integer 10. In the second, the value of the length is assigned to *number*. In the third example the length of *name* is written out. In the fourth example the value is used as an index to access an individual character of *name*. This statement will assign the last character of *name* to *ch*. In the last example, the function is used as a parameter in a call to the procedure *blanklines* of Problem 8.7. The effect of this statement would be to write out the same number of blank lines as there are characters in *name*.

In each example the occurrence of *length(name)* is a **function call** but, unlike procedure calls, the value produced is available only for immediate use. For a function, the result is not assigned to a parameter but is assigned to the function identifier itself. This will become apparent when we look at a function design. The final example above also emphasizes another difference between function calls and procedure calls. A procedure call is a statement in its own right – such a statement does not involve assignments or inequalities or whatever. It has the form

> *ProcedureIdentifier(parameter1, parameter2, . . .)*

that is, an identifier followed by a list of parameters enclosed in brackets. A function call never appears in this form.

A specification for the function *length* would be:

length

instring	A string	string parameter
{Return the length of *instring*, that is return the number of characters it contains. If *instring* is uninitialized return the value zero.}		
length	The length of the string	integer function value

The main difference between this and a procedure specification is that there is a single result and it is given the same identifier as that of the function itself. That is because the value returned by a function call is assigned to the function identifier. An implication of this is that within the function body there will have to be a statement which assigns the correct numerical value to the identifier *length*. Also note that the type of the result is specified here as *integer function value*. The following example brings all these points together.

The procedure *totalvalid* from Problem 8.9 can be specified as a function. We have done so below.

validate

question1	Score on Question 1	integer parameter
question2	Score on Question 2	integer parameter
question3	Score on Question 3	integer parameter
total	Recorded total grade	integer parameter
{If the sum of the three question scores is the same as the recorded total grade then return the value true, otherwise return the value false and write out an error message that the total is not the sum of the individual question scores.}		
validate	True if *total* is correct	boolean function value

The only difference between this specification and the earlier one is that the routine identifier is different (because it is essentially a different routine) and that the function identifier is used for the results. A design for this function would be:

validate
question1, *question2*, *question3*, *total*
{Validate *total*} 1 if *total* = *question1* + *question2* + *question3* then 2   *validate* := true 3 else 4   *validate* := false 5   write out 'Total is not the sum of individual scores' 6 ifend
validate

Notice how it is necessary to assign the result to the function identifier within the **function body**. All functions must include such an assignment statement. The data table below shows how this function would be declared by a program which used it.

Identifier	Description	Type
validate	(*question1*, *question2*, *question3*, *total*)	boolean function(integer, integer, integer, integer)
qu1	Score on Question 1	integer variable
qu2	Score on Question 2	integer variable
qu3	Score on Question 3	integer variable
overallgrade	Total score	integer variable

The form of this declaration is similar to that of procedures, except that the type of the results is written as an adjective just prior to the word *function* in the type column. An example of a call to the function is:

```
1  repeat
2      read in values
3  until totalvalid(qu1, qu2, qu3, overallgrade)
```

The body of this loop would execute until the sum of *qu1*, *qu2* and *qu3* was equal to *overallgrade*.

This example illustrates a problem with subtasks which have a single result – they can be specified as procedures or as functions. Many authors, and some programming languages, would insist that subtasks with single results must be designed as functions. We shall *not* insist on this but will make a choice determined by the way in which the subtask is to be referenced. Furthermore, not all programming languages allow functions to return values other than integer, real, char or boolean types and so their function types are restricted to these types. This means that not all subtasks with single results can be designed as functions. We shall not impose any explicit restrictions of this kind, but most functions will tend to be of one of the types just listed.

Exercise 8.12

(a) The procedure *confirm* of Problem 8.5 had a single boolean result. Can it be respecified as a function? If so give the function specification and design together with a data table for the function and its calling program.

(b) The procedures *reversecopy* and *reverse* of Problem 8.3 both have a single result parameter which is an array. Should they be respecified as functions?

8.6.4 Standard functions

Most programming languages provide certain functions as standard, the function *length* being one example. We shall introduce some other functions which are typically supplied but before you use any of them in a particular language you will need to check that the same identifier has been used and that the specification matches that given here. We begin with two functions with which you are familiar from Section 7.7.

pred

x	Any enumerated type	enumerated type parameter
{Return the predecessor of *x*. It is a fatal error to call this function if the predecessor does not exist.}		
pred	The predecessor value	enumerated type function value

succ

x	Any enumerated type	enumerated type parameter
{Return the successor of *x*. It is a fatal error to call this function if the successor does not exist.}		
succ	The successor value	enumerated type function value

abs

x	Any real number	real parameter
{Return the absolute value of *x*. (For example, *abs*(−3.4) = 3.4, *abs*(4.2) = 4.2).}		
abs	The absolute value of *x*	real function value

round

x	Any real number	real parameter
{Round *x* to the nearest integer and return the value to *round*. If *x* is halfway between two integers, the result is the integer with greatest absolute value. So, for example, *round*(−2.5) has value −3, *round*(2.5) has value 3.}		
round	Rounded value of *x*	integer function value

trunc

x	Any real number	real parameter
{Return the truncated value of *x*, that is its whole part. (For example, *trunc*(7.1) = 7, *trunc*(−7.6) = −7.)}		
trunc	The truncated value	integer function value

odd

x	Any integer value	integer parameter
{Return true if *x* is odd, false otherwise.}		
odd	True if *x* is odd	boolean function value

The final two functions convert character type to integer type and conversely. The function *ord* computes for each character a non-negative integer value called its **ordinal value**. Every character in the character set has an ordinal number which is determined by the ordering of the characters used. We have assumed ASCII ordering in this book in which case the following are examples of what *ord* returns: *ord*('0') = 48, *ord*('2') = 50, *ord*('A') = 65, *ord*('Z') = 90, *ord*('a') = 97 and so on. The function *chr* is the inverse of *ord* and converts integer values into characters. Hence *chr*(99) = 'c', *chr*(65) = 'A' and so on. The fact that these two functions are inverses of each other can be expressed in the following way:

$$ord(chr(n)) = n$$

for any integer *n* and

$$chr(ord(ch)) = ch$$

for any character *ch*. The specifications are:

ord

ch	Any character	char parameter
{Return the ordinal value of *ch*.}		
ord	The ordinal value of *ch*	integer function value

chr

n	An integer value	integer parameter
{Return the character whose ordinal value is *n*. A fatal error occurs if there is no character corresponding to *n*.}		
chr	The character corresponding to *n*	char function value

In fact *ord* can also be used with a source parameter which is a user defined ordinal type. So if

$$days = (mon, tue, wed, thur, fri)$$

then *ord*(*mon*) = 0, *ord*(*tue*) = 1 and so on. The specification for *ord* above can be adapted to include enumerated type source parameters.

A program or procedure which uses one of the standard functions does not have to declare it. We shall see why in the next subsection, but for now, we can continue with the principle that we have adopted so far with the functions like *length* and assume that all standard functions are available anywhere within a program. The list of standard functions given here is by no means exhaustive. Most programming languages provide many more but this selection will serve our purposes.

Exercise 8.13 Write a design, which calls one of the standard functions, for the following function specification:

getdigit

{Read in a character from the keyboard until a character corresponding to a digit in the range 0..9 is entered. Return the integer corresponding to the character input. It is the responsibility of the calling program to provide prompts. Error messages are not be included in the validation process.}		
getdigit	A number in the range 0..9	integer function value

8.7 SCOPE AND NESTED ROUTINES

In Section 8.4 a design was developed which used the procedure *numericdate2*. Below we have reproduced the data tables for the main program and the procedure:

Identifier	Description	Type
daytype	Subrange type definition	1..31
monthtype	Subrange type definition	1..12
yeartype	Subrange type definition	1..365
numericdate2	(*day, month, daynumber*)	procedure(*daytype, monthtype, yeartype*)
day1	Day of first date	*daytype* variable
day2	Day of second date	*daytype* variable
month1	Month of first date	*monthtype* variable
month2	Month of second date	*monthtype* variable
numeric1	Numeric version of first date	*yeartype* variable
numeric2	Numeric version of second date	*yeartype* variable
elapsed	Days between dates	*yeartype* variable

Identifier	Description	Type
dayselapsed	Cumulative days elapsed	*yeartype* variable

The data table shows that the main program declares procedure *numericdate2*. We shall say that *numericdate2* is **nested** within the main program. Shortly we shall see a generalization of this situation where a *routine* has another routine nested within it. Indeed, we shall then extend the ideas of nested routines to any level of complexity.

A question that arises with the data table for *numericdate2* is: why does the reference to *yeartype* in the definition of *dayselapsed* not result in an undeclared identifier error? To see why this is a reasonable question we need to look at the definitions quite closely. The data table for *numericdate2* declares only the identifier *dayselapsed* and so, from what we have said earlier, the only things that the procedure ought to reference are *dayselapsed* and the three parameter identifiers *day*, *month* and *daynumber*. Yet the data table for *numericdate2* references *yeartype*, which is not in this list. In other words, there seems to be an undeclared identifier error. What we shall do in this section is to explain why there is not an error. The explanation involves the idea of the **scope** of an identifier, that is, the places where it can be referenced. The main point which you must grasp from the explanation is that constant and type definitions made in a main program can be used in the declarations of local variables in routines nested within it. This may be generalized, so that if a routine makes constant and type definitions, then any routines nested within it can also reference them.

We shall begin by explaining why the data table for *numericdate2* is not in error. Throughout we must remember that all identifiers are being considered, whether they refer to constants, type definitions, routines or variables. The term **referencing environment** will be used for the collection of all identifiers that a program or routine may legitimately reference. The referencing environment for the main program consists of all the identifiers appearing in the Identifier column of its data table. So the referencing environment here is:

> from *main* : *daytype, monthtype, yeartype, numericdate2, day1, day2, month1, month2, numeric1, numeric2, elapsed*

The reason for the description from *main* in this list will become apparent shortly. The referencing environment also tells us, by implication, what the main program cannot reference. It cannot reference the formal parameters *day, month* and *daynumber*. Neither can it reference the local variable *dayselapsed* of *numericdate2*. The referencing environment is, of course, subject to the declare before use rule. So, for example, *daytype* must be defined before *day1* because it is referenced in the latter's declaration.

The referencing environment for *numericdate2* can be determined in a similar way. It consists of all the parameters together with all the identifiers in *its* data table. Thus it includes:

> from *numericdate2* : *day, month, daynumber, dayselapsed*

But a nested routine is also allowed to reference all the identifiers in the routines in which it is nested and which are declared before it. This is called a **scope rule**. Here, *numericdate2* is nested within the main program and so, by the scope rule, it can reference all the identifiers declared in the main program up to and including its own appearance. Thus *daytype, monthtype, yeartype* and *numericdate2* are all **inherited identifiers** from the main program. This gives a referencing environment for *numericdate2* of:

> from *numericdate2* : *day, month, daynumber, dayselapsed*
> from *main*   : *daytype, monthtype, yeartype, numericdate2*

This immediately answers the question we raised at the beginning of the section. Clearly *yeartype* is in the referencing of *numericdate2* and so its use in the data table to define *dayselapsed* is legitimate. In fact, *yeartype* could be referenced in any procedure within the main program. This is because main program identifiers are always in the referencing environment of routines which they contain. Identifiers like this, which can be referenced anywhere, are referred to as **global identifiers**.

The application of this scope rule does raise other issues. Firstly, it would appear from the referencing environment of *numericdate2* that it can reference itself. That means it is allowed to call itself! This may seem very strange but it is a very powerful technique called **recursion** which we shall be studying in Chapter 15. Secondly, the way the scope rule operates means that the order in which definitions and declarations are made is of paramount importance because the order influences what is and what is not included in the referencing environment of a routine. From what we have done so far you may have got the impression that the order in which identifiers are listed in a data table is totally chosen by the designers. This is not quite so. The designer has considerable freedom but there are constraints. All the data tables in this book declare identifiers in the following order:

> constant definitions
> type definitions
> routine declarations
> variable declarations

Within these constraints the designer has total freedom. So, if there are many constant definitions the designer chooses the order of definition, bearing in mind the declare before use rule. However, all constant definitions must precede type definitions. Again these could be numerous and must obey the declare before use rule and must precede any routine declarations. Finally routine declarations precede variable declarations. A consequence of this ordering is that no routine can inherit a variable from the routine in which it is nested. This is exemplified by the referencing environment of *numericdate2* which does not contain any of the variables from the main program because their declaration comes after that of *numericdate2* in the main program data table.

Many programming languages adopt a slightly different declaration ordering from that above in that variable declarations precede routine declarations. This means that a routine can inherit, and therefore reference, variables in the calling program. But if it can reference such variables then it can update their value, which means that any variable in the calling program can be updated including those which do not correspond to actual parameters of the routine. In other words, side effects become possible. We have taken the view that only variables passed as parameters should be updated by a procedure and so to avoid side effects we have chosen a different declaration order from that often encountered.

Referencing environments become more complex as the level of routine nesting increases. To illustrate this we shall look at a simple guessing game which we shall design using nested routines. In the game the first player enters a target number in the range 0 to 99. The object of the game is for a second player to guess the number entered by the first player. A top level design for this problem is:

1 read in *target* using procedure *getnumber*
2 repeat
3   read in *guess* using procedure *getnumber*
4   write out result of the guess using the procedure *message*
5 until *guess* = *target*

The procedure *getnumber* is to validate the input to check that only digits are entered. It is specified as a procedure rather than a function because of the way it is referenced by the main program. Its specification in which *inputtype* is the subrange 0..99 is given by:

getnumber

{Read in a number, character by character, in the range 0..99 inclusive and assign the result to *x*. All characters which do not correspond to digit are to be ignored but error messages in this case need not be provided. Prompts are the responsibility of the calling program.}		
x	A number in the range 0..99	*inputtype* parameter

The procedure *message* is to report whether the guess is too big, too small or exactly correct. Its specification is:

message

first	Parameter corresponding to target	*inputtype* parameter
second	Parameter corresponding to guess	*inputtype* parameter
{If *first* > *second* then write out 'Target is bigger than guess'. If *first* < *second* then write out 'Target is smaller than guess'. If *first* = *second* then write out 'You have guessed correctly'.}		

In order to refine *getnumber* we shall use the function *getdigit* developed in Exercise 8.13. The first valid digit character entered by the user will become the tens figure of the final number and the second valid digit will become its units part. This observation leads to the following top level design and data table for *getnumber*:

getnumber

{Read in a number in range 0..99}
1   *tens* := *getdigit*
2   *units* := *getdigit*
3   *x* := 10*tens + *units*

---

x

Identifier	Description	Type
getdigit	( )	integer function( )
tens	Digit representing tens digit	integer variable
units	Digit representing units digit	integer variable

The design of the procedure *message* is straightforward and so we shall not bother with the details. The final design and data table for the main program is then:

```
1.1     write out 'Enter target'
1.2     getnumber(target)
2       repeat
3.1         write out 'Enter a guess'
3.2         getnumber(guess)
4.1         message(target, guess)
5       until guess = target
```

Identifier	Description	Type
inputtype	Subrange type definition	0..99
getnumber	(*x*)	procedure(*inputtype*)
message	(*first*, *second*)	procedure(*inputtype*, *inputtype*)
target	Number to be guessed	*inputtype*
guess	Guess of target	*inputtype*

We can see from this data table that *getdigit* cannot be referenced by the main program. This is just as it should be because *getdigit* was designed as a subtask of *getnumber* and so is of no concern to the main program. Thus *getdigit* is nested within *getnumber*, which itself is nested within the main program.

For most purposes careful organization like this will enable routines to be declared in the correct order. However, there may be occasions when it is necessary to work out the referencing environments in order to check the validity of identifier references. The technique for this has already been described but not for a routine nested to the level of the function *getdigit*. We shall therefore find its referencing environment. First, it includes its parameters and local variables. This function has no parameters and so we get:

from *getdigit* : *ch*

Next are included all the identifiers in the routine in which it is nested, up to and including its own declaration. The function *getdigit* is nested within *getnumber* and so this yields:

from *getnumber* : *getdigit*

Finally the process is repeated because *getnumber* is nested within the main program and so all the identifiers up to and including *getnumber* are added to the list.

from main : *inputtype*, *getnumber*

Note how in this last case it is the procedure *getnumber* which is of importance and not the function *getdigit*. The referencing environment for *getdigit* is therefore: *ch*, *getdigit*, *inputtype* and *getnumber*. From this it can be deduced that *getdigit* can reference any of these identifiers. In particular, it could declare a variable of type *inputtype*. In fact, *getdigit* does not require to reference any of the identifiers in its referencing environment other than *ch*.

The scope rule we have been using in this section also enables us to explain why it is not necessary to declare any of the standard routines when they are used in applications programs. The main program itself is nested in an invisible outer collection of definitions and declarations which contains the definition of all the standard procedures and functions of the language. Using the method just described for working out the referencing environment of a routine we can deduce that all the identifiers in this outer collection of definitions are in the referencing environment of the main program and of any routines which it contains. Of course, all this outer collection of identifiers would not normally be listed and they are taken as being always available.

Exercise 8.14 Would it matter if the declarations of *getnumber* and *message* were interchanged in the data table for the main program above? Explain your answer.

Exercise 8.15 Suppose the specification of *message* was changed so that it was required to call *getdigit*. What changes, if any, would have to be made to the data tables of the main program, *getnumber* and *message*?

8.8 PROBLEMS

8.11 A data table for the main program of the stock control problem on page 110 includes the following declarations:

Identifier	Description	Type
entry	Record type definition	
	description	string variable
	quantity	integer variable
	price	real variable
	recordend	
stocktype	Array type definition	array[1..500] of *entry*

Complete the data table so that it contains declarations of all the procedures and actual parameters of the problem.

8.12   Using your answer to Problem 8.1 refine the design of the stock keeping program (page 110). Your answer should use procedure calls wherever possible.

8.13   Refine the design of Problem 8.2. You need not define any of *moneytype*, *ratetype*, *accounttype*.

8.14   Write a design for the following procedure specification:

swap

a	First number	real parameter
b	Second number	real parameter
{Exchange the values stored by *a* and *b*}		
a	Has *b*'s original value	real parameter
b	Has *a*'s original value	real parameter

8.15   Write a design corresponding to the procedure specification below. The part of the procedure which asks the user to confirm that the input is correct should be designed using the function *confirm* of Exercise 8.12.

readstring

{Prompt for a string of characters to be input from the keyboard. Accept the string to the parameter *instring*. Write out *instring* and ask the user if it is correct. Repeat until the user confirms the input is correct.}		
instring	String input by user	string parameter

8.16   Write a design for the following specification:

inrange

start	Lower bound of a char range	char parameter
finish	Upper bound of a char range	char parameter
between	Any character	char parameter
{Determine whether *between* is in the range *start*..*finish* inclusive. If it is, then *inrange* is set to true, otherwise it is set to false.}		
inrange	Result of test	boolean function value

8.17 Write a design for the following specification:

newrange

start	Lower bound of char subrange	char parameter
target	Character within subrange	char parameter
finish	Upper bound of char subrange	char parameter
shot	Any character in subrange	char parameter

{Replace the subrange *start..finish* by one of the subranges *start..shot, shot..finish* or *shot..shot* determined by whether *shot* comes after *target*, *shot* comes before *target* or *shot* equals *target* respectively. For example, if *start, target* and *finish* have values 'a', 'g' and 'z' respectively and *shot* has value 'k' then, since 'k' comes after 'g', the new subrange will be 'a'..'k' so that *start* will be returned with value 'a' and *finish* with value 'k'. Notice that the new subrange still contains *target* but is smaller than the original subrange.}

start	New lower bound of subrange	char parameter
finish	New upper bound of subrange	char parameter

8.18 Write a program, which uses the routines in Problems 8.16 and 8.17, to play the following game. Player 1 chooses a letter, which we shall call the target, in the range 'a' to 'z' and player 2 has to discover the target in as few guesses as possible. In order to help player 2 a prompt is to be given indicating the subrange in which the target letter lies. Initially this subrange is 'a' to 'z' but after each guess it will be updated by replacing one of the end points by the guess, in such a way that the new subrange contains the target. The game concludes as soon as player 2 guesses the target. When this happens the number of guesses required is to be output. All input is to be validated, which means that any input that does not lie in the prompted range is to be ignored and does not contribute to the game. Typical output from the program, in which user responses are underlined, would be:

> First player: Enter a letter in the range a to z r
> Second player: Enter a guess in the range a to z c
> Second player: Enter a guess in the range c to z b
> Guess is not in stated range – guess is ignored
> Second player: Enter a guess in the range c to z m
> Second player: Enter a guess in the range m to z r
> You took 3 attempts

8.19 This question concerns the following data tables:

For the main program

Identifier	Description	Type
maxsize	Constant definition	Integer constant value 50
valrange	Subrange type definition	0..100
arraytype	Array type definition	array[*minsize..maxsize*] of *valrange*
routine1	(*first, second*)	procedure(*valrange, valrange*)
routine2	(*givenarray*)	integer function(*arraytype*)
survey	An array of data	*arraytype* variable

For the procedure *routine1*:

Identifier	Description	Type
temp	A temporary variable	integer parameter

For the function *routine2*:

Identifier	Description	Type
largest	Largest element of *givenarray*	integer parameter
smallest	Smallest element of *givenarray*	integer parameter

(a) Write down the referencing environments for the main program and *routine1*.
(b) Would it be possible for *temp* to be redefined to be of type *valrange*?
(c) Can *routine1* call *routine2*?
(d) Can *routine2* call *routine1*?
(e) Can *routine1* reference *largest*?
(f) Can *routine2* reference *temp*?

8.9 SUMMARY

In this chapter we have introduced the idea of a procedure. Procedures enable a large task to be broken down into a number of smaller subtasks, each of which can be designed independently of the others. The procedures need to communicate with each other. This is done by passing data between them. Data which is required in order for a procedure to perform its task is called source data. That which is produced by a procedure is called results.

The source data and results of procedures are represented by formal parameters. It is these parameters in which the detailed design of the procedure is expressed. When a procedure is called it must be supplied with actual parameters which will replace the formal parameters. Procedures may be called with lots of different actual parameters. Procedures which have a single results parameter can be specified as a function. Functions are called in a different way from procedures in that the result of a procedure call is immediately available and does not have to be assigned to a variable. Routines which are nested within each other can reference identifiers which are in their referencing environments. The referencing environments can be evaluated by applying the scope rule to the data tables of the routines.

9

CASE STUDY

In this chapter we shall extend the ideas of Chapter 8 in the context of a case study. Many of the tasks performed by computers involve the processing of non-numeric data – the manipulation of names and addresses in commercial data processing, the editing of program statements in software development, the editing of text in letters produced on word processors. In all of these applications the underlying data structure is a sequence, or string, of characters. The case study we shall look at is concerned with string handling and in particular with the development of a very simple text editor. This will illustrate the importance of procedures in program design. The chapter begins with a look at some basic string manipulation procedures which are built into most languages. Section 9.3 extends the range of string procedures and the case study itself starts in Section 9.5.

9.1 STRING PROCEDURES

We are already familiar with the data type string and its declaration. We remind you that a string variable can be declared with a specific static length. A string variable for which no static length is declared will be assumed to be capable of storing up to 255 characters. This upper limit is common to many programming languages. Throughout this chapter we shall assume that no attempt is made to assign more than 255 characters to an individual string variable.

In order to manipulate strings we already have at our disposal the index method of identifying individual characters of a string; concatenation to join two or more strings together and the *length* function to determine the dynamic length of a string. We shall now introduce additional built-in string manipulation procedures. This means that they do not appear in the data tables of programs or procedures which use them. A list of all the built-in string procedures will be given in the chapter summary.

The function *copy* A common activity in string handling is to extract a substring from a given source string. The specification below shows one way in which this can be done.

copy

mainstring	The source string	string parameter
index	Index at which string to be copied starts	integer parameter
span	Number of characters to copy	integer parameter
{Return the substring of *mainstring* whose length is *span* characters starting with the character at position *index*. If *index* is larger than the dynamic length of *mainstring* or if *span* is such that the dynamic length of *mainstring* would be exceeded then return the null string.}		
copy	An extract from *mainstring*	string function value

Exercise 9.1 Write down the value of the result parameter after each of the following calls:

(a) *word* := *copy*('An▽introduction▽to▽design', 4, 12)

(b) *forename* := *copy*(*name, start, bridge*) where *name* has value 'Henry David Thoreau', *start* has value 7 and *bridge* has value 5.

The procedure *delete* The procedure *delete* removes characters from a string. Its specification is given below.

delete

anystring	The source string	string parameter
index	Index at which deletion starts	integer parameter
span	Number of characters to be deleted	integer parameter
{Return to *anystring* the substring obtained by deleting *span* characters from *anystring* beginning at the character at position *index* . If *index* is larger than the dynamic length of *anystring* or if *span* is such that the dynamic length of *anystring* would be exceeded then do not delete any characters and return *anystring* unaltered.}		
anystring	The source string with characters deleted	string parameter

Exercise 9.2 Write down the value of the result parameter after each of the following calls:

(a) (i) *delete*(*title*, 4, 6) where *title* is a string variable which has been initialized with the value 'The▽first▽amendments'

    (ii) *delete*(*name, start, bridge*) where *name* has value 'David', *start* has value 4 and *bridge* has value 3.

(b) Starting on each occasion with the string variable *sentence* whose value is given by

'A▽shot▽in▽the▽dark', write down calls to *delete* which will result in *sentence* taking the values:

(i)   'A▽shot'
(ii)   'in▽the▽dark'
(iii) 'shot'

The procedure *insert* The procedure *insert* enables a string to be inserted at any point within another string. The specification is:

insert

anystring	String into which insertion is made	string parameter
implant	String to be inserted	string parameter
index	Index at which insertion starts	integer parameter
{Return to *anystring* the string obtained by inserting the string *implant* into *anystring* in such a way that the first character of *implant* is placed at position *index* of the result. If *index* exceeds the dynamic length of *anystring* by more than 1 or if the combined length of *anystring* and *implant* is more than 255 then return *anystring* unaltered.}		
anystring	Source string with *implant* inserted	string parameter

The condition that *index* can exceed the dynamic length of *anystring* by 1 means that *implant* can be inserted at the end of *anystring*. Note that adding strings to the end of existing strings is the same as concatenating them.

Exercise 9.3

(a)   Write down the value of the result parameter after each of the following calls:
   (i)   *insert(title*, 'se', 4) where *title* is the string variable whose value is 'The▽Principles▽of▽Design'
   (ii)   *insert(name, middle,* 6) where *name* has value 'David▽Sargent' and *middle* has value '▽Robert'.

(b)   Starting on each occasion with the string variable *sentence* whose value is 'design' write down calls to *insert* which will result in *sentence* taking the values:
   (i)   'A▽design'
   (ii)   'design▽methods'

The function *pos* The function *pos* returns the position of a substring in a given string and is specified below.

pos

pattern	String whose position is sought	string parameter
anystring	String in which pattern is sought	string parameter
{Return the index of the start of the pattern string in the string *anystring*. If the pattern does not exist or is null, return the value zero.}		
pos	The index of *pattern* in *anystring*	integer function value

Exercise 9.4 Write down the value of the integer variable *position* after each of the following statements:

(a) *position* := *pos*('is', 'where▽is▽it')

(b) *position* := *pos*(*fruit*, *phrase*) where *fruit* has value 'banana' and *phrase* has value 'an'.

(c) *position* := *pos*('is', 'Not▽there')

9.2 PROBLEMS

9.1 Write a design for each of the functions *copy* and *pos*, and for each of the procedures *delete* and *insert*.

9.2 *copy* was developed as a function. Write a procedure, *copy2*, which has the same description as *copy* but which is specified and designed as a procedure. Your answer should include both the specification and the design.

9.3 Write a procedure called *delete2* which has a slightly different specification from *delete* in that if *span* specifies more characters than remain, starting at the *index*th position, then all the characters after this position are deleted.

9.3 FURTHER STRING PROCEDURES

The procedures we developed in Section 9.1 were built-in procedures and they provide some basic string manipulation tools. In this section we want to develop procedures which have a more specific role. The first new procedure we shall consider is one which splits a string into two. For example the string '32▽Meadow▽Way,▽Middleton' which represents an address can be split into the two strings

'32▽Meadow▽Way,'
'Middleton'

where the first string corresponds to the road of the address and the second to the town. These two components can be extracted from the original string using the *copy* procedure as follows:

road := *copy*('32▽Meadow▽Way,▽Middleton', 1, 14)
town := *copy*('32▽Meadow▽Way,▽Middleton', 16, 9)

The variables *road*, and *town* would then hold the two components of the string. The difficulty with these calls is that the index and span parameters required by the procedure *copy* have to be calculated beforehand. It would be so much easier if there was a procedure which would split the string into a left and right substring, the split occurring at the first comma.

This requirement to split a string, particularly one representing an address is quite common. Addresses are often held in what is known as free format form which means they are stored in a string (of some maximum length) with the individual components of the address being separated from each other by a punctuation character not normally found in an address. The address above could be stored as

'32▽Meadow▽Way,*Middleton'

where a * has been used to separate the road part of the address from the town. A format like this has the advantage that it caters for a whole variety of different address styles which may include one or more components like house name, house number, road, village, town, city, county and so on. Procedures can be developed which extract components of addresses stored in free format form.

The procedure *split* A procedure to split a source string at a place determined by a pattern is given below.

split

subject	The source string	string parameter
pattern	Pattern at which *subject* is split	string parameter
{Split *subject* into *left* and *right* at the first occurrence of the *pattern* string. The pattern string is not included in either the *left* or *right* parts. If the *pattern* string is not in *subject* or is the null string then assign *subject* to *left* and the null string to *right*.}		
left	Left part of the split string	string parameter
right	Right part of the split string	string parameter

Exercise 9.5 If *long* = 'a▽few▽quite▽short▽words' write down the values of *leftpart* and *rightpart* after the call

split(*long*, *code*, *leftpart*, *rightpart*)

for each of the following values of *code*:
(a) 'short';   (b) '▽';   (c) 'paragraph'.

A top level design for the procedure *split* will require an *if* statement which considers each of the two possibilities: the pattern is in the source string; the pattern is not in the source string or is null.

split

---

subject, pattern

  {Split *subject* at *pattern*}
1 initialize variables
2 if *pattern* is not in *subject* or is null then
3   *left* := *subject*
4   *right* := null
5 else
6   split subject into *left* and *right*
7 ifend

---

left, right

Step 6 of this design can be refined using the function *copy*. Source parameters have to be supplied in calls to this function. The identifiers *leftstart* and *leftlength* will be used to denote these parameters for the substring *left,* and *rightstart* and *rightlength* will be used for those associated with the substring *right*. The next exercise asks you to calculate these values for specific strings. The results will then be generalized for arbitrary strings and patterns.

Exercise 9.6 Using the identifiers above, what are the values of *leftstart*, *leftlength*, *rightstart*, *rightlength* for the string 'An▽example▽of▽a▽string' if the pattern string is '▽of▽a▽'? In addition to giving numerical answers express them using the values of *length(pattern)* and *pos(pattern, subject)*.

Exercise 9.7 Use the results from the previous exercise to write a final design for the procedure *split*.

The procedure *replace* The built-in procedure *delete* allows characters within a string to be deleted. Often deleted characters are replaced by other characters. A procedure which deletes characters and then replaces them by others is specified below.

replace

subject	The source string	string parameter
pattern	The pattern to be replaced	string parameter
object	The replacement string	string parameter
{Replace the first occurrence of *pattern* in *subject* by *object*. If *pattern* does not exist in *subject* or if the replacement would result in an overlength string, leave *subject* unaltered.		
subject	The result string	string parameter

For example, if *subject* = 'This▽procedure▽replaces▽pattern▽by▽object', *pattern* = 'by' and *object* = 'with' then the call

    replace(subject, pattern, object)

would result in *subject* having the value 'This▽procedure▽replaces▽pattern▽with▽object'. In developing a design for this procedure we shall assume that the static length of *subject* is given by the integer constant *stringsize*. A top level design for this procedure is then:

replace

---

subject, pattern, object

    {Replace *pattern* in *subject* by *object*}
1 if replacement would not exceed *stringsize* then
2   if *pattern* is in *subject* then
3   carry out replacement
4   ifend
5 ifend

---

subject

Exercise 9.8 Complete the design of the procedure *replace*.

9.4 PROBLEMS

9.4   Write a design for the following procedure specification:
replacechar

givenstring	A source string	string parameter
patternchar	A character to be replaced	char parameter
newchar	The replacement character	char parameter
{Replace every occurrence of *patternchar* in *givenstring* by *newchar*.}		
givenstring	String with replacements	string parameter

9.5   Write a design for the procedure specified below:

split2

subject	The source string	string parameter
pattern	Pattern at which *subject* is split	string parameter
{Split *subject* into *left* and *right* at the first occurrence of the *pattern* string. The pattern string *is* to be included in the *left* part. If the *pattern* string is not in *subject* or is the null string then assign *subject* to *left* and the null string to *right*.}		
left	Left part of the split string	string parameter
right	Right part of the split string	string parameter

9.5 SPECIFYING A TEXT EDITOR

In this section a very simple and somewhat crude text editor will be developed. This will enable us to look at some of the problems associated with creating a larger piece of design than hitherto. However, there are two very important features of text editors and word processors that we shall not attempt to include. The first relates to the way the cursor is used in standard word processing packages. Typically, special keys are used to position the cursor at the place in the text where an editing task is to be undertaken. Word processors and text editors which have this facility are called screen-based editors and to design such a system requires the use of screen coordinates to specify locations on the screen. Rather than become involved in defining screen locations we shall take the simpler option and develop what is known as a line-orientated editor. We shall see what this means shortly. Secondly, word processors and text editors 'work on' files, that is they manipulate data held on backing store. As files will not be covered in this book an array of string will be used to store the text, each index of the array corresponding to an individual line. This imposes the immediate restriction on the number of lines which the document can contain. In fact we shall make the number of elements in the array very small. This will simplify design testing and will enable the whole of the text to be displayed at one time should you wish to implement the design. The static length of the array elements will also be chosen so that each line of text can be output on a single line of a hypothetical screen.

9.5.1 Editor specification

The editor will be restricted to the following tasks:

- *Enter new text* – to input characters from the keyboard into the array, thereby creating the text.
- *Display the text* – to output the text to the screen.
- *Change the text* – to enable changes to be made to individual lines of the text.
- *Delete a line* – to enable a complete line of text to be removed.
- *Justify text* – to enable the user to right justify the text on a chosen width.

Each of these tasks will be specified in more detail shortly but we shall first describe how the user is to interact with the editor as a whole. The editor is to be menu-driven and upon execution of the program the user should see the screen output shown in Figure 9.1:

```
    MAIN MENU

1   Enter new text
2   Display the existing text
3   Change a word in a line
4   Delete a line of text
5   Justify the document
6   Quit

Enter your choice _
```

Figure 9.1 Text editor menu

The underscore in this diagram represents the cursor. Upon completion of any of the editor tasks the user should be returned to this menu. An option is chosen by entering the appropriate option number. Only the values 1 to 6 should be recognized by the main menu and any other choice should be ignored.

9.5.2 Specifying Enter

Text is to be entered one line at a time. No single line may contain more than *stringsize* characters where *stringsize* is an integer constant with value 40. (Most screen outputs allow more than this but 40 will make the illustrations in the text easier to read.) If a user inputs more than 40 characters to a line then only the first 40 will be taken as input and the user should be warned that this has happened. Within a line a word will be defined to be any sequence of non-space characters. No word should contain more than 20 characters but the onus will be on the user to ensure that this limit is not exceeded – the design will not check for this. (This restriction is imposed in order to simplify the justification option where we wish to avoid problems associated with hyphenating words.) Only *maxlines* lines of text may be entered where *maxlines* is an integer constant whose value is 10. (This restriction means that the whole of the text can be displayed on the screen in one go.) Exit from the Enter option is either by entering the maximum number of permitted lines of text, in which case exiting should be done automatically by the design, or by the user entering the null string. Figure 9.2 illustrates a typical dialogue for the Enter option. The symbol <ret> represents the return key and underlined text denotes user responses.

```
Enter the text one line at a time up to a maximum of 10 lines.
Only 40 characters are permitted per line.
No single word should have more than 20 characters.
Terminate input by typing <ret> twice.

Enter line 1
This is the first line.<ret>

Enter line 2
This line contains more than 40 characters.<ret>
Your input is too long and has been cut to the following:
This line contains more than 40 characte

Enter line 3
This is the third line.<ret>

Enter line 4
<ret>
```

Figure 9.2 Using the Enter option

9.5.3 Specifying Display

This option should display the current contents of the array. For the input of Figure 9.2 the Display option should produce the output shown in Figure 9.3. Only the elements which have non-null string contents should be output. In the event that an attempt is made to display the text before any has been entered, then the message that 'No text has been entered' should be displayed instead. The display should remain on the screen until the user presses any keyboard character.

```
1 This is the first line.
2 This line contains more than 40 characte
3 This is the third line.

Press any key to continue _
```

Figure 9.3 Using the Display option

9.5.4 Specifying Change

This option will allow the user repeatedly to edit an individual line of existing text. The number of the line to be edited must be specified by the user – hence the term 'line-orientated editor' referred to above. Only a line which contains text can be changed and so the line number entered by the user must be validated to ensure that this is the case. We shall assume that the input is an integer but shall check that it lies in the range 0 to *maxlines*. The input of 0 for the line number is to indicate that the user wishes to quit the option. When this happens control should be returned to the main menu.

The amount of editing that this option allows is fairly limited. The user is to be prompted for a pattern string and then for an object string which is to replace the pattern. Should the specified pattern not be there, or the replacement result in an overlength string, then no changes should be carried out. Similarly, no changes should be carried out if either the pattern string or object string is null. Figure 9.4 illustrates a dialogue when the Change option is chosen. It includes the output which is required when an invalid line number is input and when an overlength string is entered.

```
1 This is the first line.
2 This line contains more than 40 characte
3 This is the third line of text.

Lines 1 - 3 contain text and may be Changed
Enter number in this range or 0 to return to MAIN menu 2<ret>
Enter pattern :
This line contains more than 40 characters.<ret>
Your input is too long and has been cut to the following:
This line contains more than 40 characte

Enter object  :
This is now a shorter line.<ret>
New line 2 is :
This is now a shorter line.

Press any key to continue _
```

Figure 9.4 Using the Change option

Note how the existing text is displayed first, followed by the information on which lines contain text, which in turn is followed by the prompt for a line number. Figure 9.5 shows the required output when an attempt is made to use Change before any text has been entered.

```
No text has been entered.

You must Enter text before you can Change it.

Press any key to continue _
```

Figure 9.5 Using Change when there is no text entered

9.5.5 Specifying Delete

This option will allow the user to remove text one line at a time. The number of the line to be deleted must be specified by the user and it must be validated to ensure that the line does contain text. An input of 0 for a line number will indicate that further deletions are not required and control should return to the main menu. After a line has been deleted the revised text is to be displayed with the line numbers adjusted appropriately. Figure 9.6 illustrates a typical dialogue for deleting a line.

```
1 This is the first line.
2 This line contains more than 40 characte
3 This is the third line.

Lines 1 - 3 contain text and may be Deleted
Enter number in this range or 0 to return to MAIN menu 4<ret>
Number must be in range 0 - 3. Re-enter? 2<ret>
1 This is the first line.
2 This is the third line.

Press any key to continue _
```

Figure 9.6 Using the Delete option

If no text has been entered and an attempt is made to use the Delete option then a dialogue similar to that in Figure 9.5 should take place but with the references to 'change' being replaced by 'delete'.

9.5.6 Specifying Justify

If you look at the right-hand edge of most of the paragraphs in this book you will see that they are aligned with the possible exception of the last line of a paragraph. The print is said to be **right-justified**. Designers of printed text have to decide whether or not to right justify. Narrow columns tend to look rather odd if right-justified but a text as wide as this paragraph has its look improved if right justification is applied. Most text is left-justified, that is it is aligned along a left-hand margin. However, the design language of this book provides an example of text which is not left-justified because the lines often begin with space characters. A piece of text which is both left- and right-justified will be called **justified** text, otherwise it will be described as **ragged**.

Text is right-justified by adding additional space between the words on a line. This can be done in a variety of ways but we shall consider the simplest situation in which all the characters in the text are assumed to occupy the same space. Typefaces with this property are called mono pitch typefaces and are typically found on typewriters and computer screen outputs. Figures 9.1 to 9.6 all use a mono pitch typeface. The symbol Δ will be used to denote a space character, rather than the usual symbol ∇, in order to emphasize that a mono pitched typeface is being used.

To justify some text which uses a mono pitch typeface we need to know the number of characters which are to be printed on each line. The method is not as straightforward as it might seem. For example, suppose we wanted to justify

$$In\Delta order\Delta to\Delta justify\Delta some\Delta text\Delta which\Delta uses\Delta a\Delta mono$$

using a line width of 15 characters. We cannot simply break the text so that each line contains 15 characters because we would get the following:

```
InΔorderΔtoΔjus
tifyΔsomeΔtextΔ
whichΔusesΔaΔmo
no
```

The second line is not right-justified and the method splits words in the middle. For lines which have leading space characters or multiple spaces between words the situation is even worse. To simplify matters Justify will ignore leading spaces in lines and will treat multiple spaces as single space characters. This means that the text will first have to be converted into this form. This can be done by extracting successive words to form new ragged lines in the following way. Each new line is constructed so that it begins with a word and subsequent words are separated by single space characters. Words are added to the new line until its length is such that adding another word would make it longer than the line width for justification. For the text above this reforming process would result in the following lines of text being created.

```
InΔorderΔto
justifyΔsome
textΔwhichΔuses
aΔmono
```

Each line contains only complete words and has 15 or fewer characters. Spaces will now be added to each of these lines so that the text becomes right-justified. The first line requires four spaces to be added. As there are just two gaps in the line two extra spaces are assigned to each gap. The second line requires three spaces to be distributed to one gap. The third line is already justified and the last is not to be justified. This results in:

```
InΔΔΔorderΔΔΔto
justifyΔΔΔΔsome
textΔwhichΔuses
aΔmono
```

It will not always be the case that the number of additional spaces will divide equally into the number of available spaces. When the division does not work out evenly the extra spaces are to be distributed from the beginning of the line. The following exercise illustrates the technique.

Exercise 9.9 Justify the string at the bottom of page 152 using a line width of 23.

The user will choose the line width but it must lie in the range 20 to *stringsize* inclusive. When the Justify option is chosen with the text shown in Figure 9.7, then the dialogue illustrated in Figure 9.8 is expected.

```
1  InΔorderΔtoΔjustifyΔsomeΔtextΔwhichΔuses
2  aΔmonoΔpitchΔtypefaceΔweΔneedΔtoΔknow
3  theΔnumberΔofΔcharactersΔwhichΔareΔtoΔbe
4  printedΔonΔeachΔline.
```

Figure 9.7 Text before it is justified

```
Enter width for justified text in range 20 - 40? 50<ret>
Width must be in range 20 - 40, re-enter? 30<ret>

InΔΔorderΔtoΔjustifyΔsomeΔtext
whichΔΔΔusesΔΔΔaΔΔΔmonoΔΔpitch
typefaceΔΔweΔΔneedΔtoΔknowΔthe
numberΔofΔcharactersΔwhichΔare
toΔbeΔprintedΔonΔeachΔline.

Press any key to continue _
```

Figure 9.8 Text justified on a line width of 50 characters

An attempt to use the Justify option before any text has been entered should result in a dialogue similar to that in Figure 9.5 but with the reference to 'Change' being replaced by 'Justify'. A user is permitted to enter multiple space characters anywhere in a line and may have a line consisting entirely of spaces. However, multiple spaces will be treated as described above. This means that if line 2 in Figure 9.7 was replaced by a line of space characters then the Justify option would treat the text as if it consisted of only the lines 1, 3 and 4. Furthermore, if line 1 begins with space characters then Justify will remove them when justifying the text. In short, Justify is to interpret the text as a sequence of words separated by single space characters, irrespective of how many space characters may be between the words.

9.6 DECIDING WHAT TO MODULARIZE

The first stage is to decide which parts of the editor to design as routines and then to specify them. An obvious choice would be to modularize each of Enter, Display, Change, Delete and Justify leading to the following top level design for the editor:

```
    {A text editor program}
 1  initialize variables
 2  repeat
 3     display menu and read in choice
 4     select case depending on choice
 5        '1' :  Enter data using procedure enter
 6        '2' :  Display text using procedure display
 7        '3' :  Change text using procedure change
 8        '4' :  Delete a line using procedure deleteline
 9        '5' :  Justify text using procedure justify
10        '6' :  Quit editor
11     selectend
12  until choice is quit
```

But are there any other parts of this program that we could consider developing as separate routines? There are three guidelines which can help make this decision.

- Is there an existing procedure available somewhere which could usefully be exploited?
- Is there a task which is common to different parts of the design?
- Is there a part of the design which is self-contained and large enough that designing it as a procedure would clarify the overall design.

In order to answer the first question we have to take a closer look at the top level design. One task that will have to be undertaken regularly is clearing the screen – indeed the initial step of every procedure will be to create a clear screen. We have been using the design step *clear screen* to do this. This statement could be designed as a procedure – an adaption of the procedure *blanklines* developed in Chapter 8 would be one possible approach. However, all languages provide some built-in procedure for clearing the screen and there are considerable advantages in using an existing routine whenever possible. First, it avoids duplication of design effort and cuts down on the development time. Secondly, and perhaps most significantly, an existing routine will have been tested and so will have a better chance of being free from errors than one which has been developed from scratch. In this example the existing routine happened to be a built-in one. This does not have to be the case – routines from existing applications should also be exploited.

To answer the second question we need to identify pieces of design which are common to different parts of the design. The options Display, Change and Delete are all required to display the current text on the screen. The specification of Display will therefore need to take account of this. The task of reading in a line number and validating that it lies in a certain range occurs in both the Change and Delete options. This task will be developed as the procedure *GetLineNumber*. The task of entering a line of text is common to both the Enter and Change options. This will be developed as the procedure *GetString*.

The final guideline is perhaps the most difficult and open to different interpretations. Modular design enables large problems to be broken down into smaller ones but some of these smaller ones may themselves be quite large. It may be possible to identify part of the design which could usefully be designed as a separate procedure. For example, step 3 of the top level design above could be developed as part of the main program or as a separate routine. For illustrative purposes it will be developed as a procedure whose task is to display the menu and read in the user's choice of option.

At this stage there are no other tasks at this level of design which can be identified as potential procedures. In a situation like this where we are dealing with a fairly simple problem and one which can be dealt with by a single designer, the guidelines above are a reasonable method of deciding what to modularize. In a more complex problem which involves many designers, more sophisticated methods are required which are beyond the scope of an introductory text.

9.6.1 Specifying the identified procedures

Specifications for each of the routines should now be drawn up. This will involve identifying the source data and results and providing a description of the process. Many of the routines have been described in some detail in Section 9.5 and so to avoid unnecessary repetition only those routines so far not discussed will be specified in detail. The routines *GetLineNumber*, *GetString* and *display* are specified below in which *TextArray* is the type of the array holding the data, *linetype* is the type corresponding to a line number and *sentence* is a type corresponding to a line of text.

GetLineNumber

linesinput	Number of lines currently stored	*linetype* parameter
{Write out the prompt 'Enter number in this range or 0 to return to MAIN menu' and read in *linenumber* until it lies in the range 0 to *linesinput*. Use modified prompt if invalid data is entered.}		
linenumber	Validated line number input by user	*linetype* parameter

GetString

{Read in a string and if necessary cut it to *stringsize* characters. Assign the result to *instring*.}		
instring	A line of text having *stringsize* or fewer characters	*sentence* parameter

display

prose	Array holding the text	*TextArray* parameter
linesinput	Number of lines currently stored	*linetype* parameter
{Display all *linesinput* lines of the array *prose*. If *linesinput* has value zero write out the message that 'No text has been entered'. Calling programs will have the responsibility of clearing the screen and keeping the output from this procedure on the screen.}		

Exercise 9.10 Using the type identifiers just introduced, write down the source data and results for each of the procedures *menu, change, deleteline* and *justify*.

We leave as a task for the reader the detailed specification of the remaining routines. Each routine will be responsible for its own screen display. The descriptions in Section 9.5 and the solution to Exercise 9.10 should enable you to create the specifications. The design for the main program can now be refined as follows:

```
    {A text editor program}
1       initialize variables
2       repeat
3.1       menu(choice)
4         select case depending on choice
5.1         '1' : enter(prose, linesinput)
6.1         '2' : clear screen
6.2               display(prose, linesinput)
6.3               write out 'Press any key to continue '
6.4               read in ch
7.1         '3' : change(prose, linesinput)
8.1         '4' : deleteline(prose, linesinput)
```

9.1	'5' : *justify(prose, linesinput)*
10.1	'6' : do nothing
11	selectend
12	until *choice* = '6'

The order in which the routines are declared has to ensure that *GetLineNumber, GetString* and *display* are in the referencing environments of the routines which call them. The data table below takes account of this.

Identifier	Description	Type
stringsize	Maximum characters per line	integer constant value 40
maxlines	Maximum number of lines of text	integer constant value 10
sentence	String type definition	string[*stringsize*]
linetype	Subrange type definition	1..*maxlines*
TextArray	Array type definition	array[*linetype*] of *sentence*
menu	(*choice*)	procedure(char)
display	(*prose, linesinput*)	procedure(*TextArray, linetype*)
GetLineNumber	(*linesinput, linenumber*)	procedure(*linetype, linetype*)
GetString	(*instring*)	procedure(*sentence*)
enter	(*prose, linesinput*)	procedure(*TextArray, linetype*)
change	(*prose, linesinput*)	procedure(*TextArray, linetype*)
deleteline	(*prose, linesinput*)	procedure(*TextArray, linetype*)
justify	(*prose, linesinput*)	procedure(*TextArray, linetype*)
prose	The text being processed	*TextArray* variable
linesinput	Number of lines of existing text	*linetype* variable
choice	Main menu choice	char variable
ch	Used for freezing display	char variable

The same identifiers have been used for formal and actual parameters because in this instance it makes the design easier to read.

9.7 PROBLEMS

The problems in this subsection are all concerned with the design of the procedures introduced above. An understanding of their detailed design is not required in order to continue with your study of the chapter, hence they have been presented as problems rather than exercises.

9.6 Write a design for the procedures *menu, enter, display, change* and *deleteline*. You should use the procedure *GetLineNumber* in your designs for *change* and *deleteline*, and the procedure *GetString* in your designs for *enter* and *change*.

9.7 Write a design for the procedure *GetLineNumber*.

9.8 Write a design for *GetString*.

9.8 COMPLETING THE DESIGN

We shall now complete the editor by looking at the design of *justify*. Given the width of the line on which the text is to be justified there are two approaches which could be adopted for this design using the reforming technique described in Section 9.5. First, the whole array could be reformed to get an array of ragged lines and then each element of the array of ragged lines could be justified by adding spaces. To do this would require the declaration of an array which would hold the ragged lines. What should its index range be? In Exercise 9.9 we had a single line of text which required three lines when it was reformed into ragged lines. So for this example the reformed text required more lines and hence more array elements to store it. Thus the reformed text of ragged lines might require a larger array than the original text. Of course given the constraints imposed on line width, line length and the number of lines capable of being stored, there is a theoretical maximum size for the reformed text which could be evaluated. Hence an array to hold the reformed text could be defined large enough to store this theoretical number of lines. But if any of these constant values were to be changed, for example to allow more text to be stored, then this theoretical maximum would need to be recalculated and the array redefined. To avoid potential maintenance problems like this we choose not to adopt this approach. Instead, only one ragged line will be extracted at a time. It will be justified and then the next ragged line will be extracted, and so on. The top level design below expresses this more precisely. In it the variable *linewidth* denotes the number of characters in a line of justified text.

justify
_____

prose, linesinput
_____

{justify *prose* on an input line width}
1   if *linesinput* > 0 then
2   initialize variables and read in *linewidth*
3   loop while there is text to be processed
4   extract a ragged line
5   justify ragged line on *linewidth*
6   write out justified line
7   loopend
8   else
9   write out message
10 ifend
11 hold output on the screen until a key is pressed
_____

Steps 4 and 5 will be developed as separate procedures called *extract* and *spacefill*. The procedure *extract* will have created a ragged line consisting of complete words, each being separated by a single space character, and its length will not exceed the number of characters on which the line is justified, but it must have the maximum number of words in it consistent with this property. It will have to deal with the situation where the original text contains words which are separated by more than one space, with lines that end in space characters and with lines that consist solely of space characters. As an extreme example it will have to cope with a text which is all space characters. The following example should enable you to see how *extract* can be designed. A line width of 11 rather than 1 in the range 20 – *stringsize* will be used in order that characters may be more easily counted. Suppose *prose* contains the following text:

prose[1] = 'InΔthisΔsection'
prose[2] = 'weΔshallΔlook'
prose[3] = 'atΔtheΔjustifyingΔofΔtext'

With this line width the loop at step 2 of the design for *justify* will be executed six times and the ragged lines shown below will be created by step 4. (The numbers are not part of the text but will be used for ease of reference below.)

   1   'InΔthis'
   2   'sectionΔwe'
   3   'shallΔlook'
   4   'atΔthe'
   5   'justifying'
   6   'ofΔtext'

Note that the individual words in a ragged line may not necessarily come from the same element of the array *prose*. In order to design *extract* we shall need a way of recording which words have already been extracted and what remains to be extracted. This information will have to be passed as source data to *extract* each time it is called and will have to be passed out as results in preparation for the next call. The words of the current array element of *prose* which have yet to be extracted will be recorded in the parameter *remains* and the index of the next element of *prose* to be processed will be recorded in the parameter *nextline*. Thus after ragged line 1 has been extracted *extract* and *ragged* will have values

   remains = 'section', *nextline* = 2

This records the fact that 'section' remains to be extracted to a ragged line and that thereafter subsequent text will come from prose[*nextline*], that is *prose*[2]. The ragged line will then be justified by step 5 of the design and step 6 will write it out.

The next execution of the loop would then create ragged line 2. To do this *remains* and *nextline* are passed as source data into *extract*. This call illustrates why both variables are required. It begins by inserting as many words of *remains* into ragged line 2 as will fit the given line width. The whole of *remains* fits, leaving four characters of the ragged line to be filled. These are to be filled using words taken from the next element of the array *prose*. The variable *nextline* records the index of the next element and so *remains* is assigned the value 'weΔshallΔlook' and the value of *nextline* is incremented to 3. The first word in *remains* is now 'we' and this will fit into the current ragged line to give 'sectionΔwe' and this leaves one character to be filled. Clearly no further words can be fitted into this space and so the call to *extract* is complete and the values

   ragged = 'sectionΔwe', *remains* = 'shallΔlook', *nextline* = 3

are passed out as results.

Finally, the procedure must indicate when all the text in prose has been extracted. We shall use a boolean parameter for this. The specification of *extract* is given below:

extract

prose	Array holding the text	*TextArray* parameter
linesinput	Number of lines currently stored	*linetype* parameter
linewidth	Width of justified text	*stringsize* parameter
remains	Unprocessed words of current element of *prose*	*sentence* parameter
nextline	Index of next element of *prose* to be processed	*integer* parameter

{Extract a ragged line of text from *prose*. The ragged line should begin with a word and should consist of complete words, each being separated by a single space character. Its length must not exceed *linewidth* but it must have the maximum number of words in it consistent with this property. When all the elements of *prose* have been processed *textend* is returned with value true.}

ragged	The ragged line of text	*sentence* parameter
remains	Unprocessed words of current element of *prose*	*sentence* parameter
nextline	Index of next element of *prose* to be processed	integer parameter
textend	True indicates all text processed	boolean parameter

Exercise 9.11 Write a design for *extract* based on the following top level design:

extract
prose, linesinput, linewidth, remains, nextline
{Extract words from *prose* into *ragged*}
1   initialize variables
2   loop while *ragged* is not full and not all text has been processed
3   obtain the first word in *remains*
4   if the word will not fit into *ragged* then
5   put it back into *remains*
6   else
7   process extracted word
8   ifend
9   update remains
10 loopend
remains, nextline, ragged, textend

We now turn our attention to step 5 of the design for *justify*. This is the procedure *spacefill* which inserts extra space characters into the ragged line that has just been created. Its specification is:

spacefill

ragged	The ragged line of text	*sentence* parameter
linewidth	Width on which to justify	*stringsize* parameter
{If *ragged* is not empty then justify it by calculating the *shortfall* – that is (*linewidth* – *length(ragged)*) and distributing *shortfall* space characters to the gaps in *ragged*. Distribution is to be even, with extras being distributed to gaps from the front of the string. The justified line is to be returned to *justifiedline*.}		
justifiedline	A right justified line	*sentence* parameter

The distribution of the space characters is not as easy as it might seem. It turns out that starting at the end of *ragged* and working backwards is easier than starting from the front. We illustrate the process in Figure 9.9 starting with *ragged*, whose value is the string 'aΔbΔcΔd' and justifying it on a width of 12 characters. We shall use the symbol ♦ to denote the new space characters added to the string. There are five new space characters to be distributed among the three gaps in the string. The new space characters are inserted using the procedure *insert* developed in Section 9.1. The figure shows the values of the parameters required to do the insertion. Notice that by starting at the end the parameter corresponding to the position of the insert has values which are the positions of the original gaps.

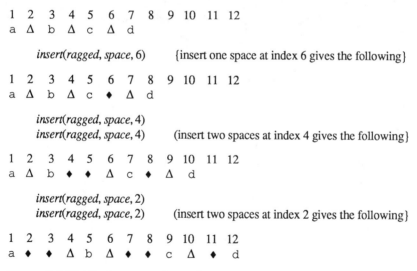

Figure 9.9 Distributing spaces in a string

Exercise 9.12 Write a design for *spacefill* based upon the following top level design in which *gapcount* is the number of gaps in *ragged* and *shortfall* is the total number of extra space characters to be inserted:

spacefill
ragged, linewidth

	{Justify *ragged*}
1	if *ragged* <> *null* then
2	calculate *gapcount* and *shortfall*
3	if *ragged* needs justifying then
4	start at end of *ragged*
5	loop while there are spaces to distribute
6	distribute *shortfall* spaces to the gaps of *ragged*
7	loopend
8	ifend
9	ifend
10	*justifiedline := ragged*

justifiedline

That completes the major part of the editor's design. There are one or two loose ends which we leave you to complete. There is no Problem section to conclude this chapter but the editor could be extended and this would be a source of additional problems which you can specify for yourself. For example, the specification used for justifying text could be altered so that lines which consist only of spaces are not removed. Additionally, leading spaces on lines could be left as they are so that text could include paragraph indents. The possibilities are almost endless.

9.9 SUMMARY

In this chapter we have looked at string operations in more detail. In particular, we introduced the procedures *delete* and *insert* and the functions *copy* and *pos* which are found as standard built-in routines in most programming languages. We then looked at some purpose-designed procedures for doing things like splitting strings at a point determined by a pattern string. The standard procedures were used to build these new routines.

Finally we looked at a case study of designing a simple text editor. We examined the specification with a view to determining which parts of the editor should be modularized and gave some guidelines for this task. We then designed each of the procedures.

ABSTRACT DATA TYPES

10.1 INTRODUCTION

In Chapter 6 we looked at a problem which involved the following table:

Town	Churches
Tonbridge	15
Elgin	10
Buxton	15
Chard	8
Harwich	19

Data presented in table form like this church survey data is a very common occurrence in our everyday lives. Tables are encountered in timetables, holiday brochures, financial pages of newspapers and so on. We shall refer to data which we encounter in our everyday lives as real-world data. When real-world data has to be entered into a computer a representation of it must be found in order to convert it into a form which can be stored and manipulated by machine. The church survey data was the first piece of real-world data that we encountered for which there is not a built-in data type in our design language by which it could be represented. Our approach to this difficulty in Chapter 6 was to represent the table by two parallel arrays and manipulate them directly in order to solve the required problem. What we failed to do there was to separate the design of the data from the design of the program. A major reason for wanting to separate data design from program design is cost. A software design fault which is not detected until the maintenance stage of its development will be extremely costly. If that error arises in code which is both implementing a complex data structure and manipulating its contents, then all of that work will have to be repeated at great expense. Separation of data design from the program which manipulates the data is an approach which helps to detect errors early and reduces the amount of corrective work to be done when an error is found. Data design will involve representing the real-world data in an abstract way and then implementing that abstraction using the data types available in our language.

We now have the design tools at our disposal which will enable us to take this approach. It will probably help if you think of the data design and program design being carried out by two different people. The person who wants to use the representation of the real-world data in the solution to some problem will be called the data structure user, or more simply the user. The second person will provide the user with the implementation of the data structure and will be referred to as the data structure implementor, or implementor for short. (Neither of these terms are technical terms, they are just being used for the purpose of emphasizing the two tasks which are to be carried out.) In fact this distinction of roles is not unrealistic; on a large project there may actually be a team of people working on each aspect.

The first stage of data design is to decide what the data item is and how it is to be manipulated. For variables of standard data type, the operations provided by the system are used to manipulate them. So, for example, integer variables are manipulated using integer operations. In this new situation *we* must decide what operations are required in order to manipulate the data items. They must be chosen in such a way that all the tools necessary for the user to create a program design are provided. We are not suggesting that the choice is easy and we will tend to present operations to you without going into reasons why they were chosen.

Let us suppose that the user and implementor decide that the list of operations below are required for manipulating data items which have the structure of the church survey table. Note that in deciding upon this choice of operations we are not just creating the possibility of defining a single data variable. We are creating a type, thereby giving rise to the opportunity of defining many items of this type. We have deliberately chosen a small number of operations in order to keep the data design simple.

- An operation, called *insert*, to insert a new entry into a table.
- An operation, called *isfull*, which enables the user to determine whether or not a table is full, that is, whether there is space for additional entries.
- An operation *gettown* which prompts for and reads in the name of a town.
- An operation, called *churchnumber*, which has as source data the name of a town and which will write out the number of churches in that town, or a message saying that the town was not in the table.
- An operation, called *display*, to display the table on the screen.
- An operation to create a table. This operation will be called *create* and we shall return to it in the next section.

The identifier *tabletype* will be used to denote the abstract data type we are defining here. That the operation *isfull* has been specified implies that *tabletype* data can hold only a restricted number of entries. The collection of items, together with the operations defined on them, is called an **abstract data type**. The same identifier will be used when we wish to specify that a particular item, for example a variable or procedure parameter, is to be of this type. Thus in terms of the abstract data type, *tabletype* refers to both the items and their related operations.

The operations will be defined more precisely by means of procedure specifications. It is not necessary to know the details of the representation of *tabletype* in order to do this, even though parameters of this type occur as either source data or results.

isfull

table	Representation of table data	*tabletype* parameter
{Return the boolean false if the table is not full and true if it is full.}		
isfull		boolean function value

insert

table	Representation of table data	*tabletype* parameter
{Prompt for and read in the name of a town and the number of churches it contains. Insert the data into the bottom row of the table. It is the responsibility of the user to check there is room for the insertion before using this operation.}		
table	Updated table	*tabletype*

gettown

{Prompt for and read in the name of a town.}		
intown	The name of the town input by user	string parameter

churchnumber

table	Representation of table data	*tabletype* parameter
searchtown	Town for which number of churches is sought	string parameter
{Search the town column of the table for the *searchtown*. If it is found then write out the number of churches it contains, otherwise write out a message saying the town is not in the table.}		

display

table	Representation of table data	*tabletype* parameter
{Display the contents of the table on the screen. Difficulties such as there being more entries in the table than will fit on the screen should be ignored. If the table is empty this procedure does nothing.}		

create

{Return a new empty table of type *tabletype*.}		
table	A new table	*tabletype* parameter

A specification of an abstract data type like this enables its implementation details to be separated from the application which uses it. This means that maintenance of an implementation can take place without affecting the user's application program and this reduces the costs mentioned earlier. Another beneficial effect is that the implementation can be changed without a knock-on effect to the applications program. An example of this will be given in the Problem section. To be totally effective the implementation details of an abstract data type ought to be hidden from the user so the user should not have access to them. The reason for this is that if the details are known then the user is free to design additional operations or to manipulate the data representation directly. If this happens then the implementation of the abstract data type would no longer match the specification and this would result in increased maintenance problems. Thus an objective of an abstract data type is to limit access to the agreed operations in the specification. Keeping the implementation design details hidden is an example of **data hiding**. Details of an implementation which are hidden from a user are said to be **invisible**. We shall return to the idea of data hiding later.

10.2 USING THE ABSTRACT DATA TYPE

Having decided upon the operations, we shall now see how the abstract data type they define can be used in a program. As we develop the program you should note that it is not necessary for the design details of the data type *tabletype* to be known. We shall consider a more general problem than in Exercise 6.6. Here the main program should prompt the user with a menu which provides a list of the available options:

I   Insert new data
D   Display the table
S   Search the table

The identifier *churchsurvey,* of type *tabletype*, will be used for the data structure representing the church survey table and a top level design for this program is:

```
 1  initialize variables
 2  repeat
 3      write out menu
 4      read in choice
 5      select case depending on choice
 6          'I' :  insert new data
 7          'D' :  display existing data
 8          'S' :  search the table
 9      selectend
10  until choice = 'Q'
```

At this stage, prior to the design of the abstract data type *tabletype*, this design would not be developed in great detail but would perhaps be progressed to one more level of refinement. We shall see why only a high level design for the main program is developed at this stage in Section 10.5, but for now we shall carry out this next refinement. Essentially what the refinement does is to replace the descriptions in the top level design by calls to the operations of the abstract data type. The design and data table below does this – read it through and then read the commentary which follows.

```
1.1     create(churchsurvey)
2       repeat
3          write out menu
4          read in choice
5          select case depending on choice
6.1           'I'  :  if not isfull(churchsurvey) then
6.2                      insert(churchsurvey)
6.3                   else
6.4                      write out 'Table is full'
6.5                   ifend
7.1           'D'  :  display(churchsurvey)
8.1           'S'  :  gettown(searchtown)
8.2                   churchnumber(churchsurvey, searchtown)
9          selectend
10      until choice = 'Q'
```

Identifier	Description	Type
churchsurvey	Representation of the survey table	*tabletype* variable
searchtown	Town for which number of churches is sought	string variable
choice	User's menu choice	char variable

The first thing to notice is that the data table does not contain any of the procedures corresponding to the operations. We shall see the reason for this shortly. The purpose of step 1.1 is to create a new empty table which will be referenced using the identifier *churchsurvey*. The refinement of step 6 checks to see if the table is full by calling *isempty*, and if not, makes a call to *insert* to insert the new details. Steps 7 and 8 are refined to calls to the appropriate procedures. It is now necessary to look at the design of the abstract data type before developing this design further.

10.3 DESIGNING THE ABSTRACT DATA TYPE

We now turn our attention to the problems which the implementor of the abstract data type faces. First, the method by which the table is to be represented has to be decided and then the procedures and functions which define the operations have to be designed. We shall represent the table as we did in Chapter 6, using two parallel arrays. The maximum number of rows already agreed between the user and implementor will give the upper bound for the size of the table. At any given time not all rows of the table might be in use and so a variable will be required which records the number of rows currently in use. The identifier *size* will be used to denote this quantity. We are now in a position to make a first stab at defining a representation of the table:

Identifier	Description	Type
maxsize	Maximum number of rows in the table	integer constant
TownArray	Array of town names	array[0..*maxsize*] of string variable
ChurchArray	Array of church numbers	array[0..*maxsize*] of integer variable
size	Number of entries in the table	0..*maxsize* variable

The index lower bound of the arrays has been defined to be 0 in order to allow the arrays to be searched using the index zero. Unfortunately this design has a number of deficiencies:

1. Consider the procedure *insert*. This procedure has as source data the table into which the insertion is to take place. How is the user to pass this source data with this representation? Essentially the representation consists of three pieces of information, the two arrays and the value of *size*. All three items would have to be passed and so the user would need to know the precise details of the representation in order to do this. So the procedure would have to be respecified with these items as source data along the following lines:

insert

TownArray	First column of table	array[0..*maxsize*] of string variable
ChurchArray	Second column of table	array[0..*maxsize*] of integer variable
size	Number of entries in table	0..*maxsize* variable

This clearly defeats the object of information hiding, that is, of making the representation invisible to the user because the precise details of the representation have to appear in the operation's specification in order that it can be used at all.

2. Since the user knows the details of the representation then the data structure could be manipulated directly. For example, the value of *size* could be changed without calling one of the provided operations. Indeed the user could construct further operations on the data structure. The result of permitting this is potentially insecure software.

3. If for some reason a different representation is chosen at some future time then the parameters illustrated in 1 would have to be altered. This would mean the user would have to change all the calls to the routines and this would have serious knock-on effects.

The way to overcome this problem is to conceal the structure of the table within a record. The data table below shows how.

Identifier	Description	Type
maxsize	Maximum number of rows in the table	integer constant
tabletype	Record type definition	
	town	array[0..*maxsize*] of string variable
	church	array[0..*maxsize*] of integer variable
	size	0..*maxsize* variable
	recordend	

How does this overcome the deficiencies described above? First, the user having been told that *tabletype* is the identifier to be used in order to declare variables to represent tables can do so without knowing the internal structure of *tabletype*. This enables the user to think of such variables as complete tables. Furthermore, by not informing the user of the record's field identifiers its details remain hidden and so cannot be manipulated directly. Lastly, if an alternative design for the data structure is subsequently required, then none of the user's design has to be changed in order to accommodate the alteration to the representation. All that the implementor has to do is to redefine *tabletype* and provide implementations of the operations using this new type. We shall see an example of this shortly. Note that we have not included a field description column in this data table. When the fields have been discussed in the text we shall omit this column in order to save space.

Exercise 10.1 An alternative way of representing the table is to use an array of records where each record corresponds to a row of the table. Write down a data table for a representation using this approach. You will still need to include a variable to record the number of entries in the table.

The alternative representation developed in Exercise 10.1 can be used to see why none of the user's design needs to be altered if it is used instead of the parallel arrays version. None of the design on page 167 refers to the representation. In particular, the identifier *churchsurvey* will be declared as before but what would have to change is the design of the procedures representing the operations which use it.

It is worth taking stock of how far we have got. The user and implementor agreed a specification of the abstract data type *tabletype*. In particular, they agreed on the maximum number of entries which could be in the table and the operations which would be provided for manipulating items of *tabletype*. Details of the operations were drawn up in the form of procedure and function specifications. At this point a high level design for the main program could be generated. The implementor's task was then considered and two possible alternative representations of *tabletype* were given. It was noted that either representation could be used and that the user's design would not need to be altered in the event that it became necessary to change one representation for the other.

We shall now continue the implementor's task of writing designs for each of the operations defined on the data type. We shall use the parallel array representation and leave as exercises designs based on the array of records representation. Only final designs are given, data tables being supplied only when there are local variables to declare.

isfull
table
1 *isfull := (table.size = maxsize)*
isfull

gettown
1 write out 'Enter the name of a town'   2 read in *intown*
intown

insert
table

1 with *table* do
   2   *size := size + 1*
   3   write out 'Enter the name of the town '
   4   read in *town[size]*
   5   write out 'Enter the number of churches in the town '
   6   read in *church[size]*
   7 withend

table

---

churchnumber

---

table, searchtown

```
 1   table.town[0] := searchtown
 2   index := table.size
 3   with table do
 4       loop while town[index] <> searchtown
 5           decrement index
 6       loopend
 7       if index <> 0 then
 8           write out searchtown, ' has ', church[index], ' churches'
 9       else
10           write out searchtown, ' is not in the table'
11       ifend
12   withend
```

Data table for *churchnumber*

Identifier	Description	Type
index	Loop control variable	0..*maxsize* variable

display

---

table

```
 1   write out 'Town', 'Churches'
 2   with table do
 3       loop for index := 1 to size
 4           write out town[index], church[index]
 5       loopend
 6   withend
```

Data table for *display*

Identifier	Description	Type
index	Loop control variable	0..*maxsize* variable

There is one last operation to design and that is the procedure *create*. This is perhaps the most subtle of the operations. There is one major but very simple task that it must do. When a variable of type *tabletype* is declared by the user a record containing the two array fields and the field *size* is created. These fields remain uninitialized until data is entered into them. The procedure *enter* provides a means of entering data into the array fields but how does *size* get its initial value? Clearly it needs initializing to 0, but equally clearly this task cannot be the responsibility of the user because the user is not even aware that such a variable exists. Hence the task of the procedure *create* is to initialize *size* to zero.

create
{No source data}
{This initializes *table*}
1 *table.size* := 0
table

We can now gather together all the work that the implementor has done. There are the definitions for the data type *tabletype,* the definitions of the procedures and the details of the designs for these procedures. We can think of these items as comprising a program. We shall temporarily refer to them as an **implementation program**. The data table below contains all the details of this implementation program. It includes a list of all the procedures which have been developed and as usual we have used the Description column to list their formal parameters.

Identifier	Description	Type
maxsize	Maximum number of rows in the table	integer constant
tabletype	Record type definition	
	town	array[0..*maxsize*] of string variable
	church	array[0..*maxsize*] of integer variable
	size	0..*maxsize* variable
	recordend	
isfull	(*table*)	boolean function(*tabletype*)
insert	(*table*)	procedure(*tabletype*)
gettown	(*intown*)	procedure(string)
churchnumber	(*table, searchtown*)	procedure(*tabletype*, string)
display	(*table*)	procedure(*tabletype*)
create	(*table*)	procedure(*tabletype*)

10.4 PRACTICAL LANGUAGE CONSIDERATIONS

In this section we want to give you a feel for how the main program and the implementation program could be coded into a programming language. The explanation is not meant to be rigorous, as such an approach would necessitate discussing details of particular programming languages. It contains generalities which are not necessarily entirely accurate when considered in the context of a particular language. Nevertheless, we hope the explanation gives you a flavour of what is required of a language which is able to support the separate development of program and data design. Do not feel that you have to master all the details and terminology as we shall not be referring to them again in future sections.

All high level programming languages are required to convert the text in which they are written into a form which can be understood by the processor of the computer being used. For simplicity we shall call this translation process **compiling**. Thus to execute a design in this book, the design would first have to be converted into a particular programming language and the result then compiled. Since the first of these tasks is relatively straightforward we say that *designs* (or *programs* as we have sometimes called them) can be compiled. So what facilities need a programming language have in order that it can support the implementation of abstract data types? Clearly both the main program and the implementation program have to be compiled.

One way of doing this would be to combine the two parts to make one large program. This is an unrealistic solution, given the care with which we have separated program design from data design, because the user would be able to see how the implementor had implemented the data design. In these circumstances the data design would be described as being **transparent** to the user. The word transparent is used because all the structure of the implementor's type is visible to the user and is thus accessible and capable of being altered.

A partial solution to this transparency problem can be obtained with languages which support **separate compilation**. Separate compilation means precisely what it says – that the main program and the implementation program would be compiled separately and the two compiled parts would then be **linked** together. Programming languages tend to use a word other than *program* to refer to two separately compiled pieces of code, but we shall persevere with the terms program and implementation program. In order to make the linking possible the main program has to contain an instruction informing the compiler that the implementation program is to be linked in with the main program. In this way the main program gets access to the implementation program.

In many languages this access means that the main program can refer to any identifier declared in the implementation program. In terms of scope, the declarations in the implementation program become global identifiers in the main program. Of course, access to some of them is what we want because the main program makes calls to *isfull*, *insert*, *gettown*, *churchnumber*, *display* and *create*. But the declarations in the data table on page 171 also contain the details of the representation as given by the definition of *tabletype* and so this information is available to the main program also. But this then means that the implementation is transparent. However, a considerable amount of independence is achieved and this is certainly a partial solution to the problem. Certainly a large bonus is that if the representation of the data type has to be changed at some stage then only the implementation program has to be updated – the main program can remain unaltered. Furthermore, if the user is well disciplined and uses only the procedures provided for the data manipulation then this solution is a reasonable compromise. Versions of the programming language Pascal tend to fall into this category of solution.

For a complete solution we need a facility whereby the declarations in the implementation program can be specified as **public** or **private**. Something which is declared as public in the implementation program would then become a global identifier in the main program and so be available for use there. Something declared private would not be known to the main program and so could not be referenced by it. In the data table opposite (for the module *surveytable*) we have made this distinction. Examine its contents and then read the commentary below.

First, you should note that all the procedures and functions corresponding to the operations have been collected together and defined as public. This is what we want because the main program is going to call them. Secondly, the identifier *tabletype* has been declared public because the user must be able to declare variables to be of this type and so this identifier must be available to the main program. However, its structure is declared as private

Identifier	Description	Type
	PUBLIC	
tabletype	Type definitions representing the table	private
isfull	(*table*)	boolean function(*tabletype*)
insert	(*table*)	procedure(*tabletype*)
gettown	(*intown*)	procedure(string)
churchnumber	(*table, searchtown*)	procedure(*tabletype*, string)
display	(*table*)	procedure(*tabletype*)
create	(*table*)	procedure(*tabletype*)
	PRIVATE	
maxsize	Maximum number of rows in the table	integer constant
tabletype	Record type definition	
	town	array[0..*maxsize*] of string variable
	church	array[0..*maxsize*] of integer variable
	size	0..*maxsize* variable
	recordend	

in the Type column. This maintains its structural anonymity from the viewpoint of the user. The private declarations then define the representation that the implementor has chosen. Finally you may have noticed that we now refer to a **module** rather than an implementation program. The word module has been borrowed from the programming language Modula2 which, along with the language ADA, are two of the languages which support the notion of public and private declarations. All the abstract data types in this book will have their declarations listed in a module data table. The top half of such a table will contain the public identifier declarations and will consist of the identifiers corresponding to the operations which have been defined in the abstract data type. The bottom half of the table will include the private declaration of the structure of the data type.

In order to reinforce the fact that the public declarations in a module are available to the main program which uses it we shall amend the data table of the main program as follows to reflect this:

Identifier	Description	Type
churchsurvey	Representation of the survey table	variable of *tabletype* from module *surveytable*
searchtown	Town for which number of churches is sought	string variable
choice	User's menu choice	char variable

Here, the type of *churchsurvey* has been modified to include the information that *tabletype* is itself defined in the module *surveytable*. This carries with it the implication that all the public data in this module is thereby available to this main program.

As a conclusion you may be wondering why the user cannot inspect the implementation of the procedures, that is the code corresponding to our procedure designs, and hence discover how the data type has been implemented. It is because this code is automatically private when separate compilation is used. This is certainly the case for Pascal, Modula2 and ADA.

Exercise 10.2 Write a data table for a module *surveytable2* which implements the data type *tabletype* using the representation developed in Exercise 10.1 and then write designs for each of the operations based upon this representation.

10.5 DESIGNING A WHOLE SYSTEM

So far no account has been given as to how the operations which define an abstract data type are determined. One way of deciding is to use what is known as an **object-oriented design** methodology. An object is a data item to be manipulated and abstract data types can be thought of as examples of objects. We shall give an illustrative example of this method of design in Chapter 16, but there remains the issue of when to design the main program and when to write the details which will implement the objects or abstract data types. It is normal practice to build the abstract data type model first and delay detailed design of the main program for as long as possible. The reason for this is not, as you might expect, that the main program uses the operations in its design. Once the specification of the operations has been fixed there is in fact no theoretical reason why the main program design could not be started. The reason that it is not started and is left as late as possible is pragmatic. It is a fact of life that customers' requirements tend to change as a project develops. What tends not to change are the objects being operated upon. So for example, the solution to a bank account problem in which there are objects like current balances, overdrafts, debits, credits etc., is unlikely to need to change these data structures, even if the requirements of the system are altered during program development. This is because these objects are fundamental to the banking system and can be thought of as having an existence of their own independent of any application which uses them. It is for this reason that the design in Section 10.2 was only developed to a second level of refinement which essentially made calls to the operations provided by the abstract data type.

A final remark on objects and abstract data types is that there may be other constraints which have to be taken into consideration in their design. The amount of memory available, the response time, the complexity of the data design are just three examples of constraints which may affect how the objects are designed. Frequently, constraints like this conflict with each other and the final data design is a compromise between them. However, we shall not be concerned with such issues in this text. In the remaining chapters we shall study some well-known abstract data types for which the operations are well established. It will therefore not be necessary to go through the design process in order to determine the operations. Each of the data types will be specified but before they are designed their use will be illustrated in the context of an application. This will give you the opportunity of getting to grips with the operations before their detailed design is considered. For clarity of exposition it may be necessary to develop the design of the application to a more refined stage than has been recommended above. We trust you will bear this in mind as you read on.

10.6 PROBLEMS

10.1 The notation 3:45.6 is often used to denote the length of time 3 minutes 45.6 seconds where .6 is the decimal part of a second. In this problem you are asked to think about the definition of an abstract data type which could be used to represent periods of time consisting of minutes and seconds having, at most, one decimal place. List the operations that you might think would be useful in the definition of such an abstract data type and briefly describe their purpose.

10.2 In this problem, which uses the same notation as Problem 10.1, you are asked to design an abstract data type *timetype* as a module called *timemodule*. The operations below, some of which were discussed in Problem 10.1, define the abstract data type *timetype*. The specifications do not allow the notion of negative times and so all times are positive or zero. Furthermore, the number of operations is very restricted in order that you may concentrate on the module rather than the design of the individual procedures. You should use a record structure for *timetype* having the three fields *minutes*, *seconds*, *decimalpart*, each of an appropriate type to hold the minutes, seconds and decimal part of a second.

readin

{Read in a time expressed in the form m:s.d where m is any number of digits representing minutes, s consists of at most two digits representing seconds and d is a single digit representing the decimal part of a second. No validation is required on the input which may be assumed to be in exactly the correct format and so will always contain a single colon and a single (decimal) point.}		
time	Time read in	*timetype* parameter

writeout

time	Time to be written out	*timetype* parameter
{Write out the time in the format m:s.d where m is the number of minutes, s the whole number of seconds and d the decimal part of the number of seconds. A time like 2.5 seconds should be output in the form 0:02.5.}		

add

a	Operand of operator	*timetype* parameter
b	Operand of operator	*timetype* parameter
{Add time *a* to time *b* and assign to *result*.}		
result	Sum of *a* and *b*	*timetype* parameter

10.3 In Section 8.4 we discussed the representation of money valued data and the problems of multiplying an amount of money by a real value. This operation would be required when an interest calculation has to be done using an interest rate which is a real number. Clearly evaluating the interest due on amounts like $13.45 or £72.98 cannot result in anything other than whole numbers of cents or pence respectively. This suggests that the type real is not the best possible to represent amounts of money. This is because $13.45 is a notation for $13 dollars and 45 cents so that .45 is not a true decimal. Most currencies have a major unit (like the dollar, pound, franc) which is made up of 100 subunits (cents, pence, centimes respectively) and the decimal notation is just a convenient way of denoting the two parts. In attempting to define an abstract data type which would represent currency, what operations would *you* include in its definition? Try to describe your operations.

10.4   The notation of Problem 10.3 is used in this problem in which we shall define and design an abstract data type *moneytype* to represent amounts of money. The operations below, some of which were discussed in Problem 10.3, define the abstract data type *moneytype*. The specification of *readin* exploits a real variable in order to simplify the design of this operation. In *writeout* we use the symbol $ to denote the unit of currency – you may prefer to use a symbol more familiar to you such as £.

readin

{Read in an amount of money to *amount*. The amount is to be entered as a real number having at most 2 decimal places. No validation is to be carried out on this input.}		
amount	An input amount	*moneytype* parameter

writeout

a	An amount of money	*moneytype* parameter
{Write out *amount* together with the appropriately placed symbol $. For example, the amounts 3 units 45 cents and minus 4 units 8 cents should be written out as $3.45 and −$4.08 respectively.}		

add

a	An amount of money	*moneytype* parameter
b	An amount of money	*moneytype* parameter
{Add the sum of money *a* to the sum of money *b* and assign to *result*.}		
result	The sum of *a* and *b*	*moneytype* parameter

subtract

a	An amount of money	*moneytype* parameter
b	An amount of money	*moneytype* parameter
{Assign to *results* the sum of money *a* − *b*.}		
result	The difference *a* − *b*	*moneytype* parameter

Write designs for each of the operations where *moneytype* is implemented using the type integer, that is, all amounts of money are to be stored as integer values. You may assume that integers are sufficiently large to represent all *moneytype* values. Why would this implementation of *moneytype* not be a good one in terms of information hiding?

10.5   The data hiding in Problem 10.4 is not good because *moneytype* is compatible with integer type and so variables of type *moneytype* could be supplied as parameters to routines which require integer parameters. A way of avoiding this is to *wrap up* the details of the implementation in a record as shown in the data table below. This has the effect of hiding the implementation from the user. Modify the designs in Problem 10.4 for this alternative implementation.

Identifier	Description	Type
moneytype	Record type definition *cents* recordend	integer variable

10.6   In order to contrast the implementations of *moneytype* above, this problem asks you to write an implementation using a totally different representation. No changes are required as far as the user is concerned. Here, dollars and cents are to be represented as two field values. For positive amounts of money both field values are positive and for negative amounts both will be negative. So, for example, the field values representing −$4.56 will be −4 and −56 respectively. The data table below defines the fields. Note that data hiding occurs naturally here because *moneytype* is a record and so cannot be manipulated without a detailed knowledge of its fields. You may like to refer to the first part of the solution if the design of the procedure *add* causes you difficulty.

Identifier	Description	Type
	PUBLIC	
moneytype	Type definition for money	private
	PRIVATE	

moneytype	Record type definition
	    dollars {Number of units}
	    cents {Number of cents}
	recordend
		integer variable
		−99..99 variable

10.7 SUMMARY

In this chapter we have introduced the idea of an abstract data type. Abstract data types are used to separate data design from the program design which manipulates the data. They are defined by giving specifications for all the operations which are to be carried out on the data.

An important feature of abstract data types is that their implementation must be kept hidden from the user. By so doing the user is unable to either design addition operations or to manipulate the data directly. This results in designs which are far more easily maintained. A further advantage is that the method of implementation can be altered without this having any effect on the program which uses it.

11

STACKS

11.1 INTRODUCTION

In this chapter we are going to introduce the concept of a sequence. We have seen that an array can be used to store a fixed number of data items. There are many occasions in which we do not know in advance how many items are required to be stored. Furthermore, the number of such stored items may vary during program execution. A sequence is a data structure which allows for these possibilities. All sequences start off empty and items are added to it and removed from it through time.

An example is a sequence of membership records of people in a bridge club. As people join the club so the sequence grows and when they leave the sequence shrinks. An important property of a sequence is that the insertion of a new item is not random – there must be some rule by which it can be determined where in the sequence the new item must go. For the bridge club, an alphabetic ordering on name might suffice.

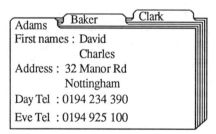

In contrast to an array there is no index access method for a sequence. In general an item in a sequence is retrieved by working through the sequence from the beginning until the item is found or all items in the sequence have been inspected.

The sequence is almost certainly the most common structure in data processing and a substantial proportion of time is spent in data processing applications programs manipulating them. Many of the sequences are very long – for example product codes for parts in the motor industry, account records in a bank, employee records in a large industry and so on. Sequences like this are often so long that they cannot be held in the working store of a computer. In this case permanent backing store has to be used to manipulate the sequence. We shall not be considering sequences of this size, but the principles we introduce here would be applicable in such circumstances. We begin with a more rigourous definition of a sequence:

> A **sequence** is a data structure with zero or more items of data of a predefined fixed type placed one after the other in an order determined by some predefined relationship.

Note that all the items in a sequence must be of a fixed type. Typically they are all records but each record must have the same record structure. There are many different types of sequence but we can identify basic operations which are associated with them.

- Creation of a sequence
- Retrieval of an item from a sequence
- Insertion of a new item into a sequence
- Deletion of a specified item from a sequence
- Updating the contents of an item in the sequence
- Testing whether there are any items in a sequence
- Although the definition does not constrain the number of items in a sequence, memory is finite and so there might be a need to test whether there is room for more items in a sequence

11.2 DEFINING A STACK

The first kind of sequence we shall look at is a **stack**. The predefined relationship which determines the order of items in a stack is the order in which they are inserted. More precisely, a new item can be inserted only at the end of a sequence. Furthermore the last item only in the sequence can be retrieved or deleted. A physical occurrence of a stack is a column of coins on a table. Only the top coin can be retrieved from the column and a coin can only be added to the column by placing it on the top of the column (Figure 11.1).

Figure 11.1 A stack of coins

A common use for stacks is in the evaluation of arithmetic expressions. All electronic calculators use a stack in order to perform their calculations. We are going to look at the problem of writing a design which uses a stack and which will perform the simple arithmetic tasks of adding, subtracting and multiplying integers. To simplify the problem further we shall only allow the integers 0..9 to be operands in the arithmetic expression we are trying to evaluate. So for example our program will be able to evaluate the following types of expression:

$$2 + 3, \ 5 - 2, \ (2 + 4)*5, \ (6 - 2)*(3 - 7)$$

Expressions like these, which use a combination of arithmetic operators, numbers and brackets, are said to be expressed in **infix** notation because the operators come *between* the operands. The brackets are required to avoid potential ambiguities in the expression. Expressions can of course also contain variables, but we shall concentrate on those containing only integer constants.

In order to evaluate an infix expression the calculator needs to re-arrange it in **reverse Polish** notation sometimes referred to as **postfix** notation. This means placing the operands before the operators. We shall not explain how this is done but will give you examples which you can use as test data. The expression 2 + 3 would appear in reverse Polish as 2 3 +. Here, the operands 2 and 3 come first followed by the operator +. The expression 5 − 2 in reverse Polish is 5 2 −. Other examples are:

Standard notation	Reverse Polish notation
(2 + 4)*5	2 4 + 5 *
(6 − 2)*(3 − 7)	6 2 − 3 7 − *

Reverse Polish expressions are evaluated from left to right as follows:

- When an operand is scanned it is put onto a stack
- When an operator is scanned
  the last two numbers are removed from the stack
  the indicated operator is performed on the two numbers
  the result is put back on the stack

Figure 11.2 illustrates the evaluation of 2 3 4 * + which represents the expression 2 + (3*4). In the figure the stack grows from lower down the page up the page. Thus the most recently entered value is the one highest up the page.

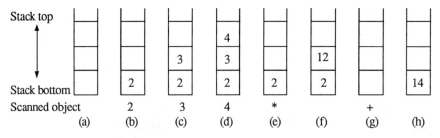

Figure 11.2 Stack evaluation of 2 + (3*4)

Initially the stack is empty at step (a). The first object scanned is the number 2 and so it is placed on the top of the (empty) stack to give (b). The next object is the number 3 and so it is placed on the stack at (c). Similarly 4 is placed on the stack at (d). The next object is the operand *. The top two numbers are removed from the stack, 4 first then 3 to give (e). They are then multiplied and the result placed back on the stack at (f). The next scanned object is + and so 12 is removed followed by 2 to give (g). These two numbers are added and the result is placed on the stack at (h). The scan is now complete and the final result can be removed from the stack and output on the screen.

Care has to be exercised when subtraction is involved to make sure it is done the correct way round. Consider the expression 4 2 − which is the same as 4 − 2. The number 4 is placed on the stack first followed by 2. When the subtraction operator is scanned it is the number 2 which is removed first and 4 second. Thus the result is given by 'second number removed from stack minus first number removed from stack'.

We can now summarize the problem for which a design is required. A single reverse Polish expression is to be entered from the keyboard into a string variable. The expression is to be evaluated character by character and its value is to be output to the screen. Expressions are assumed to be valid Polish expressions and only digits are allowed as operands. (The latter constraint will simplify the problem of converting the characters '0', '1', .., '9' into the integers 0, 1, 2, .., 9. Had we allowed multiple digit integers the problem would have been too complex.)

The identifier *integerstack* will be used to denote the abstract data type which consists of integer stacks described above. The data type *integerstack* may be defined by the following operations:

push

| *stack* | Representation of integer stack | *integerstack* parameter |
item	Integer to be entered onto the stack	integer parameter
{Place the item on top of *stack* and return the updated *stack*. If the stack is full write out 'stack overflow' and return *stack* unaltered.}		
stack	Updated stack	integerstack *parameter*

pop

stack	Representation of integer stack	*integerstack* parameter
{Remove and return the item on top of *stack* and return the updated *stack*. If the stack is empty write out 'stack underflow'.}		
stack	Updated stack	integerstack *parameter*
item	Integer removed from top of stack	*integer parameter*

isempty

stack	Representation of integer stack	*integerstack* parameter
{Return the value true if the stack is empty, false otherwise.}		
isempty		*boolean function value*

create

{Return a new empty stack of type *integerstack*.}		
stack	A new stack	integerstack *parameter*

11.3 USING A STACK

A high level design for the main program can now be written which will make calls on these operations. A top level design is:

{A calculator simulation program}
1 create a stack
2 request a Polish string
3 loop for all characters
4   process character
5 loopend
6 write out results

This design will be refined to a lower level than would normally be the case at this stage in order to illustrate the workings of a stack. This will give you familiarity with the stack operations in preparation for their design in Section 11.4. To refine step 3 we note there are different actions to be taken when the character is one of the three allowed integer operators and when it is a digit. This would suggest a case statement.

```
        {A calculator simulation program}
1       create a new stack
2.1     write 'Enter a reverse Polish string '
2.2     read in polish
3.1     loop for index := 1 to length(polish)
4.1         select case depending on polish[index]
4.2             '+'    :  process addition
4.3             '−'    :  process subtraction
4.4             '*'    :  process multiplication
4.5           '0'..'9' :  process digit
4.6         selectend
5       loopend
6       write out results
```

The identifier *calculator* will be used to denote a variable of type *integerstack* which will be used in the refinement of step 1. We have already seen that when a digit is encountered it is *pushed* onto the stack. This will require character values to be converted to integer values, specifically the characters '0' will have to be converted to the integer 0, '1' to the integer 1 and so on. We shall adopt the simple approach of expanding the case statement to treat each character individually. (There are more general and better methods than this but it is the stack operations we are concerned with here rather than the conversion of one data type into another.) To deal with an operator the top two items are *popped*, the calculation is performed and the result is *pushed* back onto the stack. Care has to be taken with the subtraction operator to subtract the items in the correct order. These observations lead to the following refinement:

```
1.1     create(calculator)
2.1     write 'Enter a reverse Polish string '
2.2     read in polish
```

3.1	loop for *index* := 1 to *length(polish)*
4.1	select case depending on *polish*[*index*]
4.2.1	'+' : *pop(calculator, FirstOff)*
4.2.2	*pop(calculator, SecondOff)*
4.2.3	*result* := *SecondOff* + *FirstOff*
4.2.4	*push(calculator, result)*
4.3.1	'−' : *pop(calculator, FirstOff)*
4.3.2	*pop(calculator, SecondOff)*
4.3.3	*result* := *SecondOff* − *FirstOff*
4.3.4	*push(calculator, result)*
4.4.1	'*' : *pop(calculator, FirstOff)*
4.4.2	*pop(calculator, SecondOff)*
4.4.3	*result* := *SecondOff* * *FirstOff*
4.4.4	*push(calculator, result)*
4.5.1	'0' : *push(calculator, 0)*
4.5.2	'1' : *push(calculator, 1)*
4.5.3	'2' : *push(calculator, 2)*
4.5.4	'3' : *push(calculator, 3)*
4.5.5	'4' : *push(calculator, 4)*
4.5.6	'5' : *push(calculator, 5)*
4.5.7	'6' : *push(calculator, 6)*
4.5.8	'7' : *push(calculator, 7)*
4.5.9	'8' : *push(calculator, 8)*
4.5.10	'9' : *push(calculator, 9)*
4.6	selectend
5	loopend
6.1	*pop(calculator, result)*
6.2	write out 'The value of the expression is ', *result*

Identifier	Description	Type
calculator	Representation of integer stack	variable of *integerstack* from the module *stackmodule*
polish	Reverse Polish expression	string variable
index	Loop control variable	integer variable
FirstOff	First item popped off stack	integer variable
SecondOff	Second item popped off stack	integer variable
result	Calculation result	integer variable

11.4 DESIGNING THE ABSTRACT DATA TYPE STACK

We can now play the role of the implementor and design the module *stackmodule*. To do so, each of the operations which define *integerstack* will have to be designed. We shall represent the type *integerstack* using an array of base type integer. This immediately imposes an upper limit on the number of items that may be on the stack. The size of the stack is therefore determined by the representation rather than by a constraint of the stack's specification. It also means that whenever the stack is used, memory space for the whole array must be set aside irrespective of the number of elements on the stack and this may be very wasteful of storage space. In the next section we shall see how to overcome these restrictions, but to do so requires the use of a data type which we have not yet introduced. With an array representation it is necessary to hold a further piece of information, the index corresponding to the top of the stack. The index 0 will be used to denote an empty stack and so the item at the top of a stack containing one item will be referenced by index 1, the item at the top of a stack of two items will be referenced by index 2 and so on.

In order that these two components, the array and the index denoting the top of the stack, do not have to be passed separately as parameters to the stack operations, they are combined together in a record in just the same way as we did for the table in Chapter 10. Furthermore, the details of the record structure are declared to be private, which leads to the following data table for the module *stackmodule*:

Identifier	Description	Type
	PUBLIC	
integerstack	Type definition representing a stack	private
push	(*stack*, *item*)	procedure(*integerstack*, *integer*)
pop	(*stack*, *item*)	procedure(*integerstack*, *integer*)
isempty	(*stack*)	boolean function(*integerstack*)
create	(*stack*)	procedure(*integerstack*)
	PRIVATE	
maxsize	Maximum stack size	integer constant
integerstack	Record type definition	
	stackarray {Stack item array}	array[1..*maxsize*] of integer variable
	stacktop {Top of stack}	0..*maxsize*
	recordend	

We can now complete the task by writing the designs for each of the operations. We give only final designs.

push	*pop*
stack, *item*	*stack*
1 with *stack* do	1 with *stack* do
2 if *stacktop* = *maxsize* then	2 if *isempty*(*stack*) then
3 write out 'stack overflow'	3 write out 'stack underflow'
4 else	4 else
5 *stacktop* := *stacktop* + 1	5 *item* := *stackarray*[*stacktop*]
6 *stackarray*[*stacktop*] := *item*	6 *stacktop* := *stacktop* − 1
7 ifend	7 ifend
8 withend	8 withend
stack	*stack*, *item*

isempty		*create*	
stack			
1 *isempty* := (*stack.stacktop* = 0)		1 *stack.stacktop* := 0	
isempty		*stack*	

Note the design for *create*. It initializes the top of the stack. That concludes the design of the module *stackmodule*. The parameters should be checked carefully to ensure those in the designs correspond to those in the specification and the individual designs should be tested.

11.5 PROBLEMS

In some problems in this section we shall modify the definition of *integerstack* to include new operations and to define those above in a slightly different way. Since any change to the definition given above gives rise to a new abstract data type, then a name other than *integerstack* has to be used for each new type. We shall call them *integerstack1*, *integerstack2* and so on. Other than this change of identifier (and unless stated otherwise) you may assume that the details given in the data table for the module *stackmodule* are available for use.

11.1 A new abstract data type *integerstack1* is defined to include a new operation called *print*. This operation takes a stack as source data and writes out its contents, starting at the top of the stack and working towards the bottom. In other words, the output on the screen will have the top of the stack at the top of the screen. The operation has no results and it is the responsibility of the calling program to ensure that the stack is not empty prior to *print* being called. Write a design for the operation *print*.

11.2 The abstract data type *integerstack2* is defined to include an operation *revprint*. This operation takes a stack as source data and writes out its contents, starting at the bottom of the stack and working towards the top. In other words, the bottom of the stack will appear at the top of the screen. The operation has no results and it is the responsibility of the calling program to ensure that the stack is not empty prior to *revprint* being called. Write a design for the operation *revprint*.

11.3 Write a design for the abstract data type *integerstack3* which is defined to have the operations *push*, *isempty* and *create* as defined above but which has a different *pop* operation. In addition there is a new operation called *top*. The specifications of these operations are:

pop

stack	Representation of integer stack	*integerstack3* parameter
{Remove the item on top of *stack* and return updated stack. If the stack is empty write out 'stack underflow'.}		
stack	Updated stack	*integerstack3* parameter

top

stack	Representation of integer stack	*integerstack3* parameter
{Return the item at the top of the stack. If the stack is empty write out 'stack underflow'.}		
item	Integer removed from top of stack	integer parameter

11.4 In Problem 7.6 we looked at a design for determining whether or not a sequence of brackets of the type '[' or ']' were well formed. We shall now generalize that problem by allowing different sorts of parentheses, including the brackets '[' and ']', to appear in arithmetic expressions. The parentheses may be nested to any level and the problem is to determine whether or not an expression is well formed. For example, the expression {1 + (5*[8 + 3])}/4 is well formed and has value {1 + 55}/4, that is 14. Compare it with the following expressions, all of which are invalid: ((2 + 4), 7 + 4], ([2 + 6}*5). If we assume that an expression is scanned from left to right then a stack can be used to do this checking process by pushing opening parentheses onto the stack. When a closing parenthesis is encountered it must match the last parenthesis pushed onto the stack. This can be checked by popping the stack and checking for a match. If at any stage what is popped does not match the closing parenthesis then the expression is not well formed. Write a design which requests an expression and which reports whether or not it is well formed. Should an expression be not well formed then this is to be reported immediately and no further characters should be examined. Your design should allow for parentheses of the type '(' '{' or '[' together with their closing equivalents. You should first give a module design for the representation of the stack and then a main program design. To test that two brackets match you should use a routine which will be part of the main program design.

11.6 POINTER VARIABLES

In Section 11.4 we used an array to implement a stack. We remarked at the time that this imposed the restriction that the stack was thereby limited to some maximum number of elements which it could contain. A problem then arises if it becomes necessary to exceed this maximum number because extra items have to be inserted. The data type then has to be redefined in its module. In this section we shall introduce a new built-in data type which overcomes this problem. This is called a **pointer** data type and it will enable us to implement a stack whose size is limited only by the memory capacity of the machine. In this section we shall concentrate on pointer variables before seeing how they can be used to implement a stack in the next section.

A variable of type pointer is one which can contain a pointer to another variable. Essentially what a pointer contains is an address at which is found the variable pointed to. We say a pointer **references** store locations. Figure 11.3 shows how pointer variables will be represented diagrammatically.

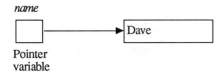

name

Pointer
variable

Figure 11.3 Pointer variable

This figure introduces some naming conventions. The identifier *name* refers to the pointer variable itself. The identifier *name^* (i.e. the identifier followed by a circumflex) identifies the variable to which *name* points. In this example the variable *name^* has string value 'Dave'.

In order to give you a mental image of a pointer variable we ask you to picture the memory of a computer as a sequence of consecutively numbered storage locations. The locations will be numbered #1, #2, #3... (The symbol # helps distinguish address locations from integers which might well be stored at a memory location.) The memory can then be pictured as a collection of numbered pigeon holes which can be arranged in groups to hold data of different types and which consequently require different amounts of storage space (Figure 11.4).

#1   #2   #3   #4   #5   #6   #7   #8   #9

Figure 11.4 Computer memory model

Each of the variables *name* and *name^* will be stored in the memory somewhere. We shall assume that only one memory location is required to store the value of the pointer variable, but the variable to which it points may require several memory locations, depending upon what type it is. Figure 11.5 illustrates this for a particular example with a string defined to be of static length 4. The pointer variable *name* contains the start address, #8, of the variable *name^* which is a string variable whose individual characters have been assumed to require one storage location.

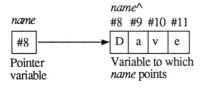

*name^*
#8 #9 #10 #11

name

Pointer
variable

Variable to which
name points

Figure 11.5 Pointer variable with hypothetical addresses

Hence *name^* requires storage locations #8 to #11 for its data value. But, in general, how is it known how many storage locations are required? The definition of a pointer variable must specify the type of the data to which it points. The data table below does this using both a type definition and a pointer variable declaration.

Identifier	Description	Type
nametype	String type definition	string[4]
name	Pointer variable	pointer variable to *nametype*

Here, the type column declares *name* to be a pointer variable and specifies that the data type to which it points is *nametype*, that is, string[4]. We say that *name* is a pointer type **bound** to the type *nametype*. This enables the system to calculate how many storage locations must be reserved for *name*^. Since this calculation is not of further concern we shall only label the start address of variables like *name*^ and diagrams will not identify individual storage locations. Thus Figure 11.5 will take the form shown in Figure 11.6.

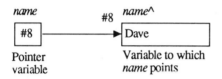

Figure **11.6** Pointer variable with hypothetical address

Exercise 11.1 Write a data table which declares two pointer variables which are bound to data of the following types respectively:
(a) an integer; (b) a real.

The solution to Exercise 11.1 did not use type definitions because the types to which the pointers were bound were of simple type. For pointers which are bound to structured types the use of a type definition is mandatory. We have already seen one example above when the type *nametype* was introduced for the definition of the pointer *name*. The data table below declares a pointer variable bound to a record type:

Identifier	Description	Type
threefields	Record type definition	
	stringfield	string variable
	booleanfield	boolean variable
	integerfield	integer variable
	recordend	
PtrToRecord	Pointer type definition	pointer to *threefields*
recordpointer	Pointer variable	*PtrToRecord* variable

As a result of this declaration, space will be reserved for a *pointer* but not as yet for the record to which it will point. Although space for the pointer variable has been reserved it is still unitialized and will not hold an address until the variable is initialized. A pointer variable is initialized by using a standard procedure called **new**. The design statement to initialize *recordpointer* would be:

  new(*recordpointer*)

This statement allocates the storage required for the *record* and assigns to *recordpointer* the address of this storage. Thus *new* allocates storage for *recordpointer*^ and stores the location of the latter in *recordpointer*. Hence *recordpointer* is now initialized but the record to which it points is not. The statements below would initialize it.

recordpointer^.stringfield := 'Dave'
recordpointer^.booleanfield := true
recordpointer^.integerfield := 24

Figure 11.7 represents the state of the variables at this stage, together with some hypothetical addresses.

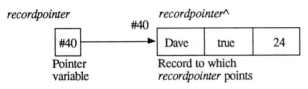

Figure 11.7 An initialized pointer variable

Exercise 11.2 Write down design statements which will initialize the pointer variables *intpointer* and *realpointer* declared in the solution to Exercise 11.1 and which will assign to their referenced variables the values 100 and 34.5 respectively.

As we shall see when we return to stack designs using pointers, it must be possible for a pointer variable to be in a state where it does not point to anything and yet is defined. This is catered for by assigning the special value **nil** to the pointer. This may be assigned to a pointer irrespective of the type to which it is bound. However, note that nil is not a string. Figure 11.8 shows how this will be represented diagrammatically for the pointer variable *charpointer* which is bound to type char.

charpointer

| nil |

Figure 11.8 A pointer with value *nil*

Another facility that will be required is the ability to make two pointers point to the same data. This can be achieved by assignment. In the design fragment below, *intpointer* and *wholepointer* are both pointer variables bound to integer type. Look at the design and then read the commentary below.

```
1  new(wholepointer)
2  wholepointer^ := 6
3  write 'Do you want a second pointer to reference same data y/n '
4  read in response
5  if response = 'n' then
6      intpointer := nil
7  else
8      intpointer := wholepointer
9  ifend
```

10 if *intpointer* = *wholepointer* then
11   write out 'Second pointer variable references the value ', *wholepointer*^
12 else
13   write out 'Second pointer variable does not reference a variable'
14 ifend

Here *intpointer* and *wholepointer* are both initialized and the value which *wholepointer* references is assigned the value 6. The variable *intpointer* will be initialized in one of two ways depending upon the user's response at step 5. If the response is 'n' then *intpointer* is assigned *nil* and so it is a valid pointer variable but it does not reference a variable. If the response is 'y' the *intpointer* is assigned the value of *wholepointer*. This has the effect of making *intpointer* reference the same data as *wholepointer*, in other words both variables point to the same address. This situation is represented diagrammatically in Figure 11.9.

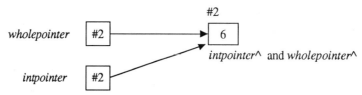

Figure 11.9 Pointer variables referencing the same location

Here, both pointers contain the same address and so reference the same data. Notice that the data which is referenced can be referred to as either *intpointer*^ or *wholepointer*^.

Step 10 illustrates one of the two operations that can be performed on pointer variables. This one is to test equality, that is it tests whether or not *intpointer* and *wholepointer* reference the same variable. Another use for equality is to test whether a pointer variable has value *nil*, in which case it does not reference a variable. The other operation on pointer variables is <>, the test for inequality. To use either comparison operator the pointer variables must either be bound to the same type or the comparison must be with the value *nil*.

To conclude this introduction to pointer variables we must emphasize that the value a pointer variable takes is an address. This value cannot be read in, printed out or used in any arithmetic expressions to perform calculations. However, the variables referenced by it can be manipulated according to the operators defined on their type.

Exercise 11.3 Draw diagrams similar to Figure 11.9 to show the state of the pointer variables at each write out statement in the following design:

 1 new(*firstpointer*)
 2 *firstpointer*^ := 'A'
 3 write out *firstpointer*^
 4 *secondpointer* := *firstpointer*
 5 write out *firstpointer*^, *secondpointer*^
 6 *secondpointer*^ := 'B'
 7 write out *firstpointer*^, *secondpointer*^
 8 new(*secondpointer*)
 9 *secondpointer*^ := 'C'
10 *firstpointer* := *secondpointer*
11 write out *firstpointer*^, *secondpointer*^

Identifier	Description	Type
charpointer	Pointer type definition	pointer to char
firstpointer	Pointer variable	*charpointer* variable
secondpointer	Pointer variable	*charpointer* variable

Exercise 11.3 illustrates how it is possible to assign, to memory, data which subsequently becomes *lost* because its address is no longer held by a pointer. The creation of lost data like this can become a problem when pointer variables are used, but only when all the available memory space has been exhausted. If this happens then a further request for a *new* pointer cannot be satisfied and the program will cease to execute. In order to avoid this happening most languages have a mechanism whereby pointer variables can be released as soon as they are no longer needed. Of course this release mechanism has to be used before the situation depicted in Exercise 11.3 arises. The release mechanism is often called **dispose** or a variant on that theme. However, the use of dispose has its own difficulties and so we shall ignore the problem of running out of memory space for pointer variables.

The most useful application of pointer variables is their use in record structures. We have already seen an example of a pointer variable which pointed to a record. Figure 11.10 uses a similar record structure but it has an extra field called *linkfield*. This field is a pointer bound to the same record structure and so it points to another record.

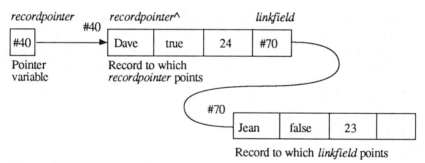

Figure 11.10 Linked records

We shall first see how such a structure can be declared and then see how the individual fields are accessed and initialized. The data table below gives the declarations. Study it and then read the commentary that follows.

Identifier	Description		Type
ptype	Pointer type definition		pointer to *details*
details	Record type definition		
	name	{Name field}	string variable
	married	{Marital status}	boolean variable
	age	{Age}	integer variable
	linkfield	{Link to next record}	*ptype* variable
	recordend		
recordpointer	Pointer variable		*ptype* variable

We shall begin by examining the record type definition. The first three fields are straightforward. The field *linkfield* is declared to have type *ptype* and so this field is a pointer to a record of *details*. In other words, this field contains a pointer to another record of the same type. The variable *recordpointer* is then defined as a pointer variable which points to a record of type *details*. So by initializing *recordpointer* using *new* we get a pointer to a record. The first three fields can be initialized in the usual way and the fourth field can be initialized to point to a second record. We shall see the precise details below but before we do so there is one subtlety in this data table that you should notice. The identifier *details* occurs in the top row of the table and is thereby used before it is defined. This is permissible for pointer variable types but only for these types. This use of *details* before it is defined is often referred to as an **implicit forward reference**.

The design fragment below would have the effect of initializing the first record to correspond to that given in Figure 11.10.

```
1   new(recordpointer)
2   with recordpointer^ do
3       name := 'Dave'
4       married := true
5       age := 24
6       new(linkfield)
7   withend
```

At this stage the first record is initialized and *linkfield* points to another record which, as yet, has all its fields uninitialized. We can gain access to these fields using the identifier *recordpointer*. Now *recordpointer^.linkfield* is the pointer which references the second record and so *recordpointer^.linkfield^* identifies the record to which it points, that is, the record at location #70 in the diagram. The fields of this record can then be accessed using the usual dot notation. Hence we can continue the initialization as:

```
 8   recordpointer^.linkfield^.name := 'Jean'
 9   recordpointer^.linkfield^.married := false
10   recordpointer^.linkfield^.age := 23
```

Exercise 11.4 Rewrite steps 8, 9 and 10 using the *with* statement.

Exercise 11.5 Write a program fragment which will attach a third record to the records in Figure 11.10 and which initializes the first three fields to values of your own choosing.

11.7 POINTER-BASED REPRESENTATION OF STACKS

We shall now use pointer variables to give an alternative design of the stack of integer which we defined in Section 11.4. The specification of the stack will be as before, except that we shall not include an error message for the operation *push* as we shall assume the memory is large enough to accommodate the stacks which will be used. The new specification of *push* is thus:

push

stack	Representation of integer stack	*integerstack* parameter
item	Integer to be entered onto the stack	integer parameter
{Place the item on top of *stack* and return the updated *stack*.}		
stack	Updated stack	integerstack *parameter*

The other three operations, *pop*, *isempty* and *create*, have the same specification as before. Figure 11.11 illustrates diagrammatically how we can use a record containing a pointer field to implement a stack. The diagrams show the contents of a stack being built up and the corresponding state of the pointer representation. The identifier *stack* represents the pointer variable which points to the linked sequence.

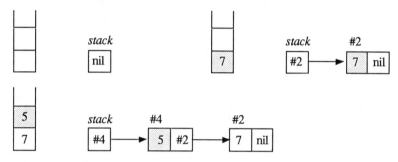

Figure 11.11 Linked representation of a stack

Notice where the top and bottom of the stack are in the linked sequence of records. When a new item is entered it goes to the front of the sequence so that it is the record directly referenced by the pointer variable *stack*. Reading the diagram from the bottom upwards shows what effect *pop* must have on the sequence. You should also notice that for an empty sequence the variable *stack* has value *nil*. The following data table for the module *stackmodule* gives the declarations corresponding to the pointer representation of a stack. Examine its contents and then read the commentary that follows.

Identifier	Description	Type
	PUBLIC	
integerstack	Type definition representing a stack	private
push	(*stack*, *item*)	procedure(*integerstack*, *integer*)
pop	(*stack*, *item*)	procedure(*integerstack*, *integer*)
isempty	(*stack*)	boolean function(*integerstack*)
create	(*stack*)	procedure(*integerstack*)
	PRIVATE	
integerstack	Type definition	pointer to *stackrecord*
stackrecord	Record type definition	
stackitem		integer variable
link		*integerstack* variable
	recordend	

The public part is exactly as it was before. This is just what we would expect, because the user sees this part and it must not contain any data type design details. In the private part *integerstack* is now not a record but is defined to be of type pointer to *stackrecord*.

We can now concentrate on designing the four operations. We shall begin with *create*. This module has no source data but must return the parameter *stack*, suitably initialized. Hence *stack* must be initialized using *new* and its value must be set to *nil* to indicate an empty sequence.

Exercise 11.6 Write a design for the procedure *create*, the function *isempty* and the procedure *pop*.

Figure 11.12 shows hypothetical values of the pointer variables when a new item is pushed onto the stack. Study the figure to work out how to update the values.

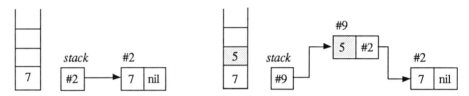

Figure 11.12 Inserting a new record into a stack

A new temporary pointer variable will have to be introduced in the design. We then need to initialize the record to which it points with the pushed data value and then link in this new record at the front of the sequence by adjusting pointer values appropriately. A design and data table is as follows:

push

stack, item

  1 new(*TempPointer*)
  2 *TempPointer.stackitem := item*
  3 *TempPointer.link := stack*
  4 *stack := TempPointer*

stack

Identifier	Description	Type
TempPointer	Temporary record pointer	*integerstack* variable

11.8 TESTING ABSTRACT DATA TYPE DESIGNS

As with any design, the design of the operations of an abstract data type needs to be tested. When the design uses pointer variables there are often particular difficulties that need to be guarded against. We know that it is an error to reference a variable which has not been initialized. The same is true of pointer variables, but with the latter we have to consider both the variable itself and the variable to which it points. This can be further complicated in abstract data types which are sequences in that the operations may involve access to the beginning of the sequence or the end of the sequence or operations which must take particular action when the sequence is empty or full.

In this section we shall introduce some general guidelines which should be used to test the design of abstract data types. The guidelines will need interpreting in the context of the data type being developed, but examples of their use over the next few chapters should make it clear how this can be done. The guidelines can be summarized by the words *empty*, *full*, *first* and *last*. We shall illustrate their use by testing the designs of the operations developed in Section 11.7.

We shall consider the operation *push* first. Here the word *empty* triggers the question: Does the design of the operation *push* work correctly on an empty stack? The sequence of diagrams in Figure 11.13 traces the design of *push* as each step is executed.

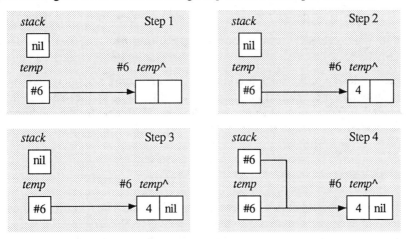

Figure 11.13 Testing *push* when stack is empty

This trace shows that the design does work when the stack is empty.

The second guideline word is *full*. This should trigger the question: Does *push* work correctly when the stack is full? For the pointer representation we assumed that there was an infinite amount of memory available and so the question is not appropriate. However, for the array representation the question is relevant and the design explicitly took care of this possibility.

The third guideline concerns the word *first*, from which the question arises: Does *push* work correctly when the item is to be pushed before the first item on the existing stack? In this case the definition of *push* specifies that the item must go at the beginning of the existing items. For general sequences the analogue of *push* is *insert* and the question of inserting before the first existing item is then more relevant. We shall return to this in the next chapter.

The final guideline *last* is similar to first, except it is dealing with the other end of the sequence. However, it also is not relevant to stack operations because they do not allow items to be inserted after all existing items.

Exercise 11.7 What questions would be triggered by the guideline words in respect of the operation *pop*?

11.9 PROBLEMS

11.5 Write a pointer-based design for the operation *print* described in Problem 11.1.

11.6 Write a design for an operation *count* which has the following specification:

count

stack	Representation of integer stack	*integerstack* parameter
{Count the number of items in the stack. If the stack is empty return the value 0.}		
count	Number of items in *stack*	*integer function value*

11.7 Write a pointer-based design for the operation *revprint* described in Problem 11.2.

11.8 Write a pointer-based design for the operations *pop* and *top* described in Problem 11.3.

11.9 Rewrite the design of the stack used in Problem 11.4 using a pointer representation. The main program developed in that problem will still be applicable with this new representation. Your solution should include a new data table for the module design, together with designs for all the operations.

11.10 SUMMARY

In this chapter we have looked at two representations of a stack. The first involved using an array. Two items of data were required with this representation, the array itself and a variable that recorded which index in the array corresponded to the top of the stack. These two pieces of information were hidden from the user by enclosing them in a record in the stack representation. The second approach used pointer variables in which the top of the stack was pointed to by a pointer variable. Subsequent items on the stack were held as a linked list of records, one of whose fields was a pointer to the next record in the list. When using pointer variables care has to be taken in testing the designs, paying particular attention to operations which may involve an empty or full list or which require the first or last item to be inspected.

12

QUEUES

12.1 INTRODUCTION

In this chapter we shall look at another kind of sequence in which the predefined relationship governing the order of the elements is determined strictly by the order in which they are inserted. The method of insertion is that a new item can be inserted at one specified end of the sequence which we shall call its **tail**. An item can only be retrieved or deleted from the other end of the sequence which is called the **head** of the sequence. You may have recognized that what we have just described is a **queue**. An illustration of a queue with which we are all familiar from our everyday lives is a queue for a bus.

Figure 12.1 A bus queue

People join the queue at its end furthest away from the bus stop sign, that is they join at the tail of the queue. When a bus arrives then people are admitted to it from the front or head of the queue.

We shall begin by looking at a queue of string, in fact a queue of names. The abstract data type *stringqueue* will be defined by five operations whose specifications are given below.

In these specifications *queue* is a parameter of type *stringqueue* and *item* is a string parameter and we shall assume that they are to be implemented in a module called *queuemodule*.

create

{Return a new empty queue of type *stringqueue*.}		
queue	A new string queue	*stringqueue* parameter

front

queue	Representation of string queue	*stringqueue* parameter
{Return the item at the head of the queue leaving *queue* unaltered. If *queue* is empty then write out 'The queue is empty'.}		
item	Item at head of queue	string parameter

insert

queue	Representation of string queue	*stringqueue* parameter
item	Item to be inserted at tail	string parameter
{Insert *item* at the tail of *queue* and return updated *queue*.}		
queue	Updated string queue	*stringqueue* parameter

remove

queue	Representation of string queue	*stringqueue* parameter
{Remove the item at the head of *queue* and return updated *queue*. If *queue* is empty write out 'Cannot remove from an empty queue'.}		
queue	Updated string queue	*stringqueue* parameter

isempty

queue	Representation of string queue	*stringqueue* parameter
{Return the value true if the queue is empty, false otherwise.}		
isempty		boolean function value

The operations involving the head of the queue are subtly different from the corresponding operation on stacks. Here, *front* returns the item at the head of the queue but leaves the queue unaltered. In other words, *front* allows the item at the head of the queue to be inspected without removing it. In order to remove an item from the head of the queue the operation *remove* has to be used. Notice that *remove* does not return the removed item. It is not a peculiarity of queues which gives rise to this method of removal – we have chosen this definition in order to contrast it with the definition of *pop* used in Chapter 11. The point is that there are many ways in which we can model a queue, or indeed any data structure. Here we have chosen five operations. As this discussion shows, we could have chosen slightly different ones to represent the queue. Each different choice of operations gives rise to a different abstract data type because of the different operations involved but each collection of operations would be a model for the queue.

12.2 USING A QUEUE

Now that the operations defining a queue have been specified we shall develop a high level design for a problem which uses them. This will give you the opportunity to become familiar with the operations prior to working on their design. The problem we are going to look at is that of maintaining a standby list at a domestic airport but it will be considerably simplified in order that we can concentrate on the use of the queue rather than get involved in the complexities of a real problem.

We shall suppose that an airline offers regular flights to a given destination and seats on these flights may be booked in advance. Passengers may also turn up at the check-in desk without a ticket and be asked to be put on a standby list. This gives them a reduced price ticket, but they have to wait until just before departure to find out whether a seat is available. Just before departure, the number of seats which have not been pre-booked is calculated and that number of seats is made available to the standby list. Seats are allocated to people on the list on a first come-first served basis. Furthermore, of those people who are allocated standby seats the person at the top of the list gets first choice of where to sit in the standby allocation, the second on the list gets second choice and so on. The standby list will be maintained by a menu-driven program which gives the user the following choices:

I Insert a new name onto the standby list
A Allocate seats from the list for a flight
Q Quit

A top level design for this program is:

```
    {Standby list}
1   initialize variables
2   repeat
3       write out menu
4       read in choice
5       select case depending on choice
6           'I' :   insert name into queue
7           'A' :   allocate seats to a flight
8       selectend
9   until choice = 'Q'
```

The standby list will be represented by a queue called *standby*. This enables the following refinement to be developed:

```
        {Standby list}
1.1     create(standby)
2       repeat
3           write out menu
4           read in choice
5           select case depending on choice
6.1             'I' :   prompt for and read in name
6.2                         insert(standby, name)
7.1             'A' :   if isempty(standby) then
```

7.2		write out 'No standby seats required on this flight'
7.3		else
7.4		prompt for and read in number of available seats
7.5		loop while there are seats to allocate and not *isempty(standby)*
7.6		*front(standby, name)*
7.7		write out *name*
7.8		*remove(standby)*
7.9		decrement number of seats to allocate
7.10		loopend
7.11		ifend
8	selectend	
9	until choice = 'Q'	

Identifier	Description	Type
standby	Representation of standby queue	variable of *stringqueue* type from module *queuemodule*
choice	User's menu choice	char variable
name	Name of a passenger	string variable

The problem will be left at this point as it gives an outline solution to the problem. Before further design is carried out the design of the abstract data type *stringqueue* must be completed.

12.3 DESIGNING THE ABSTRACT DATA TYPE QUEUE

A pointer-based design for the queue will be developed. Diagrams representing queues and pointers will use hypothetical address values in order to make the explanation easier. We remind you that these are there to help your understanding and do not reflect the amount of memory that the data depicted might require in a machine. Remember also that pointer values cannot be written out or used in arithmetic expressions. Figure 12.2 shows how a queue will be represented diagrammatically.

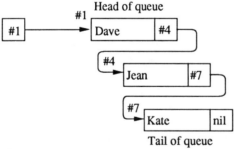

Figure 12.2 A diagrammatic representation of a queue

Here we have a queue of names each of which is in the first field of a record. The other field in the record is a pointer to the next record, what we have previously called a link field.

The queue itself is identified by a pointer variable whose value in this diagram is #1 and it points to the record at the head of the queue. Note that the record at the tail of the queue has the value *nil* in its pointer field. The hardest operation to design is *insert* because insertions have to take place at the tail of the queue. This involves sequentially searching the queue to find its end. It turns out to be easier if we have two pointers to the queue, one pointing to the head of the queue and one pointing to its tail. Figure 12.3 incorporates this modification using the identifiers *head* and *tail* in the obvious way.

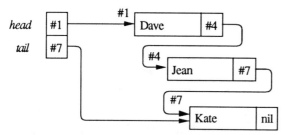

Figure 12.3 A queue with head and tail pointer

We begin by investigating what has to be done to insert a new item into the specific example given in Figure 12.3. Insertions are made at the tail of the queue and so the new item will have to go after the record containing 'Kate'. Figure 12.4 shows the result of this insertion.

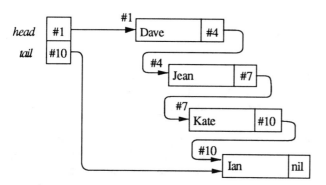

Figure 12.4 The queue after the insertion of Ian

In order to achieve this a new record has to be obtained and initialized; then the link field of Kate's record has to be updated to point to the new record and finally *tail* has to be updated to point to this new tail record. If the identifiers *queueitem* and *link* are used to denote the fields of the records then a design to accomplish this is:

```
1  new(temp)                    {temp points to new record}
2  temp^.queueitem := 'Ian'     {Initialize the queueitem field}
3  temp^.link := nil            {This will signify the end of the queue}
4  tail^.link := temp           {Make Kate record point to new one}
5  tail := temp                 {Make tail point to new record}
```

Here *temp* is a pointer variable bound to the record structure, so step 1 creates a new pointer variable (pointing to #10) and steps 2 and 3 initialize the fields of this record. Step 4 updates the link field of Kate's record, gaining access to it via the variable *tail*. Finally step 5 updates *tail* so that it points to the new tail record.

This would seem to be a correct design but it needs to be tested against critical values. Here, critical test data would include the situation where the queue is empty before insertion takes place. The queue is empty when both *head* and *tail* have value *nil*. Figure 12.5 illustrates this situation.

head | nil

tail | nil

Figure 12.5 An empty queue

Tracing through the design with this starting point and using 'Dave' as the item to be inserted, results in the situation shown in Figure 12.6 after the execution of step 3.

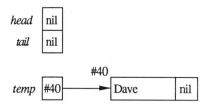

Figure 12.6 The situation after step 3

Step 4 updates *tail^.link* but the value of *tail* is *nil* and so attempting to reference the record to which *tail* points is an error. The result of this on most systems would be catastrophic and would result in a run-time error and hence the cessation of program execution. The design for insert would therefore appear to be faulty.

In fact the design only fails when the queue is empty. There are two ways to overcome this. The first would be to redesign *insert* so that it takes care of the situation when the queue is empty. All that this would require is a conditional statement which separates the two possibilities of an empty and non-empty queue. An alternative approach is to introduce a dummy record into the queue so that *head* and *tail* always point to this record. When we do this an empty queue then looks like that in Figure 12.7.

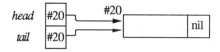

Figure 12.7 An empty queue using a dummy record

Here *head* and *tail* both point to the record at #20 and so the problem we had with the design of insert cannot arise. This time there is no difficulty updating *tail^.link* at step 4 because this value does exist and it has value *nil*. The diagram also shows that an empty sequence can be recognized by virtue of the fact that *head* and *tail* both point to the same place, in other words an empty queue has the property that *head* = *tail*.

Using a dummy record the queue of Figure 12.4 would be represented diagrammatically as in Figure 12.8.

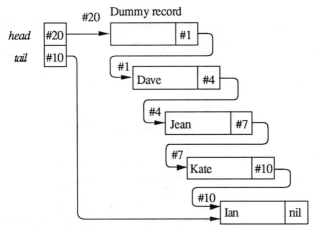

Figure 12.8 A queue with a dummy record

A consequence of using a dummy item is that the procedure *create* will have to initialize it as well as dealing with any other necessary initialization. What needs to be done is given by the following design fragment:

1 *new(head)*
2 *tail := head*
3 *head^.link* := nil

Finally, we consider the operation *remove*. This must remove the item at the head of the queue. In Figure 12.8 this would be the record containing the item 'Dave'. Figure 12.9 shows the situation after this record has been deleted.

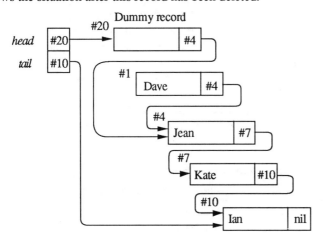

Figure 12.9 The queue with Dave removed

To carry out this deletion the link field of the dummy record has to be updated to point to the record containing 'Jean'. But the location of this record is given in the link field of the record containing 'Dave'. Hence *head^.link* has to be updated to contain *head^.link^.link*, the latter being the identifier which denotes the link field of Dave's record. The details of this are left to an exercise which follows.

In this description of the operations we have been using identifiers without defining them explicitly. In fact what we have been using are:

Identifier	Description	Type
PtrToQueueRec	Pointer type definition	pointer to *queuerecord*
queuerecord	Record type definition	
	queueitem {Data item}	*string variable*
	link {Link to next record}	*PtrToQueueRec variable*
	recordend	
head	Pointer to head of queue	*PtrToQueueRec variable*
tail	Pointer to tail of queue	*PtrToQueueRec variable*

The queue essentially consists of the two pointer variables *head* and *tail*, but of course we cannot implement it directly like this because details of the implementation would then be visible to the user. The two pointer variables are therefore collected together as a record. The following data table for the module *queuemodule* contains the details. In order to write designs for the operations the outline designs we have just considered will have to take account of this data hiding. In most instances this will mean replacing references to *head* by references to *queue.head*, a similar translation being required for *tail*. We shall ask you to provide the details in Exercise 12.1.

Identifier	Description	Type
	PUBLIC	
stringqueue	Type definition representing a string queue	private
create	(*queue*)	procedure(*stringqueue*)
front	(*queue, item*)	procedure(*stringqueue, string*)
insert	(*queue, item*)	procedure(*stringqueue, string*)
remove	(*queue*)	procedure(*stringqueue*)
isempty	(*queue*)	boolean function(*stringqueue*)
	PRIVATE	
PtrToQueueRec	Pointer type definition	pointer to *queuerecord*
queuerecord	Record type definition	
	queueitem {Data item}	*string variable*
	link {link to next record}	*PtrToQueueRec variable*
	recordend	
stringqueue	Record type definition	
	head {Head of queue}	*PtrToQueueRec variable*
	tail {Tail of queue}	*PtrToQueueRec variable*
	recordend	

Exercise 12.1 Write a design for each of the routines *create*, *front*, *insert*, *remove* and *isempty*.

12.4 PROBLEMS

12.1   The operation of printing a queue is to be added to those described in the text. The item at the head of the queue is to be output first, followed by the second and so on. In other words, the head of the queue is to be at the top of the screen with the tail of the queue towards the bottom. If the queue is empty a suitable message should be output instead.

The remaining problems are concerned with developing an abstract data type which has queue-like properties. The card game Gin Rummy uses a pack of cards in a queue-like fashion. There are two players, each of whom are dealt 10 cards; the remaining cards then form what is known as the *stock* and this will be the concern of the remaining problems. The stock contains 32 cards which are placed face down on the table. The top card is turned over and placed beside the stock. Players may exchange one of their own cards for either the face-up card or the face-down card on the top of the stock. They do so by picking up one of these two cards and then returning a discard, face uppermost, to the face-up pile beside the stock. Thus discards always go on the face-up pile so that at any time only one face is visible. There is in fact no need to have a face-up pile. The single pile will do, provided that both players can see the bottom card of the stock. This can be arranged by placing the stock on a glass-topped table arranged above the eye line. Now a player can take either the top (hidden) card of the stock or the bottom (exposed) card. Discards will be to the bottom of the stock. Note that when a player chooses to take from the bottom of the stock this exposes the card underneath it. In the remainder of this problem section an abstract data type to represent the stock and the allowable operations on it will be developed. The operations defined on the stock are given below. The problems will ask you to make definitions for the types *cardtype* and *stocktype*.

makestock

{Return a new stock containing 32 cards.}		
stock	A stock of 32 cards	*stocktype* parameter

drawtop

stock	A stock of 32 cards	*stocktype* parameter
{Remove the top card as *draw* from the stock and return the updated stock. It is the responsibility of the user to ensure that *replace* is called prior to the next request to draw a card.}		
stock	Updated stock of 31 cards	*stocktype* parameter
draw	The top card of the stock	*cardtype* parameter

drawbottom

stock	A stock of 32 cards	*stocktype* parameter
{Remove the bottom card as *draw* from the stock. Display the new bottom card exposed by this removal. It is the responsibility of the user to ensure that *replace* is called prior to the next request to draw a card.}		
stock	Updated stock of 31 cards	*stocktype* parameter
draw	The card removed from the stock	*cardtype* parameter

replace

stock	Stock of 31 cards	*stocktype* parameter
discard	Card to be replaced in the stock	*cardtype* parameter
{Replace *discard* at the bottom of the stock and return the updated stock.}		
stock	Updated stock of 32 cards	*stocktype* parameter

showbottom

stock	The stock	*stocktype* parameter
{Display the card at the bottom of the stock.}		

12.2 What data structures could be used to represent the cards in the stock? For each representation describe how the top and bottom card of the stock could be identified.

12.3 If a pointer based representation is chosen for the stock would it be necessary to include a dummy first item as was done for a queue? What problems are associated with drawing a card from the bottom of the stock with this representation and how might they be resolved?

12.4 Write down a data table for a module which defines a pointer-based representation for the stock based on the discussion in the solution to Problem 12.3. Pointers to the top, penultimate and bottom cards of the stock should be used. The definition of *cardtype* should appear in the public definitions.

12.5 Write designs for each of the operations *drawtop*, *drawbottom* and *replace* based upon the definitions given in the solution to Problem 12.4. You may assume the existence of the procedure *showbottom*.

You may like to get some further practice by designing this abstract data type without using the pointer *penultimate*. Further problems can be generated by looking at the array representation. The solution to Problem 12.2 indicated two ways in which the array representation can be implemented.

12.5 SUMMARY

In this chapter we have looked at the abstract data type queue using a pointer-based representation. Two pointers were used, one pointing to the head of the queue and the other to the tail. Although it is not strictly necessary to use two pointers it makes the design of some of the operations easier. It became apparent that it would be beneficial to use a dummy as the first item in the linked list. This was so because the operation of inserting a new item required special attention if a dummy item was not used.

13

GENERAL SEQUENCES

13.1 INTRODUCTION

In this chapter we are going to look at a more general type of sequence where the predefined relation which determines the order of the items in the sequence is to be found in the data item itself. Typically we shall be looking at sequences of records and the sequence will be ordered on one of the fields of the record. A field used for ordering a sequence is called a **key field** and it must have the property that it uniquely identifies the record. The other fields of the records are called **non-key fields**.

As an illustrative example we shall consider a computer system which maintains a list of flights due to arrive at an airport and which provides facilities for keeping this information up to date. This will involve adding new flights to the list, deleting flights which are cancelled and updating the estimated time of arrival of other flights. Output of the list will be to an information screen, an example of which is shown in Figure 13.1 in which ETA means estimated time of arrival.

Due	Flight	From	ETA
12.03	BA547	London	12.00
12.05	VA057	Dallas	Landed
12.10	AF600	Paris	Delayed

Figure 13.1 An arrivals screen

Data on the board is presented in chronological order of due arrival time which is unique for each flight. (This assumption will make the problem easier but at airports with a single runway it is the case that no two flights can arrive at exactly the same time.) The second column is a code by which individual flights are known. These codes are called flight numbers, even though they consist of both digits and characters. A flight number uniquely identifies a flight.

As in the previous chapters the problem which we shall consider is a great simplification of a real system. All that we shall require is that the operator of the flight information program be presented with a menu of five choices:

1   Add new flight information
2   Delete a flight
3   Update estimated time of arrival
4   Display the arrivals board
5   Quit

The problem of what a passenger sees on the screen when an option other than display is being used will not be considered. When option 1 is chosen the operator should be prompted for a new flight arrival time, a flight number, the place from which the flight originates and the estimated time of arrival. None of this input is to be validated and it may be assumed that the time entered is not already in the list and so is unique. For choices 2 and 3 the operator is to be prompted for a flight number. If the entered number is not in the list then a suitable message is to be output and execution of the option is to cease. When the flight number does exist then option 2 will delete that flight's information while option 3 should prompt for a new ETA and update the appropriate entry. Option 4 is to output the contents of the list but should not take account of the possibility that there may be more entries in the list than will fit a screen.

It is decided to represent the data of Figure 13.1 as a sequence of records stored in chronological order of the field corresponding to the due arrival time. This field is a key field because we have assumed that arrival times are unique. Note that the flight number is also unique and so could have been used as a key field, but the way the sequence is to be manipulated suggests that the due time is a better method of ordering. The following operator specifications define the abstract data type, *ArrivalsSeq*, which will be designed as a module called *ArrivalsModule*:

insert

arrivals	Representation of the sequence	*ArrivalsSeq* parameter
newtime	New due arrival time	real parameter
newflight	Flight number	string parameter
newfrom	Place flight originated	string parameter
neweta	Estimated time of arrival	string parameter
{Insert new flight details, due time, flight number, place of origin and estimated time of arrival, as given by the parameters *newtime*, *newflight*, *newfrom* and *neweta* respectively, into the list.}		
arrivals	Updated sequence	*ArrivalsSeq* parameter

For simplicity the time data has been specified as a real parameter. Note that the data corresponding to the estimated time of arrival is specified as a string parameter. That is because this will not always be a time, this entry may contain the string 'Landed' or 'Delayed'.

delete

arrivals	Representation of the sequence	*ArrivalsSeq* parameter
flightgiven	Flight number to be deleted	string parameter
Delete the entry whose flight number is *flightgiven*. If no such flight exists or the list is empty, report the error and take no further action.}		
arrivals	Updated sequence	*ArrivalsSeq* parameter

create

{Return a new empty sequence of type *ArrivalsSeq*.}		
arrivals	A new sequence	*ArrivalsSeq*

update

arrivals	Representation of the sequence	*ArrivalsSeq* parameter
flightgiven	Flight number whose ETA is to be updated	string parameter
{If the flight number, *flightgiven*, is in the sequence then prompt for and read in the new estimated time of arrival and enter this in the appropriate record. If the flight number does not exist report the error and take no further action.}		
arrivals	Updated sequence	*ArrivalsSeq* parameter

display

arrivals	Representation of the sequence	*ArrivalsSeq* parameter
{Clear the screen and write out the whole of the sequence. If the sequence is empty take no further action.}		

13.2 DESIGNING THE ABSTRACT DATA TYPE SEQUENCE

A pointer-based representation will be used for the sequence. As before we shall begin by representing the sequence diagramatically and use the diagrams to discover the difficulties involved in creating designs for the operations. The diagrams will include memory addresses, but their only purpose is to help your understanding and to act as convenient labels for reference in the text. (The values used do not take any account of the actual amount of memory the records might need.)

A significant difference between the sequence we are considering here and what has gone before is that the order of the records in the sequence are ordered on a key field. This means that when a record is to be inserted then the sequence must be searched to see where the new record should go. The sequence will be represented as a linked sequence of records in much the same way as we have already encountered.

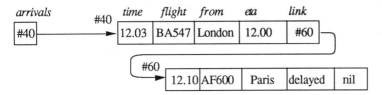

Figure 13.2 A sequence with two records

Figure 13.2 represents a sequence of two records, each of which has five fields. The first four fields correspond to the data in the columns of Figure 13.1 and the final field is a link to the next record. The last record has the value nil in its link field to denote the end of the sequence. The link fields are pointers whose type, *ArrivalsSeq,* will be defined more precisely later. The whole sequence is identified by the pointer variable *arrivals* also of type *ArrivalSeq*. In order to insert a new record in this sequence it is necessary to discover where it should be located. This will involve searching the *time* field of the sequence. Suppose we were searching to see where a record with *time* field of 12.00 should go. A potential design for such a search would be:

1 initialize variables
2 loop while *time* field < 12.00 and it is not the last record
3   move to next record
4 loopend

This may be expressed in more detail using the identifiers in Figure 13.2 together with a variable *location* of the same type as *arrivals* :

1 *location* := *arrivals*
2 loop while (*location^.time* < 12.00) and (it is not the last record)
3   *location* := *location^.link*
4 loopend

This appears to be satisfactory until the test guidelines of Section 11.8 are applied to it; that is, does it work on an empty sequence? For an empty sequence *arrivals* will have value nil (and so will not point to a record). This means an error will occur at step 2 when an attempt is made to access *location^.time*. Rather than try to deal with the special case of an empty sequence separately we shall employ the same trick that we have used before, namely we shall use a dummy first record. The sequence in Figure 13.2 would then be represented by that in Figure 13.3.

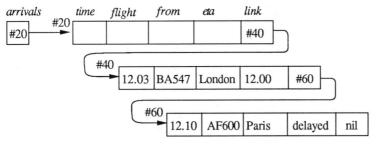

Figure 13.3 A diagrammatic representation of a sequence with dummy first record

Exercise 13.1 Flight YA057 from Dallas is due to arrive at 12.05 and its estimated time of arrival is 12.00. The details of this flight will be inserted as a record between the 12.03 and 12.10 flights. Which of the latter records do you think should be identified by the search?

It will be convenient to develop the search as a procedure, *timesearch*. Its source data will be the sequence and *timegiven*, the time of the new flight, and its results will be a pointer variable whose value is the location of the record just prior to the insertion point.

timesearch

arrivals	The sequence of flight arrivals	*ArrivalsSeq* parameter
timegiven	Time to be searched for	real parameter
{Search the *time* field of the sequence of records pointed to by *origin*. Return to *location* the pointer value which identifies the record whose time field is the last one which has a value less than *timegiven*. (All subsequent records would have a time field which is greater than *timegiven*.)}		
location	Pointer to sought record	*ArrivalsSeq* parameter

The following design is an attempt to find *location* when *timegiven* has value 12.05. Why is it incorrect?

```
1  location := arrivals^.link   {No need to examine the dummy item}
2  loop while (location^.time < 12.05) and (it is not the last record)
3      location := location^.link
4  loopend
```

The problem is that *location* points to the record at #60 after this search and that is one record too far. This can be resolved using two pointers, one of which lags one record behind the other. The technique of using two pointers in this way is very common in sequence operations. In the following design *location* would have the correct value after execution of the fragment:

```
1  lag := arrivals
2  lead := arrivals^.link      {No need to examine the dummy item}
3  loop while (lead^.time < 12.05) and (it is not the last record)
4      lag := lead
5      lead := lead^.link
6  loopend
7  location := lag
```

The designs in the following exercise are an attempt to generalize this design to search for *timegiven* rather than the specific value 12.05.

Exercise 13.2 Both the designs below would result in errors. Identify why the errors occur by drawing up a trace table in which *timegiven* has value 12.20 and the sequence is in the state depicted in Figure 13.3.

```
(a) 1  lag := arrivals
    2  lead := arrivals^.link   {No need to examine the dummy item}
    3  loop while (lead^.time < timegiven) and (lead^.link <> nil)
    4      lag := lead
```

```
5     lead := lead^.link
6   loopend
7   location := lag
```

(b) 1   *lag := arrivals*
   2   *lead := arrivals^.link*   {No need to examine the dummy item}
   3   loop while (*lead^.time < timegiven*) and (*lead <> nil*)
   4   *lag := lead*
   5   *lead := lead^.link*
   6   loopend
   7   *location := lag*

The difficulties encountered in Exercise 13.2 only arise when the time being sought comes after all the times in the sequence. This can be overcome by making the last record point back to the dummy record as shown in Figure 13.4.

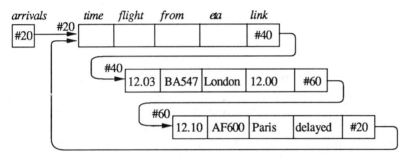

Figure 13.4 A sequence with last record pointing to the dummy record

The dummy record can then be exploited in a similar way that an array dummy index 0 element was used when searching. The time being sought is put into the time field of the dummy record. When this time exceeds all those in the sequence the search goes back from the last record to the dummy, where of course a match occurs and the search ceases. The pointer *lag* then points to the last record. In this way we do not have to worry about *falling off* the end of the sequence. The design for *timesearch* is then:

---
timesearch
---
arrivals, timegiven

```
1   arrivals^.time := timegiven
2   lag := arrivals
3   lead := arrivals^.link
4   loop while lead^.time < timegiven
5      lag := lead
6      lead := lead^.link
7   loopend
8   location := lag
```
---
location

Exercise 13.3 Write a design fragment which, starting with Figure 13.4, will insert a new record at time 12.05 as shown in Figure 13.5. The highlighted part of Figure 13.5 indicates the changes which are required. Your fragment should include a call to *timesearch*.

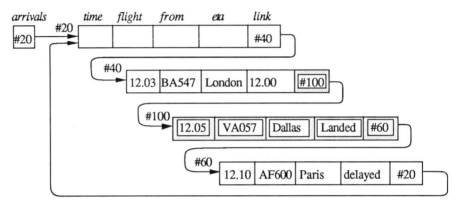

Figure 13.5 Insertion of a new record

Exercise 13.3 can be generalized into a design for the procedure *insert*. The exercises at the end of the section will ask you to complete the details. We now turn our attention to a preliminary investigation of the design of *delete* and *update*. Both of these operations are required to search the *flight* field of the records for the value *flightgiven*. This search process will be designed as a procedure, *flightsearch*, with source data *arrivals* and *flightgiven*. But what should its results be? Should the result be a pointer to the record containing *flightgiven* or to its predecessor? We can see what is required by looking at Figure 13.5 and supposing *flightgiven* is 'VA057', so that the record at #100 is the one being sought. To *update* this record the result has to be a pointer with value #100. But to *delete* it the result would need to be a pointer with value #40 in order that the 12.03 record can have its link field updated to value #60. The procedure *flightsearch* will be specified so that it returns both pointers, one to the sought item and the other to its predecessor.

flightsearch

arrivals	The sequence of flight arrivals	*ArrivalsSeq* parameter
flightgiven	Flight number sought	string parameter
{Search the flight arrivals sequence for the record containing *flightgiven* in its *flight* field. Return to *lead* the pointer value which identifies this record and to *lag* the pointer to the previous record. If no such record exists then *lead* should be assigned the value *arrivals*.}		
lead	Sought record	*ArrivalsSeq* parameter
lag	Predecessor of sought record	*ArrivalsSeq* parameter

By putting *flightgiven* in the dummy item success of the search is assured and the correct value will be assigned to *lead* if the flight number is not in the sequence. A design for *flightsearch*, which needs to be tested to ensure that it works on an empty sequence, is:

flightsearch	
arrivals, flightgiven	
1.1	*arrivals^.flight := flightgiven*
1.2	*lag := arrivals*
1.3	*lead := arrivals^.link*
2	loop while *lead^.flight <> flightgiven*
3.1	*lag := lead*
3.2	*lead := lead^.link*
4	loopend
lead, lag	

Exercise 13.4 Given the sequence in Figure 13.5 and supposing that *lead* and *lag* have values resulting from the search for flight 'VA057' write down a statement which will remove this record from the sequence.

The preliminary design for each of the operators is now complete and the detailed design can be concluded. In so doing, the declarations of *timesearch* and *flightsearch* have to be considered. Neither routine forms part of the abstract data type specification and so their declaration must be private. However, *flightsearch* is called by *update* and *delete* and so must be in both their referencing environments. This means that the declaration of *flightsearch* must precede both those of *update* and *delete*. The following data table for the module *ArrivalsModule* shows this dual requirement can be met.

The procedure *timesearch* is only required by the operation *insert*, can be declared local to it and so does not appear in the public or private parts of the data table. Thus is it inaccessible and so hidden from the user.

Identifier	Description	Type
	PUBLIC	
ArrivalsSeq	Type definition for the sequence	private
insert	(*arrivals, newtime, newflight, newfrom, neweta*)	procedure(*ArrivalsSeq*, real, string, string, string)
flightsearch	(*arrivals, flightgiven, lead, lag*)	private procedure(*ArrivalsSeq*, string, *ArrivalsSeq*, *ArrivalsSeq*)
delete	(*arrivals, flightgiven*)	procedure(*ArrivalsSeq*, string)
create	(*arrivals*)	procedure(*ArrivalsSeq*)
update	(*arrivals, flightgiven*)	procedure(*ArrivalsSeq*, string)
display	(*arrivals*)	procedure(*ArrivalsSeq*)
	PRIVATE	
ArrivalsSeq	Pointer type definition	pointer to *SeqRec*
SeqRec	record type definition	
	time	real variable
	flight	string variable
	from	string variable
	eta	string variable
	link	*ArrivalsSeq* variable
	recordend	

In the following exercises we ask you to write detailed designs for each of the operations which define the sequence. In order to do this you should use the outline designs developed in the chapter.

Exercise 13.5 Write a design for each of the routines *create*, *display* and *insert*.

Exercise 13.6 Write a design for each of the procedures *update* and *delete*. Your solutions should call the procedure *flightsearch*.

13.3 USING THE SEQUENCE

We can now play the part of the user to write a design for the problem. The major construct will be a loop as shown by the following top level design:

```
     {Arrivals board program}
 1   create a new sequence
 2   repeat
 3       write out menu
 4       read in choice
 5       select case depending on choice
 6           '1' :  add new flight information
 7           '2' :  delete flight information
 8           '3' :  update flight information
 9           '4' :  display flight information
10       selectend
11   until choice = '5'
```

This design can be refined as follows:

```
         {Arrivals board program}
1.1      create(arrivalsboard)
2        repeat
3            write out menu
4            read in choice
5            select case depending on choice
6.1              '1' :  write 'Enter the due arrival time '
6.2                     read in newtime
6.3                     write 'Enter the flight number '
6.4                     read in newflight
6.5                     write 'Enter the place where flight originated '
6.6                     read in newfrom
6.7                     write 'Enter estimated time of arrival '
6.8                     read in neweta
6.9                     insert(arrivalsboard, newtime, newflight, newfrom, neweta)
```

7.1	'2' :	write 'Enter flight number to be deleted '
7.2		read in *flightgiven*
7.3		*delete(arrivalsboard, flightgiven)*
8.1	'3' :	write 'Enter flight number to be updated '
8.2		read in *flightgiven*
8.3		*update(arrivalsboard, flightgiven)*
9.1	'4' :	*display(arrivalsboard)*
10		selectend
11		until *choice* = '5'

Identifier	Description	Type
arrivalsboard	Representation of the sequence	variable of type *ArrivalsSeq* from module *ArrivalsModule*
newtime	New due arrival time	real variable
newflight	New flight number	string variable
newfrom	Place flight originated	string variable
neweta	Estimated time of arrival	string variable
flightgiven	Flight number update	string variable
anychar	Any keyboard character	char variable
choice	Menu choice	char variable

This is as far as the program will be developed. Testing would have to include all the difficult cases that arose in the text. The test guidelines of Chapter 10 should be used to generate questions against which you should test your design. Things such as inserting into an empty sequence, deleting from an empty sequence and so on should be considered.

13.4 PROBLEMS

13.1 An administrator receives memos from colleagues and files them for processing in an intray. Each memo has a numerical code identifying its originator and the administrator files the memos in chronological order of receipt within originator number. So, for example, all files originating from colleague 10 will be filed in order with the oldest memo at the top. All of the memos from colleague 10 will precede those originating from colleague 11 and so on. The administrator processes one memo at a time by retrieving it from the pile, reading its contents and implementing any actions that the contents require. When this has been done, the memo is discarded. For a given originator, the administrator will deal with the memos in strict chronological order of receipt. Thus, for originator 10, the oldest memo will be dealt with first followed by the next oldest and so on. However, the administrator will choose the originator on whose memos to work. The system is to be computerized and an abstract data type *pileofmemo* is to be designed which models the system described above. The memos consist of two pieces of data, an originator number and text corresponding to the message. The following operations are included in the definition of *pileofmemo*:

insert

pile	A representation of the intray	*pileofmemo* parameter
originator	Originator of memo	integer parameter
giveninfo	Text of memo	string parameter
{Insert the new memo in order of originator number. Within originator number, memos are ordered in chronological order of receipt.}		
pile	Updated memo pile	*pileofmemo* parameter

remove

pile	A pile of memos	*pileofmemo* parameter
originator	Originator number	integer parameter
{Search for the first occurrence of a memo originating from *originator* in the pile, remove it from the pile and return the text of the memo to *item*. If no such memo exists assign to *item* the value 'No such memo'.}		
pile	Updated pile of mcmos	*pileofmemo* parameter
item	Text of memo from *originator*	string parameter

create

{Create a new pile of memos.}		
pile	A new pile of memos	*pileofmemo* parameter

print

pile	A pile of memos	*pileofmemo* parameter
{Write out the contents of all memos in the intray, that is the originator number and text for each memo in *pile*.}		

isempty

pile	A pile of memos	*pileofmemo* parameter
{Return the value true if the pile is empty, false otherwise.}		
isempty		boolean function value

A linked representation is to be used for the abstract data type. The type *pileofmemo* will be a record having three fields, the first two corresponding to the originator and memo text and the third being a pointer to the next record. Devise a module data table for this abstract data type and design routines for each of the operations defined above.

13.5 SUMMARY

In this chapter we have looked at general sequences using a pointer-based representation. The difficulty of finding the item at the end of a sequence represented in this way led to the trick of making the last link field point back to the dummy item. In this way searches would always be successful because the search item can be placed temporarily in the dummy item. It also avoids the difficulty of 'falling off' the end of the sequence.

14

TREES

14.1 INTRODUCTION

In this chapter we shall study an abstract data type which is not a form of sequence. A tree structure is one which is capable of representing hierarchical data. Figure 14.1 shows the job titles in a business organization and their hierarchical relation.

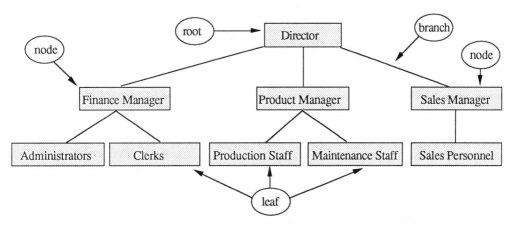

Figure 14.1 A business organization and its hierarchies

This figure introduces some terminology. The individual entries are called **nodes** and the node at the highest level is called the **root node** or more simply the **root**. Here, the root node contains the Director of the organization. Strictly speaking a node and the data it contains are different things but it gets rather cumbersome to refer to things like 'the node containing the item Director'. We shall therefore refer to a node and the data it contains by expressions like 'the node Director' or 'the Director node'.

In this figure the Director node has three **children**, the Finance Manager, Product Manager and Sales Manager. The Sales Personnel node is an example of a **leaf** node. A leaf node has no children. The Sales Manager node is the **parent** of the Sales Personnel node. The part of the tree which contains the Finance Manager node and all the nodes below it is an example of what is known as a **subtree**. You may assume that whatever is said about a tree applies to a subtree because a subtree is in fact itself a tree. What is not apparent from this example is that the nodes of a tree must all be of the same type. We can define a tree as follows:

A **tree** is a data structure which has zero or more nodes organized in a hierarchical manner, called levels, such that:

1. Except when the tree is empty there is one node at the top of the hierarchy which is called the root node.
2. Every node, except the root node, is joined by a branch to just one node at the next highest level of the hierarchy.
3. One item of a predefined type is associated with each node.
4. A predefined relationship exists between data on adjacent levels.

In general, the number of children that a node can have is unrestricted, but in the special case where a node can have at most two children, the tree is called a **binary tree**. We shall only be studying binary trees in this chapter. Since any node of a binary tree can have at most two children, then it can have at most two subtrees which are called the **left** and **right** **subtrees** of the node. Figure 14.2 shows some examples of binary trees.

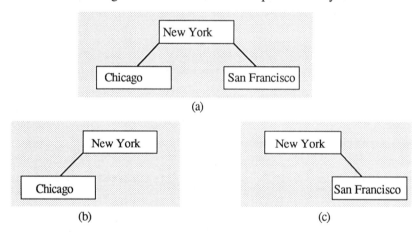

Figure 14.2 Examples of binary trees

You should note that examples (b) and (c) have different tree structure because (b) has a left subtree and no right subtree, whereas (c) has no left subtree but does have a right subtree. What the figure does not show is the predefined relationship which exists between data on adjacent levels. In fact, all the trees in Figure 14.2 are search trees and the relationship between the data on adjacent levels is that for any node:

(a) its left subtree contains only names of cities which come alphabetically *before* that in the node;
(b) its right subtree contains only names of cities which come alphabetically *after* that in the node.

We shall call trees which satisfy this relationship **binary search trees**. In the next subsection we shall look at the specification of the abstract data type binary search tree, but we first look at the operations by describing them using diagrams. We shall restrict the number of operations defining a binary search tree to a few. The operations of *create* and *isempty* will be required as will some way of building up a tree. We shall need to define an operation of insert for this purpose. Unlike the other abstract data types we have considered we shall not have an operation which allows deletions to be made. This is because we are restricting our attention to search trees and so deletion is not required. Additionally there are difficulties associated with the removal of a non-leaf node. Since the tree is to be used for searching, an operation will be required which can search the tree for a given data item and report whether or not it is there. For many applications these operations are sufficient, but we shall include one more in our definition and that is the operation of printing out the data items in a tree. There are many ways in which this can be done and this will be the subject of Section 14.4.

The method of how and where a new node is entered into a binary search tree can be illustrated by looking at how the city Dallas would be appended to the tree of Figure 14.2(a). There are three steps to the insertion:

(a) find where the node is to be inserted;
(b) create a new node containing the required data;
(c) insert the new node into the tree.

Step (a) is essentially a loop in which Dallas is repeatedly compared with the current node. The root node is where the loop starts. Since Dallas precedes New York, it must be placed in the left subtree of the New York node, so move down to the node in this left subtree. This takes us to the Chicago node. Dallas comes after Chicago alphabetically and so it must be placed in the right subtree of this node. Since Chicago is a leaf node the new node for Dallas must be inserted as a right subtree of the Chicago node. Figure 14.3 shows the resulting tree after the creation and insertion of this new node.

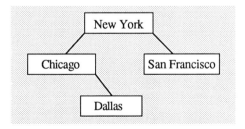

Figure 14.3 Appending a new node

Exercise 14.1 Add Atlanta, Boston and Baltimore, in that order, to the tree in Figure 14.3. Draw the tree when they are inserted in the order Baltimore, Atlanta, Boston.

If a data item to be inserted already exists in the tree then this is to be reported and no further action should be taken. Previous experience would suggest that particular care is taken to ensure that the design for insert works for the insertion of the first item into an empty tree.

Searching a tree to find a particular data item is similar to inserting a new item. Starting at the root node, the data which each node contains is compared with the sought item. If the sought item precedes the node item, then the subtree to the left of the current node is examined. If it comes after the node item, then the right subtree is examined. This continues until either the item is found or a leaf node is reached, that is, a node which has neither left nor right subtrees. In this case the item is not in the tree.

14.2 SPECIFYING A BINARY SEARCH TREE

In this section a binary tree *stringtype* will be specified and designed. The data items to be held in the tree will be strings and the operations which it uses are *create*, *isempty*, *insert* and *isthere*. The operations are specified below.

create

{Return a new empty binary search tree for data items of type string.}		
tree	A new tree of string items	*stringtree* parameter

isempty

tree	Representation of a tree	*stringtree* parameter
{Return the value true if the tree is empty, false otherwise.}		
isempty		boolean function value

insert

tree	Representation of a tree	*stringtree* parameter
item	Item to be inserted into tree	string parameter
{If *item* is in *tree* then write out 'Duplicate entry'. Otherwise insert *item* in *tree* at a leaf in the way described above.}		
tree	Updated string tree	*stringtree* parameter

isthere

tree	Representation of a tree	*stringtree* parameter
item	Item to be sought	string parameter
{If *item* is in *tree* then return true otherwise return false.}		
isthere		boolean function value

print

tree	Representation of a tree	*stringtree* parameter
{Write out the contents of a tree. (This will be discussed in Section 14.4.)}		

Records will be used to represent the nodes of the tree. They will have three different fields – a field containing a pointer to the left subtree, a field for the data item and a field for a pointer to the right subtree. Figure 14.4 illustrates the use of these records to represent the tree of Figure 14.2(a).

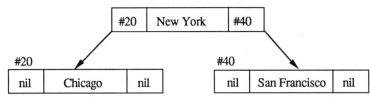

Figure 14.4 Tree representation using records

A variable *tree* will then be a pointer to this sequence of records and may be represented as in Figure 14.5.

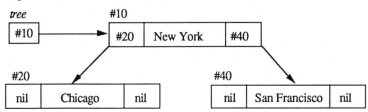

Figure 14.5 A diagram representing *tree*.

An empty tree is then represented by *tree* having the value nil. These diagrams also enable us to see how *insert* will need to be designed. To insert Detroit the node to which it is to be attached must first be found. This search would start at *tree* and so would inspect the data field of *tree*^. Since Detroit precedes New York the left subtree of this node must be searched, that is, the subtree whose address is given in the left link field (#20). The data field of this node, Chicago, is compared with Detroit, from which it can be deduced that the right subtree must be searched. But the right link field of the Chicago record has value nil indicating that there is no right subtree of this node. The search is therefore complete and the new record should be inserted as a right subtree of the Chicago record.

14.3 DESIGNING THE ABSTRACT DATA TYPE TREE

As before, the data type will be designed as a module whose data table follows:

Identifier	Description	Type
	PUBLIC	
stringtree	Type definition representing a tree	private
create	(*tree*)	procedure(*stringtree*)
isempty	(*tree*)	boolean function(*stringtree*)
insert	(*tree, item*)	procedure(*stringtree, string*)
isthere	(*tree, item*)	procedure(*stringtree, string*)
print	(*tree*)	procedure(*stringtree*)
	PRIVATE	
stringtree	Type definition	pointer to *treerecord*
treerecord	Record type definition	
	left {Left subtree pointer}	*stringtree* variable
	data {Data item}	string variable
	right {Right subtree pointer}	*stringtree* variable
	recordend	

We shall begin by looking at the design of *insert*. This will involve the same sorts of problems encountered in the design of the insert routine for general sequences. In particular the tree will have to be searched, but for trees there is nothing analogous to the dummy item of a general sequence. In Chapter 13, the searches of the sequence were developed as separate routines. As a contrast we shall not do so here but the Problem Section will give you an opportunity of doing this.

The same sort of difficulty arises in searching a tree as searching a sequence. We need to determine the last node which precedes the insertion point. The example above shows that if we use a variable to hold the address of the record currently being examined, its value at the end of the search will be nil. What we also need is the address of the record containing this nil pointer. In other words, two variables will be needed during searching, one of which lags one record behind the other. This should be a familiar technique from Chapter 13 where the two pointers were referred to as *lead* and *lag*. The following is a top level design for *insert*:

insert

tree, item

   1   create new node containing *item*
   2   if *tree* is empty then
   3   insert new node into *tree* as the root node
   4   else
   5   find where node is to be inserted
   6   if *item* is not already in *tree* then
   7   insert new node into *tree*
   8   else
   9   write out 'Duplicate entry'
 10   ifend
 11 ifend

tree

You may be wondering why the empty tree is treated as a special case by the statement at step 2. The reason is to be found in step 7. Using the insertion of Detroit into Figure 14.5 as an example, the search will result in *lag* having value #20. But this value does not tell us whether Detroit goes in the left or right subtree of Chicago. To find out, the data field of *lag* has to be referenced and compared with Chicago. But when the tree is empty, *lag* will have value nil and attempting to reference a field of the nil pointer is an error.

In the following refinement and data table the function *isempty* is assumed to be available:

insert		
tree, item		
1.1	*new(temp)*	
1.2	*temp^.left* := nil	
1.3	*temp^.right* := nil	
1.4	*temp^.data* := *item*	
2.1	if *isempty(tree)* then	
3.1	*tree* := *temp*	
4	else	
5.1	*exists* := false	
5.2	*lead* := *tree*	
5.3	*lag* := nil	
5.4	loop while *lead* <> nil and (not *exists*)	
5.5	*lag* := *lead*	
5.6	if *item* < *lead^.data* then	
5.7	*lead* := *lead^.left*	{go to left subtree}
5.8	else	
5.9	if *item* > *lead^.data* then	
5.10	*lead* := *lead^.right*	{go to right subtree}
5.11	else	
5.12	*exists* := true	{*item* is in tree already so search ends}
5.13	ifend	
5.14	ifend	
5.15	loopend	
6.1	if not *exists* then	
7.1	if *item* < *lag^.data* then	
7.2	*lag^.left* := *temp*	{insert as left subtree}
7.3	else	
7.4	*lag^.right* := *temp*	{insert as right subtree}
7.5	ifend	
8	else	
9	write out 'Duplicate entry'	
10	ifend	
11	ifend	
tree		

Identifier	Description	Type
lead	Pointer to current node	*stringtree* variable
lag	Pointer to previous node	*stringtree* variable
temp	Pointer to new node	*stringtree* variable
exists	Flag denoting duplicate entry	boolean variable

Exercise 14.2 Write designs for each of the routines *create*, *isempty* and *isthere*.

14.4 PRINTING BINARY TREES

The operation which we have, as yet, not specified or designed is that of printing out the data in all the nodes of a tree. To do so we must choose a **path** through the nodes. A path which visits each node just once is called a **tree traversal**. For a given tree there are many different tree traversals but we shall consider three different traversals called *inorder*, *preorder* and *postorder* traversals. In this section we shall explain what these terms mean and give examples of where they could be used. Designing procedures to carry out tree traversals turns out to be quite difficult and so it will be left until Chapter 15.

A traversal can be pictured as a walk around the tree, passing each node as the walk progresses. In Figure 14.6 the curved line represents such a walk.

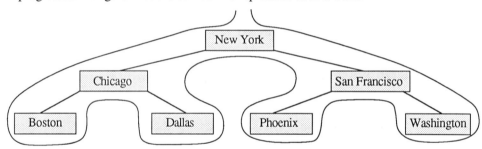

Figure 14.6 A tree traversal

We can see from this traversal that each leaf is visited once but that each non-leaf node is visited three times. An inorder traversal means that the data is written out when the walker passes *under* a node. The numbers in Figure 14.7 identify the order in which the data values are written out for an inorder traversal.

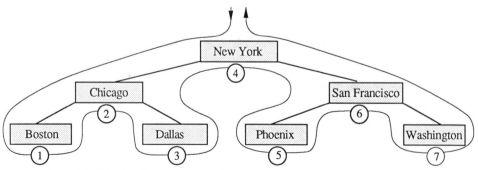

Figure 14.7 An inorder tree traversal

This shows that the cities are output in the order Boston, Chicago, Dallas, New York, Phoenix, San Francisco and Washington, that is, in alphabetical order. The reason for this is that the walk visits everything in the left subtree of a node, then the node itself and finally its right subtree. We shall return to this description in Chapter 15. We can see from this example why a binary tree is such a useful device for searching. Names can be inserted into the tree in a random order and an inorder traversal will output the data in alphabetical order.

Examples of the use of preorder and postorder traversal are found in more general binary trees. The binary tree in Figure 14.8 is a representation of the arithmetic expression

$$(2 + 3) - (4*5)$$

This diagram appears not to satisfy the condition that a tree must have nodes of the same predefined type. This is so, but in real expressions each node would be an identifier representing, in this case, either an arithmetic operator or an integer. It is easier to see what is going on if this complication is avoided, so we shall allow the nodes in the figure. Examine it before reading the commentary below.

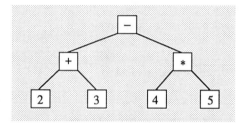

Figure 14.8 A tree representation of $(2 + 3) - (4*5)$

This tree, called an **expression tree**, enables the expression to be evaluated. We see that every non-leaf node has exactly two branches. To evaluate the expression leaf nodes having a common parent are combined and replaced by the value represented by the subtree. Figure 14.9 shows how the expression in Figure 14.8 would be evaluated.

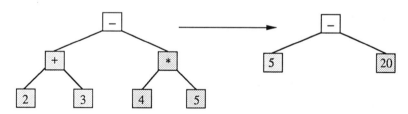

Figure 14.9 The evaluation of $(2 + 3) - (4*5)$

Here we can see that each of the lower subtrees have been evaluated and the result has replaced the item in the appropriate nodes. To complete the evaluation the calculation $5 - 20$ would be performed. In addition to their use for evaluation, expression trees can also be used to convert algebraic expressions into reverse Polish form. We have already seen in Chapter 11 that expressions like that above are usually translated into reverse Polish form for evaluation. Figure 14.10 shows the traversal which generates the reverse Polish form for the expression represented by the tree in Figure 14.8.

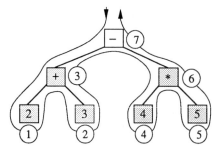

Figure 14.10 A postorder traversal

This traversal is called a postorder traversal, which means that the data is written out when the walker passes a node for the last time. Since non-leaf nodes are passed three times and leaf nodes just once, this is a fairly simple way of viewing a postorder traversal. An alternative description is to say: for a non-leaf node all its subtrees must be written out before the data it contains is output, but leaf nodes are written out as soon as they are encountered. The numbers on the diagram give the order in which the node data is output. It is

$$2\ 3 + 4\ 5 * -$$

which you may recognize as the reverse Polish expression equivalent to

$$(2 + 3) - (4 * 5)$$

You will recall that reverse Polish notation is also known as postfix notation from which this traversal gets its name.

The final traversal we shall consider is the preorder traversal. This traversal enables the prefix form of an expression to be generated. Figure 14.11 shows the order in which the nodes are processed for the preorder traversal.

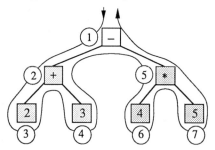

Figure 14.11 The preorder traversal

In this traversal the data in the node is written out on the first time past a node. For the tree in Figure 14.11 this would yield the **prefix expression**

$$-\ +\ 2\ 3\ *\ 4\ 5$$

in which the operators precede the operands.

In the specification of the abstract data type given in Section 14.2 the *print* procedure was not specified in detail. The three traversals we have looked at in this section could be used as a print operation specifications. We shall be considering the design of print procedures in Chapter 15.

Exercise 14.3 The expression tree of Figure 14.8 can be traversed in order to recover the infix version of the expression which it represents. The infix version will have to bracket items together. Which traversal can be modified to do this and what modifications would be required?

14.5 PROBLEMS

The problems in this section are concerned with the concordance of a piece of text. A concordance is a list of all the separate words in the text, together with the frequency with which they occur. An abstract data type *concordance* will be specified and designed as a module *concordmodule*. There are only four operations which define *concordance* and they are given below. The problems will ask you to make definitions for the type *indextype*.

create

{Return a new empty concordance.}		
concordance	A representation of a concordance	*indextype* parameter

insert

concordance	A representation of a concordance	*indextype* parameter
inword	Word to be added to concordance	string parameter
{If *inword* is in the concordance then increase its frequency count by 1 otherwise insert it into the concordance and give it a frequency of 1.}		
concordance	Updated concordance	*indextype* parameter

howmany

concordance	A representation of a concordance	*indextype* parameter
inword	Word whose frequency is required	string parameter
{Return the frequency of *inword* in the concordance. If it is not in the concordance return the value zero.}		
howmany	Frequency of *inword*	integer function value

print

concordance	A representation of a concordance	*indextype* parameter
{Write out the concordance giving the words, together with their frequency, in alphabetical order.}		

14.1   What data structures could be used to represent the concordance?

The concordance will be represented by a binary tree whose nodes, of type *nodetype*, will be records having four fields: two link fields for the left and right subtrees, one field for the word and one for its frequency. The operations *insert* and *howmany* are both required to search the concordance. A procedure *findwhere* will be developed for this purpose:

findwhere

concordance	A representation of the concordance	*indextype* parameter
inword	Word whose location is sought	string parameter
{If *inword* is in the concordance then set *exists* true and return the pointer value *location* which identifies the node containing *inword*. If *inword* is not in the concordance, set *exists* to false and return *location* with pointer value which identifies the node which would be the parent node of *inword*.}		
location	Pointer to a node	*nodetype* parameter
exists	True if *inword* is in concordance	boolean parameter

14.2 Write down the data table for the module *concordmodule* which includes the definition of the procedure *findwhere*. You will need to make suitable definitions for *indextype* and *nodetpye*.

14.3 Write a design for the procedure *findwhere*.

14.4 Write designs for each of the routines *create*, *insert* and *howmany*. The routines *insert* and *howmany* should both call *findwhere*.

14.6 SUMMARY

In this chapter we have looked at the definition and design of the abstract data type binary search tree. This was defined in terms of the operations *create*, *isempty*, *insert*, *isthere* and *print*. In order to insert a new item in a binary search tree it is necessary to compare the item to be inserted with the data item at each node. If the new item precedes the node data item then the left subtree is searched in a similar manner, otherwise the right subtree is searched.

The design of this operation required the use of two pointer variables, one which lagged one node behind the other. We looked at three ways in which the operation of *print* could be specified. They all relied on the notion of a tree traversal which can be thought of as a walk round the nodes of the tree. Three traversals were considered, the inorder, preorder and postorder traversals. Designs corresponding to these traversals will be considered in Chapter 15.

15

RECURSION

15.1 INTRODUCTION

In this chapter we shall look at a design technique called **recursion**. Broadly speaking a recursive routine is one whose design includes a call to itself. This can be a difficult concept to grasp, as it would appear that if a routine calls itself, then that call includes a further call and so on. The process would appear not to stop. In order to see how this does not happen we shall begin by using recursion to design some routines with which we are already familiar and for which we have seen non-recursive designs. There is then the problem of deciding which of the designs, the non-recursive or the recursive, is the better. We shall disuss this briefly in Section 15.4, but in order to give a gentle introduction to the subject this section will contain designs which are better done without recursion. However, in Section 15.4, we shall look at some problems which are very difficult to solve without recursion. By that stage we hope you will have mastered the techniques required and so be in a better position to appreciate the power of recursive methods.

In Chapter 11 we wrote a procedure to print out a stack. The design and data table are reproduced below.

print
_____
stack
_____

   1   *current := stack*
   2 loop while *current* <> nil
   3   write out *current^.stackitem*
   4   *current := current^.link*
   5 loopend
_____

Identifier	Description	Type
current	Current record of stack sequence	*integerstack* variable

This design processes all the items in the same way. It starts at the top of the stack and works its way down through the stack until the bottom is reached. An alternative way of looking at the printing of a stack is to think of the stack in a special way, as a top item together with the remaining items of the stack. We shall call the 'remaining items' of the stack, a substack, in order to emphasize that the items which comprise it are themselves a stack. Viewed in this way a stack of n items can be printed by first printing out the item at the top of the stack, followed by the printing of the substack consisting of the remaining $n - 1$ items. Printing the substack can again be done by printing the item at the top of the stack and then printing out the substack of $n - 2$ items. At every stage the top item is printed out and a shorter substack remains to be processed. Eventually this substack will be empty – printing it out requires no action and the task is complete. In this description printing out the substack is exactly the same process as printing out the stack! In other words we have described a method of printing which uses itself within the description. This is called **recursion**. The design below expresses the method more exactly. Read it and see if you can identify the substack and the handling of the final empty stack.

recprint

---

stack

```
1  if stack = nil then
2      do nothing
3  else
4      write out stack^.stackitem
5      recprint(stack^.link)
6  ifend
```

This design expresses the description above more succinctly. We can follow it through. A stack is passed to the procedure. If the stack is not empty then step 4 is executed and the item at the top of the stack is written out. This is immediately followed by a call to *recprint* to print out the substack given by *stack^.link*, that is the remainder of the stack. Thus *recprint* is called as part of the design of the procedure *recprint* itself, but with a stack that has one item fewer than on the original call. So eventually *recprint* will be called with an empty stack. This means *stack* will have value nil and step 2 will be executed and the process will terminate.

In order to see this in more detail we shall look at what happens when a routine is **invoked** – that is, called. In general, when a routine is invoked any existing variables must remain in the data storage area for use after the invoked routine has finished. Thus, every time a new routine is invoked a new data storage area must be set aside for the routine's local variables including any parameters it may have. (We are deliberately ignoring the precise details of how parameters are dealt with here as this is not relevant to the explanation.) We can represent this process by tracing through the design using a specific stack as an example. Figure 15.1 shows a pointer-based representation of a stack of integers, the integer data being in the first field and the links being in the second field.

As usual this diagram uses hypothetical addresses for the pointer variables. When *recprint* is called, an actual parameter, which is an address, is passed to it. The notation

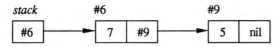

Figure 15.1 An example stack

recprint(#6) will be used to denote that *recprint* has been invoked with actual parameter #6. The series of diagrams below traces the calls to *recprint*.

recprint(#6)

1	if #6 = nil then
4	write out 7
5	*recprint*(#9)

The heading in this diagram shows that *recprint* is called with *stack* having value #6. This value results in step 1 being false and so execution continues at step 4. (We shall leave out step 3, *else*, for brevity.) This step writes out the value of *stack^.stackitem*, that is, the data field of the record at #6. Step 5 then calls *recprint* with actual parameter *stack^.link*, that is, with actual parameter #9. Another invocation of *recprint* now follows. Note that the first invocation is not yet finished because step 6 has not yet been executed. The next diagram shows how we shall deal with the second invocation:

recprint(#6)

1	if #6 = nil then
4	write out 7
5	*recprint*(#9)

    | 1 | if #9 = nil then |
    | 4 | write out 5 |
    | 5 | *recprint*(nil) |

Each invocation is surrounded by a box to emphasize its separate identity. At this stage of the processing the boxes are incomplete because none of the invocations have terminated. In this second invocation step 4 writes out the data of the record at #9 and calls *recprint*, using the link field as actual parameter. There is now a third invocation of *recprint*, this time with actual parameter nil:

recprint(#6)

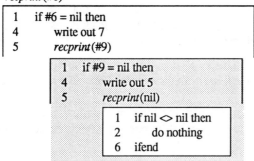

For this invocation the stack passed to the procedure is the empty stack and so execution *is* completed. This is emphasized by the box surrounding this invocation being complete. This being the case the second invocation in which the passed parameter had value #9 can now continue its execution. What remains to be done is trivial, namely the execution of step 6. However, as we shall see, this will not always be the case. The situation at this stage is:

recprint(#6)

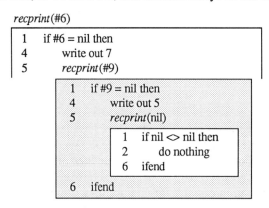

The intact box around the second invocation shows that it is now completed. All that remains is the completion of the first invocation:

recprint(#6)

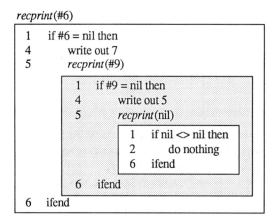

We can now stand back and see that the numbers 7 and 5, in that order, have been written out by this procedure. In other words it has printed out the stack items. This example illustrates three fundamental properties of recursive routines:

1. First there must be some stopping condition. That is, there must be some value(s) of the input for which the routine does not call itself. In the example the value corresponded to an empty stack.
2. For values of the input not covered by the stopping condition, the routine calls itself.
3. For all input values the stopping condition must be reached after a finite number of recursive calls.

This last feature is perhaps the most difficult to appreciate. We shall therefore look at it in more detail by examining a template which can be adapted to the design of most recursive routines. Of necessity it is rather vague and imprecise and the terms in which we express it are not technical ones. However, we hope that with suitable interpretation it enables you to design recursive routines.

If we examine the design of *recprint* then we can see that it works by taking an item from the stack and processing it together with the substack that remains. The substack gets smaller on each invocation and this is requirement 3 above. For any routine which you want to design recursively there is an analogy to the stack item and its substack. For convenience we shall refer in the general situation to an **article** and a **subarticle**. (The word article is used for convenience here, it is not a technical term.) We can think of a *subarticle* as being the *article* with one or more items removed from it. We shall refer to the item which is removed from the article as an **entity**. This enables us to write a template for a general recursive routine. Read through the template design below and then the commentary which follows.

recurse

article
1 if the *article* is trivial then
2   process it
3 else
4   identify the *entity* and *subarticle*
5   *recurse(subarticle)*
6   process *entity*
7 ifend
results   {details depend upon purpose of the routine}

In step 1 the word *trivial* is used to convey the meaning that the stopping condition has been reached and the article can be directly processed. That this is reached after a finite number of steps is conveyed by the notion of article and subarticle. Step 4 may not appear explicitly as a separate step but it must be there implicitly. It was not evident in *recprint* but it did appear implicitly in step 4 where the stack item was written out. Again identifying the subarticle was not a separate step in *recprint* but it did appear within the recursive call statement itself. A further difficulty with this general design template is that processing the *entity* at step 6 may have to precede the recursive call with the subarticle. When you come to design your own recursive routines it will be apparent what order is required.

We shall now demonstrate the use of this template to write a recursive procedure which reverses the characters in a string. The procedure specification is:

reverse

given	A non-empty string	string parameter
{Write out the characters of *given* in reverse order, that is, starting with the last and finishing with the first. The string *given* may be assumed to have at least one character.}		

The first task is to identify the roles of *entity*, *article* and *subarticle* in the template design. Clearly the source data *given* will be the *article*, but what are *entity* and *subarticle* here? The subarticle will in some sense have to 'get smaller' because it will eventually provide the stopping condition. If we think of how to write out a reversed string, one way is to write out the last letter, which then leaves all characters but the last to be reversed. So the *entity* would appear to be the last letter and the *subarticle* all the characters which precede it.

Exercise 15.1 What condition is equivalent to the template condition *the article is trivial*?

A top level design and refinement for *reverse* can then be written as:

reverse

---
given

---
  1 if *length(given)* = 1 then
  2   write *given*[1]
  3 else
  4   write last character of *given*
  5   reverse all but the last character of *given*
  6 ifend

---
reverse

---
given

---
  1   if *length(given)* = 1 then
  2   write *given*[1]
  3   else
  4.1   write *given*[*length(given)*]
  5.1   *reverse(copy(given, 1, length(given) − 1))*
  6   ifend

Figure 15.2 illustrates calls to *reverse* assuming that *given* has value 'bat':

reverse ('bat')

1	if 3 = 1 then
4.1	write 't'
5.1	*given* = 'ba'
5.2	*reverse* ('ba')

1	if 2 = 1 then
4.1	write 'b'
5.1	*given* = 'a'
5.2	*reverse* ('a')

1	if 1 = 1 then
2	write 'a'
6	ifend

    6   ifend

6   ifend

Figure 15.2 Invocations of *reverse* with actual parameter 'bat'

Exercise 15.2 An alternative design for *reverse* would be to remove the first character, reverse the remaining characters and then write out the removed character as in the following design.

reverse

---

given

```
1   if length(given) = 1 then
2       write given[1]
3   else
4       remove first character from given
5       reverse what is left of given
6       write first character
7   ifend
```

Refine this design and trace it through using source data 'bat' in a similar way to that shown above.

A more complicated example arises if we try to write a recursive function to test whether a given string is palindromic. You will recall that a string is palindromic if it reads the same backwards as forwards, for example the word madam. The specification below gives the details of what is required.

palindrome

given	A string	string parameter
{If *given* is palindromic then write out 'palindrome' else write out 'not a palindrome'. The source data is assumed to be a non-empty string.}		

The first task is to identify the roles for *entity*, *article* and *subarticle*. The *article* will be the given input string. To determine whether a string is palindromic its first and last characters must be compared, then the second and penultimate characters, and so on. So *entity* would need to be the first and last characters and the *subarticle* is the string with these characters removed.

Exercise 15.3 Describe the condition that the *article* is *trivial* for this procedure.

One point that ought to be borne in mind is that as soon as two end characters are found to differ there is no point examining the others because the word cannot be palindromic. The design below caters for this:

palindrome

---

given

---

 1   if (*length(given)* = 0) or (*length(given)* = 1) then
 2   write out 'palindrome'
 3   else
 4   if *given*[1] = *given*[*length(given)*] then
 5   *delete(given, 1, 1)*
 6   *delete(given, length(given), 1)*
 7   *palindrome(given)*
 8   else
 9   write out 'not a palindrome'
10   ifend
11   ifend

Exercise 15.4 Draw a diagram similar to Figure 15.2 showing the invocations of *palindrome* with actual parameter 'madam' and then with actual parameter 'reader'.

Although it would not be too difficult to write a non-recursive design for this procedure, the recursive design is very clear. It can even be described quite clearly: if the first and last characters are the same, then call *palindrome* with the string obtained by removing the first and last characters.

We shall now consider a problem where a non-recursive design is considerably more difficult than a recursive one. In Problem 11.7 we considered the task of designing a procedure, *revprint,* which writes out an integer stack in reverse order, that is starting at the bottom item and finishing at the top. The non-recursive solution was based on the following design:

 1   count the number of items in the stack
 2   loop for $i := count$ downto 1
 3   move down to ith entry
 4   write out data
 5   loopend

An alternative approach is to use two pointers in a lead and lag role so that when the bottom item is found, lag points to its predecessor. The value of lag would then determine the stopping position for lead on the next pass through the stack and so on. Neither approach is particularly obvious. Let us compare a recursive design. In terms of the recursive template, the stack is the *article.* But what takes the role of the *entity*? Printing the stack in reverse means that the top of the stack is printed last. Hence the rest of the stack is printed in reverse followed by the item at the top of the stack. Hence the top of the stack takes the role of *entity.* This implies that the *subarticle* is just the stack with the first item removed. A strategy for the design is then to *revprint*(the stack with top item removed) and then write out the first item. This leads to the following design:

revprint

---

stack

```
1  if stack = nil then
2      do nothing
3  else
4      revprint(stack^.link)
5      write out stack^.item
6  ifend
```

Exercise 15.5 Draw a diagram similar to Figure 15.2 showing the invocations of *revprint* with the stack of Figure 15.1. Use the hypothetical addresses in that diagram as actual parameters for each call.

15.2 RECURSIVE DESIGNS FOR TREE OPERATIONS

In this section we shall design procedures for printing out a tree using tree traversals introduced in Chapter 14. We shall also look at alternative recursive designs for the tree operations. We begin by completing the design of the abstract data type *stringtree* for which we have not yet designed the operation *print*. An inorder traversal will be used to print out the data in the nodes of a tree as described in the following specification:

print

tree	Representation of a tree	*stringtree* parameter
{Write out the data field of the nodes of *tree* using an inorder traversal}		

In Chapter 14 the inorder traversal was described as a walk which visits everything in the left subtree of a node, then the node itself and finally its right subtree. We have reproduced Figure 14.6 in order to illustrate the operation of *print*.

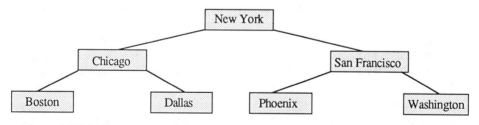

Figure 15.3 A city name search tree

To print the data in Figure 15.3 using an inorder traversal:

•   print the data in the left subtree of New York

- print the data in the root node itself, i.e. New York
- print the data in the right subtree of New York

To accomplish the first of these tasks we note that the left subtree of New York is the tree whose root node is Chicago. The same technique is therefore applied to this tree:

- print the tree in the left subtree of Chicago
- print the data in the root node itself, i.e. Chicago
- print the data in the right subtree of Chicago

What we are using here is a recursive description of the task. It gives a clue as to what should be the roles *article*, *entity* and *subarticle* in a recursive design and what condition corresponds to the *article* being trivial. The current node takes the *entity* role but what plays the role of the *subarticle*? In this instance there are two subarticles – the left and right subtrees pointed to by the parameter *tree*. The *subarticle* being trivial corresponds to the tree being empty, that is, to *tree* having value nil. This leads to the following design for *print*:

print

tree

1	if *tree* = nil then
2	do nothing
3	else
4	*print(tree^.left)*
5	write out *tree^.data*
6	*print(tree^.right)*
7	ifend

Exercise 15.6 Draw a diagram similar to Figure 15.2 showing the invocations of *print* with the tree of Figure 14.5. Use the hypothetical addresses in that diagram as actual parameters for each call.

This design shows the power of recursive techniques. Designing an inorder print routine without using recursion is very complex. This is because the design would start off by going down the leftmost subtree until it reached a leaf. The data in the leaf would then be written out. The next step would be to move up to the leaf's parent node and look at its right subtree. The leftmost leaf of this subtree would then be found, after which its parent's right subtree would be traversed. We can see from this that after each data item is printed the design has to go to the leaf's parent node. The location of the parent node must therefore be stored on the way down through the tree. But every node, except the leaf nodes, is a parent of some other subtree! Compare this description with the recursive design above. The recursive design is simple by comparison.

The tree operation *insert* can also be designed recursively. We must first decide the roles for each of *article*, *entity* and *subarticle* and what corresponds to the notion of the *article* being trivial. The general process will be to compare the new data with the data in the current node. If the new data precedes the data in the current node then it is inserted in the left subtree and if it comes after it then it is inserted in the right subtree. If neither holds then the new data is a duplicate entry. This suggests that *entity* should be the current node and that *subarticle* should be the appropriate subtree (left or right) of the current node. The *article* being trivial corresponds to the tree being empty, that is, *tree* having value nil. When this is the case the new data is attached at this subtree. This leads to the following design and data table:

insert

tree, item	
1	if isempty(tree) then
2.1	*new(temp)*
2.2	*temp^.left* := nil
2.3	*temp^.right* := nil
2.4	*temp^.data* := *item*
2.5	*tree* := *temp*
4	else
5.1	if *item* < *tree^.data* then
5.2	*insert(tree^.left, item)*
5.3	else
5.4	if *item* > *tree^.data* then
5.5	*insert(tree^.right, item)*
5.6	else
5.7	write out 'Duplicate entry'
5.8	ifend
5.9	ifend
7	ifend

tree

Identifier	Description	Type
temp	Pointer to current node	*stringtree* variable

Exercise 15.7 Draw a diagram similar to Figure 15.2 showing the invocations of *insert* when Chicago is inserted into the tree of Figure 14.4. Use the hypothetical addresses in that figure in your procedure calls.

15.3 PROBLEMS

In order to test your designs in this problem section we suggest that you draw diagrams similar to Figure 15.2 using suitable test data values.

15.1 Write a recursive procedure, *binary*, specified below:

binary

number	An integer	integer parameter
{Write out the binary equivalent of the integer.}		

15.2 Hexadecimal numbers are numbers to the base 16 and are extensively used in low level and machine language programming. The digits for hexadecimal numbers are the digits 0 to 9 together with the letters A, B, C, D, E, F which correspond to the decimal numbers 10 to 12 respectively. Hexadecimals often have the letter H written after them to denote the fact that they are hexadecimal and not base 10 numbers. Hence 13H denotes the hexadecimal number 13, which is $1 \times 16 + 3$ to base 10. Similarly 3DH is $3 \times 16 + 13$ to the base 10. Write a recursive procedure, *hex*, which converts base 10 numbers to their hexadecimal equivalent. The specification of the procedure is:

hex

number	An integer to base 10	integer parameter
{Write out the hexadecimal equivalent of the integer.}		

15.3   Write a recursive routine for the tree operation *isthere* specified in Section 14.2.

15.4   Write a recursive print routine for the tree operation *print* which writes out the data using a postorder traversal.

15.5   Write a recursive print routine for the tree operation *print* which writes out the data using a preorder traversal .

15.6   An additional operation of counting the number of nodes of a binary search tree is to be added to the abstract data type *stringtree*. Write a recursive procedure for this operation which has the following specification:

countnodes

tree	Representation of a tree	*stringtree* parameter
{Count the number of nodes in tree.}		
count	Number of nodes in *tree*	integer parameter

15.7   An alternative specification for the operation of insertion into a binary tree would allow duplicate entries. The following specification allows for this:

duplicates

tree	Representation of a tree	*stringtree* parameter
item	Item to be inserted	string parameter
{Insert *item* in *tree*. The item is inserted in the left tree of a node if it strictly precedes the data in that node. Otherwise it is inserted in the right subtree.}		
tree	Updated string tree	*stringtree* parameter

15.8   In this problem you should assume that the insertion of items into a tree allows for duplicate entries as described in Problem 15.7. A new operation is to be provided which enables the number of occurrences of a particular item to be counted. Write a recursive design for the specification given below:

howmany

tree	Representation of a tree	*stringtree* parameter
item	Item to be counted	string parameter
{Count the number of occurrences of *item* in *tree*.}		
count	The number of occurrences	integer parameter

15.4 EFFICIENCY OF RECURSION

In this chapter we have seen examples of designs which are much easier to write using recursion and some for which the recursive design had little or no advantage over its non-recursive counterpart. How can we judge whether or not a recursive approach should be adopted? We shall not attempt to give firm guidelines but the usual general design principles apply. The method adopted should be the natural and logical way of solving the problem. So, for the first example we looked at, the problem of printing the contents of a stack, the natural design is to start at the top of the stack and work down it to the bottom, writing out the data on the way. Hence a non-recursive approach is the most natural. By contrast, printing out the contents of a tree proved to be very difficult using a non-recursive approach. The recursive design is very transparent and has nowhere near the same number of complications.

Another factor that might have to be taken into account is the overheads associated with recursive designs. Diagrams like Figure 15.2 give some idea of what overheads are involved. Each time a recursive routine is called, the system has to save the current values of all the variables and parameters. This occupies space and takes time. When the recursion eventually completes with the trivial stage then all the previous invocations are completed in turn. This involves re-establishing the appropriate data values and then releasing the space they occupied when the invocation is completed. In general, a non-recursive version of a routine will execute more efficiently in terms of space and time than its recursive counterpart. This is essentially due to all these housekeeping tasks undertaken by the system.

15.5 SUMMARY

In this chapter the concept of recursion has been introduced. For some designs recursion can be used but it is not necessarily the best approach. However, for some problems recursion is a natural and clear method. This is particularly so for tree operations which involve the tree being searched or traversed in some way.

16

OBJECT-ORIENTED DESIGN

16.1 INTRODUCTION

Throughout this book we have been using a top down approach to problem solving. The essential features of this approach are to analyse the problem to identify its major components and to break it up in a modular fashion. Each of the modular components can be dealt with in a similar way until a stage is reached where each of the modules can be individually designed. This is achieved by writing a top level design which is refined in a stepwise manner. The same approach enabled abstract data types to be developed, thereby extending the range of data models which could be provided as part of the design process. However, even with the introduction of abstract data types, the data and the procedures by which it is manipulated are seen as distinct. Data hiding methods attempt to ensure that an abstract data type is manipulated by only one of the permitted operations, but that is about as close a tie as the data and their operations get. In what is known as an **object-oriented design** methodology the data (and the operations which manipulate it) are thought of as being part of the same overall structure called an **object**. Just as the design methods of this book can be described by the words *modular approach*, *top down design* and *stepwise refinement*, so the key features of the object method can be described by the words **encapsulation**, **inheritance** and **virtual methods**.

Our aim in this chapter is to attempt to explain what these words mean and what advantages they bring to a design. We shall do so by looking at an illustrative example of the object method and seeing where the approach we have adopted fits into the scheme. We shall see that the top down approach is more suited to the detail of the design process, whereas an object approach gives more help in determining what to modularize. As a result of reading the chapter we hope you will become aware of the facilities offered by the object approach, but it is not intended that the detailed methods introduced will be anything other than illustrative. For this reason, major simplifications have been introduced into the example in order to reduce the burden of reading vast amounts of detail which would not enhance your understanding of the new concepts. As you read try to remember that object methods are intended for use in complex problems, even though the example itself is totally trivial. The statement of the problem is as follows:

A program is to be designed to maintain details on undergraduate students studying at a university. A rough specification is for the program to handle data about students, the amount of data stored being minimal in order to reduce the complexity of the problem. In fact, we shall store only three pieces of information – the student name, year of entry to the university and an identifier number which is unique for each student. The latter will be called the student id. The program is to be capable of handling data on up to 1500 undergraduate students. To avoid problems with files we shall assume the program runs permanently and is accessed through the following menu:

R   Read in details of a new undergraduate
W   Write out the details of a specified undergraduate
L   List details of all the undergraduates
Q   Quit

The first option is to prompt for and read in the new data which is then to be stored. The data is to be input from the keyboard and we shall make the simplifying assumption that the user is able to allocate unique student identifiers. The second option is to prompt for a student identification number and to write out the details of the student with that number or a message to say that the number is invalid. The final option will list all the student data stored. A top level design for the program would be:

```
 1   initialize variables
 2   repeat
 3       write out menu
 4       read in choice
 5       select case depending on choice
 6            'R' :  Read in new data
 7            'W' :  Write out existing data
 8            'L' :  List all undergraduates
 9       selectend
10   until choice = 'Q'
```

By now this is all very familiar, but having achieved a top level statement of what the program is to do, we now take a different view to its development.

16.2 THE OBJECT METHOD OF DESIGN

There are two stages to the object-oriented design methodology. First, we must identify the data objects and then the operations by which they will be manipulated.

16.2.1 Identify the objects

Objects have things done to them – they are operated on. So, to identify the objects we must pick out those things (objects) from the program description which are operated on and give them names (identifiers) by which they will be known. Often, the data for a real problem will occur in collections which naturally belong together. Typically, data which belong together, either conform to a similar pattern or may arise because a manual system (for example index cards) keeps certain information together. In our problem it is natural to think of the three data elements held on each student, student id, name and year, as belonging together. A collection of data elements which belong together is called a **data object**. Objects can consist of a small or large number of data elements which may be all of the same type or they may have many different types. The identifier *undergraduate* will be used to represent the three data elements student id, name and year of entry.

Another object which is operated on by the program is the collection of all undergraduate student data. This data object will be called *allundergrads* and it will be represented by an array. It will store all the existing individual *undergraduate* elements and will be indexed 0..1500, with index 0 being reserved for searching. A variable to record how many student elements are currently stored will also be required. The two data objects of this program can now be defined in a data table. Study the table opposite and then read the commentary below.

The form of these object definitions is very similar to that of a record except that the words *object* and *objectend* are used instead of *record* and *recordend*. This similarity is not coincidental and it may help to think of an object as a special kind of record. Indeed, the word *field* will be used to refer to each of the data elements and the dot notation for accessing records will also be used for objects.

There is a fundamental flaw with the declarations in that there is no attempt to hide the representation of the data elements. We know that this is an important consideration for abstract data types and this is also the case here. Shortly we shall consider the operations which will enable the data elements to be processed. The user of a data object must be constrained to use these operations and so there is again the need to hide the data in such a way that it cannot be directly manipulated. The second version of the data table for *objectmodule* does this and assumes that the objects are being designed within a module. For *undergraduate* the fields have simply been defined as private, whereas the two items which make up *allundergrads* have been combined in a record in a way that by now should be familiar.

That completes the identification and naming of the objects. The next stage is to identify the operations.

16.2.2 Identify the methods

The operations through which the data objects are manipulated are called **methods**. We shall see why there is a change of terminology shortly. To identify the methods we must pick out the actions from the program description and associate each action with the relevant data object. By concentrating on each data object in turn we can identify the methods associated with it. Some of the methods are self-evident for this problem.

For example, consider the object type *undergraduate*. There must be a *method* whereby a variable of this type can have data entered into it and a *method* whereby the object data can be written out. For the data object type *allundergrads* a method to list all the students is required. A less obvious requirement is a method which searches the entries for a particular student's details. We shall specify that the source data for this method will be a student id and its results will be a boolean variable to indicate the outcome of the search, together with the data object corresponding to the student id. Similarly, a method will be required which places a new student data object into *allundergrads*. These two examples illustrate that the methods may not

Identifier	Description	Type
undergraduate	Object type definition	
	id {Student id}	integer variable
	name {Student name}	string variable
	year {Year enrolled}	integer variable
	objectend	
allundergrads	Object type definition	
	studarray {All student data}	array[0..1500] of *undergraduate* variable
	nrstuds {Number of students}	0..1500 variable
	objectend	

Identifier	Description	Type
	PUBLIC	
undergraduate	Object type definition	
	id {Student id}	private
	name {Student name}	private
	year {Year enrolled}	private
	objectend	
allundergrads	Object type definition	
	allitems {All student data}	private
	objectend	
	PRIVATE	
id	Student id	integer variable
name	Student name	string variable
year	Year enrolled	integer variable
allitems	Record type definition	
	studarray	array[0..1500] of *undergraduate* variable
	nrstuds	0..1500 variable
	recordend	

be immediately recognizable from the program description, but one which ought to be familiar by now is that of initialization. New objects of type *undergraduate* will be initialized by having data read in from the keyboard and an object of type *allundergrads* will be initialized by having *nrstuds* set to zero. The table below summarizes the methods we have identified:

Object type	Method identifier	Method
undergraduate	*readin*	read in new *undergraduate* object
	writeout	write out *undergraduate* object
allundergrads	*init*	initialize
	place	place a new *undergraduate* object in stored data
	retrieve	retrieve an *undergraduate* object
	list	list all the *undergraduate* objects stored

Detailed specifications of these methods will not be given as we hope their purpose is clear from the descriptions above. The definitions of the object types *undergraduate* and *allundergrads* can now be completed. To do so the methods are incorporated into the object definitions. The final data table for *objectmodule* contains the details but to save space the private definitions have been omitted:

Identifier	Description	Type
	PUBLIC	
undergraduate	Object type definition	
	id {Student id}	private
	name {Student name}	private
	year {Year enrolled}	private
	procedure *readin*	
	procedure *writeout*	
	objectend	
allitems	Type definition	private
allundergrads	Object type definition	
	studdata {All student data}	*allitems*
	procedure *init*	
	procedure *place*(*given*)	(*undergraduate*)
	procedure retrieve(*inid, student, found*)	(integer, *undergraduate*, boolean)
	procedure *list*	
	objectend	

Notice how this definition **encapsulates** the data object with its methods. This is a major departure from what has gone before, because here the data and the operations by which it is manipulated are bound together. This encapsulation enables the programmer to think of data and the way it is to be manipulated as being inseparable. So, the data can only be manipulated by the methods contained in the object's definition and the method of one object cannot be applied to a totally different object. (The latter needs some qualification hence the phrase *totally different* which will be explained shortly.) The two components, data and methods, are collectively known as an **object type**. Variables which are declared to be of object type are said to be **objects**. One thing that may have struck you as curious in these definitions is that only *place* and *retrieve* have parameters. This is because the methods operate on the whole of their object data and a variable, once defined, *carries around* with it the methods by which it is manipulated. In other words, the data object is global data for each of the methods. Compare this with the abstract data type situation where the operations and variables have their own separate identity and to apply an operation requires the variable to be passed to it as a parameter.

16.3 DESIGNING AND USING THE METHODS

Each method in the data table above can be designed as a procedure using the top down methodology. By way of illustration the designs opposite are for the methods *readin* and *writeout*. There is nothing new in the process part but the procedure headings are different.

The procedure identifier uses the dot notation and consists of the identifier of the object type followed by that of the method. A data object can also be referenced using the dot notation, so that *undergraduate.id* would refer to the student id field. However, within the process part of the design there is no need to precede each data field by the object identifier –

undergraduate.readin		*undergraduate.writeout*	
1	write 'Enter personal identifier '	1	write out 'Personal identifier ', *id*
2	read in *id*	2	write out 'Student name ', *name*
3	write 'Enter student name '	3	write out 'Year enrolled ', *year*
4	read in *name*		
5	write 'Enter year enrolled in university '		
6	read in *year*		

it is as if the outer dotting reference is a *with* statement which applies throughout the process part of the design. The designs for the two *allundergrads* methods, *place* and *init,* are straightforward and they are given below. Note how a parameter of type *undergraduate* is passed to the procedure *allundergrads.place.*

allundergrads.place		*allundergrads.init*	
given {of type *undergraduate*}			
1	with *allitems* do	1	*allitems.nrstuds* := 0
2	increment *nrstuds*		
3	*studarray*[*nrstuds*] := *given*		
4	withend		

The method *retrieve* involves a search. The item sought is the array element having *inid* in its student id field *id*. Remember the array elements are objects of type *undergraduate* and so their fields are accessed using the usual dot notation. In the design below, index 0 is used for the search item and the *with* statement at step 1 results from hiding the representation of the method of storing all student data.

allundergrads.retrieve	
inid	
1	with *studdata* do
2	*i* := *nrstuds*
3	*studarray*[0]*.id* := *inid*
4	loop while *studarray*[*i*] <> *inid*
5	decrement *i*
6	loopend
7	if *i* <> 0 then
8	*student* := *studarray*[*i*]
9	*found* := true
9	else
10	*found* := false
11	ifend
12	withend
student, found	

The design of *list* is somewhat more subtle although its basic structure is simple.

```
1   with studdata do
2       loop for i := 1 to nrstuds
3           write out current array element
4       loopend
5   withend
```

How can step 3 be refined? The object type *allundergrads* does not have any writing out methods associated with it and so we would seem to be stuck. But an array element is an object of type *undergraduate* and we have already stated that an object carries around with it the methods associated with its type and one of these methods is *writeout*. In other words, the array elements *know how to write themselves out* – all that is required is a call to the method *writeout*. Referencing an object method uses exactly the same notation as referencing one of its data fields – the dot notation. The final design below gives the details:

allundergrads.list

```
1     with studdata do
2         loop for i := 1 to nrstuds
3.1           studarray[i].writeout
4         loopend
5     withend
```

To see how a user would use the methods we have just designed, we will refine the student program shown on page 245. We need only be concerned with steps 6–8. An object of type *allundergrads* will be required for the stored data and one of *undergraduate* type will be required for an individual student. The identifiers *allstudents* and *onestudent* will be used for them respectively. Step 6 will require that *onestudent* call *readin* so that values can be read in to its fields. This data will then have to be stored in *allstudents* by means of the method *place*. In step 7 the user is to be prompted for a student id, then the array will need to be searched using *retrieve* and finally the data, if it is found, will need to be written out. Step 8 is simply a call to *list*. The refinements and data table are shown below:

```
6.1   'R' : onestudent.readin
6.2         allstudents.place(onestudent)
7.1   'W' : write 'Enter a student identifier '
7.2         read in inid
7.3         allstudents.retrieve(inid, onestudent, found)
7.4         if found then
7.5             onestudent.writeout
7.6         else
7.7             write out 'No student with that identifier'
7.8         ifend
8.1   'L' : allstudents.list
```

Identifier	Description	Type
onestudent	Representation of *undergraduate* object	variable of type *undergraduate* from module *objectmodule*
allstudents	Representation of *allundergrads* object	variable of type *allundergrads* from module *objectmodule*
inid	A student identifier	integer variable
found	True for successful search	boolean variable

In step 6.1 the object *onestudent* is initialized by the call to the method *readin*. This is followed by the object *allstudents* calling the method *place* with *onestudent* as an actual parameter. In step 7.3 the object *allstudents* calls its method *retrieve* with actual parameters *inid, onestudent* and *found*. If the search is successful the object *onestudent* holds the relevant data and it calls its *writeout* method.

16.4 EXTENDING OBJECTS AND INHERITANCE

Section 16.3 gave a brief explanation of the term encapsulation as it applies to object-oriented design. In this and the next section we want to illustrate the meaning of inheritance and virtual methods. In both sections we shall only use the object type *undergraduate* defined above. Suppose it is now decided to include graduates in the program and that the type of degree a graduate obtained is to be included in a graduate record. The data for a graduate can be thought of as consisting of undergraduate data together with an additional item *degree*. In other words a graduate is a subcategory of an undergraduate. In object terminology, a graduate is called a **descendant** of an undergraduate. Conversely, an undergraduate is an **ancestor** of a graduate. The terminology here is borrowed from *taxonomy* and is used as a method of classification. An important point to remember is that once an object has a defined characteristic, then all descendants of that object also have that characteristic. In our example, where we have defined a graduate to be a descendant of an undergraduate, all the characteristics of an undergraduate are **inherited** by the graduate. So a *graduate* inherits all the data objects of an *undergraduate*; in other words, it inherits the data fields *id*, *name* and *year*. It has one data object which is not inherited, namely the *degree* data object. None of this is too surprising and may appear to be a rather long-winded description of the way a graduate was defined in the first place. However, a descendant not only inherits the data objects, it also inherits the methods from its ancestor. This turns out to be a very powerful facility. The data table below defines the descendant object *graduate* in which *degree* is assumed to be a string field. (The private part is omitted.)

Note how the type column in the definition of *graduate* includes a reference to *undergraduate* to indicate the descendant relationship. Now suppose *agraduate* is an object of type *graduate*, that has been initialized (we shall see how shortly). Then it would be quite legal to write

agraduate.writeout

At first sight this might be surprising because the object *graduate* does not contain an explicit reference to *writeout*. The reason it is legal is because the method is inherited. The effect of

Identifier	Description	Type
	PUBLIC	
undergraduate	Object type definition	
	id {Identifier}	private
	name {Student name}	private
	year {Year enrolled}	private
	procedure *readin*	
	procedure *writeout*	
	objectend	
graduate	Object type definition	inherit *undergraduate* type
	degree {All student data}	private
	objectend	

the statement would be to write out the data fields *id*, *name* and *year* of the object *agraduate*. Note that it does not write out the *degree* field because *writeout* only *knows about* the fields defined in *undergraduate*.

The question of how a *graduate* object gets initialized must now be answered. The method *readin* is inherited and so can be referenced, even though it is not explicitly referred to in the definition of *graduate*. Hence the following statement is certainly legal.

agraduate.readin

This would have the effect of reading data into the fields *id*, *name* and *year* but that of course would leave *degree* unitialized. There are two ways of overcoming this problem. A totally new procedure called say *readgraduate*, could be defined as a method in *graduate*. This would be designed to read in values for all four fields. However, the process of reading in graduate details is essentially the same as for undergraduate details so why should it be called by a new name and why can it not exploit the inherited method? The answer is that it should and it can. What is done is to **overwrite** *readin* in the definition of *graduate* so that all the fields are read in. To do so requires that *readin* be included explicitly as a method within the definition of *graduate*. The data table below does this:

Identifier	Description	Type
	PUBLIC	
undergraduate	Object type definition	
	id {Identifier}	private
	name {Student name}	private
	year {Year enrolled}	private
	procedure *readin*	
	procedure *writeout*	
	objectend	
graduate	Object type definition	*undergraduate* type
	degree {All student data}	private
	procedure *readin*	
	objectend	

This new method now needs designing. Study the designs below before reading on.

graduate.readin

1	write 'Enter personal identifier '
2	read in *id*
3	write 'Enter student name '
4	read in *name*
5	write 'Enter year enrolled in university '
6	read in *year*
7	write 'Enter the degree '
8	read in *degree*

graduate.readin

1	*undergraduate.readin*
2	write 'Enter the degree '
3	read in *degree*

The two designs are equivalent but the second one exploits the inherited method *readin* from *undergraduate*. The call at step 1 requires the prefix *undergraduate* because without it the call would be interpreted as being to *graduate.readin* and, as we have already stated, within a design field references are taken to be prefixed by the first part of the procedure identifier. (Leaving off the prefix in step 1 would in fact result in a recursive call to the version of *readin* defined in *graduate* and clearly would be an error.) Despite this minor complication over prefixes this shorter method is to be preferred. We shall see why shortly.

To see where we have got to, suppose *astudent* and *agraduate* are objects of types *undergraduate* and *graduate* respectively. Consider the following statements:

astudent.readin
agraduate.readin
astudent.writeout
agraduate.writeout

The first statement concerns an *undergraduate* object and so the version of *readin* is that defined in *undergraduate*. This will have the effect of reading in the three fields *id*, *name* and *year* into *astudent*. In the second statement *readin* is a method defined in *graduate* and so data for the four fields *id*, *name*, *year* and *degree* will be read into *agraduate*. The third statement writes out the three fields of *astudent*. For the final statement we see that there is no method of this name in the definition of *graduate* and so this is an inherited method. Its effect is to write out the *id*, *name* and *year* fields of the graduate data.

To see why the three-step design of *graduate.readin* is to be preferred over the other version we shall suppose that the object type *undergraduate* has been provided for us in a compiled module, *studentmodule*, to which we do not have access. The only information about *studentmodule* which is made available to us is the non-private declarations – that is we know only of the existence of *readin* and *writeout* but we do not know how the information on student id, name and year is stored. Despite this we can still extend the definition of *undergraduate* in our main program to include the descendant *graduate*. The data table below shows what needs to be declared.

The descendant type is declared together with the overwriting definition for *writeout* whose design we need to provide. Since the details of the representation of the three data fields *id*, *name* and *year* is hidden from us the eight-step design for *graduate.readin* is not an option. However, *undergraduate.readin* is inherited, is available and so the three-step design can be exploited.

Identifier	Description	Type

graduate	Object type definition
	
	    degree {All student data}
	    procedure *readin*
	    objectend
		inherit *undergraduate* type from module *studentmodule*
		string variable

This final example shows how objects can be extended to descendants, even though their ancestors may be contained in a module to which the user does not have access.

16.5 VIRTUAL METHODS

The last part of the previous section showed how we could overwrite the definition of the *undergraduate* method *readin* to a descendant, despite the fact that we did not have access to the code defining *undergraduate*. Effectively what we were able to do was to extend the definition of *writeout* to include the new field. However, suppose the need arose for a graduate method which would write out just the student id, name and degree fields. If the same assumptions about the existence of *studentmodule* apply here, could this be achieved? The answer is no. The object type *graduate* inherits *writeout*; all it can do is to extend *writeout*. What is required here is to restrict *writeout* so that it outputs only the *id* and *name* fields. The design of the module *studentmodule* has not given the user the flexibility required to achieve this. What we shall do is to see how the module can be modified so this flexibility is provided.

We begin by redesigning the module *studentmodule* in a way that looks promising but which in fact will not give us what we want. In the discussion below, the method *writeout* is amended so that it performs only the task of writing out the *id* and *name* fields. A new method called *extra* is introduced which write out the *year* field. The definitions are as follows:

Identifier	Description	Type

undergraduate	PUBLIC
	Object type definition
	    id {Student id}
	    name {Student name}
	    year {Year enrolled}
	    procedure *readin*
	    procedure *writeout*
	    procedure *extra*
	    objectend
		
		private
		private
		private

The methods *writeout* and *extra* are designed as follows:

undergraduate.extra

---

  1 write out 'Year ', *year*

---

undergraduate.writeout

```
1   write out 'Identifier ', id
2   write out 'Name ', name
3   extra
```

We shall suppose that these new designs are part of the compiled module *studentmodule*. Does this now enable us to write the main program using the descendant *graduate* with the required output method? This time things look more promising because the inherited module *writeout* only writes out the two fields *id* and *name* and then calls the method *extra*. If we can overwrite the inherited call to *extra* by a method *extra* declared in *graduate* we shall be home and dry. The data table and design below are an attempt to do this:

Identifier	Description	Type

graduate	Object type definition
	
	    degree {All student data}
	    procedure *readin*
	    procedure *extra*
	  objectend
		inherit *undergraduate* type from module *studentmodule*
		
		private

graduate.extra

```
1   write out 'Degree is ', degree
```

graduate.readin

```
1   undergraduate.readin
2   write 'Enter the degree '
3   read in degree
```

Now if *agraduate* is an object of type *graduate* which has been initialized, what would be the effect of the statement *agraduate.writeout*? The object *agraduate* inherits *writeout* from its ancestor and so it inherits the design:

```
1   write out 'Identifier ', id
2   write out 'Name ', name
3   extra
```

This design writes out the identifier and name fields and then calls the method *extra*. But which version of *extra* is it? Is it that associated with *undergraduate* or *graduate*? The design is the body of the procedure *undergraduate.extra* and so unfortunately this reference is to *undergraduate* and not to *graduate* as we had hoped. What we want to happen is for this reference to *extra* to be taken to mean the one defined in *graduate* and not the compiled version associated with *undergraduate*. The facility that is provided that enables this reference to be taken as a reference to the *graduate extra* is called **virtual methods**. The effect of specifying *extra* to be a virtual method is that the version of *extra* declared in *graduate* is used in the invocation at step 3 rather than the one inherited from *undergraduate*. Effectively, this means we have been able to modify a method that appears in an already compiled piece of code! The data tables below for *studentmodule* and for the main program show how the methods called *extra* are declared to be virtual.

Identifier	Description	Type

undergraduate	PUBLIC
	Object type definition
	    id {Student id}
	    name {Student name}
	    year {Year enrolled}
	    procedure *readin*
	    procedure *writeout*
	    procedure *extra*
	objectend
		
		private
		private
		private
		
		virtual

Identifier	Description	Type

graduate	Object type definition
	
	    degree {All student data}
	    procedure *readin*
	    procedure *extra*
	objectend
		inherit *undergraduate* type from module *studentmodule*
		
		private
		
		virtual

16.6 SUMMARY

In this chapter we have seen how the object-oriented approach can be used to identify objects and their related methods. This is a particularly useful technique when dealing with large problems because of the encapsulation of data and the methods by which it is manipulated. It leads to highly modular programs which have distinct advantages in terms of maintainability. Top down design techniques can be used to develop the detailed design of the object methods and of the main program itself.

Objects are particularly useful for data which has a hierarchical structure because descendants can be defined which inherit all the attributes of their ancestors. Virtual methods enable ancestor methods to be replaced by those applicable to descendants. This means that a user of a pre-compiled piece of code can overwrite the methods which that code contains. A major consequence of this is that users can amend pre-compiled code without requiring access to the source code. A typical example of this is the provision of *tool boxes* for graphical software. Basic tools for manipulating graphics can be provided as a commercially available package. Although users would not be entitled to the source code of the tool box they would be able to extend and replace the tools which it provided. This not only protects the copyright of the tool box but gives the user the ability to tailor the package to their own needs.

SOLUTIONS TO EXERCISES

Exercise 2.1

(a) Here the user is to input precisely 15 integers, no more and no less. The type of number is specified quite unambiguously and so we would now be in a position to start designing.

(b) The user may choose not to input any data but is to be permitted to enter up to 100 numbers, but no more than that. A method will have to be devised which enables this to happen and which gives the user the opportunity of quitting input before the 100th entry. Clearly the user must not be allowed, or indeed asked, to input a 101st number. Only real numbers may be entered by the user.

(c) The user must first specify a number. We can deduce from the problem that this number must be an integer. However, there is no indication of the range of allowable number of entries. Is the user not allowed to enter any reals? Is the user allowed to enter as many as 1 000 000 reals? These issues need clarifying before designing begins because entering 1 000 000 reals might exhaust the memory capacity of a machine. If this is a problem then the maximum allowable number of entries should be part of the specification. Having entered this number the user must then be allowed to enter precisely this number of reals – no more and no less.

Exercise 2.2

When the user enters the number of reals, is it intended that the design should check that the value entered lies in the specified range 0 to 500? This would need clarifying before design could commence. Should this be a requirement we would say that the data input is to be **validated**, that is, checked to ensure that first it is an integer and second that it lies in the specified range. Another problem that needs to be resolved is whether the range includes the numbers 0 and 500.

Exercise 2.3

1.1 write out 'Enter the first integer'
1.2 read in *FirstNumber*

   1.3   write out 'Enter the second integer'
   1.4   read in *SecondNumber*

Prompts should be as helpful as possible, so here the user is told not only which number is about to be entered but is also reminded that an integer is required. The numbering used here reminds us that these steps are refinements of step 1.

Exercise 2.4

We have used a ? mark in the diagrams below to indicate that a variable is undefined.

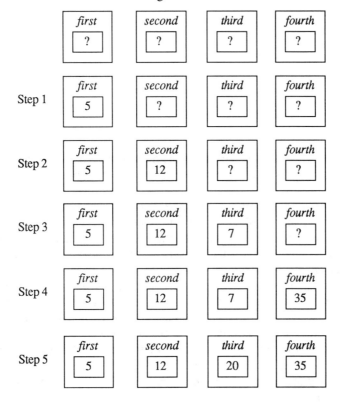

Exercise 2.5

After step 1 *count* has value 2. At step 3 its value is incremented to 3. Step 3 doubles its value to 6 and step 4 decrements it by 1 to give a final value of 5.

Exercise 2.6

UNDERSTAND THE PROBLEM

Clearly in a book it is impossible for the reader to ask for clarification of problem specifications. So we shall use this section to give hints for the design solution. They will often take the form of questions which identify key processes in the design. If you are totally stuck on a design then read this section and see if it helps you to make a start. The questions asked will often generate test data which will be used in the testing phase of the design process. You may like to use this data as a supplement to that of your own in order to test your own designs.

What is the product of the three numbers 3, 5, 2? The product is 30 – product means multiply the numbers together. The symbol for multiplication in design language is *.

DEVISE A SOLUTION

To begin with we shall nearly always give a top level design. Should the questions in the UNDERSTAND THE PROBLEM section not have helped you get started on your own solution, we suggest that you read the top level design and try to refine it before reading the rest of the solution. As you become more experienced we shall sometimes give only the final design. The numbering of the final designs should enable you to identify the major steps in the higher level design. You may find it instructive to **reverse engineer** these final designs to obtain the original top level design.

A top level design is:

1   read in the numbers
2   find the product of the numbers
3   write out the result

This may be refined as:

1.1   write out 'Enter first integer'
1.2   read in *first*
1.3   write out 'Enter second integer'
1.4   read in *second*
1.5   write out 'Enter third integer'
1.6   read in *third*
2.1   *product := first*second*third*
3.1   write out 'The product is ', *product*

Data table

Identifier	Description	Type
first	First number entered	integer variable
second	Second number entered	integer variable
third	Third number entered	integer variable
product	Product of inputs	integer variable

TEST THE DESIGN

For a more complex problem than this, your solution is unlikely to match the one we provide. To test your own design you should include in your test data any data generated in the UNDERSTAND THE PROBLEM phase and any data that we introduce in this part of the design process. In this simple design there is little to check and so we shall not go through detailed testing here.

Exercise 2.7

(a)   The condition is *the cheque exceeds £50*. This condition being true means that a cheque has a value which exceeds £50 and so a bankers card and one other form of identification is required. When the condition is false then the cheque does not exceed £50 and a bankers card is sufficient.

(b)   The condition is *today is Sunday*. If this condition is true then the sequence of actions to be performed is: get up late, have a bath and eat brunch. If it is false then the actions to be performed are: get up at 7.30, have a wash and then eat breakfast.

Exercise 2.8

The two solutions below illustrate the alternative ways in which an *if* statement which has no *else* clause may be handled.

1 write out 'Enter a non-zero integer'	1 write out 'Enter a non-zero integer'
2 read in *item*	2 read in *item*
3 if *item* is zero then	3 if *item* is zero then
4 write out 'Warning the number is zero'	4 write out 'Warning the number is zero'
5 else	5 ifend
6 do nothing	
7 ifend	

Exercise 3.1

(a)   This is a valid assignment statement.
(b)   This is incorrect because an assignment statement may not have an expression to the left of the assignment symbol.
(c)   This is not an assignment statement; it is in fact a condition for equality and so will have a value true or false depending upon the value held by *height*.
(d)   This is a valid assignment statement.
(e)   This is a valid assignment statement but care has to be taken to ensure that *breadth* does not have the value zero. If it does then execution of the statement will result in a **divide by zero** error.
(f)   This statement is invalid because the right-hand side, which evaluates to 10.0, is not an integer. (Note that 10.0 is not an integer value.) This results in a **type mismatch** error because an attempt has been made to assign to an integer variable a non-integer value; in other words, it violates the assignment compatibility rule.

Exercise 3.2

(a)   This is a valid condition.
(b)   Again it is valid.
(c)   This is not a condition because it does not involve a comparison operator. Neither is it an assignment statement because you cannot assign a value to anything other than a variable.
(d)   This is not a valid condition because it includes two comparison operators. We shall often want to express mathematical inequalities like this in designs but this cannot be done in this form. We shall see how it can be done in Chapter 7.
(e)   This is a valid condition.

Exercise 3.3

(a)   Any integer greater than or equal to 5. Note that this includes 5 itself.
(b)   Any integer less than 4. So this includes all the negative integers together with 0, 1, 2 and 3 but excluding 4.
(c)   There is only one value which makes this condition true and that is 12.

Exercise 3.4

(a) Invalid because both operands are real variables, whereas they should be of integer type for the operator MOD to be applicable.
(b) Valid. The multiplications are valid because integers are allowed in real expressions.
(c) Again this is valid.
(d) The expression (*IntegerOne* DIV *IntegerTwo*) is valid, provided *IntegerTwo* is non-zero. This evaluates to an integer value which can be used to multiply a real value.

Exercise 3.5

(a) Valid because integer expressions are allowed within real expressions.
(b) Valid.
(c) Invalid. This is a type mismatch because *IntegerOne* is of type integer and *RealTwo* is of type real.
(d) Invalid because 3.0 is a real number and so the right-hand side evaluates to a real and this statement tries to assign this to an integer variable.

Exercise 3.6

(a) Valid.
(b) Valid.
(c) Valid but care has to be taken equating real numbers if they result from arithmetic operations. As a consequence of the inherent approximations in real arithmetic, algebraically equal expressions may not hold in real arithmetic.

Exercise 3.7

(a) This is a valid condition. It takes the value true because the space character precedes the letters and digits. Note that '1' is a character and is not the integer 1. The difference is important.
(b) This is a valid condition. It takes the value false because the character '9' does not precede the character '2'. Note the reason it is false is NOT because 9 (the integer) is greater than 2 (the integer).
(c) This is a valid condition. Its value depends upon the value of the variable *ch* at the time the test for equality is done.
(d) This is not a valid condition because 'character' is not a character (it has many characters between its apostrophes).

Exercise 3.8

(a) Valid and the resulting dynamic length is 4.
(b) Valid and the resulting dynamic length is 0.
(c) The assignment to *area* is valid and gives a string of dynamic length 4.
(d) The assignment to *locality* is not valid because *area* has dynamic length 4 and this exceeds the static length of *locality*.

Exercise 3.9

(a) The string with the least first character must come first and this is '▽Dave' since the space character precedes all the letters. 'Da▽ve' comes next because its third character precedes 'v'. Finally 'Dave' precedes 'Dave▽' because it is shorter but otherwise equal.

(b) The upper-case characters precede the lower-case ones and so the order is 'COMPUTING', 'Computing', 'computing'.

Exercise 3.10

FullName has the value 'John▽Edward▽Pitt'. *NewName* is to assign this value and then has its 13th character updated to the character 'K' which gives 'John▽Edward▽Kitt'.

Exercise 4.1

UNDERSTAND THE PROBLEM

Is the user allowed to quit before entering 20 numbers?
No – exactly 20 inputs are required so the user will have to be prompted accordingly.

DEVISE A SOLUTION

One possible approach here would be to assign the 20 input values to twenty variables and then do the calculation. However, this would be a very inefficient design which would also be very inflexible if the specification was to change to allow 100 inputs. Then, a totally new design would be required because using 100 variables would be unrealistic. So, some other approach is required. Input data will not be assigned to variables but will be processed immediately. This means that a running total of the input values will have to be kept. There are many possible designs but one which corresponds to the general format we have used so far is:

    {Find the average of 20 real numbers input from keyboard}
1 initialize variables referenced in loop
2 loop while there are numbers to be input
3   read in and process a number
4 loopend
5 calculate and write out average

TEST THE DESIGN

The crucial test here is to check that the design allows for exactly 20 input values. This point is taken up in the text.

Exercise 4.2

Leaving *count* initialized to 1 at step 1.1 the loop control condition can be expressed using a strict inequality. The same user prompt as used in the text can also be used here.

  1.1 *count* := 1
  2.1 loop while *count* < 21
  3.1   write out 'Enter number ', *count*, ' now'

Alternatively *count* could be initialized to 0 in which case the loop condition needs attention as does the prompt

  1.1 *count* := 0
  2.1 loop while *count* <= 19
  3.1   write out 'Enter number ', *count* + 1, ' now'

or using a strict inequality:

1.1　*count* := 0
2.1　loop while *count* < 20
3.1　　write out 'Enter number ', *count*, ' now'

Yet another possibility is to initialize *count* to 0 and re-position the step which increments *count*.

{Find the average of 20 real numbers input from keyboard – version 2}
1.1　*count* := 0
1.2　*sum* := 0
2.1　loop while *count* < 20
3.1　　increment *count*
3.2　　write out 'Enter number ', *count*, ' now'
3.3　　read in *number*
3.4　　*sum* := *sum* + *number*
4　loopend
5.1　*average* := *sum* /20
5.2　write out 'The average is ', *average*

Within the body of the loop *count* has a value which corresponds to the number of the item being processed. Positioning the incrementation in this way makes it easier to see that the value of *count* within the loop corresponds to the item being processed. So on the first execution of step 3.1 *count* is incremented to 1, which corresponds to the first item of data. It is not always possible to re-position statements within a design without affecting their logic so care must be exercised when this is done.

Exercise 4.3

Perhaps the most obvious error is that there is no statement within the loop which updates the variable *count* and so this loop would execute for ever. We can rectify this as follows:

{This design still contains errors}
1.1　*count* := 0
1.2　*sum* := 0
1.3　write out 'Enter a number'
1.4　read in *number*
2.1　loop while *count* < 20
3.1　　increment *count*
3.2　　*sum* := *sum* + *number*
3.3　　write out 'Enter a number'
3.4　　read in *number*
4　loopend
5.1　*average* := *sum* /20
5.2　write out 'The average is ', *average*

However, that is not the end of the errors. If you trace this design through you should discover that the user is asked to input 21 numbers, even though only 20 of them contribute to the sum. This is because input is requested at the end of the loop; in fact the input request immediately precedes the test which decides whether or not the loop executes again. Asking the user for more data than is required *is* an error even though the final result *is* the average of the first 20 numbers input.

Another way of seeing this is to argue that after the first execution of the loop *count* will have value 1, two numbers will have been read in but only the first will have contributed to *sum*. So, after the last execution of the loop, *count* has value 20, twenty-one numbers will have been read in of which the first twenty contribute to *sum*.

Exercise 4.4

UNDERSTAND THE PROBLEM

What are non-negative real numbers?
They are all the positive real numbers together with zero. Note that when zero is to be included as an allowable input then the description has to be *non-negative real numbers* because the positive real numbers exclude zero.
Is the user allowed to input 100 positive numbers?
Yes.
What should happen if the user chooses not to input any numbers?
A message that the average does not exist should be output.
What data should be included in the test of the design?
It should include:
(a)   no numbers entered at all
(b)   a small number of inputs for which the result can be calculated by hand.

DEVISE A SOLUTION

The option discussed in the text and in the solution of Exercise 4.1 of assigning the inputs to variables and then doing the calculations is clearly not even a possibility here because it is not known in advance how many numbers will be entered. A top level design for this problem is:

```
    {Find average of an arbitrary number of non-negative reals}
1   initialize variables referenced in loop
2   loop while there are numbers to be input
3       process the data
4   loopend
5   calculate average and write out results
```

In order to refine the design we need to consider how the loop is to be controlled. It must cease execution as soon as the user has finished entering data. This suggests that the values entered can be used to control the loop. Since only non-negative numbers are to be entered, the user can be prompted to input a negative number to indicate that all the data has been entered. A special value (or values) like this which indicates that data entry is complete is called a **sentinel** value. We shall have to be careful here to not include the sentinel value as data to be processed.

```
      {Find average of arbitrary number of non-negative reals}
      {Terminate input with a negative number}
1     initialize variables referenced in loop
2.1   loop while number >= 0
3         process the data
4     loopend
5     calculate average and write out results
```

Data table

Identifier	Description	Type
number	Input data	real variable

This now means that *number* must be initialized prior to step 2.1. Step 3 also needs to include the process whereby *number* can be updated. Since we need to know how many numbers are entered (in order that the average can be calculated) a count will be required to record this fact. Step 5 will use this value to calculate the average, but since the count can be zero care will have to be taken to avoid a divide by zero error.

{Find average of arbitrary number of non-negative reals}
{Terminate input with a negative number}
1.1   *count* := 0
1.2   *sum* := 0
1.3   write out 'Enter a non-negative number as data or a negative number to quit'
1.4   read in *number*
2.1   loop while *number* >= 0
3.1   *sum* := *sum* + *number*
3.2   increment *count*
3.3   write out 'Enter a non-negative number as data or a negative number to quit'
3.4   read in *number*
4   loopend
5.1   if *count* = 0 then
5.2   write out 'No data has been input so the average does not exist'
5.3   else
5.4   *average* := *sum/count*
5.5   write out 'The average of your ' *count* ' numbers is ' *average*
5.6   ifend

Data table

Identifier	Description	Type
number	Input data	real variable
count	The number of numbers input	integer variable
sum	Cumulative total of inputs	real variable
average	Average of *count* inputs	real variable

TEST THE DESIGN

Testing must check that the sentinel value is not included in *sum* and that it does not contribute to *count*. A trace table with a small number of user inputs can verify this is so.

Step	*count*	*sum*	*number*	*number* <> 0	*average*
1.1	0				
1.2		0			
1.3			2.5		
2.1				true	
3.1		2.5			
3.2	1				
3.4			−1		
2.1				false	
5.4					2.5

Because the body of the loop is not executed after the sentinel has been entered its value is not added to sum. A further trace table in which the user enters the sentinel as the first piece of input data will show that the loop is not executed at all and processing goes from step 2.1 directly to step 5.1. The result of the condition in step 2.1 would then cause step 5.2 to be executed next.

Exercise 5.1

(a) The outputs are 5, 7, 9, 11, 13, and the string *end*.
(b) The output is the string *end* – the loop is not executed because the first index exceeds the second and it is not a downto loop.
(c) The outputs are 13, 11, 9, 7, 5, and the string *end*.
(d) The loop executes once giving rise to outputs −3, and the string *end*.

Exercise 5.2

UNDERSTAND THE PROBLEM

For each entry there are three things to write out. What are they?
The number of feet, which could be a blank space, the number of inches and the number of millimetres.
What sort of a loop could be used?
A *for* loop which runs through all the possible number of inches would appear to be the easiest solution.
Should the *write* and *write out* statements be within the loop or outside it?
Within the loop, because on each loop execution a row of the table will be output.

DEVISE A SOLUTION

A top level design is:

```
    {A metric ready reckoner}
 1  initialize variables referenced in loop
 2  loop for all values of inches
 3      process inches
 4  loopend
```

The initialization will need to write out the heading of the ready reckoner table. This heading must not be in the loop, otherwise each time it executes the heading will be output. For a given number of inches we need to know its equivalent form in feet and inches. We can use the integer operators DIV and MOD to get these values. Two alternative refinements are:

{A metric ready reckoner version 1}	{A metric ready reckoner version 2}
1.1 write out 'Feet ', 'Inches ', 'Millimetres '	1.1 write out 'Feet ', 'Inches ', 'Millimetres '
2.1 loop for $i := 1$ to 36	2.1 loop for $i := 1$ to 36
3.1 *metric* := 25.4*i	3.1 *metric* := 25.4*i
3.2 if $i < 12$ then	3.2 *feet* := i DIV 12
3.3 write out ' ', i, *metric*	3.3 *inches* := i MOD 12
3.4 else	3.4 if *feet* = 0 then
3.5 *feet* := i DIV 12	3.5 write out ' ', *inches*, *metric*
3.6 *inches* := i MOD 12	3.6 else
3.7 write out *feet*, *inches*, *metric*	3.7 write out *feet*, *inches*, *metric*
3.8 ifend	3.8 ifend
4 loopend	4 loopend

Step 1.1 produces the heading to the table and it consists of the three strings which make up the column headings. Note how the entry under the first column is handled when a blank is required.

Data table

Identifier	Description	Type
i	Loop control variable	integer variable
metric	Number of millimetres	real variable
feet	Number of feet	integer variable
inches	Number of inches	integer variable

TEST THE DESIGN

You should check that the format of the output changes as the number of inches goes from 11 to 12.

Exercise 5.3

UNDERSTAND THE PROBLEM

A postconditioned loop is always executed at least once. The first execution of the loop must allow for the possibility that the user does not wish to enter any data. The last execution must not include the sentinel value in the averaging process.

DEVISE A SOLUTION

A top level design would be:

{Find average of arbitrary number of non-negative reals}
1 initialize variables referenced in loop
2 repeat
3   read in and process a number
4 until no more inputs required
5 calculate and write out average of numbers

Care needs to be taken when refining step 3. The value read in is eventually going to be the sentinel value and this must not be included in the sum of the numbers. The easiest way to achieve this is to position the reading in of data as the last statement in the refinement of step 3. This leads to the intermediate design:

{Find average of arbitrary number of non-negative reals}
1   initialize variables referenced in loop
2   repeat
3.1   *sum := sum + number*
3.2   increment *count*
3.3   write out 'Enter a non-negative number as data or a negative to quit'
3.4   read in *number*
4.1   until *number* <= 0
5   calculate and write out average of numbers

This leaves the problem of the initialization of the variables. Why can step 1 not include a request for the first data item? Because a user who did not want to enter any data would have to respond to this request and also to the request at step 3.4. In other words, to quit the program immediately would require the input of *two* pieces of data. To what value should *count* be initialized? It has to be initialized to −1 because step 3.2 increments it and this happens before the first request for data. The final design is:

{Find average of arbitrary number of non-negative reals. Version 1}
1.1 *sum* := 0
1.2 *count* := −1
1.3 *number* := 0
2.1 repeat
3.1 *sum* := *sum* + *number*
3.2 increment *count*
3.3 write out 'Enter a non-negative number as data or a negative to quit'
3.4 read in *number*
4.1 until *number* <= 0
5.1 if *count* = 0 then
5.2 write out 'No data has been input so the average does not exist'
5.3 else
5.4 *average* := *sum*/*count*
5.5 write out 'The average of your ' *count* ' numbers is ' *average*
5.6 ifend

Step 3 could have been refined so that its first statement was a request for input, but as we remarked above this would imply that the sentinel value would then be included in *sum*. If this approach is adopted then after the loop ceases to execute, *sum* would have to be adjusted. An intermediate design based on this would be:

{Find average of arbitrary number of non-negative reals}
1 initialize variables referenced in loop
2 repeat
3.1 write out 'Enter a non-negative number as data or a negative to quit'
3.2 read in *number*
3.3 *sum* := *sum* + *number*
3.4 increment *count*
4.1 until *number* <= 0
5 calculate and write out average of numbers

To calculate the average in step 5 now requires the adjustment of *sum* so as to remove the sentinel value which it includes. What is the statement which adjusts *sum*? It is

sum := *sum* − *number*

To what value should *count* be initialized? As the design stands, *count* gets incremented when the sentinel value is entered but this value should not contribute to *count*. However, if *count* is initialized to −1 then it always lags one behind the number of data items entered and is corrected on the final loop execution because of the sentinel value. If on the other hand *count* is initialized to 0, then during loop execution it holds the number of actual data items entered but after the final execution it has a value one too many. This can be rectified by decrementing its value outside the loop. In the refinement below the former strategy has been adopted.

{Find average of arbitrary number of non-negative reals. Version 2}
1.1 *sum* := 0
1.2 *count* := −1
2.1 repeat

3.1   write out 'Enter a non-negative number as data or a negative to quit'
3.2   read in *number*
3.3   *sum := sum + number*
3.4   increment *count*
4.1   until *number* < 0
5.1   *sum := sum − number*
5.2   if *count* = 0 then
5.3   write out 'No data has been input so the average does not exist'
5.4   else
5.5   *average := sum/count*
5.6   write out 'The average of your ' *count* ' numbers is ' *average*
5.7   ifend

TEST THE DESIGN

This solution has considered some of the issues against which the design should be tested.

Exercise 5.4

UNDERSTAND THE PROBLEM

If the first player enters the number 10 and the second guesses 5, what sort of response should the program give?
It should respond that the guess is too small.

DEVISE A SOLUTION

There are many possible ways of designing a solution to this problem. Here, we wanted to force you to use both a *repeat* loop and a *while* loop. In fact two repeat loops can be used but this will then require the use of a nested *if* statement which we study in Section 5.7. A top level design is:

{Guessing game}
1   repeat
2   design for a single game
3   process the request for another game
4   until no more games requested

This can be refined to the following final design:

{Guessing game}
1   repeat
2.1   write 'First player enter an integer '
2.2   read in *target*
2.3   clear screen
2.4   write 'Second player make a guess '
2.5   read in *guess*
2.6   loop while *guess* <> *target*
2.7   if *guess* < *target* then
2.8   write out 'Guess is too small'
2.9   else
2.10   write out 'Guess is too large'
2.11   ifend
2.12   write 'Make another guess '

2.13   read in *target*
2.14   loopend
2.15   write out 'Well done'
3.1   write out 'Do you want to continue? y/n'
3.2   read in *response*
4.1   until *response* = 'n'

Data table

Identifier	Description	Type
target	First player's number	integer variable
guess	Second player's guess	integer variable
response	Exit program control variable	char variable

TEST THE DESIGN

Test data should include the possibility that player 2 makes a correct guess at the first attempt. The congratulations message should appear immediately thereafter. If it does not then that statement is incorrectly positioned. In other words the message should be outside the innermost loop.

Exercise 5.5

(a)   When *x* has value 15 the *then* clause is executed resulting in the output
            It is bigger than 10
      When *x* has value 5 the *else* clause is executed resulting in the output
            It is not bigger than 10
            But it could be equal to 10
(b)   When *x* has value 15 the *then* clause is executed resulting in the output
            It is bigger than 10
            But it could be equal to 10
      When *x* has value 5 the *else* clause is executed resulting in the output
            It is not bigger than 10
            But it could be equal to 10

Exercise 5.6

```
1   if ch = 'a' then
2       ch := 'A'
3   else
4       if ch = 'b' then
5           ch := 'B'
6       else
7           ch := 'C'
8       ifend
9   ifend
```

Exercise 5.7

```
1   if person is under 25 then
2       if the car is a saloon then
```

```
3        premium is 100           {under 25 saloon driver}
4      else
5        premium is 150           {under 25 sports car driver}
6      ifend
7    else
8      if the car is a saloon then
9        premium is 80            {25 and over saloon driver}
10     else
11       premium is 120           {25 and over sports car driver}
12     ifend
13   ifend
```

Exercise 5.8

We give a final design which uses the same identifiers as in Exercise 5.4.

```
         {Guessing game}
1      repeat
2.1        write 'First player enter an integer '
2.2        read in target
2.3        clear screen
2.4        write 'Second player make a guess '
2.5        read in guess
2.6          if guess < target then
2.7             write out 'Guess is too small'
2.8          else
2.9            if guess > target then
2.10              write out 'Guess is too large'
2.11           else
2.12              write out 'Well done'
2.13           ifend
2.14         ifend
2.15       until guess = target
3.1        write out 'Do you want to continue? y/n'
3.2        read in response
4.1    until response = 'n'
```

Exercise 6.1

The value 0.0 has index 5 and 3.45 is the value whose index is 1.

Exercise 6.2

The lower bound is −3, the upper bound is 1 and the values are −3, −2, −1, 0 and 1.

Exercise 6.3

The diagram labelled *identity* does not represent an array because it contains elements of different types, namely strings and integers. The other two do represent arrays and they can be declared as:

Data table

Identifier	Description	Type
names	An array of names	array[1..4] of string variable
list	An array of numbers	array[−3..0] of integer variable

Exercise 6.4

UNDERSTAND THE PROBLEM

Describe what needs to be done.
Each element of the array will have to be examined and a count will have to be kept of the number of elements which have value true.

DEVISE A SOLUTION

A design fragment is:

```
        {Count the number of married in survey}
1   married := 0
2   loop for i := 1 to 250
3       if survey[i] = true then
4           increment married
5       ifend
6   loopend
7   write out 'There are ', married, ' married people in the survey.'
```

Data table

Identifier	Description	Type
survey	An array holding survey data	array[1..250] of boolean variable
married	Count of the married people	integer variable
i	Loop control variable	integer variable

TEST THE DESIGN

That the loop executes the correct number of times should be checked.

Exercise 6.5

UNDERSTAND THE PROBLEM

Why does an index lower bound of 0 not help here?
Since output is required for all matches then all the elements of the array will have to be examined and so a *for* loop through all the elements will be required. Using a dummy item will not tell us whether there have been any matches for the other elements of the array.
How can we deal with the possibility that there will be no matches?
A boolean flag will be required to record when a match occurs. Then when all the elements of the array have been examined, the boolean flag can be inspected to see if it is required to output a message that no matches were found.

DEVISE A SOLUTION

A final design is:

{Write out index for all matches}
1.1   write 'Enter search item '
1.2   read in *searchitem*
1.3   *flag* := false
2.1   loop for *i* := 1 to *maxsize*
3.1   if *surnames*[*i*] = *searchitem* then
3.2   write out 'There is a match at index ', *i*
3.3   *flag* := true
3.4   ifend
4   loopend
5.1   if *flag* = false then
5.2   write out 'No matches were found'
5.3   ifend

Data table

Identifier	Description	Type
maxsize	Array index upper bound	integer constant
surnames	Array of surnames	array[1..*maxsize*] of string variable
searchitem	Item being sought	string variable
i	Loop control variable	integer variable
flag	Set true if a match is found	boolean variable

Notice how the flag is set true when a match is found. If no match is found then after the execution of the loop it will still have value false and so the final message will be written out.

TEST THE DESIGN

Critical data here is when no matches are found and where there is more than one match. So the design should be tested with data where there are no matches, as well as with data for which there are many matches.

Exercise 6.6

UNDERSTAND THE PROBLEM

Why is the index zero method of search appropriate here?
Because we do not necessarily have to inspect all the items in the towns array.
What kind of value should be chosen for the sentinel?
The user is to be asked for the name of a town and so the sentinel will have to be a string value which does not appear in the array *town*. A suitable value would be 'zzz'.

DEVISE A SOLUTION

A top level design is:

{Parallel array search}
1   initialize variables
2   loop while searches are required
3   search the array *town*
4   write out the result
5   request next search
6   loopend

This may be refined to:

```
        {Parallel array search}
1.1     write 'Enter the town required or zzz to quit '
1.2     read in town[0]
2.1     loop while town[0] <> 'zzz'
3.1         index := maxsize
3.2         loop while town[index] <> town[0]
3.3             decrement index
3.4         loopend
4.1         if index = 0 then
4.2             write out 'Town is not in the array'
4.3         else
4.4             write out town[0], ' has ', churches[index], ' churches'
4.5         ifend
5.1         write 'Enter the town required or zzz to quit '
5.2         read in town[0]
6       loopend
```

Data table

Identifier	Description	Type
maxsize	Array index upper bound	integer constant
town	Array of town names	array[0..maxsize] of string variable
churches	Parallel array of church numbers	array[0..maxsize] of integer variable
index	Loop control variable	integer variable

TEST THE DESIGN

As with all searches, test data should include values which result in successes and failures. In addition to the successful searches you need to ensure that the correct data is output from the parallel array.

Exercise 6.7

(a)   The entry corresponds to April 1989 and so is referenced as $births[4, 1989]$.
(b)   Reading directly from the table we see its value is 27.

Exercise 6.8

Using the same identifiers as in the text the fragment is:

```
        {Sum entries for May}
1   total := 0
2   loop for year := 1987 to 1990
3       total := total + births[5, year]
4   loopend
```

Exercise 6.9

UNDERSTAND THE PROBLEM

Does every element in the array have to be inspected in order to find the least value?
No – all the elements need not be inspected but all those corresponding to females must be.

The result is required for females only and so the index corresponding to females will remain fixed. Moreover, only those elements which have day index corresponding to Thursday, Friday and Saturday should be inspected.

DEVISE A SOLUTION

A top level design is:

{Find least hours of TV watched among females}
1   initialize variables referenced in loop
2   find the least hours watched among the females
3   write out result

A final design is:

{Find least hours of TV watched among females}

1.1	*leasthours* := *hours*[5, 5, 0]
1.2	*leastage* := 5
2.1	loop for *age* := 5 to 99
2.2	loop for *day* := 5 to 7
2.3	if *hours*[*day*, *age*, 0] < *leasthours* then
2.4	*leasthours* := *hours*[*day*, *age*, 0]
2.5	*leastage* := *age*
2.6	ifend
2.7	loopend
2.8	loopend
3.1	write out 'The age of least viewing females is ', *leastage*

Data table (additional to definitions in the text)

Identifier	Description	Type
leasthours	Smallest number of hours watched	real variable
leastage	Age of people viewing least	integer variable
age	Loop control variable for age	integer variable
day	Loop control variable for day	integer variable

TEST THE DESIGN

A check that the correct indexes have been used and that the loops are correctly specified is essential here.

Exercise 6.10

Data table

Identifier	Description		Type
employeetype	Record type definition		
	name	{employee name}	string variable
	worksid	{works number}	string variable
	age	{employee age}	integer variable
	salary	{employee salary}	real variable
	recordend		
employee	An employee's record		*employeetype* variable

We have chosen to represent the works identity number as a string because it is rare for arithmetic operations to be performed on works numbers. The following sequence of statements initializes the record *employee*:

```
with record employee do
    name := 'Smith'
    worksid := '53917'
    age := 35
    salary := 12450.50
withend
```

Exercise 6.11

Data table

Identifier	Description	Type
maxsize	Array index upper bound	integer constant
employeetype	Record type definition	
	name {employee name}	string variable
	worksid {works number}	string variable
	age {employee age}	integer variable
	salary {employee salary}	real variable
	recordend	
workers	Array of employee records	array[0..*maxsize*] of *employeetype*

Note that the record at index 0 has been left as a dummy entry in anticipation of the searches.

UNDERSTAND THE PROBLEM

What kind of loop is required?
A *for* loop

DEVISE A SOLUTION

A top level design is:

```
    {Initialize an array of records}
1   loop for all elements
2       initialize current record
3   loopend
```

We shall use the *with* notation in the refinement:

```
       {Initialize an array of records}
1.1    loop for index := 1 to maxsize
2.1        with record workers[index]
2.2            write 'Enter workers name '
2.3            read in name
2.4            write 'Enter works number '
2.5            read in worksid
2.6            write 'Enter age of worker '
2.7            read in age
2.8            write 'Enter salary of worker '
2.9            read in salary
2.10       withend
3      loopend
```

Data table (additional to that above)

Identifier	Description	Type
index	Loop control variable	integer variable

TEST THE DESIGN

You need to ensure you have got the access to the record structure correct. The *with* statement is not compulsory, but if it is not used then the dot notation must be.

Exercise 7.1

(a)   True.
(b)   False; because of the value of *count*.
(c)   False; the first inequality is strict and does not permit equality.
(d)   False; because of the value of *index*.

Exercise 7.2

(a)   True; in fact both conditions forming the compound expression are true.
(b)   True; because of the value of *index* .
(c)   True; because of the value of *index*.
(d)   False; neither expression is true and so the compound expression is false.

Exercise 7.3

(a)   Either *number* must have value 6 or more, or *total* must have value 4 or less. If both of these conditions are met then compound expression still has value true.
(b)   *number* must have one of the values 6, 7, 8, 9, 10, 11, 12, 13, 14.
(c)   This is impossible to make true. That is, this expression is always false no matter what value *number* has.
(d)   *number* must have value 16 or more, or value 4 or less. In other words, any integer value excluding 5 to 15 inclusive.
(e)   *total* must have value 6 or more and *flag* must be false. Both these conditions must apply.

Exercise 7.4

(a)   (*answer* = 'y') or (*answer* = 'Y')
(b)   (*answer* = 'y') or (*answer* = 'Y') or (*answer* = 'n') or (*answer* = 'N')
(c)   (*day* > 0) and (*day* < 32) and (*month* > 0) and (*month* < 13)
        Alternatively the expression
        (*day* >= 1) and (*day* <= 31) and (*month* >= 1) and (*month* <= 12)
        would do just as well.

Exercise 7.5

Using the same identifiers as in Problem 5.11 the corresponding designs are:

{Occurrences of 'an' using compound boolean}

1.1   *count* := 0
1.2   write out 'Enter the string '
1.3   read in *sentence*
1.4   *previous* := *sentence*[1]
2.1   loop for *current* := 2 to *length*(*sentence*)
3.1   if (*previous* = 'a') and
               sentence[*current*] = 'n' then
3.2   increment *count*
3.3   ifend
3.4   *previous* := *sentence*[*current*]
4   loopend
5.1   write out 'Number of occurrences is ' *count*

{Count occurrences of 'an' using compound boolean}

1.1   *count* := 0
1.2   write out 'Enter the string '
1.3   read in *sentence*
2.1   loop for *current* := 1 to *length*(*sentence*)–1
3.1   if *sentence*[*current*] = 'a' and
               sentence[*current* + 1] = 'n' then
3.2   increment *count*
3.3   ifend
4   loopend
5.1   write out 'Number of occurrences is ' *count*

Exercise 7.6

The data table below gives the declarations but first we make some comments:
(a)   These are numbers between 1 and 999 inclusive.
(b)   The range of numbers is 1900 to 1999 inclusive.
(c)   The grades are A, B, C, D, E, F and G.
(d)   The shortest month can have as few as 28 days but the longest can have no more than 31.
(e)   There are either 365 or 366 depending upon whether or not it is a leap year.
(f)   The number 24 never appears on such a clock but 0 does.
(g)   The number 60 never appears on such a clock but 0 does.

Data table

Identifier	Description	Type
number	Numerical part of registration plate	1..999 variable
century	Years in 20th century	1900..1999 variable
grade	Examination grade	'A'..'G' variable
monthdays	Days in a month	28..31 variable
yeardays	Days in a year	365..366 variable
hours	24-hour digital clock values	0..23 variable
minutes	Minutes on digital clock	0..59 variable

Exercise 7.7

(a)   *hoursworked*[*thursday*]
(b)   7.45

Exercise 7.8

Data table

Identifier	Description	Type
rainbow	Enumerated type definition	(*red, orange, yellow, green, blue, indigo, violet*)
suit	Enumerated type definition	(*clubs, diamonds, hearts, spades*)
months	Enumerated type definition	(*jan, feb, mar, apr, may, jun, jul, aug, sep, oct, nov, dec*)
scale	Enumerated type definition	(*do, re, me, fa, so, la, te*)

Exercise 7.9

Data table

Identifier	Description	Type
paint	A colour of the rainbow	*rainbow* variable
summer	List of summer months	*may..aug* variable
hand	Number of cards of each suit	array[*suit*] of 0..13 variable

Note that we have used the enumerated type identifier *suit* to define the index range of the array. We could have specified the index lower bound and index upper bound had we so wished. Thus an equivalent definition would be array[*clubs..spades*] of 0..13 variable.

Exercise 7.10

(a)   The predecessor is *orange*, successor *green*.
(b)   The predecessor is *hearts*. It has no successor.
(c)   The predecessor is *aug*, successor *oct*.
(d)   It has no predecessor, the successor is *re*.

Exercise 7.11

UNDERSTAND THE PROBLEM

What should be the updated values of *day*, *month* and *year* if they are initialized with each of the following values respectively:
(a) 20 *mar* 1989; (b) 28 *feb* 1989; (c) 28 *apr* 1989; (d) 30 *apr* 1989; (e) 31 *dec* 1989. They should have the values:
(a) 21 *mar* 1989; (b) 1 *mar* 1989; (c) 29 *apr* 1989; (d) 1 *may* 1989; (e) 1 *jan* 1990.

DEVISE A SOLUTION

Since leap years are to be ignored, action, other than just incrementing the value of *day*, may be required when *day* has value 28, 30 or 31 because these values may initiate a change of month. A top level design is:

```
1   select case depending on day
2       28    : process this value
3       30    : process this value
4       31    : process this value
5     default : increment day
6   selectend
```

When *day* has value 28 it should be incremented unless the month is *feb*, in which case *day* must be set to 1 and *month* should be updated to the successor of *month*. The case labels 30 and 31 can be dealt with similarly. This leads to the final design:

```
1       select case depending on day
2.1         28    : if month = feb then
2.2                     month := succ (month)
2.3                     day := 1
2.4               else
2.5                     increment day
2.6               ifend
```

```
3.1       30   : select case depending on month
3.2                   apr, jun, sep, nov  :  month := succ(month)
3.3                                          day := 1
3.4               default          :  increment day
3.5             selectend
4.1       31   : if month = dec then
4.2                   increment year
4.3                   month := jan
4.4                   day := 1
4.5             else
4.6                   month := succ(month)
4.7                   day := 1
4.8             ifend
5       default : increment day
6       selectend
```

Data table (additional to definitions in the text)

Identifier	Description	Type
year	The year of current date	integer variable

TEST THE DESIGN

The data given above should be included in your test data.

Exercise 8.1

The number input by the user has to be validated to see if it corresponds to an existing item. One way of doing this is to search the array *stock* to find the stock number of the last item and use it in the validation process. Another way is to use the procedure *findnext*, which returns a number which exceeds by one the last item number used. But *findnext* requires *stock* as source data and so whichever method is adopted *stock* will have to be source data of *update*. Furthermore, it is also required as source data because *update* must write out the description, quantity and price of the item. Since *stock* is updated by the procedure it must also be specified as results.

Exercise 8.2

January 4th corresponds to day 4 and February 3rd to day 34.

Exercise 8.3

newitem

stock	Array holding stock records	stocktype parameter
stocknumber	Index to array and stock number	integer parameter
{Prompt for and read in the description, quantity and price of the new stock item and assign the details to the record at index *partnumber* of the array *stock*.}		
stock	Updated array	stocktype parameter

Exercise 8.4

The first number, 4, corresponds to the day and the second number, 1, corresponds to the month, so it converts 4th January to its numeric value and assigns the result to the variable *today*.

Exercise 8.5

The first data item passed must correspond to the first parameter of the procedure, that is *day*. But 3 represents the month March. The data have been passed in the wrong order. The correct call is:

> *numericdate*(10, 3, *yesterday*)

Exercise 8.6

Data table for program calling *numericdate*

Identifier	Description	Type
numericdate	(*day*, *month*, *daynumber*)	procedure(integer, integer, integer)
nowday	Actual parameter corresponding to the formal parameter *day*	integer variable
nowmonth	Actual parameter corresponding to the formal parameter *month*	integer variable
todayno	Actual parameter corresponding to the formal parameter *daynumber*	integer variable
tomorrowno	Actual parameter corresponding to the formal parameter *daynumber*	integer variable

```
1  nowday := 20
2  nowmonth := 3
3  numericdate(nowday, nowmonth, todayno)
4  write out todayno
5  numericdate(nowday + 1, nowmonth, tomorrowno)
6  write out tomorrowno
```

In this solution an expression has been used as the actual parameter corresponding to the formal parameter *day* in step 5. Expressions can be used in this way for source parameters. However, a result cannot be assigned to an expression but must be assigned to a variable. Notice also how there are two variables corresponding to the formal parameter *daynumber*. That is because the procedure is called twice and has the results assigned to different variables on each call.

Exercise 8.7

The first solution uses different identifiers for the formal and actual parameters.

Data table for a program which calls *confirm*

Identifier	Description	Type
confirm	(*prompt*, *result*)	procedure(string, boolean)
line	A textual prompt	string variable
ok	Confirmation of input 'y' or 'Y'	boolean variable

The data table below would do just as well but it uses the same identifiers for the formal and actual parameters.

Data table for a program which calls *confirm* (common identifiers for parameters)

Identifier	Description	Type
confirm	(*prompt, result*)	procedure(string, boolean)
prompt	A textual prompt	string variable
result	Confirmation of input 'y' or 'Y'	boolean variable

Exercise 8.8

It would have been better to declare them both as subranges: *day* as the subrange 1..31 because there are a maximum of 31 days in a month and *daynumber* as 1..365 as this is the total number of days in a (non-leap) year.

Exercise 8.9

(a) The specification of the procedure *splitnumber* is valid.
(b) The specification of the procedure *search* has two errors. Firstly, the main data table violates the declare before use rule. Secondly, *searchitem* is declared to be an integer parameter but the array to be searched is an array of string.
(c) The procedure *errormessage* is valid.

Exercise 8.10

UNDERSTAND THE PROBLEM

How many actual variables will the main program need to declare and how should they be initialized?
One for each of the five formal parameters. The variable corresponding to the source parameter will be initialized by having the value read into it from the keyboard. The variables corresponding to the results will be initialized by the procedure call.

DEVISE A SOLUTION

The same identifiers have been used for the actual and formal parameters. The main program fragment is:

```
1.1   write out 'Enter a number in the range 0 to 9999 '
1.2   read in number
2     splitnumber(number, thousands, hundreds, tens, units)
3.1   write out thousands
3.2   write out hundreds
3.3   write out tens
3.4   write out units
```

Data table for main program

Identifier	Description	Type
splitnumber	(*number, thousands, hundreds, tens, units*)	procedure(integer, integer, integer, integer, integer)
thousands	Number of thousands in *number*	integer variable
hundreds	Number of hundreds in *number*	integer variable
tens	Number of tens in *number*	integer variable
units	Number of units in *number*	integer variable

splitnumber
number

1 *units := number* MOD 10
2 *number := number* DIV 10
3 *tens := number* MOD 10
4 *number := number* DIV 10
5 *hundreds := number* MOD 10
6 *number := number* DIV 10
7 *thousands := number* MOD 10

thousands, hundreds, tens, units

This module design does not have any local variables and so a data table is not required.

TEST THE DESIGN

Test data should include values for which *thousands*, *hundreds*, *tens* and *units* would be zero.

Exercise 8.11

(a) The procedure *swap* has common source data and results and so the procedure is declared with just two parameters. Different identifiers have been used for the actual and formal parameters.

Data table for program which calls *swap*

Identifier	Description	Type
swap	*(first, second)*	procedure(real, real)
one	Any real number	integer variable
two	Any real number	integer variable

(b) There are no common source data and results and so the procedure is declared with two parameters. The type definition must be part of the data table of the calling program.

Data table for program which calls *reversecopy*

Identifier	Description	Type
maxsize	Array index upper bound	integer constant
arraytype	Array type definition	array[1..*maxsize*] of string
reversecopy	*(givenarray, reversedcopy)*	procedure(*arraytype*, *arraytype*)
forwards	An array	*arraytype* variable
backwards	The reverse of *forwards*	*arraytype* variable

(c) The source data is the same as the results and so the procedure is declared with just one parameter. The type definition must be included in the data table.

Data table for program which uses *reverse*

Identifier	Description	Type
maxsize	Array index upper bound	integer constant
arraytype	Array type definition	array[1..*maxsize*] of string
reverse	*(given)*	procedure(*arraytype*)
itemarray	An array	*arraytype* variable

Exercise 8.12

(a) This procedure has a single boolean result and so can be specified as a function.

Data table for program using *confirm*

Identifier	Description	Type
confirm	*(prompt)*	boolean function(string)
message	A prompt	string variable

confirm

prompt	A string prompt	string parameter
{Write out *prompt* and read in a character from the keyboard. If the character is 'y' or 'Y' assign true to *confirm* otherwise assign it the value false.}		
confirm	True for 'y' or 'Y'	boolean function value

The detailed design of the function *confirm* is:

confirm

prompt

{Check response for 'y' or 'Y'}
1.1   write out *prompt*
1.2   read in *ch*
2.1   *confirm* := (*ch* = 'y') or (*ch* := 'Y')

confirm

Data table for function *confirm*

Identifier	Description	Type
ch	Input character	char variable

(b) Since the result of each of these procedures is an array it is unlikely that a whole array would appear in an expression. It may therefore be more appropriate to leave these as procedures rather than respecify them as functions.

Exercise 8.13

UNDERSTAND THE PROBLEM

If the character entered is '4' how can *getdigit* convert this to the number 4?
The *ord* function will convert it to an integer but not to the integer 4. In fact *ord* converts it to the integer 52. To recover the digit 4 the ordinal value of '0' must be subtracted from 52. Hence the character is converted to the digit equivalent by the expression

$ord('4') - ord('0')$

This function would be more realistic if the input by the user was not output to the screen until it had been validated. Invalid inputs would then not be echoed to the screen. The design language statement *read in* assumes the input appears on the screen. Facilities for inhibiting screen output are not considered as their programming language equivalents tend to differ widely.

DEVISE A SOLUTION

The final design for *getdigit is:*

getdigit

{get a validated digit}
1 repeat
2   read in *ch*
3 until *ch* in ['0'..'9']
4 *getdigit* := ord(*ch*) − ord('0')

getdigit

Data table for the function *getdigit*

Identifier	Description	Type
ch	Input character	char variable

Notice how this data table does not need to declare the function *ord*. That is because it is a built-in function and so does not need explicit declaration in a user design.

TEST THE DESIGN

Step 4 needs to be checked to ensure the correct value is returned.

Exercise 8.14

It would not matter because neither of them calls the other and so they are independent of each other and can be declared in this alternative order.

Exercise 8.15

Since *message* now requires access to *getdigit* then *getdigit* must be declared so that it appears in the referencing environment of *message*. At first sight the obvious way to achieve this is to declare *getdigit* in the data table for *message* and to leave the other data tables as they were. The data table for the main program would then be as given in the text and those for the routines would be:

Data table for procedure *getnumber*

Identifier	Description	Type
getdigit	( )	integer function( )
tens	Character representing tens digit	char variable
units	Character representing units digit	char variable

Data table for the procedure *message*

Identifier	Description	Type
getdigit	( )	integer function( )

In other words, both routines would declare *getdigit* locally. This, in fact, is very wasteful because it means declaring the same routine twice. Furthermore, in most programming languages it would mean writing the corresponding code twice as well. This would then create maintenance problems if *getdigit* had to be amended at a later date because both instances would have to be found and altered identically. A better way of proceeding is to declare *getdigit* so that it occurs in the referencing environments of both *getnumber* and *message* but is not declared locally in either. This can be achieved by declaring it in the main program before both the declarations of *getnumber* and *message* themselves. Then *message* does not declare any local variables and the other data tables are modified as shown below:

Data table for main program

Identifier	Description	Type
inputtype	Subrange type definition	0..99
getdigit	( )	integer function( )
getnumber	(*x*)	procedure(*inputtype*)
message	(*first, second*)	procedure(*inputtype, inputtype*)
target	Number to be guessed	*inputtype*
guess	Guess of target	*inputtype*

Data table for procedure *getnumber*

Identifier	Description	Type
tens	Character representing tens digit	char variable
units	Character representing units digit	char variable

Notice here how neither routine declares *getdigit* and how care has to be taken with the order of the declarations in order to make sure *getdigit* is in the referencing environment of both *message* and *getnumber*.

Exercise 9.1

(a) *word* has string value 'introduction'
(b) *forename* has string value 'David'

Exercise 9.2

(a) (i) *title* has string value 'The▽amendments'
     (ii) *name* is returned unaltered because the value of the third parameter results in an attempt to delete characters beyond the dynamic length of the source string.
(b) (i) *delete(sentence,* 7, 12)
     (ii) *delete(sentence,* 1, 7)
     (iii) This requires two calls to *delete* and can be done in two ways. Deleting 'A▽' first and then '▽in▽the▽dark' requires
           delete(sentence, 1, 2)
           delete(sentence, 5, 12)
           Alternatively deleting '▽in▽the▽dark' first and then 'A▽' requires
           delete(sentence, 7, 12)
           delete(sentence, 1, 2)

Exercise 9.3

(a) (i) *title* has value 'These▽Principles▽of▽Design'
     (ii) *name* has value 'David▽Robert▽Sargent'
(b) (i) *insert(sentence,* 'A▽', 1)
     (ii) *insert(sentence,* '▽methods', 7)

Exercise 9.4

(a) *position* has value 7.
(b) *position* has value 2. Note that it is the first occurrence of the pattern whose position is returned.
(c) *position* has value 0 because the pattern does not appear within the string.

Exercise 9.5

(a) *leftpart* = 'a▽few▽quite▽'
    rightpart = '▽words'
(b) *leftpart* = 'a'
    rightpart = 'few▽quite▽short▽words'
    Note that this is split at the first space character and that the character itself is in neither substring.
(c) *leftpart* = 'a▽few▽quite▽short▽words'
    rightpart = "
    Here the pattern is not in the source string and so leftpart is assigned the whole of the source string.

Exercise 9.6

The two substrings extracted from the source string will be given by *left* = 'An▽example' and *right* = 'string'. Hence for the left substring we have

> *leftstart* = 1
> *leftlength* = 10

and for the right string

> *rightstart* = 17
> *rightlength* = 6

Using the fact that *pos(pattern, subject)* = 11 and *length(pattern)* = 6 these values can be expressed more generally as

> *leftstart* = 1
> *leftlength* = pos(pattern, subject) − 1
> *rightstart* = pos(pattern, subject) + length(pattern)
> *rightlength* = length(subject) − rightstart + 1

You should convince yourself that these expressions are in fact valid in general.

Exercise 9.7

UNDERSTAND THE PROBLEM

Which procedure will we require in order to refine step 2 of the top level design?
The procedure *pos* can be used since it returns the value zero if the pattern is not there or the pattern is null.

DEVISE A SOLUTION

The final design is:

split
subject, pattern

	{Split *subject* at *pattern*}
1.1	{Nothing to initialize}
2.1	if *pos(pattern, subject)* = 0 then
3	*left* := *subject*
4	*right* := null
5	else
6.1	*leftstart* = 1
6.2	*leftlength* = *pos(pattern, subject)* − 1
6.3	*rightstart* = *pos(pattern, subject)* + *length(pattern)*
6.4	*rightlength* = *length(subject)* − *rightstart* + 1
6.5	*left* := *copy(subject, leftstart, leftlength)*
6.6	*right* := *copy(subject, rightstart, rightlength)*
7	ifend

left, right

Data table for procedure *split*

Identifier	Description	Type
leftstart	Index of start of left substring	integer variable
leftlength	Length of left substring	integer variable
rightstart	Index of start of right substring	integer variable
rightlength	Length of right substring	integer variable

TEST THE DESIGN

The previous text provided some test data. You should supplement this by data in which the pattern is not there and in which the pattern is null. It is also possible for *subject* to be null and your procedure needs to be tested when this is the case.

Exercise 9.8

UNDERSTAND THE PROBLEM

How do you know whether the replacement would exceed *stringsize* before carrying it out?
The lengths of all the individual strings are known and so the potential length of the string with replacement characters can be calculated prior to the replacement being done.
Which procedures from Section 9.1 will we require in order to carry out the replacement?
We shall need the procedure *delete* to get rid of the pattern and the procedure *insert* to insert the object string.
Write down the successive calls to *delete* and *insert* which will replace *pattern* in *subject* by *object* for each of the following values:

(a)   *subject* = 'a▽short▽word'
     pattern = 'short'
     object = 'four▽letter'
(b)   *subject* = 'a▽short▽word'
     pattern = 'hort'
     object = 'ensible'

In (a) we first delete the word 'short' using *delete(subject, 3, 5)* to get 'a▽ ▽word' and then insert 'four▽letter' at index 3 by the call *insert(subject, object,* 3). Notice that the number 3 here is the position of *pattern* in *subject* and that 5 represents its length. This will be a useful observation when you come to refine the design.

In (b) we first delete the word 'hort' using *delete(subject,* 4, 4) to get 'a▽s▽word' and then insert 'ensible' at index 4 by the call *insert(subject, object,* 4).

DEVISE A SOLUTION

We have chosen to introduce a variable which represents the position of the pattern in the subject string. Although the use of such a variable can be avoided, the design is clearer for its use.

---

replace

---

subject, pattern, object

	{Replace *pattern* in *subject* by *object*}
1.1	if *length(subject)* + *length(object)* − *length(pattern)* <= *stringsize* then
1.2	position := *pos(pattern, subject)*
2.1	if *position* > 0 then
3.1	*delete(subject, position, length(pattern))*
3.2	*insert(subject, object, position)*
4	ifend
5	ifend

---

subject

Data table for *replace*

Identifier	Description	Type
position	Position of deletion and insertion	integer variable

TEST THE DESIGN

The design should be tested with data similar to that in the examples above, together with data for which the pattern is not in the subject, the pattern is the null string, the subject is the null string and the object is the null string. Combinations of these should also be considered.

Exercise 9.9

The text is first split up so that none of the lines contains more than 23 characters and each line contains only complete words separated by single spaces. The symbol Δ has been used to denote a fixed font space character.

```
InΔorderΔtoΔjustify
someΔtextΔwhichΔuses
aΔmono
```

Spaces can now be added so that each line contains 23 characters. The first line requires the addition of four spaces to the three existing gaps. Each gap gets one space with the remaining addition space being positioned at the first gap. The second line requires three spaces to be distributed to three gaps, that is one space per gap. This then gives:

```
InΔΔΔorderΔΔtoΔΔjustify
someΔΔtextΔΔwhichΔΔuses
aΔmono
```

Exercise 9.10

The procedure *menu* has no source data and has results the user's choice. The type char will be used for this parameter.

The procedure *change* has *prose* and *linesinput* as source data and as it updates the entries of *prose* will return *prose* as results.

The procedure *deleteline* will require *prose* and *linesinput* as source data and as it deletes an element of *prose* will return both *prose* and *linesinput* as results.

The procedure *justify* will require *prose* and *linesinput* as source data but as it just outputs to the screen it produces no results.

Exercise 9.11

UNDERSTAND THE PROBLEM

The identifier *space* will denote the string constant whose value is a single space character and *ragged* will denote the ragged line which is being constructed.

Step 3 can be refined using the procedure *split* with pattern string *space* developed in Section 9.3. This procedure will split *remains* at the first occurrence of *space* and hence will enable the first word to be obtained. However, what would happen if *remains* had value '▽▽double▽space'?

The call *split(remains, space, word, remains)* would assign the null string to *word* and the string '▽double▽space' to *remains*. (Remember it splits at the first occurrence of the pattern and the pattern appears in neither string.) Multiple spaces must be skipped over and this can be achieved using a loop.

Step 7 requires a little care. Essentially it concatenates extracted words on to *ragged*. However, the extracted word could be the empty string, in which case concatenation is not required. Non-empty values must be concatenated onto the ragged string preceded by a space, except when the word is the first one assigned to ragged.

DEVISE A SOLUTION

A data table is given below and a final design is shown oppopsite:

Data table for procedure *extract*

Identifier	Description	Type
null	The null string	string constant value ''
space	A single space	char constant value '▽'
split	*(subject, pattern, left, right)*	(string, string, string, string)
spaceleft	Number of characters left in ragged	*linetype* variable
full	True represents ragged is full	*boolean* variable
word	Currently extracted word from remains	string variable

Exercise 9.12

UNDERSTAND THE PROBLEM

If there are five spaces to be divided among three gaps then the most right gap gets one of these spaces. How can the number 1 be derived from 5 and 3?

1 = 5 DIV 3

extract

---

prose, linesinput, linewidth, remains, nextline

	{Extract words from *prose* into *ragged*}	
1.1	*ragged := null*	
1.2	*spaceleft := linewidth*	
1.3	*full :=* false	
1.4	*textend :=* false	
2.1	loop while (not *full*) and (not *textend*)	
3.1	repeat	{get first word from *remains*}
3.2	split(*remains, space, word, remains*)	{loop allows for multiple spaces}
3.3	until (*word <> null*) or (*remains = null*)	{if *remains* consists only of spaces *word* is null on exit}
4.1	if *length(word) > spaceleft* then	{*word* will not fit into *remains*}
5.1	*remains := word + space + remains*	{concatenate it to the front of
5.2	*full :=* true	*remains* – do not forget the space}
6	else	
7.1	if *word <> null* then	{concatenate it in one of two ways}
7.2	if *ragged = null* then	{*word* is first word of new ragged line}
7.3	*ragged := word*	
7.4	else	{concat a space then *word* to *ragged*}
7.5	*ragged := ragged + space + word*	
7.6	ifend	
7.7	*spaceleft := spaceleft – length(word) – 1*	{Note this allows for a space
7.8	else	after word just concatenated}
7.9	do nothing	{see comment at step 3.3}
7.10	ifend	
8	ifend	
9.1	if *remains = null* then	{get more text from *prose*}
9.2	if *nextline > linesinput* then	
9.3	*textend :=* true	{all text has been processed}
9.4	else	
9.5	*remains := prose[nextline]*	
9.6	increment *nextline*	
9.7	ifend	
9.8	ifend	
10	loopend	

---

remains, nextline, ragged, textend

Processing would then moved to the middle gap, at which stage there would be four spaces to be divided into the two remaining gaps. What calculation is now required to work out the distribution?

4 DIV 2 gives the number of spaces to be inserted into this gap.

What condition will determine whether or not *ragged* needs justifying?

Both *shortfall* and *gapcount* will need to be positive – note both are required. This is because a line may contain exactly the correct number of characters by chance and so will not need justifying. In this situation *gapcount* will be positive and *shortfall* will be zero. On the other hand, a line which contains just one (very long) word will have a positive *shortfall* and zero *gapcount*. In this case the line cannot be right justified.

DEVISE A SOLUTION

A final design follows:

spacefill

---

ragged, linewidth

	{Justify *ragged*}	
1	if *ragged* <> *null* then	
2.1	*gapcount* := 0	
2.2	loop for *i* := 1 to *length*(*ragged*)	{calculate *gapcount*}
2.3	if *ragged*[*i*] = *space* then	
2.4	increment *gapcount*	
2.5	ifend	
2.6	loopend	{*gapcount* now calculated}
2.7	*shortfall* := *linewidth* − *length*(*ragged*)	{calculate *shortfall*}
3.1	if (*shortfall* > 0) and (*gapcount* > 0) then	{if *ragged* needs justifying}
4.1	*index* := *length*(*ragged*)	{start at end of *ragged*}
5.1	loop while *shortfall* > 0	{loop while spaces to distribute}
6.1	decrement *index*	
6.2	if *ragged*[*index*] = *space* then	
6.3	*nospaces* := *shortfall* DIV *gapcount*	{calculate no. spaces for this gap}
6.4	loop for *i* := 1 to *nospaces*	{insert that number of spaces}
6.5	insert(*ragged*, *space*, *index*)	
6.6	loopend	
6.7	*shortfall* := *shortfall* − *nospaces*	
6.8	decrement *gapcount*	
6.9	ifend	
7	loopend	
8	ifend	
9	ifend	
10	*justifiedline* := *ragged*	

---

justifiedline

Data table for *spacefill*

Identifier	Description	Type
null	The null string	string constant value "
space	A single space	char constant value '▽'
insert	(*anystring, implant, index*)	procedure(string, string, integer)
gapcount	The number of gaps in *ragged*	integer variable
i	Loop control variable	integer variable
shortfall	Number of spaces to be inserted	integer variable
index	Location of character of *ragged* being examined	*linetype* variable
nospaces	Number of spaces to distribute	integer variable

Exercise 10.1

The representation essentially consists of two items; an array of records and the variable *size* to record the number of current entries. These two items are wrapped up in a record type definition in order to hide the details of the representation from the user.

Data table for abstract data type *tabletype* (Version 2)

Identifier	Description	Type
maxsize	Maximum number of rows in the table	integer constant
rowtype	Record type definition	
	town	string variable
	church	integer variable
	recordend	
tabletype	Record type definition	
	item {The array holding rows}	array[0..*maxsize*] of *rowtype*
	size {Number of items in table}	0..*maxsize* variable
	recordend	

Exercise 10.2

UNDERSTAND THE PROBLEM

What is required to be done to the data table?
The private declaration of *tabletype* on page 173 will have to be changed to reflect the new structure.
Which routines will need rewriting?
The routines *isfull*, *insert*, *churchnumber* and *display* will have to be re-written to take account of the new representation. The routines *gettown* and *create* do not need to be changed because their design is still applicable in the new representation. The solution will therefore consist of a new module data table and new designs for the routines which have to be changed.

DEVISE A SOLUTION

The new module data table is:

Data table for module *surveytable2*

Identifier	Description	Type
	PUBLIC	
tabletype	Type definition representing the table	private
isfull	(*table*)	boolean function(*tabletype*)
insert	(*table*)	procedure(*tabletype*)
gettown	(*intown*)	procedure(string)
churchnumber	(*table, searchtown*)	procedure(*tabletype*, string)
display	(*table*)	procedure(*tabletype*)
create	(*table*)	procedure(*tabletype*)
	PRIVATE	
maxsize	Maximum number of rows in the table	integer constant
rowtype	Record type definition	
	town	string variable
	church	integer variable
	recordend	
tabletype	Record type definition	
	item {The array holding rows}	array[0..*maxsize*] of *rowtype*
	size {Number of items in table}	0..*maxsize*
	recordend	

---

insert

---

table

1	with *table* do
2	size := size + 1
3	write out 'Enter the name of the town '
4	read in *item*[*size*].*town*
5	write out 'Enter the number of churches in the town '
6	read in *item*[*size*].*church*
7	withend

---

table

---

churchnumber

---

table, searchtown

1	*table.item*[0].*town* := *searchtown*
2	*index* := *table.size*
3	with *table* do
4	loop while *item*[*index*].*town* <> *searchtown*
5	decrement *index*
6	loopend
7	if *index* <> 0 then
8	write out *searchtown*, ' has ', *item*[*index*].*church*, ' churches'
9	else
10	write out *searchtown*, ' is not in the table'
11	ifend
12	withend

---

display

---

table

1	write out 'Town', 'Churches'
2	with *table* do
3	loop for *index* := 1 to *size*
4	write out *item*[*index*].*town*, *item*[*index*].*church*
5	loopend
6	withend

---

isfull

---

table

1	*isfull* := (*table.size* = *maxsize*)

---

isfull

Data table for *churchnumber* and *display*

Identifier	Description	Type
index	Loop control variable	0..*maxsize* variable

TEST THE DESIGN

Each of the procedures and functions need to be individually tested and their parameters need to be checked that they agree with those in the specification.

Exercise 11.1

Data table

Identifier	Description	Type
intpointer	Pointer variable	pointer variable to integer
realpointer	Pointer variable	pointer variable to real

Exercise 11.2

1	*new*(*intpointer*)
2	*intpointer*^ := 100
3	*new*(*realpointer*)
4	*realpointer*^ := 34.5

Exercise 11.3

At step 3 *firstpointer* has been initialized and *firstpointer^* has been assigned the value 'A'. The variable *secondpointer*, although declared, is uninitialized and so does not point to a variable. Note it would be an error to attempt to write out *secondpointer^* or to compare *secondpointer* with *firstpointer*.

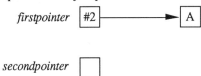

Step 4 assigns the address of *firstpointer* to the variable *secondpointer* and so this has the effect of making both pointers reference the same data. Thus at step 5 we have:

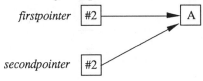

Step 6 assigns a new value to *secondpointer^* and thus both pointers still point to the same location which now contains 'B'. So at step 7 the picture is as follows:

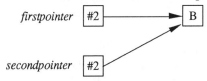

Step 8 sets aside new memory area for *secondpointer^* and step 9 initializes the value of this variable to 'C'. At this stage *firstpointer^* would have value 'B' and *secondpointer^* value 'C' but step 10 updates the value of *firstpointer* so that it points to the same location as *secondpointer*. This gives the picture below:

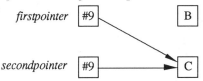

Note that the variable previously known as *firstpointer^* still has value 'B' but that now nothing points to it and it is effectively 'lost'.

Exercise 11.4

```
 8   with recordpointer^.linkfield^ do
 9       name := 'Jean'
10       married := false
11       age := 23
12   withend
```

Exercise 11.5

There are many ways of doing this. We have given two.

1 *new(recordpointer^.linkfield^.linkfield)*
2 *recordpointer^.linkfield^.linkfield^.name* := 'Susan'
3 *recordpointer^.linkfield^.linkfield^.married* := true
4 *recordpointer^.linkfield^.linkfield^.age* := 31

Alternatively we can use the *with* statement:

1 with *recordpointer^.linkfield^* do
2   new(linkfield)
3   *linkfield^.name* := 'Susan'
4   *linkfield^.married* := true
5   *linkfield^.age* := 31
6 withend

Exercise 11.6

create
1   *stack* := nil
stack

isempty
stack
1   *isempty* := (*stack* = nil)
isempty

The major difficulty with *pop* is working out the identifier corresponding to the fields of the record at the top of the stack.

UNDERSTAND THE PROBLEM

What is the identifier of the item at the top of the stack?
The variable *stack* points to the first record in the stack and so *stack^* is the record to which it points. The *stackitem* field of this record is required and its identifier is *stack^.stackitem*.

DEVISE A SOLUTION

pop
stack
1   if *isempty(stack)* then
2   write out 'stack underflow'
3   else
4   *item* := *stack^.stackitem*
5   *stack* := *stack^.link*
6   ifend
stack, item

TEST THE DESIGN

You should check that the design copies the first item in the sequence to *item* and then updates *stack* so that it points to the second record in the sequence. Note that in this design the record containing the item which is popped is lost in memory.

Exercise 11.7

The word *empty* would trigger the question: Does *pop* work on an empty stack? Since the operation of *pop* explicitly covers the case of an empty stack the design should be checked to see if it meets this specification.

The word *full* would trigger the question: Does *pop* work on a full stack? For the pointer representation we have excluded the possibility of a full stack and so the situation will not arise. In any event the definition of *pop* is unaffected by whether or not the stack is full.

The word *first* is again not relevant because *pop* can only remove the first item on the stack.

The word *last* can trigger the question: Does *pop* work correctly to remove the last item on the stack? Of course, if there is more than one item on the stack the question is meaningless because *pop* can only remove the first item. However, the question is relevant if there is only one item left on the stack. What it ought to do in these circumstances is to produce an empty stack as depicted by the box containing *nil* in step 1 of Figure 11.13. You may like to draw diagrams similar to Figure 11.13 to see that *stack* is indeed assigned the value nil in this instance.

Exercise 12.1

remove

queue

```
1  if isempty(queue) then
2      write out 'Cannot remove from an empty
            queue'
3  else
4      queue.head^.link := queue.head^.link^.link
5      if (head^.link = nil) then
6          tail := head
7      ifend
8  ifend
```

queue

front

queue

```
1  if isempty(queue) then
2      write out 'The queue is empty'
3  else
4      item := queue.head^.link^.queueitem
5  ifend
```

item

create

```
1  new(queue.head)
2  queue.tail := queue.head
3  queue.head^.link := nil
```

queue

insert

queue, item

```
1  new(temp)
2  temp^.queueitem := item
3  temp^.link := nil
4  queue.tail^.link := temp
5  queue.tail := temp
```

queue

isempty

queue

```
1  isempty := (queue.head = queue.tail)
```

isempty

Data table for procedure *insert*

Identifier	Description	Type
temp	Temporary pointer variable	*PtrToQueueRec* variable

Exercise 13.1

Since the link field of the 12.03 record will have to be updated to point to the new record, the search routine should identify the 12.03 record. Note that this record is just prior to the insertion point.

Exercise 13.2

(a)   The trace table for this design is as follows:

	lag	*lead*	*lead^.time < timegiven*	*lead^.link <> nil*
1	#20			
2		#40		
3			true	true
4	#40			
5		#60		
3			true	false
6				

At the end of the execution *lag* has value #40 instead of #60 as it ought to. The reason is that the condition *lead^.link <>* nil, which is there to avoid going beyond the end of the sequence, becomes false and so the loop is not executed and *lag* is not updated.

(b)   The trace table for this design is as follows:

	lag	*lead*	*lead^.time < timegiven*	*lead <> nil*
1	#20			
2		#40		
3			true	true
4	#40			
5		#60		
3			true	true
4	#60			
5		nil		
3			error	true

The error arises because an attempt is made to reference *lead^.time* when *lead* has value nil. This would lead to a run-time error on most systems.

Exercise 13.3

In the fragment below we have assumed that the time field is a real variable.

1.1	*timesearch(arrivals*, 12.05, *location)*	{*location* now has value #40}
1.2	new(*temp*)	{value #100 in Figure 13.5}
2.1	*temp^.time* := 12.05	
2.2	*temp^.flight* := 'VA057'	
2.3	*temp^.from* := 'Dallas'	
2.4	*temp^.eta* := 'Landed'	
2.5	*temp^.link* := *location^.link*	{assign #60 to *link* of *temp*}
3	*location^.link* := *temp*	{updates #40 *link* field to #100}

Exercise 13.4

lag^.link := *lead^.link*

Exercise 13.5

The procedure *create*

UNDERSTAND THE PROBLEM

What tasks does create have to do?

It has to return *arrivals*, which is a record representing the sequence. So it must create a pointer to the record type *SeqRec* and a dummy record whose link field must point to itself.

DEVISE A SOLUTION

create

---

1   new(*arrivals*.)
2   *arrivals^.link := arrivals*

---

arrivals

TEST THE DESIGN

The link field of the dummy record must point to itself. You should ensure that this is so.

The procedure *display*

UNDERSTAND THE PROBLEM

This procedure must work its way through the sequence writing out the field details for each record. This will require a pointer variable of type *ArrivalsSeq* which will point to the record currently being processed. How can you tell when the end of the sequence is reached?
The pointer variable will have value *arrivals* when the end of the sequence is reached.

DEVISE A SOLUTION

display

---

arrivals

1.1   clear screen
1.2   *current := arrivals^.link*
2   write out 'Due', 'Flight', 'From', 'ETA'
3   loop while *current <> arrivals*
4   with *current^* do
5   write out *time, flight, from, eta*
6   withend
7   *current := current^.link*
8   loopend

Data table for procedure *display*

Identifier	Description	Type
current	Pointer to record being written out	*ArrivalsSeq* variable

TEST THE DESIGN

This design can be tested with some of the example sequences given in the figures. It should also be tested with an empty sequence.

The procedure *insert* This procedure will need to declare *timesearch* as a local procedure.

DEVISE A SOLUTION

Data table for the procedure *insert*

Identifier	Description	Type
timesearch	*(origin, timegiven, location)*	procedure(*ArrivalsSeq*, real, *ArrivalsSeq*)
temp	Pointer to new record	*ArrivalsSeq* variable

insert

---

arrivals, newtime, newflight, newfrom, neweta

1	*timesearch(arrivals, newtime, location)*
2	new(*temp*)
3.1	*temp^.time := newtime*
3.2	*temp^.flight := newflight*
3.3	*temp^.from := newfrom*
3.4	*temp^.eta := neweta*
3.5	*temp^.link := location^.link*
4	*location^.link := temp*

---

arrivals

TEST THE DESIGN

Again the example sequences in the figures can be used as test data but the procedure must also be tested with an empty sequence and one in which the item sought is not present.

Exercise 13.6

The procedure *update*

UNDERSTAND THE PROBLEM

Is it *lead* or *lag* which will be required after the call to *flightsearch*?
The record at which *flightgiven* is located is required and so the required pointer is *lead*.

DEVISE A SOLUTION

update

---

arrivals, flightgiven

1	*flightsearch(arrivals, flightgiven, lead, lag)*
2	if *lead = arrivals* then
3	write out 'This flight is not in the list'
4	else
5	write 'Enter new estimated time of arrival '
6	read in *lead^.eta*
7	ifend

---

arrivals

TEST THE DESIGN

The guideline for testing abstract data types would suggest the following questions. Does *update* work on an empty sequence? Does it work if the record to be updated is the first one? Does it work if the record to be updated is the last one? Test data would need to be generated for each of these possibilities.

The procedure *delete*

UNDERSTAND THE PROBLEM

Which results need to be used after the call to *flightsearch*?
A clearer design is obtained if both of them are used, even though *lead = lag^.link*.

DEVISE A SOLUTION

delete

---

arrivals, flightgiven

---

1 *flightsearch(arrivals, flightgiven, lead, lag)*
2 if *lead = arrivals* then
3   write out 'This flight is not in the list'
4 else
5   *lag^.link := lead^.link*
6 ifend

---

arrivals

TEST THE DESIGN

Your test data should include examples similar to that for the procedure *update*.

Exercise 14.1

Atlanta precedes Chicago and so goes in its left subtree. Boston also precedes Chicago and so goes in its left subtree. However, it comes after Atlanta and so goes in the right subtree of Atlanta. Similarly, Baltimore goes to the left of Chicago, to the right of Atlanta and to the left of Boston. This gives the figure below:

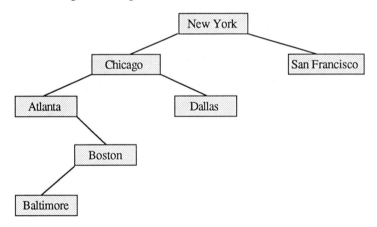

When the names are inserted in the order Baltimore, Atlanta, Boston a different tree is obtained. Baltimore goes to the left of Chicago. Atlanta goes to the left of Chicago and to the left of Baltimore. Finally Boston goes to the left of Chicago but to the right of Baltimore.

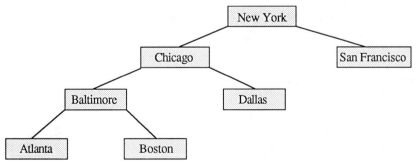

Exercise 14.2

isthere

---

tree, item

1.1	*current := tree*
1.2	*found :=* false
2.1	loop while (*current* <> nil) and not *found*
3.1	if *item = current^.data* then
3.2	*found =* true
3.3	else
3.4	if *item < current^.data* then
3.5	*current := current^.left*
3.6	else
3.7	*current := current^.right*
3.8	ifend
3.9	ifend
4	loopend
5.1	*isthere := found*

isthere

---

create

1	*tree :=* nil

tree

---

isempty

---

tree

1	*isempty :=* (*tree =* nil)

isempty

Data table for function *isthere*

Identifier	Description	Type
current	Pointer to node being accessed	*stringtree* variable
found	A boolean flag	boolean variable

Exercise 14.3

The inorder traversal would produce the symbols 2 + 3 − 4 * 5. These symbols are in the correct order but the brackets are missing. The traversal needs to be modified so that when a non-leaf node is encountered for the:
- first time, then an opening bracket is printed
- second time, then a closing bracket is printed

Exercise 15.1

It is trivial when it has length 1 because to write out a string of length 1 in reverse just requires the single character to be output.

Exercise 15.2

The design and a trace of it *given* = 'bat' is shown below.

reverse

given

1	if *length(given)* = 1 then
2	write *given*[1]
3	else
4.1	*first* := *given*[1]
4.2	*delete(given*, 1, 1)
5.1	*reverse(given)*
6.1	write *first*
7	ifend

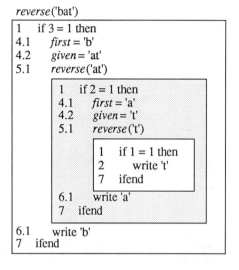

reverse ('bat')

1	if 3 = 1 then
4.1	*first* = 'b'
4.2	*given* = 'at'
5.1	*reverse* ('at')

1	if 2 = 1 then
4.1	*first* = 'a'
4.2	*given* = 't'
5.1	*reverse* ('t')

1	if 1 = 1 then
2	write 't'
7	ifend

6.1	write 'a'
7	ifend

6.1	write 'b'
7	ifend

Exercise 15.3

The *article* is *trivial* corresponds to the article having length zero or 1 because in either case it is palindromic.

Exercise 15.4

palindrome ('madam')

1	if (5 = 0) or (5 = 1) then
4	if 'm' = 'm' then
5	*given* = 'adam'
6	*given* = 'ada'
7	*palindrome* ('ada')

1	if (3 = 0) or (3 = 1) then
4	if 'a' = 'a' then
5	*given* = 'da'
6	*given* = 'd'
7	*palindrome* ('d')

1	if (1 = 0) or (1 = 1) then
2	'palindrome'
11	ifend

10	ifend
11	ifend

10	ifend
11	ifend

palindrome ('reader')

1	if (6 = 0) or (6 = 1) then
4	if 'r' = 'r' then
5	*given* = 'eader'
6	*given* = 'eade'
7	*palindrome* ('eade')

1	if (4 = 0) or (4 = 1) then
4	if 'e' = 'e' then
5	*given* = 'ade'
6	*given* = 'ad'
7	*palindrome* ('ad')

1	if (2 = 0) or (2 = 1) then
4	if 'a' = 'd' then
9	'not a palindrome'
10	ifend
11	ifend

10	ifend
11	ifend

10	ifend
11	ifend

Exercise 15.5

revprint(#6)

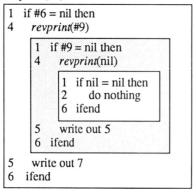

```
1   if #6 = nil then
4      revprint(#9)
        ┌──────────────────────────────────┐
        │ 1   if #9 = nil then              │
        │ 4      revprint(nil)              │
        │        ┌────────────────────────┐ │
        │        │ 1   if nil = nil then  │ │
        │        │ 2      do nothing      │ │
        │        │ 6   ifend              │ │
        │        └────────────────────────┘ │
        │ 5      write out 5               │
        │ 6   ifend                        │
        └──────────────────────────────────┘
5      write out 7
6   ifend
```

Exercise 15.6

print (#10)

```
1     if #10 = nil then
4        print(#20)  {the left subtree of New York record}
          ┌──────────────────────────────────────────────────────────┐
          │ 1   if #20 = nil then                                     │
          │ 4      print(nil)  {the left subtree of Chicago record}   │
          │        ┌────────────────────────┐                         │
          │        │ 1   if nil = nil then  │                         │
          │        │ 2      do nothing      │                         │
          │        │ 7   ifend              │                         │
          │        └────────────────────────┘                         │
          │ 5      write out Chicago                                  │
          │ 6      print(nil)  {the right subtree of Chicago record}  │
          │        ┌────────────────────────┐                         │
          │        │ 1   if nil = nil then  │                         │
          │        │ 2      do nothing      │                         │
          │        │ 7   ifend              │                         │
          │        └────────────────────────┘                         │
          │ 7   ifend                                                 │
          └──────────────────────────────────────────────────────────┘
5        write out New York
6        print(#40) {the right subtree of New York record}
          ┌────────────────────────────────────────────────────────────────┐
          │ 1   if #40 = nil then                                           │
          │ 4      print(nil) {the left subtree of San Francisco record}    │
          │        ┌────────────────────────┐                               │
          │        │ 1   if nil = nil then  │                               │
          │        │ 2      do nothing      │                               │
          │        │ 7   ifend              │                               │
          │        └────────────────────────┘                               │
          │ 5      write out San Francisco                                  │
          │ 6      print(nil) {the right subtree of San Francisco record}   │
          │        ┌────────────────────────┐                               │
          │        │ 1   if nil = nil then  │                               │
          │        │ 2      do nothing      │                               │
          │        │ 7   ifend              │                               │
          │        └────────────────────────┘                               │
          │ 7   ifend                                                       │
          └────────────────────────────────────────────────────────────────┘
7     ifend
```

Exercise 15.7

insert(#10, Chicago)

```
1        if isempty(#10) then
5.1         if Chicago < New York then      {#10^.data  = New York}
5.2           insert(#20, Chicago)          {#10^.left  = #20}

                 1        if isempty(#20) then
                 5.1         if Chicago < Chicago then      {#20^.data  = Chicago}
                 5.4            if Chicago > Chicago then    {#20^.data  = Chicago}
                 5.7              write out Duplicate entry
                 5.8           ifend
                 5.9         ifend
                 7        ifend

5.9      ifend
7        ifend
```

SOLUTIONS TO PROBLEMS

Problem 3.1

What does it mean to say that the cost of a BTU is to be input as a decimal number of pence?
It means that the cost may be a real number of pence as opposed to an integer number of pence.

Suppose that a BTU costs 38.5p and that the previous meter reading was 2120 and the current reading is 2500. What calculations are required to work out the total cost?

The difference in readings is 380 cubic feet which is 380*1.016 BTUs, that is 386.08 BTUs. At 38.5p per BTU this gives a gas used cost of 386.08*38.5p. This will need to be converted to pounds and be added to the standard charge.

DEVISE A SOLUTION

A top level design is:

> {Gas bill calculation}
> 1   read in the data
> 2   calculate the cost
> 3   write out results

This may be refined as:

> {Gas bill calculation}
> 1.1   write out 'Enter the price per BTU in pence '
> 1.2   read in *priceBTU*
> 1.3   write out 'Enter previous meter reading '
> 1.4   read in *previous*
> 1.5   write out 'Enter current meter reading '
> 1.6   read in *current*
> 2.1   *GasCost* := (*current* − *previous*)*priceBTU*1.016/100

306

2.2   *TotalCost := GasCost* + 8.70
3.1   write out 'Total gas bill is ', *TotalCost*

Data table

Identifier	Description	Type
priceBTU	Price of one BTU	real variable
previous	Previous meter reading	integer variable
current	Current meter reading	integer variable
GasCost	Cost of gas used	real variable
TotalCost	Overall bill	real variable

A design could be developed which avoids the introduction of the variables *GasCost* and *TotalCost* but it would have a different top level design.

　　　{Gas bill version 2}
1　read in the data
2　write out results

This would then refine to:

　　　{Gas bill version 2}
1.1　write out 'Enter the price per BTU in pence '
1.2　read in *priceBTU*
1.3　write out 'Enter previous meter reading '
1.4　read in *previous*
1.5　write out 'Enter current meter reading '
1.6　read in *current*
2.1　write out 'Total gas bill is ', (*current* − *previous*)*priceBTU*1.016/100 + 8.70

Here all the calculation is done as part of the write out statement. This illustrates that write out statements can include formulae. However, it is less clear in this design how the overall cost is calculated. Although the variables *GasCost* and *TotalCost* are strictly unnecessary they do add to the clarity.

TEST THE DESIGN

You should check that the formulae in this design are correct and give the same answer for the data given above.

Problem 3.2

UNDERSTAND THE PROBLEM

How should the input for each fraction be obtained?
The user will have to be asked to input the numerator and denominator separately and the input data will have to be assigned to appropriate variables.
If the numerator and denominator for the first fraction are 3 and 4 respectively and those for the second fraction are 2 and 5 respectively what are the values of the numerator and denominator of their product?
The numerator has value 3*2 and the denominator 4*5, that is, 6 and 20 respectively.

DEVISE A SOLUTION

A top level design is:

{Multiplication of fractions}
1   read in the fractions
2   calculate their product
3   write out results

This can be refined to:

{Multiplication of fractions}
1.1   write out 'Enter the numerator of the first fraction '
1.2   read in *numerator1*
1.3   write out 'Enter the denominator of the first fraction '
1.4   read in *denominator1*
1.5   write out 'Enter the numerator of the second fraction '
1.6   read in *numerator2*
1.7   write out 'Enter the denominator of the second fraction '
1.8   read in *denominator2*
2.1   *numprod := numerator1*numerator2*
2.2   *denomprod := denominator1*denominator2*
3.1   write out 'The numerator of the product is ', *numprod*
3.2   write out 'The denominator of the product is ', *denomprod*

Data table

Identifier	Description	Type
numerator1	First fraction numerator	integer variable
denominator1	First denominator	integer variable
numerator2	Second numerator	integer variable
denominator2	Second denominator	integer variable
numprod	Product numerator	integer variable
denomprod	Product denominator	integer variable

TEST THE DESIGN

You should test your design against the data above.

Problem 3.3

UNDERSTAND THE PROBLEM

What will be the cost of 48 boxes?
There are 4 lots of 10 boxes and 8 single boxes and so the purchase price is 4*£45 + 8*£5 and this is then subject to tax.

DEVISE A SOLUTION

A top level design is:

{Floppy disk price calculation}
1   read in number of boxes purchased
2   calculate number of multiples of boxes of 10
3   calculate number of single boxes
4   calculate total cost
5   write out results

This may be refined as:

{Floppy disk price calculation}
1.1   write out 'Enter the number of boxes bought '
1.2   read in *boxes*
2.1   *cheap* := *boxes* DIV 10
3.1   *expensive* := *boxes* MOD 10
4.1   *cost* := 1.15*(45**cheap* + 5**expensive*)
5.1   write out 'Total cost inclusive of tax is ', *cost*

Data table

Identifier	Description	Type
boxes	Number of boxes bought	integer variable
cheap	Number of sets of 10 boxes	integer variable
expensive	Number of single boxes	integer variable
cost	Overall cost	real variable

Note how the cost has to be of real type, whereas the various box numbers are all of integer type.

TEST THE DESIGN

In addition to the data above you should check that your design works with a number of boxes which is less than 10, in which case no special reduction takes place.

Problem 3.4

UNDERSTAND THE PROBLEM

How many units will be charged for a 361 second call?
This call goes one second over a single unit and so there is a charge of 2 units.
If *duration* represents the length of a call why does the formula 1 + *duration* DIV 360 not give the correct answer for the number of units used?
Because a call of exactly 360 seconds costs 1 unit whereas the formula gives 2 units.

DEVISE A SOLUTION

A top level design is:

    {Cost of a telephone call}
1   read in data
2   calculate cost
3   write out results

This design can be refined in many different ways. Two alternatives are given in detail.

	{Cost of a telephone call version 1}		{Cost of a telephone call version 2}
1.1	write out 'Enter duration of call '	1.1	write out 'Enter duration of call '
1.2	read in *duration*	1.2	read in *duration*
2.1	*wholeunits* := *duration* DIV 360	2.1	*wholeunits* := *duration* DIV 360
2.2	*timeleft* := *duration* MOD 360	2.2	if (*duration* MOD 360 > 0) then
2.3	if *timeleft* > 0 then	2.3	increment *wholeunits*
2.4	increment *wholeunits*	2.4	ifend
2.5	ifend	2.5	*cost* := 1.15*4.4**wholeunits*
2.6	*cost* := 1.15*4.4**wholeunits*	3.1	write out 'The cost of the call is ', *cost*
3.1	write out 'The cost of the call is ', *cost*		

Data table (for both designs)

Identifier	Description	Type
duration	Length of call	integer variable
wholeunits	Number of units used	integer variable
timeleft	Time elapsed of current charged unit	integer variable
cost	Cost of call	real variable

In version 1 if *timeleft* is greater than zero this indicates that the caller has gone into another unit of time and so the number of units used is incremented. If *timeleft* is zero then the call has used an exact multiple of 360 seconds and so is not liable for another unit's charge. In version 2, the variable *timeleft* is avoided by the use of the expression (*duration* MOD 360 > 0) as the condition in the *if* statement.

Yet another possibility using the same top level design is to add 259 to the value of *duration*. Then the number of units used is given by *duration* DIV 360. You may need to convince yourself of this.

TEST THE DESIGN

Clearly you need to take care that your design produces the correct cost when the duration of a call is a multiple of 360 or is a value like 361 which just goes into the next charge unit.

Problem 3.5

UNDERSTAND THE PROBLEM

What should be output if the number 5 is entered?
A message saying that 5 is not exactly divisible by 3.

DEVISE A SOLUTION

A top level design is:

```
    {Test for divisibility by 3}
1   read in an integer
2   test for divisibility
3   write out results
```

This may be refined to:

```
        {Test for divisibility}
1.1     write out 'Enter an integer '
1.2     read in number
2.1     remainder := number MOD 3
3.1     if remainder = 0 then
3.2         write out 'The number is exactly divisible by 3'
3.3     else
3.4         write out 'The number is not exactly divisible by 3'
3.5     ifend
```

Data table

Identifier	Description	Type
number	Input integer	integer variable
remainder	Remainder on division by 3	integer variable

The introduction of the variable *remainder* was not strictly necessary here and could be avoided. To do so requires a slightly different top level design.

> {Test for divisibility by 3}
> 1 read in an integer
> 2 write out results

This is then refined to:

> {Test for divisibility}
> 1.1 write out 'Enter an integer '
> 1.2 read in *number*
> 2.1 if (*number* MOD 3 = 0) then
> 2.2   write out 'The number is exactly divisible by 3'
> 2.3 else
> 2.4   write out 'The number is not exactly divisible by 3'
> 2.5 ifend

TEST THE DESIGN

Test data should consist of numbers which are divisible by 3 and those which are not divisible by 3.

Problem 3.6

UNDERSTAND THE PROBLEM

The 14th February 1995 will be entered by a user as day 14, month 12 and year 1994. For this date what are the values of century and decade?
They have values 19 and 94 respectively.
What day code is generated by the formula?
(13*month −1) DIV 5 is 155 DIV 5, that is 31; decade DIV 4 is 94 DIV 4, that is 23; century DIV 4 is 19 DIV 4, that is 4. The whole expression for the day code is therefore

> (31 + 23 + 4 + 94 + 14 − 2*19) MOD 7

that is, 128 MOD 7 which is 2.

DEVISE A SOLUTION

A top level design is:

> {Find day of the week}
> 1 read in the date
> 2 calculate the century and the decade
> 3 evaluate formula
> 4 write out result

This may be refined to:

> {Find day of the week}
> 1.1 write out 'Enter the number of the day '
> 1.2 read in *day*
> 1.3 write out 'Enter the coded month '
> 1.4 read in *month*
> 1.5 write out 'Enter the year, coded if necessary '
> 1.6 read in *year*

2.1   *century := year* DIV 100
2.2   *decade := year* MOD 100
3.1   *daycode := ((13*month − 1)* DIV 5 + *decade* DIV 4 + *century* DIV 4 + *decade* + *day*
            − 2*century) MOD 7
4.1   write out 'Your date falls on day ', *daycode*

Data table

Identifier	Description	Type
day	See the text in the statement of the	integer variable
month	problem for a description of all these	integer variable
year	variables	integer variable
century		integer variable
decade		integer variable
daycode		integer variable

TEST THE DESIGN

A check should be made to see that the formula has been correctly expressed. The major problem here is with the generation of the two variables *century* and *decade*.

Problem 3.7

UNDERSTAND THE PROBLEM

A user will now input a date like 14th February 1995 as day 14, month 2 and year 1995. What will the design have to do to this data before the formula is applied?
The month will have to be converted to 12 and the year to 1994.
Try some other dates to see how they are to be converted.

DEVISE A SOLUTION

The top level design of Problem 3.6 must be slightly modified here.

      {Find day of the week with standard month coding}
1   read in the date
2   code the number representing the month
3   calculate the century and the decade
4   evaluate formula
5   write out result

This leads to the following final design:

      {Find day of the week}
1.1   write out 'Enter the number of the day '
1.2   read in *day*
1.3   write out 'Enter the month '
1.4   read in *month*
1.5   write out 'Enter the year '
1.6   read in *year*
2.1   if *month* <= 2 then
2.2   *month := month* + 10
2.3   *year := year* − 1
2.3   else

2.4   *month := month − 2*

2.5   ifend

3.1   *century := year* DIV 100

3.2   *decade := year* MOD 100

4.1   *daycode :=* ((13∗*month −* 1) DIV 5 + *decade* DIV 4 + *century* DIV 4 + *decade* + *day*
                  − 2∗*century*) MOD 7

5.1   write out 'Your date falls on day ', *daycode*

The data table is as given in Problem 3.6.

TEST THE DESIGN

As the major part of this design has already been tested it is only necessary to test that the coding process has been done correctly.

Problem 4.1

UNDERSTAND THE PROBLEM

If a user enters 0 for the initial value what should happen?
A message saying that the input is in error should be output followed by a prompt to try again.
What should happen if the user's next try is also in error?
Exactly the same thing.
What control structure does this suggest for the validation of the initial value?

DEVISE A SOLUTION

The same top level design as used on page 37 can be used, but step 1.2 must be refined in a different way. The same identifiers as used in the text have been used in the design below.

         {Validate user input for only positive values}

1.1   write out 'Enter initial value of micro '

1.2.1   read in *value*

1.2.2   loop while *value* <= 0

1.2.3   write out 'The initial value must be positive, please try again'

1.2.4   read in *value*

1.2.5   loopend

Note that the loop at step 1.2.2 is not executed at all if the user inputs a positive number at the first request. Moreover if the first attempt is not positive then the loop will execute repeatedly until a positive input is received.

TEST THE DESIGN

You may wish to draw a trace table for the part of the design shown above.

Problem 4.2

UNDERSTAND THE PROBLEM

How should the input string 'Problem' be output?
It should appear as:

P
r
o
b
l
e
m

A top level design is:

```
    {write out input string one character per line}
1   initialize variables referenced in loop
2   loop while there are characters to process
3       process character
4   loopend
```

This can be refined to

```
        {write out input string one character per line}
1.1     write out 'Input your string '
1.2     read in line
1.3     index := 1
2.1     loop while index <= length(line)
3.1         write out line[index]
3.2         increment index
4       loopend
```

Data table

Identifier	Description	Type
line	The input string	string variable
index	Loop control variable	integer variable

Test data needs to check that the loop executes the correct number of times and that *index* does not go out of range. The trace table below checks this with an input value of 'An'.

Step	*line*	*index*	*index := length(line)* [†]	Step 3.1
1.2	An			
1.3		1		
2.1			true	
3.1				A
3.2		2		
2.1			true	
3.1				n
3.2		3		
2.1			false	
4				

† Here *length(line)* = 2

Problem 4.3

The user could just press the <return> key in response to the request for input. This would have the effect of assigning the null string to *line*. The length of the null string is zero and so the loop at step 2.1 would not execute and program execution would terminate. No output at all would be generated by the program and the user would probably be confused by the apparent lack of activity caused by the input. If the assumption is removed a step 5 could be included which would output a suitable message to cover the possibility of a null input. It would need to be an *if* statement.

Problem 4.4

```
        {Depreciation with zero rate as a possibility}
1.1     write out 'Enter the depreciation rate as a number in range 0–100'
1.2     read in rate
2.1     if rate = 0 then
3           write out 'No depreciation ever takes place'
4       else
5.1       year := 0
5.2       NewValue := OriginalValue
5.3       loop while NewValue > 50
5.4           NewValue := (100 – rate)*NewValue/100
5.5           increment year
5.6       loopend
5.7       write out 'Original value will have halved by the year ', year
6       ifend
```

The data table is the same as that used in the text. Note that here there is a loop within the *else* clause of an *if* statement.

TEST THE DESIGN

Trace tables should be drawn with various values of *rate* including zero.

Problem 4.5

UNDERSTAND THE PROBLEM

The basic structure of the design will be a loop while there are menu items to process. The loop will be controlled by a sentinel value for the unit price. After the sentinel value is entered the user should not be asked for a quantity. How can this be achieved?

There are many methods. One way is to read in the unit price just before the end of the loop statements so that the loop condition is encountered immediately afterwards. Positioning of the statement to read in the quantity then has to be carefully considered. Another method is to input the unit price and follow it with an *if* statement which is executed only when the unit price is non-zero.

DEVISE A SOLUTION

A top level design is:

```
        {Produce a bill for fast-food outlet}
1   initialize variables referenced in the loop
2   loop while there are inputs to process
```

```
3      process input
4   loopend
5   write out results
```

Two refinements of this design are given which reflect the discussion above:

	{Produce a bill for fast-food outlet}		{Produce a bill for fast-food outlet}
1.1	*bill* := 0	1.1	*bill* := 0
1.2	*totalno* := 0	1.2	*totalno* := 0
1.3	write out 'Enter unit price or 0 to quit '	1.3	*UnitPrice* := 1
1.4	read in *UnitPrice*	2.1	loop while *UnitPrice* > 0
2.1	loop while *UnitPrice* > 0	3.1	write out 'Enter unit price or 0 to quit '
3.1	write out 'Enter quantity for this price '	3.2	read in *UnitPrice*
3.2	read in *quantity*	3.3	if *UnitPrice* > 0 then
3.3	*bill* := *bill* + *quantity*∗*UnitPrice*	3.4	write out 'Enter quantity for this price '
3.4	*totalno* := *totalno* + *quantity*	3.5	read in *quantity*
3.5	write out 'Enter unit price or 0 to quit '	3.6	*bill* := *bill* + *quantity*∗*UnitPrice*
3.6	read in *UnitPrice*	3.7	*totalno* := *totalno* + *quantity*
4	loopend	3.8	ifend
5.1	write out *totalno*, ' items ordered'	4	loopend
5.2	write out 'Total cost ', *bill*	5.1	write out *totalno*, ' items ordered'
		5.2	write out 'Total cost ', *bill*

Data table

Identifier	Description	Type
bill	Total bill of the order	real variable
UnitPrice	Cost of a food item	real variable
quantity	Quantity required of given menu item	integer variable
totalno	Total number of items ordered	integer variable

TEST THE DESIGN

We shall not provide a trace table for this design. Potential critical data would include the possibility that the first unit price entered is zero.

Problem 4.6

UNDERSTAND THE PROBLEM

We cannot just assign the real number to an integer variable but we can count the number of times 1 has to be subtracted from the real number before we get zero.

DEVISE A SOLUTION

We give only a final design.

```
        {reals with no fractional part}
1.1   write out 'Enter a real number with zero decimal part'
1.2   read in realnumber
1.3   wholenumber := 0
2.1   loop while realnumber > 0
2.2       increment wholenumber
2.3       decrement realnumber
3     loopend
4     write out wholenumber
```

Data table

Identifier	Description	Type
realnumber	A real number	real variable
wholenumber	Integer equivalent of *realnumber*	integer variable

TEST THE DESIGN

The major test is to confirm that the loop executes the correct number of times.

Step	*realnumber*	*wholenumber*	*realnumber* > 0
1.2	3.0		
1.3		0	
2.1			true
2.2		1	
2.3	2.0		
2.1			true
2.2		2	
2.3	1.0		
2.1			true
2.2		3	
2.3	0.0		
2.1			false

As the specification refers only to positive real numbers we do not need to test the design for an input of 0.0.

Problem 4.7

The condition at step 2.1 would need to be changed to:

2.1   loop while *realnumber* >= 1

Try drawing a trace table for the real number 3.45 if you cannot see this. In fact this condition would work equally well in Problem 4.6.

Problem 4.8

UNDERSTAND THE PROBLEM

The average length of the words in the text will be the total number of non-space characters divided by the number of words. What are the word length averages for each of the following strings?
(a)   'Introduction▽'
(b)   'Two▽words▽'
(c)   'This▽is▽a▽sentence▽'
(d)   'colon:▽'
The values are 12, 4, 3.75 and 6. Note how in the last example the punctuation is considered to be part of the word.
When averages are required care must be taken to avoid potential divide by zero errors. Is this a difficulty here?
No – the specification says that the user must input at least one non-space character which

means that the average will always be defined.
How can the constraint that the input must terminate with a space be used?
Every word, including the last is identified by a space character.

DEVISE A SOLUTION

A top level design is:

> {word count program}
> 1   read in the text
> 2   initialize variable referenced in the loop
> 3   loop while there are characters to process
> 4   process character
> 5   loopend
> 6   calculate average word length
> 7   write out results

In order to refine this we note that the loop must terminate once the end of the text is encountered. We shall use the *length* function to control the loop. Variables will be required to hold the number of characters (excluding space characters) and the number of words in the input string. An index variable will be required for accessing the individual characters of the input. In the final design the char constant *space* has been used to denote the space character.

> {word count program}
> 1.1   write out 'Enter your line of text with single spaces between words'
> 1.2   write out 'Terminate input with a single space '
> 1.3   read in *line*
> 2.1   *index* := 1
> 2.2   *wordcount* := 0
> 2.3   *lettercount* := 0
> 3.1   loop while *index* <= *length(line)*
> 4.1   if *line[index]* = *space* then
> 4.2   increment *wordcount*
> 4.3   else
> 4.4   increment *lettercount*
> 4.5   ifend
> 4.6   increment *index*
> 5   loopend
> 6.1   *average* := *lettercount/wordcount*
> 7.1   write out 'Average word length is ', *average*

Data table

Identifier	Description	Type
space	Space character	char constant value '▽'
line	A line of text	string variable
index	Loop control variable	integer variable
wordcount	Number of words in *line*	integer variable
lettercount	Number of letters in *line*	integer variable
average	Average word length	real variable

TEST THE DESIGN

Access to a character beyond the dynamic length of the input string must be avoided. The trace table below assumes that the input data is 'I▽am▽' which has dynamic length 5.

Step	index	wordcount	lettercount	index <= length(line)	line(index) = space
2.1	1			†	
2.2		0			
2.3			0		
3.1				true	
4.1					false
4.4			1		
4.6	2				
3.1				true	
4.1					true
4.2		1			
4.6	3				
3.1				true	
4.1					false
4.4			2		
4.6	4				
3.1				true	
4.1					false
4.4			3		
4.6	5				
3.1				true	
4.1					true
4.2		2			
4.6	6				
3.1				false	

† *length(line)* has value 5

We can see from this table that once *index* has the value 6 no attempt is made to use this index to access *line*, thus an out of range error does not occur.

Problem 4.9

UNDERSTAND THE PROBLEM

What is the value of the new string if the input string is 'a▽short▽sentence'?
The new string is 'a▽▽short▽▽sentence'.
Can the input string begin with a space?
Yes, in which case the output string will begin with two spaces.
Can it end in a space?
Yes, in which case the output string will end with two spaces.

DEVISE A SOLUTION

A top level design is

```
      {Insert extra space characters in a string}
  1   initialize variables referenced in the loop
  2   loop for all characters in old string
  3      copy current character to new string
```

4   process current character
5   loopend
6   write out results

Step 4 will have to determine whether or not the current character is a space and take the appropriate action. It will then have to move on to the next character in the input string. This leads to the final design:

{Insert extra space characters in a string}
1.1   write out 'Enter the string with no adjacent space characters '
1.2   read in *oldstring*
1.3   *newstring* := "
1.4   *position* := 1
2.1   loop while *position* <= *length*[*oldstring*]
3.1   *newstring* := *newstring* + *oldstring*[*position*]
4.1   if *oldstring*[*position*] = *space* then
4.2   *newstring* := *newstring* + *space*
4.3   ifend
4.4   increment *position*
5   loopend
6.1   write out 'The new string is ' *newstring*

Data table

Identifier	Description	Type
space	The space character	char constant value '▽'
oldstring	User input string	string variable
position	Loop control variable	integer variable
newstring	String with extra spaces	string variable

TEST THE DESIGN

We shall use the string 'a▽b▽' as the input string in the trace table opposite. We can see from this table that loop execution ceases at the correct place and that the new string has the correct value at this point. You may have wondered why the restriction that the input string must not contain adjacent space characters was imposed. If you trace through this design with an input string of 'a▽short▽ ▽sentence' then the output string will be 'a▽▽short▽ ▽ ▽sentence'. This would not be a good way of allocating additional spaces because what was already a large gap becomes a very large gap and this looks unsightly. One way of overcoming this is to distribute to the double space just a single additional space but to do this requires a more sophisticated design strategy which we have not yet covered.

Problem 5.1

The number of executions is known at execution time because if, say the user enters the string 'Problem' then the loop must execute 7 times, that is, *length*('Problem') times. A design using a *for* loop is:

{write out input string one character per line}
1.1   write out 'Input your string '
1.2   read in *line*
2.1   loop for *index* := 1 to *length*(*line*)
3.1   write out *line*[*index*]
4   loopend

Step	oldstring	newstring	position	position <= length(oldstring)	oldstring [position] = space
1.2	'a▽b▽'				
1.3		''			
1.4			1		
2.1				true	
3.1		'a'			
4.1					false
4.4			2		
2.1				true	
3.1		'a▽'			
4.1					true
4.2		'a▽▽'			
4.4			3		
2.1				true	
3.1		'a▽▽b'			
4.1					false
4.4			4		
2.1				true	
3.1		'a▽▽b▽'			
4.1					true
4.2		'a▽▽b▽▽'			
4.4			5		
2.1				false	

Problem 5.2

UNDERSTAND THE PROBLEM

What should be the output if the user does just enter an asterisk?
Essentially two null strings each preceded by its prompt.
What sort of data should you use to test your design? Are there any critical values?

DESIGN A SOLUTION

A top level design is

```
    {Split a string at a *}
1   read in the string
2   initialize variables referenced in loop
3   loop while current character is not a *
4       concatenate current character to firstword
5   loopend
6   skip over the *
7   assign remaining characters to secondword
8   write out results
```

Since the location of the asterisk is unknown, the loop at step 3 has to be designed as a *while* loop because the number of loop executions is not known. Since the *length* function gives the length of the input string, step 7 can be designed as a *for* loop running from the index of the character following the asterisk to the end of the string.

    1.1   write out 'Enter two words separated by a single asterisk'

1.2   read in *TwoWords*
2.1   *firstword* := "
2.2   *secondword* := "
2.3   *index* := 1
3.1   loop while *TwoWords*[*index*] <> '*'
4.1   *firstword* := *firstword* + *TwoWords*[*index*]
4.2   increment *index*
5   loopend
6.1   increment *index*
7.1   loop for *j* := *index* to *length*(*TwoWords*)
7.2   *secondword* := *secondword* + *TwoWords*[*j*]
7.3   loopend
8.1   write out 'First word is ' *firstword*
8.2   write out 'Second word is ' *secondword*

Data table

Identifier	Description	Type
TwoWords	User input string	string variable
firstword	Characters preceding * in input string	string variable
secondword	Characters after * in input string	string variable
index	Index into string variable	integer variable
j	Loop control variable	integer variable

TEST THE DESIGN

You should trace through the design with data which includes the following types of input: 'one*two', '*', '*two', 'one*'.

Problem 5.3

UNDERSTAND THE PROBLEM

What is the score of a skater whose marks from the eight judges are 5.2, 5.4, 5.3, 6.2, 5.3, 5.3, 4.8, 5.0?
The two discarded scores are 6.2 and 4.8. The remaining six scores have an average of 5.25. As the data is entered what running values need to be stored?
A running total of all the scores entered plus a record of the highest and lowest scores so far entered. The highest and lowest scores can then be deducted from the running total once all the data has been entered. Care must be taken initializing the highest and lowest scores.

DEVISE A SOLUTION

A top level design is:

     {Ice skating judging}
  1   initialize variables referenced in loop
  2   loop for all judges
  3   process current judge's score
  4   loopend
  5   calculate average
  6   write out result

We give two refinements which initialize the highest and lowest scores in different ways:

{Ice skating judging version 1}
1.1   *lowest* := 6
1.2   *highest* := 0
1.3   *total* := 0
2.1   loop for *i* := 1 to 8
3.1   write out 'Enter score for judge ', *i*
3.2   read in *score*
3.3   *total* := *total* + *score*
3.4   if *score* > *highest* then
3.5   *highest* := *score*
3.6   ifend
3.7   if *score* < *lowest* then
3.8   *lowest* := *score*
3.9   ifend
4   loopend
5.1   *total* := *total* − *highest* − *lowest*
5.2   *average* := *total* /6
6.1   write out 'Skater has scored ', *average*

{Ice skating judging version 2}
1.1   write out 'Enter score for judge 1'
1.2   read in *score*
1.3   *total* := *score*
1.4   *lowest* := *score*
1.5   *highest* := *score*
2.1   loop for *i* := 2 to 8
3.1   write out 'Enter score for judge ', *i*
3.2   read in *score*
3.3   *total* := *total* + *score*
3.4   if *score* > *highest* then
3.5   *highest* := *score*
3.6   ifend
3.7   if *score* < *lowest* then
3.8   *lowest* := *score*
3.9   ifend
4   loopend
5.1   *total* := *total* − *highest* − *lowest*
5.2   *average* := *total* /6
6.1   write out 'Skater has scored ', *average*

Data table

Identifier	Description	Type
lowest	Lowest of 8 scores	real variable
highest	Highest of 8 scores	real variable
total	Sum of all 8 scores	real variable
score	An individual judges score	real variable
average	Skater's overall score	real variable
i	Loop control variable	integer variable

Care has to be taken to initialize *highest* and *lowest* correctly. In the first version *highest* is initialized to 0. Any non-zero score will update this value. If all scores are zero then the value is correct. Similarly *lowest* is initialized to 6. Any score less than 6 will update this value but if all eight judges award 6 then *lowest* has the correct value.

TEST THE DESIGN

The scores used above should be included in the test data. Your design should also be tested for the critical data where all eight judges score the same value. In particular, all eight scores of zero and then all eight scores of 6.

Problem 5.4

UNDERSTAND THE PROBLEM

Taking particular note of the space characters what will be output if the user enters the following text: 'Begin here.▽This sentence is on a new line.▽The number 2.5 is a real number.'?
The output will be:
      Begin here.
      ▽This sentence is on a new line.
      ▽The number 2.
      5 is a real number.

DEVISE A SOLUTION

A top level design is:

{Output sentences on a new line}
1 read in the text
2 loop for all characters
3   write out the character on appropriate line
4 loopend

This may be refined to:

{Output sentences on a new line}
1.1 write 'Enter the text '
1.2 read in *paragraph*
2.1 loop for *i* := 1 to *length(paragraph)*
3.1   if *paragraph[i]* = '.' then
3.2   write out *paragraph[i]*
3.3   else
3.4   write *paragraph[i]*
3.5   ifend
4   loopend

Data table

Identifier	Description	Type
paragraph	Input text	string variable
i	Loop control variable	integer variable

TEST THE DESIGN

Data similar to that above should be used. Possible critical data here is an input string consisting of only a single full stop and one with no full stops at all.

Problem 5.5

UNDERSTAND THE PROBLEM

What day number does the user have to enter for the month above?
Day 3 corresponds to Tuesday.
What is the relationship between the day entered and the number of initial spaces in the calendar?
The number of spaces is one less than the day on which the month starts.
A new line must be produced after the numbers 5, 12, 19 and 26 are written out in the example above. How can this be done?
This can be achieved by keeping a count of the number of columns written out, or by deriving a formula which uses the current day and the day on which the first of the month falls.

DEVISE A SOLUTION

A top level design is:

{Write out a calendar}
1 initialize variables
2 write out headings
3 write out leading blanks
4 write out numbers

A final design is then:

	{Write out a calendar version 1}		{Write out a calendar version 2}
1.1	write 'Enter day on which the 1st falls	1.1	write 'Enter day on which the 1st falls
	1 = Sunday, 2 = Monday etc '		1 = Sunday, 2 = Monday etc '
1.2	read in *firstday*	1.2	read in *firstday*
1.3	write 'How many days in the month? '	1.3	write 'How many days in the month? '
1.4	read in *monthdays*	1.4	read in *monthdays*
1.5	*column* := 1	2.1	write out 'Sun ', 'Mon ', 'Tues ', 'Wed ',
2.1	write out 'Sun ', 'Mon ', 'Tues ', 'Wed ',		'Thurs ', 'Fri ', 'Sat '
	'Thurs ', 'Fri ', 'Sat '	3.1	loop for i := 1 to *firstday* −1
3.1	loop for i := 1 to *firstday* −1	3.2	write ' '
3.2	write ' '	3.3	loopend
3.3	increment *column*	4.1	loop for i := 1 to *monthdays*
3.4	loopend	4.2	write i
4.1	loop for i := 1 to *monthdays*	4.3	if $(i + firstday)$ MOD 7 = 1 then
4.2	if *column* := 7 then	4.4	write out
4.3	write out i	4.5	ifend
4.4	*column* := 1	4.6	loopend
4.5	else		
4.6	write i		
4.7	increment *column*		
4.8	ifend		
4.9	loopend		

Data table (for both designs)

Identifier	Description	Type
firstday	Day on which 1st falls	integer variable
monthdays	Days in the month	integer variable
i	Loop control variable	integer variable
column	Column in which next day is output	integer variable

Note how this design uses write and write out to control whether or not a new line is produced. The statement *write out* has the effect of writing nothing out but it does produce a new line.

TEST THE DESIGN

Some critical vales here are when *day* has value 1 or 7.

Problem 5.6

UNDERSTAND THE PROBLEM

Since the user must terminate input with a '*' we can assume that the input consists of at least one character.
To what type of variable should the input characters be assigned?
A char variable.

DEVISE A SOLUTION

The two top level designs and their refinements are shown below:

{Occurrences of 'a' version 1}
1   initialize variables referenced in the loop
2   loop while there are characters to process
3   process character
4   loopend
5   write out results

{Occurrences of 'a' version 2}
1   initialize variables referenced in the loop
2   repeat
3   process character
4   until no more characters to process
5   write out results

{Occurrences of 'a' version 1}
1.1   write out 'Enter characters terminating
       with a *'
1.2   read in *letter*
1.3   *count* := 0
2.1   loop while *letter* <> '*'
3.1   if *letter* = 'a' then
3.2   increment *count*
3.3   ifend
3.4   read in *letter*
4   loopend
5.1   write out 'Number of occurrences of
       the letter a is ' *count*

{Occurrences of 'a' version 2}
1.1   *count* := 0
1.2   write out 'Enter characters terminating with
       a *'
2.1   repeat
3.1   read in *letter*
3.2   if *letter* = 'a' then
3.3   increment *count*
3.4   ifend
4   until *letter* = '*'
5.1   write out 'Number of occurrences of the
       letter a is ' *count*

Data table (for both designs)

Identifier	Description	Type
letter	Character input by user	char variable
count	Count of occurrences of 'a'	integer variable

Since at least one character has to be processed, the loop controlling data entry must execute at least once. Thus a postconditioned loop is the more appropriate.

TEST THE DESIGN

Test data should include strings which do not contain the letter 'a'.

Problem 5.7

UNDERSTAND THE PROBLEM

If the rate of inflation is 36 per cent what is $100 worth after 1 year?
It is worth $100*(100 − 36)/100, that is $64.
How many years is it before it has depreciated to half its value or less?
After another year it is worth 64 per cent of $64, that is $40.96. So it depreciates to less than half its value in 2 years.
How does this compare with the rule of 72 estimate and does it matter that $100 was used as the initial fixed sum?
The rule of 72 predicts 72 DIV 36 years and so the estimate agrees with the actual value. That a fixed sum of $100 was chosen does not affect the outcome.

DEVISE A SOLUTION

The design must loop through all values of inflation rates from 1 to 36 per cent. Hence a top level design is:

{The rule of 72}
1   initialize variables
2   loop for all values of inflation rate
3   calculate precise number of years
4   write out estimate and precise value of years
5   loopend

Final designs based on this are:

	{The rule of 72}		{The rule of 72}
1.1	write out 'Rate ', 'Actual ', 'Estimate '	1.1	write out 'Rate ', 'Actual ', 'Estimate '
2.1	loop for *rate* := 1 to 36	2.1	loop for *rate* := 1 to 36
3.1	*value* := 100	3.1	*value* := 100
3.2	*ActualYrs* := 0	3.2	*ActualYrs* := 0
3.3	loop while *value* > 50	3.3	repeat
3.4	*value* := *value**(100 – *rate*)/100	3.4	*value* := *value**(100 – *rate*)/100
3.5	increment *ActualYrs*	3.5	increment *ActualYrs*
3.6	loopend	3.6	until *value* <= 50
4.1	write out *rate* , *ActualYrs*, 72 DIV *rate*	4.1	write out *rate* , *ActualYrs*, 72 DIV *rate*
5	loopend	5	loopend

Data table

Identifier	Description	Type
rate	Annual inflation rate	integer variable
value	Current value of fixed sum	real variable
ActualYrs	Actual years to depreciate to half value	integer variable

TEST THE DESIGN

The output should be checked against a few values calculated by hand.

Problem 5.8

UNDERSTAND THE PROBLEM

What estimate does the modified rule give if the rate of inflation is 16 per cent?
72/16 = 4.5 and as the fractional part is .5 the number is rounded up to 5.
How can you calculate the fractional part of such a division?
Subtract the result of integer division from that of real division.

DEVISE A SOLUTION

A top level design is:

{The modified rule of 72}
1   initialize variables
2   loop for all values of inflation rate
3   calculate precise number of years
4   calculate estimated number of years
5   write out results
6   loopend

A final design is:

{The modified rule of 72}
1.1   write out 'The differences are:'
1.2   write out 'Rate ', 'Actual ', 'Estimate '
2.1   loop for *rate* := 1 to 36
3.1   *value* := 100
3.2   *ActualYrs* := 0
3.3   loop while *value* > 50
3.4   *value* := *value**(100 − *rate*)/100
3.5   increment *ActualYrs*
3.6   loopend
4.1   if 72/*rate* − 72 DIV *rate* >= 0.5 then
4.2   *estimate* := (72 DIV *rate*) + 1
4.3   else
4.4   *estimate* := 72 DIV *rate*
4.5   ifend
5.1   if *ActualYrs* <> *estimate* then
5.2   write out *rate*, *ActualYrs*, 72 DIV *rate*
5.3   ifend
6   loopend

{The modified rule of 72}
1.1   write out 'The differences are:'
1.2   write out 'Rate ', 'Actual ', 'Estimate '
2.1   loop for *rate* := 1 to 36
3.1   *value* := 100
3.2   *ActualYrs* := 0
3.3   repeat
3.4   *value* := *value**(100 − *rate*)/100
3.5   increment *ActualYrs*
3.6   until *value* <= 50
4.1   if 72/*rate* − 72 DIV *rate* >= 0.5 then
4.2   *estimate* := (72 DIV *rate*) + 1
4.3   else
4.4   *estimate* := 72 DIV *rate*
4.5   ifend
5.1   if *ActualYrs* <> *estimate* then
5.2   write out *rate*, *ActualYrs*, 72 DIV *rate*
5.3   ifend
6   loopend

Data table

Identifier	Description	Type
rate	Annual inflation rate	integer variable
value	Current value of fixed sum	real variable
ActualYrs	Actual years to depreciate to half value	integer variable
estimate	Estimated period to halve value	integer variable

TEST THE DESIGN

You will need to find some inflation rates for which the estimate and actual values differ. Try 29 per cent and 16 per cent.

Problem 5.9

UNDERSTAND THE PROBLEM

Using *daycode* to represent the day code what should be output if *daycode* has value 4?
The string 'Thursday'.

DEVISE A SOLUTION

The numbering we have used in the following design represents a refinement of step 5 of Problem 3.7. The same identifiers are used as before.

5.1   if *daycode* = 0 then
5.2   write out 'Sunday'
5.3   else
5.4   if *daycode* = 1 then
5.5   write out 'Monday'
5.6   else
5.7   if *daycode* = 2 then
5.8   write out 'Tuesday'
5.9   else

```
5.10          if daycode = 3 then
5.11              write out 'Wednesday'
5.12          else
5.13              if daycode = 4 then
5.14                  write out 'Thursday'
5.15              else
5.16                  if daycode 5 then
5.17                      write out 'Friday'
5.18                  else
5.19                      write out 'Saturday'
5.20                  ifend
5.21              ifend
5.22          ifend
5.23      ifend
5.24  ifend
5.25  ifend
```

When using nests of *if* statements you should check that the number of *if*s is the same as the number of *ifend*s. A missing *ifend* will destroy the logic of the statements. Here, the *if* statements are arranged so as to select one of seven possible alternatives. In Chapter 7 we shall see a better way of selecting between alternative possibilities.

TEST THE DESIGN

Each of the possible values of *daycode* should be used in a trace through the design.

Problem 5.10

UNDERSTAND THE PROBLEM

If the input string is:
          'This▽▽text▽▽▽has▽multiple▽▽▽spaces▽▽▽between▽its▽▽words'
what should be output?
The string 'This▽text▽has▽multiple▽spaces▽between▽its▽words'.
What is wrong with the following design?

```
1   read in the text
2   loop for all characters
3       if current character is a space then
4           write a space
5           skip over any subsequent spaces
6       else
7           write current character
8   loopend
```

Step 2 is a *for* loop which inspects each and every character in turn. Therefore it is impossible for the body of the loop to skip over characters, as this would require the variable controlling the *for* loop to be updated within the loop's body.

DEVISE A SOLUTION

A *while* loop overcomes this difficulty. An intermediate and final level design is shown below. The loop at step 3.3 is guaranteed to terminate because the specification says that the input string must terminate with a non-space character.

{Remove multiple spaces; intermediate}

1.1 read in the text
1.2 i := 1
2 loop while i <= length(paragraph)
3.1   if paragraph[i] = space then
3.2   write paragraph[i]
3.3   skip space characters
3.4   else
3.5   write paragraph[i]
3.6   move to next character
3.7   ifend
4 loopend

{Remove multiple spaces; final}

1.1 write 'Enter your text '
1.2 read in paragraph
1.3 i := 1
2 loop while i <= length(paragraph)
3.1   if paragraph[i] = space then
3.2   write paragraph[i]
3.3.1   loop while paragraph[i] = space
3.3.2   increment i
3.3.3   loopend
3.4   else
3.5   write paragraph[i]
3.6   increment i
3.7   ifend
4 loopend

Data table

Identifier	Description	Type
space	The space character	char constant value '▽'
paragraph	Input text	string variable
i	Loop control variable	integer variable

TEST THE DESIGN

Data similar to that above should be used. Possible critical data here is an input string consisting of only a single full stop.

Problem 5.11

UNDERSTAND THE PROBLEM

How many occurrences of 'an' are there in each of the following:
(a) 'banana'
(b) 'A man and his animal'
(c) 'An opera nut'?
There are two in (a) three in (b) and none in (c). Note that 'An' has an upper-case A and there is a space character between the end of opera and the beginning of nut.
Each character of the input string will have to be examined in turn. What kind of loop should be used?
Since the number of characters to be examined is known from the *length* function, a for loop should be used.

DEVISE A SOLUTION

A top level design is:

1 read in data and initialize variables
2 loop for all characters
3   process current character
4 loopend
5 write out results

Step 3 can be refined by introducing a char variable *previous* which will hold the character immediately preceding the current character. Then if *previous* has value 'a' and the current character is an 'n' the count must be incremented. These additional variables can be avoided but care is required in getting the termination of the *for* loop correct.

	{Count occurrences of 'an' in input string}		{Count occurrences of 'an' in input string}
1.1	*count* := 0	1.1	*count* := 0
1.2	write out 'Enter the string '	1.2	write out 'Enter the string '
1.3	read in *sentence*	1.3	read in *sentence*
1.4	*previous* := *sentence*[1]	2.1	loop for *current* := 1 to *length(sentence)*–1
2.1	loop for *current* := 2 to *length(sentence)*	3.1	if *sentence*[*current*] = 'a' then
3.1	if *previous* = 'a' then	3.2	if *sentence*[*current* + 1] = 'n' then
3.2	if *sentence*[*current*] = 'n' then	3.3	increment *count*
3.3	increment *count*	3.4	ifend
3.4	ifend	3.5	ifend
3.5	ifend	4	loopend
3.6	*previous* := *sentence*[*current*]	5.1	write out 'Number of occurrences is ' *count*
4	loopend		
5.1	write out 'Number of occurrences is ' *count*		

Data table

Identifier	Description	Type
count	Occurrences of pattern 'an'	integer variable
sentence	Input string	string variable
previous	Character before one being currently examined	char variable
current	Index of character being currently examined	integer variable

TEST THE DESIGN

The data above would be a minimal set. Note that if only one character is entered the design still works – the *for* loop is then not executed at all because in both designs the initial value of the loop control variable is larger than the final value.

Problem 5.12

UNDERSTAND THE PROBLEM

The numbers 9 and 4 do not fit the pattern described in the specification. How should they be dealt with?
Step 3 will have to be refined as an *if* statement which treats the case 9 separately. Similarly, step 5 will have to be refined as an *if* statement to deal with the case of value 4.

DEVISE A SOLUTION

We give only a final design:

Data table

Identifier	Description	Type
number	An integer in the range 1 to 9	integer variable
roman	Roman equivalent of *number*	string variable

	{convert a number in range 1 to 9 to Roman numeral}
1.1	*roman* := "
2	if *number* >= 5 then

3.1   if *number* = 9 then
3.2   *roman* := 'IX'
3.3   else
3.4   *roman* := 'V'
3.5   *number* := *number* − 5
3.6   loop while *number* > 0
3.7   *roman* := *roman* + 'I'
3.8   decrement *number*
3.9   loopend
3.10   ifend
4   else
5.1   if *number* = 4 then
5.2   *roman* := 'IV'
5.3   else
5.4   loop while *number* > 0
5.5   *roman* := *roman* + 'I'
5.6   decrement *number*
5.7   loopend
5.8   ifend
6   ifend

TEST THE DESIGN

This particular design can be tested exhaustively as there are only 9 cases to consider.

Problem 5.13

UNDERSTAND THE PROBLEM

What should be output if the input string is
        'A▽big▽ ▽bat▽ ▽ ▽hit▽me'
The new space characters have been denoted by Δ, their position might give you a clue to the design strategy.
        'A▽Δbig▽Δ▽bat▽Δ▽ ▽hit▽Δ me'
The original problem used a *for* loop to examine each character in turn. When a space character was encountered it, together with an additional space, were copied to the result string. A *for* loop can also be used here, but a flag will be required to distinguish single spaces from multiple spaces. The alternative is to use a *while* loop, so that when a space is encountered the subsequent spaces (if any) can be copied to the new string without the addition of further spaces. You are reminded that the input could begin with a space or sequence of spaces.

DEVISE A SOLUTION

Top level designs for both possibilities are opposite with data table as follows:

Data table

Identifier	Description	Type
space	The space character	char constant value '▽'
oldstring	User input string	string variable
position	Loop control variable	integer variable
newstr	String with extra spaces	string variable
openingspace	Flag denoting an opening space	boolean variable

{Insert extra space characters in a string
with potential multiple spaces}
1   initialize data
2   loop while there are characters to process
3   if current character is a space then
4   append an additional space
5   copy current and subsequent spaces
6   else
7   copy current character
8   move to next character position
9   ifend
10   loopend
11   write out results

{Insert extra space characters in a string
with potential multiple spaces}
1   initialize data
2   loop for all characters
3   if current character is a space then
4   if it is an opening space then
5   process start of space sequence
6   else
7   process remaining space sequence
8   ifend
9   else
10   process non-space
11   ifend
12   loopend
11   write out results

The corresponding final designs are :

{Insert extra space characters in a string
with potential multiple spaces}
1.1   write out 'Enter the string '
1.2   read in *oldstring*
1.3   *newstr* := "
1.4   *position* := 1
2.1   loop while *position* <= length[*oldstring*]
3.1   if *oldstring*[*position*] = *space* then
4.1   *newstr* := *newstr* + *space*
5.1   loop while *oldstring*[*position*] = *space*
5.2   *newstr* := *newstr* + *space*
5.3   increment *position*
5.4   loopend
6   else
7.1   *newstr* := *newstr* + *oldstring*[*position*]
8.1   increment *position*
9   ifend
10   loopend
11   write out 'The new string is ', *newstr*

{Insert extra space characters in a string
with potential multiple spaces}
1.1   write out 'Enter the string '
1.2   read in *oldstring*
1.3   *newstr* := "
1.4   *openingspace* := (*oldstring*[1] = *space*)
2.1   loop for *position* := 1 to length[*oldstring*]
3.1   if *oldstring*[*position*] = *space* then
4.1   if *openingspace* then
5.1   *newstr* := *newstr* + *space* + *space*
5.2   *openingspace* := false
6   else
7.1   *newstr* := *newstr* + *space*
8   ifend
9   else
10.1   *newstr* := *newstr* + *oldstring*[*position*]
10.2   *openingspace* := true
11   ifend
12   loopend
13   write out 'The new string is ', *newstr*

TEST THE DESIGN

In the *while* loop solution, the condition that the input string does not terminate with a space is exploited in step 5. Had this condition not been there then a space character at the end of the string would have caused an index out of range error when this loop was executed. Thus the test data should not include input strings which terminate with a space.

Problem 5.14

UNDERSTAND THE PROBLEM

Explain how 600 millimetres is the same as 1 foot 11.6 inches.
1 inch is 25.4 millimetres and so 1 millimetre is 1/25.4 inches. Hence 600 millimetres is 600/25.4 inches or 23.6 inches (to 1 decimal place). This must now be converted to an integer

number of feet together with a number of inches, the latter being a real number.

A top level design is:

> {Ready reckoner, millimetres to feet and inches}
> 1   initialize variables
> 2   loop for all required values
> 3   convert millimetres to inches
> 4   express result in feet and inches
> 5   write out row of table
> 6   loopend

This may be refined to:

> {Ready reckoner, millimetres to feet and inches}
> 1.1   write out 'Millimetres', 'Feet', 'Inches'
> 2.1   loop for *i* := 1 to 10
> 3.1   *millimetres* := 100**i*
> 3.1   *inches* := *millimetres*/25.4
> 4.1   *wholefeet* := 0
> 4.2   loop while *inches* >= 12
> 4.3   increment *wholefeet*
> 4.4   *inches* := *inches* − 12
> 4.5   loopend
> 5.1   if *wholefeet* > 0 then
> 5.2   write out *millimetres, wholefeet, inches*
> 5.3   else
> 5.4   write out *millimetres*, ' ', *inches*
> 5.5   ifend
> 6   loopend

Data table

Identifier	Description	Type
i	Loop control variable	integer variable
millimetres	Number of millimetres	integer variable
wholefeet	Number of feet	integer variable
inches	Number of inches	real variable

All 10 values could be checked but you should certainly include values for which the whole number of feet is zero.

Problem 5.15

Individual characters are to be analysed as they are entered. What data type would be appropriate to this situation?
The type char.
What kind of a loop would the problem suggest is required?

As the number of input characters is not known in advance, a *for* loop is not appropriate and so a *while* loop or *repeat* loop will be required.

DEVISE A SOLUTION

A design is given for each of the *while* and *repeat* loops. The design which uses the *repeat* loop forces the user to enter at least two characters before the program can be terminated. Although this does not violate the specification it could be a difficulty for the user. Of course the initial prompt could be changed to say that at least two characters must be entered.

1	read in first character		1	read in first character
2	initialize variables referenced in loop		2	initialize variables referenced in loop
3	loop while there are characters to process		3	repeat
4	read in next character		4	read in next character
5	process character		5	process character
6	loopend		6	until no more characters
7	write out results		7	write out results

The corresponding final designs are:

	{Occurrences of 'an' from keyboard}			{Occurrences of 'an' from keyboard}
1.1	write 'Enter characters terminated with * '		1.1	write 'Enter characters terminated with * '
1.2	read in *previous*		1.2	read in *previous*
2.1	*count* := 0		2.1	*count* := 0
3.1	loop while *previous* <> '*'		3.1	repeat
4.1	read in *current*		4.1	read in *current*
4.2	if *previous* = 'a' then		4.2	if *previous* = 'a' then
5.1	if *current* = 'n' then		5.1	if *current* = 'n' then
5.2	increment *count*		5.2	increment *count*
5.3	ifend		5.3	ifend
5.4	ifend		5.4	ifend
5.5	*previous* := *current*		5.5	*previous* := *current*
6	loopend		6	until *previous* = '*'
7.1	write out 'Number of occurrences ', *count*		7.1	write out 'Number of occurrences ', *count*

Data table

Identifier	Description	Type
count	Occurrences of pattern 'an'	integer variable
previous	Character before one being currently examined	char variable
current	Character being examined	char variable

TEST THE DESIGN

The same test data as was used for Problem 5.11 could be used here.

Problem 5.16

UNDERSTAND THE PROBLEM

How is the average in the question calculated?
The number of completed innings is 24 − 4, that is 20. It is this number which then divides the total runs scored.
How is a score of '37 not out' entered by the user and how must it be processed?

The score is entered as 1037 to indicate that the innings was 'not out'. The processing must use the fact that the entered score is greater than 1000 to record the fact that it was a 'not out' score. The actual score must be recovered from 1037 by subtracting 1000 from it.

DEVISE A SOLUTION

A top level design is:

```
    {Prepare cricket batting average}
1   initialize variables
2   loop for all innings
3       process scores of each innings
4   loopend
5   write out results
```

Step 3 will have to record the number of not out innings and manipulate the scores. Step 5 will have to cater for the different possible outcomes of the processing. A final design is:

```
    {Prepare cricket batting averages}
1.1    notout := 0
1.2    runs := 0
1.3    write 'How many innings to input? '
1.4    read in innings
2.1    loop for i := 1 to innings
3.1        write 'Enter score for innings ', i, ' entering score + 1000 for not out innings'
3.2        read in score
3.3        if score >= 1000 then
3.4            increment notout
3.5            runs := runs + score − 1000
3.6        else
3.7            runs := runs + score
3.8        ifend
4      loopend
5.1    if innings > 0 then
5.2        completed := innings − notout
5.3        if completed > 0 then
5.4            average := runs/completed
5.5            write out innings, notout, runs, average
5.6        else
5.7            write out innings, notout, runs, 'N/A'
5.8        ifend
5.9    else
5.10       write out 'Cricketer did not bat'
5.11   ifend
```

Data table

Identifier	Description	Type
notout	Number of times 'not out'	integer variable
runs	Total runs scored	integer variable
innings	Total times batted	integer variable
i	Loop control variable	integer variable
score	Score for a single innings	integer variable
completed	Number of completed innings	integer variable
average	Average score over season	real variable

The input of the data and its output can be treated separately as far as testing goes. The input needs to be checked to see that it handles not out scores correctly and all three different possibilities for output also need testing.

Problem 5.17

UNDERSTAND THE PROBLEM

The major difficulty is in interpreting the table used in the calculation of the epact.

DEVISE A SOLUTION

A top level design is:

```
     {Easter day for years 1900 to 1999}
1    loop for all years
2        calculate day using the design in the text
3        write out results
4    loopend
```

This may be refined to:

```
       {Easter day for years 1900 to 1999}
1.1    loop for year := 1900 to 1999
2.1        Century := (year DIV 100) + 1
2.2        Golden:= (year MOD 19) + 1
2.3        Gregorian := (3*Century) DIV 4 − 12
2.4        Clavian := (8*Century + 5) DIV 25 −5 − Gregorian
2.5        factor := (5*year) DIV 4 − Gregorian − 10
2.6        Epact := (11*Golden + 20 + Clavian) MOD 30
2.7        if Epact = 24 then
2.8            Epact := Epact + 1
2.9        else
2.10           if Epact = 25 then
2.11               if Golden > 11 then
2.12                   Epact := Epact + 1
2.13               ifend
2.14           ifend
2.15       ifend
2.16       day := 44 − Epact
2.17       if day < 21 then
2.18           day := day + 30
2.19       ifend
2.20       day := day + 7 − (day + factor) MOD 7
3.1        if day <= 31 then
3.2            write out 'In ', year, 'Easter is on ', day, 'March'
3.3        else
3.4            write out 'In ', year, 'Easter is on ', day − 31, 'April'
3.5        ifend
4      loopend
```

Data table

Identifier	Description	Type
year	Loop control variable	integer variable
Century	See text	integer variable
Golden	See text	integer variable
Gregorian	See text	integer variable
Clavian	See text	integer variable
factor	See text	integer variable
Epact	See text	integer variable
day	See text	integer variable

TEST THE DESIGN

The arithmetic becomes quite hard here and it may be difficult to find out when Easter was in some of the years! To help you the following table gives the value of *Epact* and the date on which Easter fell for four of the years in question.

Year	*Epact*	Easter
1990	3	15 April
1991	14	31 March
1992	26	19 April
1993	6	11 April

Problem 5.18

UNDERSTAND THE PROBLEM

'How many words of length six or more occur in this sentence?'
Just two – 'length' and 'sentence?'.
What indicates the end of a word?
A space character signifies the end of a word. However, adjacent space characters are permitted but a second or subsequent adjacent space can be thought of as terminating a word of length zero. The last word will probably not be followed by a space so this word cannot be dealt with in this way.

DEVISE A SOLUTION

A top level design is:

```
     {How many words of 6 or more characters}
 1   initialize variables referenced in loop
 2   loop while there are characters to process
 3       if current character is a space then
 4           process end of word
 5       else
 6           process mid-word character
 7       ifend
 8   loopend
 9   calculate and write out results
```

A final design is:

{How many words of 6 or more characters}
1.1   write 'Enter the text to be analyzed '
1.2   read in *paragraph*
1.3   *lettercount* := 0
1.4   *longcount* := 0
2.1   loop for *position* := 1 to *length(paragraph)*
3.1   if *paragraph[position]* = '▽' then
4.1   if *lettercount* >= 6 then
4.2   increment *longcount*
4.3   ifend
4.4   *lettercount* := 0
5   else
6.1   increment *lettercount*
7   ifend
8   loopend
9.1   if *lettercount* >= 6 then {check last word}
9.2   increment *longcount*
9.3   ifend
9.4   write out 'The text had ', *longcount*, ' words with 6 or more letters'

Data table

Identifier	Description	Type
paragraph	Input text	string variable
lettercount	Number of letters in current word	integer variable
longcount	Number of words with 6 or more characters	integer variable
position	Loop control variable	integer variable

TEST THE DESIGN

Critical data here includes a string consisting of only space characters, a string with a terminating space and a string with no spaces in it .

Problem 5.19

UNDERSTAND THE PROBLEM

We can anticipate that the design will have to *skip* over multiple space characters. Does this suggest that a *for* loop or a *while* loop is likely to be effective?
It is not known in advance how many multiple space characters there will be and as a *for* loop executes a fixed number of times it is less likely to be effective.

DEVISE A SOLUTION

An intermediate level design is:

{Output sentences on a new line}
1.1   initialize variables and read in the text
1.2   skip over any initial space characters
2   loop while there are characters to process
3.1   if current character is a full stop then
3.2   process the full stop
3.3   if not the end of the text then
3.4   skip to next non-space character

```
3.5        ifend
3.6     else
3.7        if current character is a space then
3.8           write a space
3.9           skip to next non-space character
3.10       else
3.11          write current character
3.12          move to next character
3.13       ifend
3.14    ifend
4     loopend
```

Here the steps which skip to next character are exploiting the fact that the input must terminate with a full stop. On each occasion the next non-space character is therefore guaranteed to exist. The design may be refined to:

```
           {Output sentences on a new line}
1.1.1   write 'Enter the text '
1.1.2   read in paragraph
1.1.3   i := 1
1.2.1   loop while paragraph[i] = space
1.2.2      increment i
1.2.3   loopend
2.1.1   loop while i <= length(paragraph)
3.1.1      if paragraph[i] = fullstop then
3.2.1         write out fullstop
3.2.2         increment i
3.3.1         if i < length(paragraph) then
3.4.1            loop while paragraph[i] = space
3.4.2               increment i
3.4.3            loopend
3.5           ifend
3.6        else
3.7.1         if paragraph[i] = space then
3.8.1            write space
3.9.1            repeat
3.9.2               increment i
3.9.3            until paragraph[i] <> space
3.10          else
3.11.1           write paragraph[i]
3.12.1           increment i
3.13          ifend
3.14       ifend
4        loopend
```

Data table

Identifier	Description	Type
fullstop	The full stop character	char constant value '.'
space	The space character	char constant value '▽'
paragraph	Input text	string variable
i	Loop control variable	integer variable

TEST THE DESIGN

Possible critical data includes text having a single sentence, text having multiple initial space characters and text like that shown above.

Problem 5.20

UNDERSTAND THE PROBLEM

Re-read the solution to Problem 5.11 and try to generalize its solution here.

DEVISE A SOLUTION

The same top level design can be used here and so only a final design has been provided. The use of the identifiers *first* and *second* can be avoided in a similar way to that of the earlier solution.

```
        {Count occurrences of 'the' in input string}
1.1     count := 0
1.2     write 'Enter the string '
1.3     read in sentence
1.4     first := sentence[1]
1.5     second := sentence[2]
2.1     loop for current := 3 to length(sentence)
3.1         if first = 't' then
3.2             if second = 'h' then
3.3                 if sentence[current] = 'e' then
3.4                     increment count
3.5                 ifend
3.6             ifend
3.7         ifend
3.8         first := second
3.9         second := sentence[current]
4       loopend
5.1     write out 'Number of occurrences is ' count
```

Data table

Identifier	Description	Type
count	Occurrences of pattern 'the'	integer variable
sentence	Input string	string variable
first	First character of the 3 currently being examined	char variable
second	Second character of 3 currently being examined	char variable
current	Index of the third character being examined	integer variable

TEST THE DESIGN

This should include strings which result in a count of zero as well as strings which give a non-zero count.

Problem 5.21

UNDERSTAND THE PROBLEM

What should be output if the input string is

'▽▽▽A▽big▽▽bat▽▽▽hit▽me'

The first three spaces are left unaltered. The additional spaces have been denoted by Δ.

'▽▽▽A▽Δbig▽Δ▽bat▽Δ▽▽hit▽Δ me'

DEVISE A SOLUTION

The same designs as used in Problem 5.13 will work here except for a modification to their initialization step 1. Each of the alternatives would need to be refined as follows. (*start* is an integer variable.)

	{Insert extra space characters in a string with potential multiple spaces}			{Insert extra space characters in a string with potential multiple spaces}
1.1	write out 'Enter the string '		1.1	write out 'Enter the string '
1.2	read in *oldstring*		1.2	read in *oldstring*
1.3	*newstr* := "		1.3	*newstr* := "
1.4	*position* := 1		1.4	*start* := 1
1.5	loop while *oldstring[position]* = *space*		1.5	loop while *oldstring[start]* = space
1.6	*newstr* := *newstr* + *space*		1.6	*newstr* := *newstr* + *space*
1.7	increment *position*		1.7	increment *start*
1.8	loopend		1.8	loopend
2.1	loop while *position* <= *length[oldstring]*		1.9	*openingspace* := (*oldstring[start]* = *space*)
			2.1	loop for *position* := *start* to *length[oldstring]*

TEST THE DESIGN

The modification needs to be checked to ensure that initial spaces are dealt with correctly.

Problem 5.22

UNDERSTAND THE PROBLEM

The strategy adopted in the solution to Problem 4.8 was to increment the wordcount every time a space character was encountered. How can this strategy be amended to meet the constraints here?

Once the wordcount has been updated any subsequent space characters must be skipped until a non-space is encountered. This is always guaranteed by the constraint that the input string terminates in a non-space character.

How can any initial spaces be dealt with?

Since there is at least one non-space character, initial spaces can be skipped prior to the processing just described.

DEVISE A SOLUTION

A top level design is:

1   read in text
2   initialize variables
3   skip over initial spaces
4   loop while there are characters to process
5   if current character is a space then
6   increment word count
7   move to next non-space character
8   else

```
9        increment letter count
10          move to next character
11      ifend
12   loopend
13   calculate and write out results
```

This may be refined to:

```
1.1    write out 'Enter your line of text terminating in a non-space character'
1.2    read in line
2.1    index := 1
2.2    wordcount := 0
2.3    lettercount := 0
3.1    loop while line[index] = space
3.2        increment index
3.3    loopend
4.1    loop while index <= length(line)
5.1        if line[index] = space then
6.1            increment wordcount
7.1            loop while line[index] = space
7.2                increment index
7.3            loopend
8          else
9.1            increment lettercount
10.1           increment index
11         ifend
12     loopend
13.1   increment wordcount  {count the last word of input}
13.2   average := lettercount/wordcount
13.3   write out 'Average word length is ', average
```

Data table

Identifier	Description	Type
space	Space character	char constant value '∇'
line	A line of text	string variable
index	Loop control variable	integer variable
wordcount	Number of words in line	integer variable
lettercount	Number of letters in line	integer variable
average	Average word length	real variable

TEST THE DESIGN

Test data should include strings which have initial spaces, those which do not and those which have multiple spaces between words. It should also include strings which have a word count of 1 and which have a letter count of 1.

Problem 5.23

UNDERSTAND THE PROBLEM

What should be output if the input string is 'A dark black kite'?

There is one occurrence of *ck* and one of *rk* and so the report should be that the counts are equal. Notice that the *k* in the word kite does not contribute to the process because it is not preceded by a letter. Also note that the problem is only concerned with lower-case letters.

What general strategy can be adopted here?

Pairs of characters must be examined to see if they have the form *ck* or **k* where * is any other letter. This can be done by examining successive pairs of characters in the input string.

DEVISE A SOLUTION

There are two ways of examining each pair of characters. The first character of the pair can be examined first, followed by the second. Alternatively, the second character of the pair can be examined first. The latter leads to a simpler design but we give both in case you want the challenge of implementing them in a programming language. The designs are:

1	initialize variables		1	initialize variables
2	loop while there are pairs to process		2	loop while there are pairs to process
3	if first character of pair is 'c' then		3	if second character of pair is 'k' then
4	process pair beginning with 'c'		4	process pair ending in 'k'
5	else		5	ifend
6	process pair beginning with '*'		6	move to next pair
7	ifend		7	loopend
8	move to next pair		8	write out results
9	loopend			
10	write out results			

			1.1	write out 'Enter text'
1.1	write out 'Enter text'		1.2	read in *sample*
1.2	read in *sample*		1.3	*index* := 1
1.3	*index* := 1		1.4	*ckcount* := 0
1.4	*ckcount* := 0		1.5	*anykcount* := 0
1.5	*anykcount* := 0		2.1	loop while *index* < *length*(*sample*)
2.1	loop while *index* < *length*(*sample*)		3.1	if *sample*[*index* + 1] = 'k' then
3.1	if *sample*[*index*] = 'c' then		4.1	if *sample*[*index*] = 'c' then
4.1	if *sample*[*index* + 1] = 'k' then		4.2	increment *ckcount*
4.2	increment *ckcount*		4.3	else
4.3	ifend		4.4	increment *anykcount*
5	else		4.5	ifend
6.1	if *sample*[*index* + 1] = 'k' then		5	ifend
6.2	increment *anykcount*		6.1	increment *index*
6.3	ifend		7	loopend
7	ifend		8.1	if *ckcount* < *anykcount* then
8.1	increment *index*		8.2	write out 'ck is less frequent than *k'
9	loopend		8.3	else
10	{see steps 8.1 to 8.9 on adjacent design}		8.4	if *ckcount* > *anykcount* then
			8.5	write out 'ck is more frequent than *k'
			8.6	else
			8.7	write out 'There is no difference'
			8.8	ifend
			8.9	ifend

Data table

Identifier	Description	Type
sample	The input string	string variable
index	Index of first of character pair	integer variable
ckcount	Count of occurrences of *ck*	integer variable
anykcount	Count of any letter then *k*	integer variable

TEST THE DESIGN

Test data should check against all three possible outcomes and should include strings which have no occurrences of either pattern as well as those which have one or more occurrences.

Problem 6.1

UNDERSTAND THE PROBLEM

A user wishes to fill locations 15 to 20 and inputs a start address of 20 and a final address of 15. What should the program do?
Issue an error message informing the user that the final address must be larger than the start address. Program execution then terminates.

DEVISE A SOLUTION

A top level design is:

```
    {Fill a memory address range with a value}
1   read in start and finish addresses
2   if the address range is valid then
3       read in value to fill the address range
4       assign the value to the address range
5   else
6       write out error message
7   ifend
```

This can be refined to:

```
        {Fill a memory address range with a value}
1.1     write 'Enter initial address of range to be filled '
1.2     read in initial
1.3     write 'Enter final address of range to be filled '
1.4     read in final
2.1     if initial <= final then
3.1         write 'Value to fill memory is? '
3.2         read in FillValue
4.1         loop for i := initial to final
4.2             memory[i] := FillValue
4.3         loopend
5       else
6           write out 'Initial address is larger than final address'
7       ifend
```

Data table

Identifier	Description	Type
maxsize	Array index upper bound	integer constant
memory	Array simulating machine memory	array[1..maxsize] of integer variable
initial	First address of range to be filled	integer variable
final	Last address of memory to be filled	integer variable
FillValue	Value to fill range	integer variable
i	Loop control variable	integer variable

TEST THE DESIGN

A critical value here is when the initial value is the same as the final value. This is perfectly legitimate and the result should be that a single address should be filled with the value input by the user.

Problem 6.2

UNDERSTAND THE PROBLEM

If *maxsize* had value 25 and locations 15 to 20 were to be moved to location 23 what should happen?

An error message saying there was insufficient room should be generated and the program should terminate.

For moves for which there is sufficient space, the range of address values cannot simply be assigned to the elements beginning at the destination location. Why not?

An example should make this clear. The figure below represents memory locations in which are stored characters. We have used characters rather than integers in order not to confuse memory addresses and memory contents.

1	2	3	4	5	6	7
z	a	b	c	x	x	x

Suppose locations 2 to 4 inclusive had to be moved to address beginning at location 4. (The specification does not preclude the destination address being in the range of addresses to be moved.) If we tried to move them in order, we would move the contents of location 2 to location 4, those of 3 to 5 and finally those of 4 to 6. But if we did this the contents of the memory after the first move would be:

1	2	3	4	5	6	7
z	a	b	a	x	x	x

and after the second

1	2	3	4	5	6	7
z	a	b	a	b	x	x

and finally

1	2	3	4	5	6	7
z	a	b	a	b	a	x

The first move has overwritten the contents of location 4 – not what we want. You will have to work out how to avoid this.

Does it make any difference to the strategy of moving the data if the destination address precedes the initial address of the range to be moved? What happens if it comes after the final address of the range?

DEVISE A SOLUTION

A top level design is:

> {Move a range of memory}
> 1   read in range to be moved

```
2   if the range is valid then
3       read in destination start address
4       if the destination address is valid then
5           move the data
6       else
7           write out invalid destination error message
8       ifend
9   else
10      write out invalid range message
11  ifend
```

In order to refine this design we need a strategy for moving the data. The strategy that we have adopted is that if the destination location precedes the initial address of the range to be moved then just copy the data directly in its address order. If the destination address does not satisfy this condition then movement must be carried out backwards, that is, starting at the highest memory address of the range to be moved and working down towards its initial value. This leads to the following refinement:

```
        {Move a range of memory}
1       read in range to be moved
2       if the range is valid then
3           read in destination start address
4.1         if there is room for the move then
5.1             if the destination address precedes the range then
5.2                 move contents in order
5.3             else
5.4                 move contents in reverse order
5.5             ifend
6           else
7               write out invalid destination error message
8           ifend
9       else
10          write out invalid range message
11      ifend
```

To refine steps 4.1 and 5.4 we shall need to work out the destination address corresponding to the final location of the range.

```
        {Move a range of memory}
1.1     write 'Enter initial address of range to be filled '
1.2     read in initial
1.3     write 'Enter final address of range to be filled '
1.4     read in final
2.1     if initial <= final then
3.1         write 'Enter the destination start address '
3.2         read in destination
4.1.1       if (destination + final − initial) <= maxsize then
5.1.1           if destination < initial then              {there is space for move}
5.2.1               loop for i := 0 to (final − initial)   {move in normal order}
5.2.2                   memory[destination + i] := memory[initial + i]
5.2.3               loopend
5.3             else
```

```
5.4.1              loop for i := (final − initial) downto 0    {move in reverse order}
5.4.2                  memory[destination + i] := memory[initial + i]
5.4.3              loopend
5.5            ifend    {end of moving}
6          else
7.1            write out 'Out of memory with that destination'
8          ifend
9        else
10.1         write out 'Initial value cannot be larger than final value of range'
11       ifend
```

Data table

Identifier	Description	Type
maxsize	Array index upper bound	integer constant
memory	Array simulating machine memory	array[1..*maxsize*] of integer variable
initial	First address of range to be moved	integer variable
final	Last address of memory to be moved	integer variable
destination	Address to which range to be moved	integer variable
i	Loop control variable	integer variable

TEST THE DESIGN

We need to check that the loops execute the correct number of times and that the movement of the data is done correctly. In the test data below we assume that *maxsize* has value 10. Although this is a ridiculously small value it does enable checks to be done by hand. A more realistic value would be harder to test. You should include data of the following type when you test your design:

	initial value	final value	destination
(a)	3	5	2
(b)	3	5	4
(c)	3	5	7
(d)	3	5	9
(e)	4	1	Not required for this data

The first three result in data being moved. The first test data set has the property that the destination location precedes the initial value of the range, the second data set has the property that the destination location is within the range of values to be moved, and the third data set has the destination location after the final value of the range. The last two data sets test the error checking parts of the design.

Problem 6.3

UNDERSTAND THE PROBLEM

If the array contains the four elements Shakespeare, Brookner, Bragg and Robbins what should be written out?
The name Bragg should be output as it precedes the others alphabetically.

DEVISE A SOLUTION

A top level design is:

{Find least element}
1   initialize variables referenced in loop
2   loop for all elements in the array
3   find the least element
4   loopend
5   write out results

This can be refined to:

{Find least element of array}
1.1   *least* := *authors*[1]
2.1   loop for *i* := 2 to *maxsize*
3.1   if *authors*[*i*] < *least* then
4.1   *least* := *authors*[*i*]
4.2   ifend
5   loopend
6.1   write out 'Least element is ' *least*

Data table

Identifier	Description	Type
maxsize	Size of the array *authors*	integer constant
least	Least element of *authors*	string variable
authors	Array of names of authors	array[1..*maxsize*] of string variable
i	Loop control variable	integer variable

TEST THE DESIGN

The data used above could be used as part of the test data here. Critical test data would include the possibility that all the array elements had the same value.

Problem 6.4

UNDERSTAND THE PROBLEM

Suppose the sorted arrays contained the following integer data:

    3   5   7   12   23   35
    2   4   8   11   15   16

What would the merged array contain?
It would contain 2 3 4 5 7 8 11 12 15 16 23 35. The merged array takes its elements from the appropriate sorted array until one of the sorted arrays is exhausted. Then the remaining elements of the other sorted array are appended to the merged array.
This process suggests a loop. What will the condition controlling the loop have to test?
It will have to indicate that one of the sorted array's elements has been exhausted. Try using a flag to indicate this occurrence.

DEVISE A SOLUTION

A top level design is:

{Merge two sorted arrays}
1   initialize variables referenced in loop
2   repeat

3   copy from appropriate sorted array to merged array
4   until one of the sorted arrays is exhausted
5   copy the remaining elements of unexhausted sorted array to merged array

This can be refined to:

```
      {Merge two sorted arrays}
1.1   index1 := 1
1.2   index2 := 1
1.3   MergedIndex := 1
1.4   exhaustedflag := false
2     repeat
3.1       if sorted1[index1] < sorted2[index2] then
3.2           merged[MergedIndex] := sorted1[index1]
3.3           increment index1
3.4           exhaustedflag := (index1 > 6)
3.5       else
3.6           merged[MergedIndex] := sorted2[index2]
3.7           increment index2
3.8           exhaustedflag := (index2 > 6)
3.9       ifend
3.10      increment MergedIndex
4     until exhaustedflag
5.1   if index1 > 6 then
5.2       loop for i := index2 to 6          {copy remaining elements of sorted2}
5.3           merged[MergedIndex] := sorted2[i]
5.4           increment MergedIndex
5.5       loopend
5.6   else
5.7       loop for i := index1 to 6          {copy remaining elements of sorted1}
5.8           merged[MergedIndex] := sorted1[i]
5.9           increment MergedIndex
5.10      loopend
5.11  ifend
```

Data table

Identifier	Description	Type
SortedType	Array type definition	array[1..6] of integer
sorted1	First sorted array	*SortedType* variable
sorted2	Second sorted array	*SortedType* variable
index1	Current position in *sorted1*	integer variable
index2	Current position in *sorted2*	integer variable
merged	The merged array	array[1..12] of integer variable
MergedIndex	Current position in *merged*	integer variable
exhaustedflag	Indicates one of the sorted arrays is exhausted	boolean variable
i	Loop control variable	integer variable

Here we have declared the two sorted arrays using a type definition.

TEST THE DESIGN

The data used above should certainly be traced through. Critical data here would include the possibility that all the values in one of the sorted arrays preceded the values in the other. Also the design should be tested with data which has common values in the two sorted arrays – notably if both arrays have identical values.

Problem 6.5

UNDERSTAND THE PROBLEM

If *dictionary* contained the words: *ifend, increment, loopfor, readin, loopend, loopwhile, implement, ifthen, looprepeat, decrement, ifthenelse*; what should be output if the word *ifbegin* is checked for correct spelling?
A message saying the word is not in the dictionary should be output.

DEVISE A SOLUTION

A final design based upon the general linear search algorithm above is:

```
        {Check spelling of a word from an array dictionary}
1.1   read in word
1.2   dictionary[0] := word
1.3   index := size
2.1   loop while dictionary[index] <> word
3.1       decrement index
4     loopend
5.1   if index = 0 then
5.2       write out 'The word is not in the dictionary'
5.3   else
5.4       write out 'The word is correctly spelled'
5.5   ifend
```

Data table

Identifier	Description	Type
dictionary	Dictionary array	array[0..]† of string variable
size	Number of entries in the dictionary	integer variable (whose value is set prior to this extract)
word	Word whose spelling is to be checked	string variable
index	Loop control variable	integer variable

† since this design is part of a larger program we do not need to know the index upper bound since we are told the array has *size* elements initialized.

TEST THE DESIGN

You should test the design using one word which is in the dictionary and one which is not.

Problem 6.6

UNDERSTAND THE PROBLEM

For the data given in the church survey table (page 74) what should be output if the user enters the number 15?
The towns Buxton and Tonbridge as these both have 15 churches.

DEVISE A SOLUTION

A top level design is:

{Write out towns which have given number of churches}
1   initialize variables
2   loop for all elements of *churches*
3   process element
4   loopend
5   write out message

This may be refined to:

{Write out towns which have given number of churches}
1.1   write 'How many churches? '
1.2   read in *searchitem*
1.3   *flag* := false
2.1   loop for *i* := 1 to *maxsize*
3.1   if *churches* [*i*] = *searchitem* then
3.2   write out *town*[*i*]
3.3   *flag* := true
3.4   ifend
4   loopend
5.1   if *flag* = false then
5.2   write out 'There were no towns having that number of churches'
5.3   ifend

Data table

Identifier	Description	Type
maxsize	Array index upper bound	integer constant
searchitem	Number of churches for which towns are sought	integer variable
town	Array of town names	array[0..*maxsize*] of string variable
churches	Parallel array of church numbers	array[0..*maxsize*] of integer variable
i	Loop control variable	integer variable
flag	Set true if match found	boolean variable

TEST THE DESIGN

Again, choose data which will ensure that all parts of the design are tested.

Problem 6.7

UNDERSTAND THE PROBLEM

Assuming the dictionary has the contents listed in Problem 6.5 and that the word *loopeend* is checked for spelling what should be output?
Since this is incorrectly spelled (probably a typing error) then a list of suggestions should be output. The list should be the words; *loopfor, loopend, loopwhile, looprepeat*.
What should be output if *case* is checked?
The dictionary will think that this is incorrectly spelled and so will try to offer some suggestions. However, none match the criteria and so a message saying that the word is potentially incorrect and that there are no suggestions in the dictionary should be output.
Write down the identifier which represents the second character of the word held at index 3 of *dictionary*.
dictionary[3] denotes the word at index 3 and so *dictionary*[3][2] denotes its second character.

DEVISE A SOLUTION

We can base part of the design on Problem 6.5. We need to amend step 5.2. Using the identifiers already defined we can do this as follows:

5.2.1	*CantSuggest* := true
5.2.2	loop for *index* := 1 to *size*
5.2.3	if *word*[1] = *dictionary*[*index*][1] then
5.2.4	if *word*[2] = *dictionary*[*index*][2] then
5.2.5	write out *dictionary*[*index*]
5.2.6	*CantSuggest* := false
5.2.7	ifend
5.2.8	ifend
5.2.9	loopend
5.2.10	if *CantSuggest* then
5.2.11	write out 'Sorry – cannot suggest an alternative '
5.2.12	ifend

A data table additional to that above is:

Data table

Identifier	Description	Type
CantSuggest	Flag set false when suggestion has been made	boolean variable

Notice in particular the access to the individual characters of the array elements. The notation *dictionary*[*index*][2] looks confusing at first but remember *dictionary*[*index*] denotes the *index*'th array element (a string) and the subsequent 2 accesses the second character of the string.

TEST THE DESIGN

Using the data above a good test value would be *loopend*, just to check that all words beginning *lo* were output as suggestions. A critical value here would be one for which there were no suggestions, such as *case*.

Problem 6.8

UNDERSTAND THE PROBLEM

How many rivers are there in the diagram below which represents a page of text consisting of four lines of text each of which contains five characters?

```
▽   A   B   C   ▽
D   E   ▽   F   ▽
G   ▽   ▽   H   I
J   ▽   ▽   L   M
```

Three.

What are their start and finish coordinates? (Remember the top row is line 1, the second line 2 and so on. Similarly, the leftmost column is column 1, the rightmost being column 5.)

Their coordinates are: (3, 2) to (4, 2), (2, 3) to (4, 3) and (1, 5) to (2, 5).

In which order is it best to scan this array?

Since we are looking for vertical rivers it is best to scan the array column-by-column.

The end of the river in column 5 is detected when the character at (3, 5) is examined. How can the start and end row coordinates of this river be deduced from the coordinates (3, 5)?

The row coordinate of the start of the river is given by (the row coordinate at which the end of the river is detected − the length of the river). The row coordinate of the end is given by (the row coordinate at which the end of the river is detected − 1).

DEVISE A SOLUTION

A top level design is:

```
    {Find rivers in text}
 1   initialize variables referenced in the loop
 2   loop for all columns
 3       look for and report rivers in current column
 4   loopend
```

We shall concentrate on refining step 3 first. We have seen that to specify a river we need the coordinate at which the end is detected and the length of the river. So as we scan down a column we shall need to record the current length of a river. Once the end of the river is detected we output its details. So a refinement of step 3 is:

```
 3.1    initialize variables referenced in the loop
 3.2    loop for all rows
 3.3        if the current character is a space then
 3.4            increment river length
 3.5        else
 3.6            if a river has just terminated then
 3.7                write out its details
 3.8                set river length to 0
 3.9            ifend
 3.10       ifend
 3.11   loopend
```

Trace through this refinement with the river from (2, 3) to (4, 3) and see if you can see a problem. A difficulty arises when a river finishes on the last line of the page because the loop for all rows terminates with the river length being non-zero and without the details of that river having been output. To overcome this we need a final *if* statement which traps this possibility and calculates the coordinates correctly. Our final design for the problem is then:

```
        {Find rivers in text. Nothing to initialize prior to outer loop so no step 1}
 2.1    loop for col := 1 to maxcols
 3.1.1      riverlength := 0
 3.2.1      loop for row := 1 to maxrows
 3.3.1          if page[row, col] = '▽' then
 3.4.1              increment riverlength
 3.5            else
 3.6.1              if riverlength > 1 then
 3.7.1                  write out 'There is a river from ', row − riverlength, col , ' to ', row − 1, col
 3.8.1                  riverlength := 0
 3.9                ifend
 3.10           ifend
 3.11       loopend
 3.12       if riverlength > 1 then
 3.13           write out 'There is a river from ', maxrows − riverlength + 1, col, ' to ', maxrows , col
 3.14       ifend
 4          loopend
```

Data table

Identifier	Description	Type
maxrows	Number of lines on the *page*	integer constant
maxcols	Number of characters per line	integer constant
page	Page of text	array[1..*maxrows*, 1..*maxcols*] of string variable
col	Loop control variable	integer variable
row	Loop control variable	integer variable
riverlength	Length of a river	integer variable

TEST THE DESIGN

You should test your design using small values for the constants representing the number of rows and columns. You should ensure that the array is initialized in such a way that there is a river which finishes at the bottom row. The 4 row by 5 column example we did earlier would provide a useful test data example.

Problem 6.9

UNDERSTAND THE PROBLEM

Define the data structure to hold a representation of the chosen letter.
It should be a two-dimensional array of boolean having index ranges 1..9 and 1..7.
Given that there are no direct screen control commands – just *write* and *write out* – should the array be processed row-by-row or column-by-column?
Because write works row-by-row the processing should be by row.

DEVISE A SOLUTION

A top level design is:

```
       {Array representation of dot matrix letters}
  1  initialize variables referenced in loop
  2  loop for all rows
  3      loop for all columns
  4          write a dot or space as appropriate
  5      loopend
  6      move to a new line
  7  loopend
```

This can be refined to:

```
       {Array representation of dot matrix letters}
  1.1    initialize array elements
  2.1    loop for row := 1 to 9
  3.1        loop for column := 1 to 7
  4.1            if dots[row, column] then
  4.2                write dot
  4.3            else
  4.4                write space
  4.5            ifend
  5          loopend
  6.1        write out        {Move to a new line}
  7      loopend
```

Data table

Identifier	Description	Type
dot	The character representing a dot	char constant value '*'
space	The space character	char constant value '▽'
dots	Array holding letter representation	array[1..9, 1..7] of boolean variable
row	Row loop control variable	integer variable
col	Column loop control variable	integer variable

To initialize the array it would be necessary to assign true or false to each of the elements. Perhaps the quickest way of doing this is to assign them all the value false using nested *for* loops and then to reassign true to those elements which represent the dots.

TEST THE DESIGN

To test this design a trace table is probably the most reliable method. You should include as test data a space all of whose array elements are false.

Problem 6.10

UNDERSTAND THE PROBLEM

What index ranges should be used for the array and what should be its base type?
The first index can be used to represent the rows and so will need to be 1..5 and the second index can represent the columns and so will need to be 1..4. The elements will need to be of type char.
Bearing in mind that once the cursor has moved to a new line there is no facility for moving it back up, in what order should the array be written out – by row or by column?
Row-by-row.

DEVISE A SOLUTION

The same top level design as used in Problem 6.9 can be used here. The array will be initialized to represent the upper-case A in the diagram in the question. To save space these steps have been written across the page.

```
        {Write out A}
1.1   letter[1,1] := '▽'  1.2   letter[1,2] := 'A'   1.3   letter[1,3] := 'A'   1.4   letter[1,4] := '▽'
1.5   letter[2,1] := 'A'   1.6   letter[2,2] := '▽'   1.7   letter[2,3] := '▽'   1.8   letter[2,4] := 'A'
1.9   letter[3,1] := 'A'   1.10  letter[3,2] := 'A'   1.11  letter[3,3] := 'A'   1.12  letter[3,4] := 'A'
1.13  letter[4,1] := 'A'   1.14  letter[4,2] := '▽'   1.15  letter[4,3] := '▽'   1.16  letter[4,4] := 'A'
1.17  letter[5,1] := 'A'   1.18  letter[5,2] := '▽'   1.19  letter[5,3] := '▽'   1.20  letter[5,4] := 'A'
2.1   loop for row := 1 to 5
3.1      loop for col := 1 to 4
4.1         write letter[row, col]
5        loopend
6.1      write out
7        loopend
```

Data table

Identifier	Description	Type
letter	Array representation of big character	array[1..5, 1..4] of char variable
row	Loop control variable	integer variable
col	Loop control variable	integer variable

TEST THE DESIGN

You need to ensure that the array is written out row-by-row.

Problem 6.11

Data table

Identifier	Description	Type
maxsize	Array index upper bound	integer constant
holidaytype	Record type definition	
	place {Holiday location}	string variable
	people {Number in party}	string variable
	car {Make of car}	string variable
	doors {Number of car doors}	integer variable
	cost {Cost per week for car}	real variable
	recordend	
brochure	Array of holiday records	array[1..*maxsize*] of *holidaytype* variable

The field representing the number of people in the party has been defined to be of type string because data like '1 to 4' has to be stored.

Problem 6.12

UNDERSTAND THE PROBLEM

You must decide how to represent the table, bearing in mind the kind of search which is to be undertaken. Which search method should be used here?

The linear search using a dummy item and so the table must be represented by an array whose lower index bound is 0.

How can you represent the colour monitor option column?

You could use a string but essentially each entry in this column has only one of two values and so a boolean would be more appropriate.

DEVISE A SOLUTION

The table can be represented as follows:

Data table

Identifier	Description	Type
size	Array index upper bound	integer constant value 100
rowtype	Record type definition	
	model {Model number}	string variable
	memory {Size of memory}	integer variable
	disk {Disk capacity}	string variable
	colour {Colour option}	boolean variable
	price {Price of model}	real variable
	recordend	
table	Array of records	array[0..*size*] of *rowtype* variable

A top level design is:

    {Search for model number}
 1   initialize variables referenced in loop

2   loop while search item is not found
3   search the table
4   loopend
5   report the results

This may be refined to:

{Search for model number}
1.1   write out 'Enter model number '
1.2   read in *searchmodel*
1.3   *table*[0]. *model* := *searchmodel*
1.4   *index* := *size*
2.1   loop while *searchmodel* <> *table*[*index*].*model*
3.1   decrement *index*
4   loopend
5.1   if *index* = 0 then
5.2   write out 'No data for that model'
5.3   else
5.4   with *table*[*index*] do
5.5   write *model, memory, disk*
5.6   if *colour* then
5.7   write ' colour option available '
5.8   else
5.9   write ' colour option not available '
5.10   ifend
5.11   write out *price*
5.12   withend
5.13 ifend

Data table (addition to above)

Identifier	Description	Type
searchmodel	Item to be found	string variable
index	Loop control variable	integer variable

TEST THE DESIGN

The design needs to be traced with values that are in the table and values which are not.

Problem 6.13

UNDERSTAND THE PROBLEM

What types of output could be expected here and what sort of loop is required?
The output could consist of many model numbers or there could be no models satisfying the users' requirements. Since every item has to be inspected, a *for* loop should be used.

DEVISE A SOLUTION

The same top level design as used in Problem 6.12 can be used here but refined differently. As the array is searched, successful comparisons will be written out immediately. But there may be no machines satisfying the requirements. To record this possibility we have used a flag in the refinement.

1.1   write out 'Enter size of memory required '
1.2   read in *memorysize*
1.3   *found* := false
2.1   loop for *index*] := 1 to *size*
3.1   if *table*[*index*].*memory* >= *memorysize* then
3.2   write out *table*[*index*].*model*, ' has a memory of at least ', *memorysize*
3.3   *found* = true
3.4   ifend
4   loopend
5.1   if *found* = false then
5.2   write out 'No model has that size of memory'
5.3   ifend

Data table (additional to the definition of the table)

Identifier	Description	Type
memorysize	Memory size to be searched	integer variable
found	Flag indicating match	boolean variable
index	Loop control variable	integer variable

TEST THE DESIGN

The design needs to be tested with values of memory size that are known to occur several times and values for which there would be no machines which satisfy the criteria.

Problem 6.14

UNDERSTAND THE PROBLEM

Try to recover all the titles from the keywords in the table by hand paying particular attention to the location of space characters.

DEVISE A SOLUTION

A top level design is:

1   initialize variables referenced in loop
2   loop for all items in table
3   if *keysearch* is found then
4   reconstruct title
5   ifend
6   loopend
7   report the results

Step 7 will need to output a suitable message in the event that no matches are found and this will require the use of a flag within the loop. However, the major problem is refining step 4. As a first step we note that every character in the remainder must be examined and that what is to be done depends upon whether or not a slash character has been encountered. This leads to the following refinement of step 4:

4.1   initialize variables referenced in loop
4.2   loop for all characters in remainder
4.3   if current character is a slash then
4.4   process it

4.5	else
4.6	process non slash character
4.7	ifend
4.8	loopend
4.9	write out result of this construction

The refinement of step 4.4 will involve setting a flag to record the fact that a slash has been encountered and skipping over the slash character itself. The refinement of step 4.6 will require different actions dependent upon whether the current character is part of the title after the keyword or before it. This, of course, depends upon whether the slash character has been encountered and so the refinement will need to test the state of the flag. For simplicity we have chosen to use two variables to hold these characters; *prefix* will store all the characters which precede the keyword and *suffix* will hold those which follow it. Finally, step 4.9 will need to take care with spaces between the three components which will have to be concatenated to form the overall title.We thus get the following final design:

	{Reconstruct title from keyword index}	
1.1	*foundmatch* := false	
1.2	write out 'Enter a key word '	
1.3	read in *keysearch*	
2.1	loop for *item* := 1 to *size*	
3.1	if *keysearch* = *keyindex*[*item*].*keyword* then	
4.1.1	*foundmatch* := true	
4.1.2	*prefix* := ''	
4.1.3	*suffix* := ''	
4.1.4	*slashfound* := false	
4.2.1	loop for *i* := 1 to *length*(*keyindex*[*item*].*remainder*)	{all the remainder}
4.3.1	*current* := *keyindex*[*item*].*remainder*[*i*]	{current character}
4.3.2	if *current* = '/' then	
4.4.1	*slashfound* := true	
4.5	else	
4.6.1	if *slashfound* then	
4.6.2	*prefix* := *prefix* + *current*	{concatenate to *prefix*}
4.6.3	else	
4.6.4	*suffix* := *suffix* + *current*	{concatenate to *suffix*}
4.6.5	ifend	
4.7	ifend	
4.8	loopend	
4.9.1	if *prefix* <> '' then	
4.9.2	*title* := *prefix* + *keysearch* + *suffix*	
4.9.3	else	
4.9.4	*title* := *keysearch* + *suffix*	
4.9.5	ifend	
4.9.6	write out *title*	
5	ifend	
6	loopend	
7.1	if *foundmatch* = false then	
7.2	write out 'No matches for this keyword'	
7.3	ifend	

Data table (additional to that in the text)

Identifier	Description	Type
foundmatch	Flag, denotes search success	boolean variable
item	Index to current record	integer variable
prefix	Phrase preceding *keysearch*	string variable
suffix	Phrase after *keysearch*	string variable
i	Loop control variable	integer variable
current	Current character	char variable
slashfound	Flag, denotes slash found	boolean variable
title	Reconstructed title	string variable

TEST THE DESIGN

The data given above lists some critical values; namely remainders which begin with a slash, those which do not contain a slash and those which have a slash in the middle. You should also test for empty remainders to allow for book titles like 'Pascal'.

Problem 6.15

UNDERSTAND THE PROBLEM

The array *directory* holds all the information. Should every element of the array be output? No – some entries contain deleted files; others have never been used and so these entries should not be output.

DEVISE A SOLUTION

A top level design is:

```
      {A directory listing}
  1   loop for all elements
  2       if element has active file then
  3           write out details
  4       ifend
  5   loopend
```

This may be refined to:

```
        {A directory listing}
  1.1   loop for i := 1 to 112
  2.2       if directory[i].filename[1] <> '∇' then
  3.1           with directory[i]
  3.1               write out filename, extension, size, date, time
  3.3           withend
  4         ifend
  5     loopend
```

Data table (additional to the definition of *directory*)

Identifier	Description	Type
i	Loop control variable	integer variable

TEST THE DESIGN

The data above provides some test data here.

Problem 6.16

Data table

Identifier	Description		Type
datetype	Record type definition		
	day	{Day of the month}	integer variable
	month	{Month number}	integer variable
	year	{Year}	integer variable
	recordend		
entry	Record type definition		
	filename	{File name}	string[8] variable
	extension	{File extension}	string[3] variable
	attribute	{File attribute}	char variable
	time	{Time file was saved}	integer variable
	date	{Date file was saved}	*datetype* variable
	cluster	{First cluster number}	integer variable
	filesize	{File size}	integer variable
	recordend		
directory	Array of directory entries		array[0..112] of *entry* variable

Problem 7.1

5.1.1	select case depending on *daycode*
5.1.2	0 : write out 'Sunday'
5.1.3	1 : write out 'Monday'
5.1.4	2 : write out 'Tuesday'
5.1.5	3 : write out 'Wednesday'
5.1.6	4 : write out 'Thursday'
5.1.7	5 : write out 'Friday'
5.1.8	6 : write out 'Saturday'
5.1.9	selectend

Here we have left out the default option because *daycode* can only have one of the values 0 to 6 inclusive. It would however not be wrong to include the default as we have below:

5.1.1	select case depending on *daycode*
5.1.2	0 : write out 'Sunday'
5.1.3	1 : write out 'Monday'
5.1.4	2 : write out 'Tuesday'
5.1.5	3 : write out 'Wednesday'
5.1.6	4 : write out 'Thursday'
5.1.7	5 : write out 'Friday'
5.1.8	6 : write out 'Saturday'
5.1.9	default : do nothing
5.1.10	selectend

Problem 7.2

UNDERSTAND THE PROBLEM

Is 12 13 a valid pair of inputs for the day and month respectively?
No – there is no 13th month and so the date is invalid.

DEVISE A SOLUTION

In the top level design which follows we have chosen to examine the month data first:

{Test for valid date}
1 initialize variables
2 select case depending on *month*
3   process *month*
4 selectend
5 write out results

We shall need to use a flag to record the outcome of step 3 for use in step 5.

{Test for valid date}
1.1   write 'Enter day as an integer '
1.2   read in *day*
1.3   write 'Enter month as an integer '
1.4   read in *month*
1.5   *dateok* := true
2   select case depending on *month*
3.1   1, 3, 5, 7, 8, 10, 12 : if *day* > 31 then
3.2   *dateok* := false
3.3   ifend
3.4   2   : if *day* > 28 then
3.5   *dateok* := false
3.6   ifend
3.7   4, 6, 9, 11   : if *day* > 30 then
3.8   *dateok* := false
3.9   ifend
3.10   default   : *dateok* := false
4   selectend
5.1   if *dateok* then
5.2   write out 'Date may be valid'
5.3   else
5.4   write out 'Date is not valid'
5.5   ifend

Data table

Identifier	Description	Type
day	Day of the month	integer variable
month	Month expressed as an integer	integer variable
dateok	Flag set true if date is OK	boolean variable

TEST THE DESIGN

Test data should include values which will test all possible case labels. The date 12 13 will check the default label. For the other case labels you will require both a valid date and an invalid date and so six more test data items need to be generated.

Problem 7.3

UNDERSTAND THE PROBLEM

Do the integers 29 02 1990 represent a valid date?

No – the 29th of February only exists in leap years and since 1990 is not exactly divisible by four it is not a leap year.

DEVISE A SOLUTION

The same top level design as in Problem 7.2 can be used here.

```
        {Test for valid date including leap years}
1.1     write 'Enter day as an integer '
1.2     read in day
1.3     write 'Enter month as an integer '
1.4     read in month
1.5     write 'Enter year as an integer '
1.6     read in year
1.7     dateok := true
2       select case depending on month
3.1        1, 3, 5, 7, 8, 10, 12  : if day > 31 then
3.2                                    dateok := false
3.3                                 ifend
3.4                    2           : if year MOD 4 = 0 then
3.5                                    if day > 29 then
3.6                                       dateok := false
3.7                                    ifend
3.8                                 else
3.9                                    if day > 28 then
3.10                                      dateok := false
3.11                                   ifend
3.12                                ifend
3.13       4, 6, 9, 11    : if day > 30 then
3.14                           dateok := false
3.15                        ifend
3.16        default     : dateok := false
4       selectend
5.1     if dateok then
5.2        write out 'Date may be valid'
5.3     else
5.4        write out 'Date is not valid'
5.5     ifend
```

Data table

Identifier	Description	Type
day	Day of the month	integer variable
month	Month expressed as an integer	integer variable
year	Year as an integer	integer variable
dateok	Flag set true if date is OK	boolean variable

TEST THE DESIGN

The month of February now needs four test data values; a valid date in February, the date 29th February in a non-leap year, the date 29th February in a leap year and a date like 30th February in a leap year.

Problem 7.4

If the first input is correct what should happen?
The second and third lines of the dialogue would not happen.

Since a different prompt is required for second and subsequent attempts at input, the following top level design is suggested:

    {Validate integer input is in range 2 to 5}
1   read in the data
2   loop while the data is not valid
3   obtain valid data
4   loopend

This may be refined to:

    {Validate integer input is in range 2 to 5}
1.1   write 'Enter an integer in the range 2 to 5 inclusive? '
1.2   read in *number*
2.1   loop while (*number* < 2) or (*number* > 5)
3.2   write 'You must enter an integer in the stated range 2 to 5. Try again? '
3.3   read in *number*
4   loopend

Data table

Identifier	Description	Type
number	Integer input by user	integer variable

The crucial thing here is to test that the operator *or* is used correctly. Test data should include values less than 2, values between 2 and 5 and values greater than 5.

Problem 7.5

What should be output if the input string is
    'Write▽a▽{top▽level▽{and▽refined}▽but▽not▽final}▽design'?
The output should be the string 'Write▽a▽▽but▽not▽final}▽design'.

There are two basic approaches. The first is to examine each character in turn and as soon as an opening brace is encountered skip over subsequent characters until the closing brace or the end of the string is encountered. This requires the use of nested loops; the outer one to progress through each character and the inner one to skip characters. The alternative approach is to examine each character in turn and to use flags to indicate when a character falls within an open and closed brace pair. The two designs below express these approaches:

{Remove text between braces}
1 initialize variables referenced in loop
2 loop while there are characters to process
3   if current character is '{' then
4   skip until '}' or all characters processed
5   else
6   copy current character to new string
7   ifend
8   move to next character
9 loopend
10 write out results

{Remove text between braces}
1 initialize variables referenced in loop
2 loop for all characters
3   if character within a brace pair then
4   if character = '}' then
5   *withinpair* := false
6   ifend
7   else
8   if character = '{' then
9   *withinpair* := true
10   else
11   copy character to new string
12   ifend
13   ifend
14 loopend
15 write out results

These designs may be refined as follows:

{Remove text between braces}
1.1 $i := 1$
1.2 *newstr* := "
1.3 write 'Enter text '
1.4 read in *given*
2.1 loop while $i <= length(given)$
3.1   if *given*[i] = '{' then
4.1   repeat
4.2   increment i
4.3   until *given*[i] = '}' or $i = length(given)$
5   else
6.1   *newstr* := *newstr* + *given*[i]
7   ifend
8.1   increment i
9 loopend
10.1 write out 'New string is ', *newstr*

{Remove text between braces}
1.1 *newstr* := "
1.2 write 'Enter text '
1.3 read in *given*
1.4 *withinpair* := false
2.1 loop for $i := 1$ to $length(given)$
3.1   if *withinpair* then
4.1   if *given*[i] = '}' then
5   *withinpair* := false
6   ifend
7   else
8.1   if *given*[i] = '{' then
9   *withinpair* := true
10   else
11.1   *newstr* := *newstr* + *given*[i]
12   ifend
13   ifend
14 loopend
15.1 write out 'New string is ', *newstr*

Combined data table for both designs

Identifier	Description	Type
i	Index of character in *given*	integer variable
newstr	New string with braces removed	string variable
given	Old input string	string variable
withinpair	Flag denoting open/closed brace pair	boolean variable

TEST THE DESIGN

Test data should include strings which do not contain any braces, those which contain only opening braces, those containing only closing braces and those containing a mixture like the example above.

Problem 7.6

UNDERSTAND THE PROBLEM

Is the expression [2 + 3]*[[[2 + 4]*[5 − 2] + 3]*2 + 1] well formed?
Yes – the number of opening brackets never exceeds the number of closing brackets and there are five of each type in the string.
Is the expression [2+1]] * [6 well formed?
No – although there are equal numbers of opening and closing brackets there are two closing brackets to one opening bracket at the time the third character of the string is examined. The output should indicate that the number of closing brackets exceeds the number of opening brackets at the sixth character of the input string.
Is the expression [5 − 2[*] [4+2] well formed?
No – there are more opening brackets than closing ones. The message that the sequence is not well formed should be output.
Should a *for* loop be considered for the design? If at any stage the number of closing brackets exceeds the number of opening ones, then the expression is not well formed, the fact should be reported and execution should cease. A *for* loop is therefore not appropriate.

DEVISE A SOLUTION

A top level design is:

    {Well-formed expression?}
1   initialize variables
2   loop while not end of expression and closing brackets do not exceed open brackets
3   process character
4   loopend
5   write out results

A boolean flag will be used to indicate that the number of closing brackets does not exceed the number of opening brackets. This flag will be used to control the loop and will be used again in step 5 to produce a final message if one is required.

    {Well-formed expression}
1.1   write out 'Enter an expression '
1.2   read in *expression*
1.3   *moreclosing* := false
1.4   *position* := 1
1.5   *opencount* := 0
1.6   *closecount* := 0
2.1   loop while *position* <= *length(expression)* and not *moreclosing*
3.1   if *expression*[*position*] = '[' then
3.2   increment *opencount*
3.3   else
3.4   if *expression*[*position*] = ']' then
3.5   increment *closecount*
3.6   if *closecount* > *opencount* then
3.7   *moreclosing* := true
3.8   write 'Number of closed brackets exceeds number of open brackets '
3.9   write out 'at character ', *position*
3.10   ifend
3.11   ifend

3.12   ifend
3.13   increment *position*
4   loopend
5.1   if not *moreclosing* then
5.2   if *closecount* = *opencount* then
5.3   write out 'The expression is well formed'
5.4   else
5.5   write out 'The expression is not well formed – too many left brackets'
5.6   ifend
5.7   ifend

Data table

Identifier	Description	Type
expression	Expression being tested	string variable
moreclosing	True indicates closing bracket error	boolean variable
position	String index	integer variable
opencount	Number of opening brackets	integer variable
closecount	Number of closing brackets	integer variable

Note how the message that the expression is not well formed is not written out when processing has terminated because the number of closing brackets exceeded the number of opening brackets.

TEST THE DESIGN

The test data above would check all the selections in this design. Your design ought to work with expressions consisting only of brackets and so your test data could just consist of strings of brackets.

Problem 7.7

UNDERSTAND THE PROBLEM

What are the two possible outcomes of any search?
Either the item is found or all items in the array are examined and the item is not there.

DEVISE A SOLUTION

A top level and refined design are shown below:

{Linear search version 2}
1   initialize variables
2   repeat
3   move to next item
4   update *found*
5   until (*found*) or (end of the array is reached)
6   write out results

{Linear search version 2}
1.1   write 'Enter item to be searched for '
1.2   read in *item*
1.3   *index* := 0
2   repeat
3.1   increment *index*
4.1   *found* := (*item* = *names*[*index*])
5.1   until (*found*) or (*index* > *maxsize*)
6.1   if *found* then
6.2   write out 'Item is at index ', *index*
6.3   else
6.4   write out 'Item is not in list'
6.5   ifend

Data table

Identifier	Description	Type
maxsize	Array index upper bound	integer constant
names	Array of names	array[1..*maxsize*] of string variable
item	Item being searched for	string variable
index	Index to element being examined	integer variable
found	True if item is found	boolean variable

Note how *found* is updated in this design. We remind you that step 3.1 is equivalent to

    if *item* = *names*[*index*] then
        found := true
    else
        found := false
    ifend

TEST THE DESIGN

You will need to generate some hypothetical data to test this design. Both successful and unsuccessful outcomes should be tested.

Problem 7.8

The difficulty arises if the search is unsuccessful. Suppose *maxsize* has value 10. Eventually *index* will be incremented until it has value 10 and step 2 will be executed. Since *item* is not equal to *names*[10], step 3.1 is executed again, which results in *index* having value 11. A problem now arises with step 2 because the first condition *index* <= *maxsize* evaluates to false and this of course means that the whole expression must be false. If we relied upon left to right evaluation all would be well but to do so is unsafe as many systems do not support this type of evaluation. So, examining the second part of the condition, we have to evaluate the expression *item* <> *names*[*index*] with *index* having the value of 11. But *names*[11] is an index out of range error. Note that the problem cannot be avoided simply by making the inequality involving *maxsize* a strict inequality, because then the element with index *maxsize* is not examined to see if it matches the search item.

One way of avoiding potential out of range errors like this is to not reference the array in the loop control condition but to use a boolean flag instead. We have done so in the design below.

```
        {Linear search using a while loop and a boolean flag}
1.1     write 'Enter item to be searched for '
1.2     read in item
1.3     index := 0
1.4     found := false
2       loop while index < maxsize and not found
3.1         increment index
3.2         found := (item = names[index])
4       loopend
5.1     if found then
5.2         write out 'Item is at index ', index
5.3     else
5.4         write out 'Item is not in list'
5.5     ifend
```

Problem 7.9

UNDERSTAND THE PROBLEM

What should happen if *maxsize* had value 512 and the user enters as initial and final values the two numbers 25 and −10 respectively?

The first number is in the given range and so is a valid input. The second is not in the required range and a message to this effect should be output. (That it also violates the additional constraint that the final address must not precede the initial address is of no concern because the program terminates before this is considered.)

DEVISE A SOLUTION

Two alternative designs, both top level and refined, are given below.

	{Fill memory, validating input addresses}
1	read in initial address
2	if it is in error then
3	report the error in initial address
4	else
5	read in the final address
6	if it is in error then
7	report the error in final address
8	else
9	process the inputs
10	ifend
11	ifend

	{Fill memory, validating input addresses}
1	read in initial address
2	if it is valid then
3	read in the final address
4	if it is valid then
5	process the inputs
6	else
7	report the error in final address
8	ifend
9	else
10	report the error in initial address
11	ifend

	{Fill memory, validating input addresses}
1.1	write 'Enter initial address '
1.2	read in *initial*
2.1	if (*initial* <= 0) or (*initial* > *maxsize*) then
3.1	write out 'Initial address is not in address range '
4	else
5.1	write 'Enter final address '
5.2	read in *final*
6.1	if (*final* <= 0) or (*final* > *maxsize*) then
7.1	write out 'Final address is not in address range'
8	else
9.1	if *initial* <= *final* then
9.2	write 'Value to fill memory is? '
9.3	read in *FillValue*
9.4	loop for *i* := *initial* to *final*
9.5	memory[*i*] := *FillValue*
9.6	loopend
9.7	else
9.8	write out 'Initial address is larger than final address'
9.9	ifend
10	ifend
11	ifend

	{Fill memory, validating input addresses}
1.1	write 'Enter initial address '
1.2	read in *initial*
2.1	if (*initial* >= 0) and (*initial* <= *maxsize*) then
3.1	write 'Enter final address '
3.2	read in *final*
4.1	if (*final* >= 0) and (*final* <= *maxsize*) then
5.1	if *initial* > *final* then
5.2	write out 'Initial address is larger than final address'
5.3	else
5.4	write 'Value to fill memory is? '
5.5	read in *FillValue*
5.6	loop for *i* := *initial* to *final*
5.7	memory[*i*] := *FillValue*
5.8	loopend
5.9	ifend
6	else
7.1	write out 'Final address is not in address range'
8	ifend
9	else
10.1	write out 'Initial address is not in address range '
11	ifend

Data table

Identifier	Description	Type
maxsize	Array index upper bound	integer constant
memory	Array simulating machine memory	array[1..maxsize] of integer variable
initial	First address of range to be filled	integer variable
final	Last address of memory to be filled	integer variable
FillValue	Value to fill range	integer variable
i	Loop control variable	integer variable

TEST THE DESIGN

Tests carried out for Problem 6.1 are appropriate here but in addition this design needs to be tested to check that the invalid data inputs are handled correctly.

Problem 7.10

UNDERSTAND THE PROBLEM

Re-read the solutions to Problem 5.20 and Problem 5.11.

DEVISE A SOLUTION

The final design given below uses three variables for the characters being examined. The use of these variables can be avoided in a similar way to that used in Problem 5.11.

```
        {Count occurrences of 'the' in input string using a compound boolean}
1.1   count := 0
1.2   write 'Enter the string '
1.3   read in sentence
1.4   first := sentence[1]
1.5   second := sentence[2]
2.1   loop for current := 3 to length(sentence)
3.1       if (first = 't') and (second = 'h') and (sentence[current] = 'e') then
3.2           increment count
3.3       ifend
3.4       first := second
3.5       second := sentence[current]
4     loopend
5.1   write out 'Number of occurrences is ' count
```

Data table

Identifier	Description	Type
count	Occurrences of pattern 'the'	integer variable
sentence	Input string	string variable
first	First character of the 3 currently being examined	char variable
second	Second character of 3 currently being examined	char variable
current	Index of the third character being examined	integer variable

TEST THE DESIGN

This should include strings resulting a count of zero as well as strings giving a non-zero count.

Problem 7.11

As well as the two items mentioned above, subranges should be used to define day, month, hours and minutes. The data table below gives the modified definition:

Data table

Identifier	Description	Type
datetype	Record type definition	
	day {Day of the month}	1..31 variable
	month {Month number}	1..12 variable
	year {Year}	0..99 variable
	recordend	
timetype	Record type definition	
	hours {Hour of time}	0..23 variable
	minutes {Minute of time}	0..59 variable
	recordend	
entry	Record type definition	
	filename {File name}	string[8] variable
	extension {File extension}	string[3] variable
	attribute {File attribute}	char variable
	time {Time file was saved}	*timetype* variable
	date {Date file was saved}	*datetype* variable
	cluster {First cluster number}	integer variable
	filesize {File size}	integer variable
	recordend	
directory	Array of directory entries	array[0..112] of *entry* variable

Problem 7.12

Data table

Identifier	Description	Type
weekday	Enumerated type definition	*monday..friday*
weeklywork	Array of weekday hours worked	array[*weekday*] of real variable

Problem 7.13

UNDERSTAND THE PROBLEM

What will be the major structure of the top level design?
Two loops, one nested inside the other, which enable each of the elements of the two-dimensional array to be initialized in turn.
Headings for the table ought to be given but the lines it contains can be ignored.

DEVISE A SOLUTION

A top level design is:

```
    {Weekly production figures}
1   initialize variables referenced in loops
2   loop for all days
3       loop for all shifts
4           read in data
5       loopend
```

6 loopend
7 write out table

The parallel arrays to handle the generation of the prompts are initialized as part of the refinement of step 1:

{Weekly production figures}
1.1 *dayname*[*mon*] := 'Monday'   1.2 *dayname*[*tue*] := 'Tuesday'
1.3 *dayname*[*wed*] := 'Wednesday'   1.4 *dayname*[*thur*] := 'Thursday'
1.5 *dayname*[*fri*] := 'Friday'   1.6 *shiftname*[*early*] := 'Early'
1.7 *shiftname*[*late*] := 'Late'   1.8 *shiftname*[*night*] := 'Night'
2.1 loop for *day* := *mon* to *fri*
3.1   loop for *shift* := *early* to *night*
4.1   write 'Enter production for the ', *dayname*[*day*], *shiftname*[*shift*], ' shift'
4.2   read in *week*[*day*, *shift*]
5   loopend
6   loopend
7.1 write out ' ', 'Monday', 'Tuesday', 'Wednesday', 'Thursday', 'Friday'
     {The table headings}
7.2 loop for *shift* := *early* to *night*
7.3   write *shiftname*[*shift*]   {The row heading}
7.4   loop for *day* := *mon* to *fri*
7.5   write *week*[*day*, *shift*]
7.6   loopend
7.7   write out   {Create a new row}
7.8 loopend

Data table

Identifier	Description	Type
DayType	Enumerated type definition	(*mon, tue, wed, thur, fri*)
ShiftType	Enumerated type definition	(*early, late, night*)
week	Array holding weekly production	array[*DayType, ShiftType*] of integer variable
day	Day of the week	*DayType* variable
shift	Shift within a day	*ShiftType* variable
dayname	Array of weekday names	array[*DayType*] of string variable
shiftname	Array of shift names	array[*ShiftType*] of string variable

TEST THE DESIGN

For the data input the order in which the loops are nested is not crucial. We have chosen the order so that the user enters data for all three shifts on a given day. The day then moves on to the next day. You may have ordered your loops so that data for all the early shifts is entered, then all the late shifts and finally all the night shifts. When it comes to the output data there is no flexibility. That is because the top row of the table must be produced first, then the second row and finally the last. A trace of the input section will confirm the input order. A more careful scrutiny of the output may be required to check that it is produced row by row.

Problem 7.14

UNDERSTAND THE PROBLEM

What happens to punctuation marks?
Nothing – they remain in the string.

DEVISE A SOLUTION

A top level design is:

> {Small ads abbreviation}
> 1 initialize variables
> 2 loop for all characters
> 3   process character
> 4 loopend
> 5 write out results

The processing of each character will involve creating a new abbreviated string. To do so we shall concatenate only the non-vowel characters of the input string to it.

> {Small ads abbreviation}
> 1.1 write out 'Enter the advert '
> 1.2 read in *advert*
> 1.3 *abbreviation* := "
> 1.4 *vowels* := ['a', 'c', 'i', 'o', 'u']
> 2.1 loop for *position* := 1 to *length(advert)*
> 3.1   if not (*advert*[*position*] in *vowels*) then
> 3.2   *abbreviation* := *abbreviation* + *advert*[*position*]
> 3.3   ifend
> 4   loopend
> 5.1 write out 'Abbreviation is ', *abbreviation*

Data table

Identifier	Description	Type
advert	Input string	string variable
vowels	Set of vowel characters	set of char variable
abbreviation	Input string with vowels removed	string variable
position	Loop control variable	integer variable

TEST THE DESIGN

You should include in your test data strings which do not have any vowels, as well as those that do.

Problem 7.15

UNDERSTAND THE PROBLEM

What is the minimum length of an abbreviated word?
One – if the word begins with a vowel then the vowel is not removed. Vowels are removed from the second character onwards in each word.
What do you think is the significance of the restriction that words are separated by single spaces?
A space signals that the next character is the start of a word and this character must be given special treatment because it must not be removed.

DEVISE A SOLUTION

We can use the same top level design as before:

{Small ads abbreviation version 2}
1   initialize variables
2   loop for all characters
3   process character
4   loopend
5   write out results

An obvious first refinement of this design is:

{Small ads abbreviation version 2}
1   initialize variables
2   loop for all characters
3.1   if current character is the start of a word then
3.2   append it to the abbreviation
3.3   else
3.4   process character
3.5   ifend
4   loopend
5   write out results

We have already decided that the existence of a space indicates that the next character is the start of a word. We can therefore anticipate that Step 3.4 will have to deal with this possibility and set a flag to indicate the start of a word. But it will also have to deal with the situations that the character is a vowel or a non-vowel. This suggests that step 3.4 should be refined as a case statement whose labels are the possible values of the current character.

{Small ads abbreviation version 2}
1.1   write out 'Enter the advert '
1.2   read in *advert*
1.3   *abbreviation* := "
1.4   *NewWord* := true
2.1   loop for *position* := 1 to *length*(*advert*)
3.1   if *NewWord* then
3.2.1   *abbreviation* := *abbreviation* + *advert*[*position*]
3.2.2   *NewWord* := false
3.3   else
3.4.1   select case depending on *advert*[*position*]
3.4.2   'a', 'e', 'i', 'o', 'u' : do nothing
3.4.3   '▽'   : *abbreviation* := *abbreviation* + *advert*[*position*]
3.4.4   *NewWord* := true
3.4.5   default   : *abbreviation* := *abbreviation* + *advert*[*position*]
3.4.6   selectend
3.5   ifend
4   loopend
5.1   write out 'Abbreviation is ', *abbreviation*

Data table

Identifier	Description	Type
advert	Input string	string variable
abbreviation	Input string with vowels removed	string variable
NewWord	Flag denoting start of a word	boolean variable
position	Loop control variable	integer variable

In this refinement we have not used a set as in the earlier problem. While the earlier problem may have helped in forming a strategy for this design it would have proved cumbersome to try to attempt to modify it to fit this situation. Here, a fresh approach to the refinement of step 3.4 leads to a straightforward solution.

TEST THE DESIGN

Test data should include words which have a vowel as initial letter as well as those that do not. Inputs consisting of a single word should be used, with the values for the words being chosen so that some have a vowel as an initial letter and others have a consonant as an initial letter.

Problem 7.16

UNDERSTAND THE PROBLEM

What are the pairs and the counts arising from the string 'pipe of peace'?
The pairs are *pi, ip, pe, of, pe, ea, ac, ce* of which *pe* occurs twice.
Space characters and punctuation marks must not appear in the pair counts. How can this be avoided?
A pair of adjacent characters will have to be tested to see if they contain only lower-case letters. Those that are not both lower-case do not contribute to the count.
How can the test for lower-case be done?
The easiest way is to use a set.
All adjacent pairs of characters will have to be examined. What sort of loop is therefore required?
A *for* loop should be used to progress the pair being examined from the start of the string to its end.

DEVISE A SOLUTION

A top level design is:

```
      {Count the pairs in a string}
  1   initialize variables referenced in loop
  2   loop for all pairs of characters
  3       if the pair are both lower-case letters then
  4           update the count
  5       ifend
  6       move to next pair
  7   loopend
  8   write out results
```

A final design is:

```
      {Count the pairs in a string}
  1.1   write 'Enter the text to be analysed '
  1.2   read in paragraph
  1.3   lowercase := ['a'..'z']
  1.4   loop for first := 'a' to 'z'
  1.5       loop for second := 'a' to 'z'
  1.6           paircount[first, second] := 0
  1.7       loopend
  1.8   loopend
```

1.9   *first := paragraph*[1]
2.1   loop for *position := 2* to *length(paragraph)*
3.1   *second := paragraph*[*position*]
3.2   if (*first* in *lowercase*) and (*second* in *lowercase*) then
4.1   *paircount*[*first, second*] *:= paircount*[*first, second*] + 1
5   ifend
6.1   *first := second*
7   loopend
8.1   write out ' a b c d e f g h i j k l m n o p q r s t u v w x y z'
8.2   loop for *first* := 'a' to 'z'
8.3   write *first*, ' '
8.4   loop for *second* := 'a' to 'z'
8.5   write paircount[*first, second*], ' '
8.6   loopend
8.7   write out   {go to new line}
8.8   loopend

Data table

Identifier	Description	Type
alpha	Subrange type definition	'a'..'z'
lowercase	Set of lower-case characters	set of char variable
paragraph	Input text	string variable
first	First character of a pair	char variable
second	Second character of a pair	char variable
paircount	Array holding the counts	array[*alpha, alpha*] of integer variable
position	Index to the characters in *paragraph*	integer variable

TEST THE DESIGN

You should check that the design does not include counts for characters other than lower-case pairs. The order of the pairs is important and the output should correctly report the order. For example the illustration in the question has a pair *ab* but not a pair *ba*.

Problem 7.17

UNDERSTAND THE PROBLEM

The top level design will be the same as Problem 7.13, as will be much of the refinement. What will be different is the way the prompts will be generated. How can the input prompt 'Enter the production for Sunday' be produced using the value of *day*?

A case statement can be used which has as case labels the enumerated type values *mon, tue* etc., and which has the string values 'Monday', 'Tuesday' and so on as the respective statements for each label.

DEVISE A SOLUTION

The final design (based upon the top level design in Problem 7.13) is:

       {Weekly production version 2}
1   {No initializing required}
2.1   loop for *day := mon* to *fri*
3.1   loop for *shift := early* to *night*

4.1   write 'Enter production for the '
4.2   select case depending on *day*
4.3   *mon*   : write 'Monday '
4.4   *tue*   : write 'Tuesday '
4.5   *wed*   : write 'Wednesday '
4.6   *thur* : write 'Thursday '
4.7   *fri*   : write 'Friday '
4.8   selectend
4.9   select case depending on *shift*
4.10   *early* : write 'Early shift'
4.11   *late*   : write 'Late shift'
4.12   *night* : write 'Night shift'
4.13   selectend
4.14   read in *week*[*day*, *shift*]
5   loopend
6   loopend
7.1 write out ' ', 'Monday', 'Tuesday', 'Wednesday', 'Thursday', 'Friday'
     {The table headings}
7.2 loop for *shift* := *early* to *night*
7.3   write *shift*   {The row heading}
7.4   loop for *day* := *mon* to *fri*
7.5   write *week*[*day*, *shift*]
7.6   write out   {Create a new row}
7.7   loopend
7.8 loopend

The data table is as before with the exception that the parallel arrays holding the names of the days and shifts are not declared here.

TEST THE DESIGN

The new method of prompting needs testing. The rest of the design is the same as before.

Problem 7.18

UNDERSTAND THE PROBLEM

We shall use the same user defined ordinal types as used in Problem 7.13 together with the parallel arrays used in its solution, which we shall assume are already initialized and so are available for use.
What function will be required in order to find the shift following the best shift?
The *succ* function which finds the successor to a user defined ordinal value.
Can we just apply this function to the shift which has the best production?
No – if that shift is the night shift then we know that *night* has no successor, it is the last value of the user defined ordinal type *ShiftType*.

DEVISE A SOLUTION

A top level design is:

```
      {Best production shift}
1   initialize variables referenced in loop
2   loop for all shifts
3       find best shift
4   loopend
5   write out results
```

This may be refined to:

```
        {Best production shift}
1.1   bestprod := 0
2.1   loop for day := mon to fri
2.2       loop for shift := early to night
3.1           if week[day, shift] >= bestprod then
3.2               bestprod := week[day, shift]
3.3               bestday := day
3.4               bestshift := shift
3.5           ifend
4.1       loopend
4.2   loopend
5.1   write out 'The best production was on the ', dayname[bestday], shiftname[bestshift], ' shift.'
5.2   write out 'It produced ', bestprod, ' items.'
5.3   if bestshift <> night then
5.4       write out 'The next shift produced ', week[bestday, succ(bestshift)], ' items.'
5.5   else
5.6       write out 'The next shift produced ', week[succ(bestday), early], ' items.'
5.7   ifend
```

Data table (additional to Problem 7.13)

Identifier	Description	Type
bestprod	Best production of the week	integer variable
bestday	Day on which *bestprod* was produced	*DayType* variable
bestshift	Shift in which *bestprod* was produced	*ShiftType* variable

Notice how we have used the *succ* function here. It is evaluated and the resulting value becomes the index of the array.

TEST THE DESIGN

You should check that in the event that there is no unique best production then it is the last shift which produces the largest number of items which is output. You should also make sure that no attempt is made to find the successor which does not exist. Step 5.3 ensures that the successor of *shift* is handled correctly but what about the successor of *day* in step 5.6? If the Friday night shift produced the best production of the week then step 5.6 would attempt to find the successor of *fri*, which does not exist and this would be an error. But the problem specifies that the Friday night shift cannot produce the best output of the week because it is concerned with routine maintenance and so this possibility does not arise.

Problem 8.1

load

{Retrieve *stock* from backing store.}		
stock	The stock list	*stocktype* parameter

menu

{Write out the menu to the screen.}		

choice

{Read in a menu choice from the keyboard. All inputs other than 1, 2, 3 or 4 should be ignored.}		
menuchoice	User's chosen option	char parameter

update

stock	The stock list	*stocktype* parameter
{Prompt for a stock number. If the stock number is valid write out the details of the stock number item, prompt for a new quantity in stock and update *stock*. Otherwise write out a message that stock number is invalid.}		
stock	Updated stock list	*stocktype* parameter

findnext

stock	The stock list	*stocktype* parameter
{Find the next item number for a new stationery item. If the array *stock* is full then return the value 0.}		
itemnumber	The new item number	integer parameter

display

stock	The stock list	*stocktype* parameter
{Display the complete contents of *stock* on the screen.}		

save

stock	The stock list	*stocktype* parameter
{Save *stock* on file in backing store.}		

Problem 8.2

We adopt the usual convention of not including the file name as source data or results in any procedure which involves file access.

getaccount

{Read in an account number to *accountno*. Validate the input against a file of current account numbers. If the number corresponds to an account set *valid* true and return *accountno*. If the number does not correspond to an account set *valid* to false.}		
accountno	An individual account	*accounttype* parameter
valid	Flag to denote validity of number	boolean parameter

getbalance

accountno	An account number	*accounttype* parameter
{Retrieve the balance for the account with number *accountno* from backing store.}		
balance	The balance in this account	*moneytype* parameter

getrate

balance	An amount of money	*moneytype* parameter
{Return the interest rate applicable for a deposited amount of size *balance*.}		
rate	The applicable interest rate	*ratetype* parameter

addinterest

balance	An amount of money	*moneytype* parameter
interest	An amount of interest	*moneytype* parameter
{Add the *interest* to *balance* and return as *newbalance*.}		
newbalance	Updated balance	*moneytype* parameter

print

accountno	The account number	*accounttype* parameter
oldbalance	Balance before interest calculated	*moneytype* parameter
interest	Interest due	*moneytype* parameter
newbalance	Updated balance with interest	*moneytype* parameter
{Write out the current balance and details of the the interest due and the new balance.}		

save

accountno	An account number	*accounttype* parameter
balance	Balance for that account	*moneytype* parameter
{Save on backing store *balance* in the account with account number *accountno*. }		

Problem 8.3

(a) This procedure has the same source data as results.

swap

first	A real number	real parameter
second	A real number	real parameter
{Exchange the values held by *first* and *second*.}		
first	Has *second's* original value	real parameter
second	Has *first's* original value	real parameter

(b) This requires a type definition.

Identifier	Description	Type
maxsize	Array upper bound	integer constant
arraytype	Type definition	array[1..*maxsize*] of string

reversecopy

givenarray	Array to be copied in reverse order	*arraytype* parameter
{Produce a copy of *givenarray* but with its elements in reverse order from those of *givenarray*.}		
reversedcopy	The reversed array	*arraytype* parameter

(c) Again we need a type definition. We shall use the same one as in (b). Note here that the result has the same parameter as the source data. In (b) a separate copy of the array was made; here the original copy is reassigned values in reverse order and so its source data and results must use the same parameter.

reverse

given	Array to be reversed	*arraytype* parameter
{Reverse the elements of *given* so that the element indexed 1 is stored at index *maxsize*, that at index 2 is stored at *maxsize* − 1 and so on.}		
given	The reversed array	*arraytype* parameter

Problem 8.4

Your specification needs to include source data and results as well as the specification of the purpose of the procedure. The latter can be taken from the description in the question.

leapyear

year	20th century year	integer parameter
{If *year* is a leap year assign *currentleap* the value true otherwise set it false. In either event assign to *nextleap* the next occurrence of a leap year. }		
currentleap	True if *year* is a leap year	boolean parameter
nextleap	Next leap year occurrence	integer parameter

UNDERSTAND THE PROBLEM

The year 1952 is a leap year because it is exactly divisible by four. What values should be assigned to the results parameters?

The value true should be assigned to *currentleap* and the value 1956 to *nextleap*.

What is the remainder when 1987 is divided by four and how can this be used to determine the next leap year?

The remainder is three and any year which leaves remainder three on division by four requires the addition of one year to get the next leap year.

What integer operator enables remainders to be calculated?

The operator MOD. It was described in Chapter 3.

DEVISE A SOLUTION

Two final designs to this problem are given. The numbering used should enable you to deduce the major steps used in their top level design.

leapyear	
year	
1	select case depending on (*year* MOD 4)
2.1	0 : *currentleap* := true
2.2	*nextleap* := *year* + 4
2.3	1 : *currentleap* := false
2.4	*nextleap* := *year* + 3
2.5	2 : *currentleap* := false
2.6	*nextleap* := *year* + 2
2.7	3 : *currentleap* := false
2.8	*nextleap* := *year* + 1
3	selectend
currentleap , *nextleap*	

leapyear	
year	
1	if *year* MOD 4 = 0 then
2.1	*currentleap* := true
2.2	*nextleap* := *year* + 4
3	else
4.1	*currentleap* := false
4.2	select case depending on (*year* MOD 4)
4.3	1 : *nextleap* := *year* + 3
4.4	2 : *nextleap* := *year* + 2
4.5	3 : *nextleap* := *year* + 1
4.6	selectend
5	ifend
currentleap , *nextleap*	

As no local variables have been used this procedure does not require a data table.

TEST THE DESIGN

To test a procedure design, the formal parameters have to be passed actual parameter values. The easiest way to do this here is to assign the formal parameter *year* the actual values used above and to trace through the procedure with these values. Values should be chosen so as to test each possibility in the case statement. A data table for a program which uses this procedure is given below:

Data table for program using the procedure *leapyear*

Identifier	Description	Type
leapyear	(*year*, *currentleap*, *nextleap*)	procedure(integer, boolean, integer)
givenyear	The year being investigated	integer variable
isleapyr	True if *givenyear* is a leap year	boolean variable
nextleapyr	The first leap year after *givenyear*	integer variable

Problem 8.5

UNDERSTAND THE PROBLEM

Describe what happens when the call *confirm*('Do you wish to continue? y/n ', *answer*) is executed and the user responds with Y.

First the prompt would be output to the screen and then, as a result of the user input, *answer* would be returned with value true.

DEVISE A SOLUTION

We give only a final design:

confirm

prompt

	{Check response for 'y' or 'Y'}
1.1	write out *prompt*
1.2	read in *ch*
2.1	*result* := (*ch* = 'y') or (*ch* = 'Y')

result

Data table for procedure *confirm*

Identifier	Description	Type
ch	Input character	char variable

TEST THE DESIGN

We leave the details to you.

Problem 8.6

UNDERSTAND THE PROBLEM

If the arrays are as follows, what value should be returned?

2	12	23	41

2	12	32	41

The value false because the elements indexed 3 are different.

DEVISE A SOLUTION

Two designs are given, one of which tests all the elements and the other which stops execution as soon as an unmatched pair is encountered. The latter is to be preferred, particularly if the arrays are large.

compare

first, second

	{compare the two arrays}
1.1	*result* := true
2.1	loop for *i* := 1 to *maxsize*
3.1	if *first*[*i*] <> *second*[*i*] then
3.2	*result* := false
3.3	ifend
4	loopend

result

compare

first, second

	{compare the two arrays}
1.1	*result* := true
2.1	loop while *i* <= *maxsize* and *result*
3.1	if *first*[*i*] <> *second*[*i*] then
3.2	*result* := false
3.3	ifend
3.4	*i* := *i* + 1
4	loopend

result

Data table for procedure *compare*

Identifier	Description	Type
i	Loop control variable	1..*maxsize* variable

TEST THE DESIGN

We leave the details to you.

Problem 8.7

UNDERSTAND THE PROBLEM

We remind you that the statement *write out* will produce a blank line.

DEVISE A SOLUTION

A final design is:

blanklines
___

n
___

    {Output *n* blank lines}
1   loop for $i := 1$ to n
2   write out
3   loopend
___

Data table for procedure *blanklines*

Identifier	Description	Type
i	Loop control variable	integer variable

TEST THE DESIGN

We leave the details to you.

Problem 8.8

UNDERSTAND THE PROBLEM

The example in the problem would suggest that a different process is required depending upon whether x is positive or negative. For the number -3.45, how many times must you add 1 to it before it becomes positive? What is the relationship between this number of times and the integer part of -3.45?

1 must be added to -3.45 four times before a positive number is obtained. The number 4 is the integer part of -3.45.

Check this works for other negative numbers and generate a similar tactic for positive numbers. What is the integer part of zero?

DEVISE A SOLUTION

The above preamble enables the following top level and final designs to be deduced:

integerpart
x

	{Find the integer part of x}
1	initialize variables
2	if x is positive then
3	calculate the integer part of a positive real
4	else
5	calculate the integer part of a negative real
6	ifend

intx

integerpart
x

	{Find the integer part of x}
1	$intx := 0$
2.1	if $x > 0$ then
3.1	loop while $x >= 1$
3.2	decrement x
3.3	$intx := intx + 1$
3.4	loopend
4	else
5.1	loop while $x < 0$
5.2	increment x
5.3	$intx := intx - 1$
5.4	loopend
6	ifend

intx

TEST THE DESIGN

Test values should include positive and negative reals, positive and negative integers and zero.

Problem 8.9

UNDERSTAND THE PROBLEM

If the values 25, 30, 10, 55 are passed to this procedure what value will be returned?
The three question scores are 25, 30 and 10, which have sum 65. This should be the value of the last parameter. Since it is not, then *valid* will be returned with value false and the message will be written out.

DEVISE A SOLUTION

We give a final design and leave the testing to you.

totalvalid
question1, question2, question3, total

	{Validate *total*}
1	if *total* = *question1* + *question2* + *question3* then
2	*valid* := true
3	else
4	*valid* := false
5	write out 'Total is not the sum of individual scores'
6	ifend

valid

Problem 8.10

UNDERSTAND THE PROBLEM

What denominations are required to make up the sum £3.45?
Three pound coins, two 20p coins and one 5p coin.

In which order did you calculate the denominations required?

The number of pound coins required must be calculated first. Three are required leaving a sum of 45p for which change is still required. The number of 50p coins required can now be calculated. None are required. Two 20p coins will leave a sum of 5p and so on down through the other denominations.

DEVISE A SOLUTION

The problem above should give a clue to a method of solution – namely work down through the denominations, subtracting the number of coins of each denomination from the change to be given at each stage. Thus a top level design is:

change

---

money

  {Change machine problem}
1 calculate number of pound coins required
2 calculate number of 50p coins required
3 calculate number of 20p coins required
4 calculate number of 10p coins required
5 calculate number of 5p coins required
6 calculate number of 2p coins required
7 calculate number of 1p coins required

---

pounds, fifties, twenties, tens, fives, twos, ones

This may be refined to:

change

---

money

  {Change machine problem}
1.1 *pounds := money* DIV 100
1.2 *SumLeft := money* MOD 100
2.1 *fifties := SumLeft* DIV 50
2.2 *SumLeft := SumLeft* MOD 50
3.1 *twenties := SumLeft* DIV 20
3.2 *SumLeft := SumLeft* MOD 20
4.1 *tens := SumLeft* DIV 10
4.2 *SumLeft := SumLeft* MOD 10
5.1 *fives := SumLeft* DIV 5
5.2 *SumLeft := SumLeft* MOD 5
6.1 *twos := SumLeft* DIV 2
6.2 *SumLeft := SumLeft* MOD 2
7.1 *ones := SumLeft*

---

pounds, fifties, twenties, tens, fives, twos, ones

Data table

Identifier	Description	Type
SumLeft	Change required	integer variable

TEST THE DESIGN

Input values which result in no coins of the denominations should be used as well as values which result in all denominations being required.

Problem 8.11

Data table for main program of Figure 8.2

Identifier	Description	Type
entry	Record type definition	
	description	string variable
	quantity	integer variable
	price	real variable
	recordend	
stocktype	Array type definition	array[1..500] of *entry*
findnext	(*stock, itemnumber*)	procedure(*stocktype*, integer)
display	(*stock*)	procedure(*stocktype*)
menu	( )	procedure( )
choice	(*menuchoice*)	procedure(char)
update	(*stock*)	procedure(*stocktype*)
newitem	(*stock, itemnumber*)	procedure(*stocktype*, integer)
save	(*stock*)	procedure(*stocktype*)
load	(*stock*)	procedure(*stocktype*)
stocklist	Items in stock	*stocktype* variable
newnumber	New item number	integer variable
userchoice	Menu choice	char variable

Problem 8.12

```
1.1    load(stocklist)
2      repeat
3.1        menu
4.1        choice(userchoice)
5.1        select case depending on userchoice
6.1            '1' : update(stocklist)
7.1.1          '2' : findnext(newnumber)
7.2.1                newitem(stocklist, newnumber)
8.1            '3' : display(stocklist)
9          selectend
10.1   until userchoice = '4'
11.1   save (stocklist)
```

Problem 8.13

```
1      repeat
2.1        getaccount(accountno, valid)
3.1        if valid then
4.1            getbalance(accountno, balance)
5.1            getrate(balance, rate)
6.1            calcinterest(balance, rate, interest)
7.1            addinterest(balance, interest, newbalance)
8.1            print(accountno, balance, interest, newbalance)
9.1            save(accountno, newbalance)
10         ifend
11     until transactions for the day are completed
```

Data table

Identifier	Description	Type
moneytype	Type definition of money	Not defined here
ratetype	Type definition of interest rates	Not defined here
accounttype	Type definition of account number	Not defined here
getaccount	(*accountno, valid*)	procedure(*accounttype*, boolean)
getbalance	(*accountno, balance*)	procedure(*accounttype, moneytype*)
getrate	(*balance, rate*)	procedure(*moneytype, ratetype*)
addinterest	(*balance, rate, interest*)	procedure(*moneytype, ratetype, moneytype*)
calcinterest	(*balance, interest, newbalance*)	procedure(*moneytype, moneytype, moneytype*)
print	(*accountno, balance, interest, newbalance*)	procedure(*accounttype, moneytype, moneytype, moneytype*)
save	(*accountno, newbalance*)	procedure(*accounttype, moneytype*)
accountno	An account number	*accounttype* variable
valid	Flag for valid account number	boolean variable
balance	Current account balance	*moneytype* variable
rate	Applicable interest rate	*ratetype* variable
interest	Interest due	*moneytype* variable
newbalance	Updated balance	*moneytype* variable

Problem 8.14

UNDERSTAND THE PROBLEM

If *first, second* are two real variables which have the values 1.0 and 2.0 respectively, what is the result of a call to *swap* with these variables as actual parameters?
first would have value 2.0 and *second* would have value 1.0.

DEVISE A SOLUTION

The solution is very straightforward:

swap
_____
a, b
_____
    {swap values of *a* and *b*}
  1 *temp* := *a*
  2 *a* := *b*
  3 *b* := *temp*
_____
a, b
_____

Data table for procedure *swap*

Identifier	Description	Type
temp	Temporary storage variable	real variable

TEST THE DESIGN

We leave the details to you.

Problem 8.15

UNDERSTAND THE PROBLEM

What sort of a loop is appropriate here?

Since the user must input at least one string but may wish to insert it again if an error is made, then a postconditioned loop is appropriate.

DEVISE A SOLUTION

We give a final design only:

readstring

	{Receive *confirmed* input string from keyboard}
1	repeat
2.1	write 'Enter a string '
2.2	read in *instring*
2.3	write out 'Your entry was ', *instring*
3	until *confirm*('Enter y to confirm input is correct ')

instring

Data table for procedure *readstring*

Identifier	Description	Type
confirm	(*prompt, result*)	(string, boolean)
answer	Flag	boolean variable

TEST THE DESIGN

The test data should include cases where the user enters a character other than 'y' at step 2.2.

Problem 8.16

UNDERSTAND THE PROBLEM

This routine is specified as a function and so at least one assignment must be made. What identifier will be involved?

An assignment must be made to *inrange*.

DEVISE A SOLUTION

A final design is:

inrange

start, finish, between

1	*inrange* := (*start* <= *between*) and (*between* <= *finish*)

inrange

TEST THE DESIGN

Test values for *between* should include the end points of the subrange, *start* and *finish* as well as values which lie inside and outside the subrange.

Problem 8.17

UNDERSTAND THE PROBLEM

There are three cases to consider. What construct should be used?

A case statement cannot be used because the cases are determined by inequalities and so a nest of *if* statements is required.

DEVISE A SOLUTION

A final design is:

newrange
start, finish , target, shot

```
  1   if shot > target then
  2       finish := shot
  3   else
  4       if shot < target then
  5           start := shot
  6       else
  7           start := target
  8           finish := target
  9       ifend
 10   ifend
```

start, finish

TEST THE DESIGN

Test values should be chosen so that all possible cases are tested.

Problem 8.18

UNDERSTAND THE PROBLEM

What design construct will be required in order to read in valid data?
A *repeat* loop.

DEVISE A SOLUTION

A top level design is:

```
  1   initialize variables
  2   repeat
  3       prompt for and read in target from player 1
  4   until target is valid
  5   repeat
  6       prompt for and read in guess
  7       process guess
  8   until player 2 guesses target
  9   write out results
```

This may be refined to:

```
  1.1   count := 0
  1.2   first := 'a'
  1.3   last := 'z'
  2     repeat
  3.1       write out 'First player: Enter a letter in the range ', first, ' to ' , last
  3.2       read in target
  4.1   until inrange('a', 'z', target)
```

```
5      repeat
6.1        write out 'Second player: Enter a guess in the range ', first, ' to ', last
6.2        read in guess
7.1        if not inrange(first, last, guess) then
7.2            write out 'Guess is not in the stated range – guess is ignored'
7.3        else
7.4            newrange(first, last, target, guess)
7.5            count := count + 1
7.6        ifend
8.1    until last = first
9.1    write out 'You took ', count, ' attempts'
```

Data table

Identifier	Description	Type
inrange	(*start, finish, target*)	boolean function(char, char, char)
newrange	(*start, finish , target, shot*)	procedure(char, char, char, char)
count	Number of guesses	integer variable
first	Lower bound of subrange	char variable
last	Upper bound of subrange	char variable
target	Character to be guessed	char variable
guess	The guess of player 2	char variable

TEST THE DESIGN

The validation of the inputs needs to be checked and so values outside the valid range should be included in the test data. Test data should also include the cases where the target is guessed at the first attempt and when it takes several attempts to guess it.

Problem 8.19

(a) The referencing environment for the main program:
      from main : *maxsize, valrange, arraytype, routine1, routine2, survey*
      The referencing environment for *routine1*
      from main   : *maxsize, valrange, arraytype, routine1*
      from *routine1* : *first, second, temp*
(b) Since *valrange* is in the referencing environment of *routine1* then *temp* could be redefined in this way.
(c) No – *routine2* is declared after *routine1* and so this call cannot be made.
(d) Yes – it is declared after *routine1* and so can be called by *routine2*.
(e) No – largest is a local variable of *routine2* and so cannot be referenced outside this routine.
(f) No – *temp* is a local variable of *routine1* and so cannot be referenced outside it.

Problem 9.1

The function *copy*

UNDERSTAND THE PROBLEM

The design will have to check the values of *index* and *span* to check that the conditions in the specification are not violated. For valid values, a *for* loop can be used to loop from the first character to be copied for the required number of characters. The concatenation operator can

be used to do the copying. If the value of *index* is 4 and the value of *span* is 6, what index values of the source string would need to be accessed?
The index values 4, 5, 6, 7, 8 and 9.

DEVISE A SOLUTION

A final design is:

copy
___
mainstring, index, span
___
1.1	*substring* := ''
1.2	*copy* := ''
2.1	if (*index* > 0) and (*span* > 0) and (*index* + *span* − 1 <= *length*(*mainstring*)) then
3.1	loop for *j* := 0 to (*span* − 1)
3.2	*substring* := *substring* + *mainstring*[*index* + *j*]
3.3	loopend
4	*copy* := *substring*
5	ifend

copy
___

Data table for the function *copy*

Identifier	Description	Type
j	Loop control variable	integer variable
substring	String for copied characters	string variable

TEST THE DESIGN

The data of Exercise 9.1 provides some test data to which should be added data to test invalid values of the numeric parameters.

The function *pos*

UNDERSTAND THE PROBLEM

There are many approaches to this problem. This solution extracts from *anystring* a string which has the same number of characters as *pattern* and then compares this string with the pattern string. This process will form the body of a loop which starts at the beginning of *anystring* and works its way through its characters until either the pattern is found or the end of *anystring* is reached.
If *anystring* has value 'abcde' write down the succession of two character strings which would be extracted if the position of the pattern string 'cd' was being sought.
The sequence would be 'ab', 'bc' and 'cd', at which point a match is found.
What would the sequence be if the pattern 'xy' was sought?
The sequence would be 'ab', 'bc', 'cd', and 'de', at which point the end of *anystring* is reached and so the pattern is not there.
Express in terms of the numbers *length*(*anystring*) and *length*(*pattern*) the number of inspections which are required when the pattern is not there. You may find it helpful to do more examples than that just done in order to get an answer.
The number of inspections is *length*(*anystring*) − *length*(*pattern*) + 1.

DEVISE A SOLUTION

A final design is:

---

pos

---

anystring, pattern

1.1	*found* := false or (*length*(*pattern*) = 0)
1.2	*pos* := 0
1.3	*inspections* := 1
2.1	loop while (not *found*) and (*inspections* <= *length*(*anystring*) − *length*(pattern) + 1)
3.1	*temp* := *copy*(*anystring*, *inspections*, *length*(*pattern*))
3.2	if *temp* = *pattern* then
3.3	*found* := true
3.4	*pos* := *inspections*
3.5	ifend
3.6	increment *inspections*
4	loopend

---

pos

Data table for the procedure *pos*

Identifier	Description	Type
found	Set true if pattern is found	boolean variable
inspections	The number of inspections made	integer variable
temp	A substring of *anystring* whose length is the same as *pattern*	string variable

TEST THE DESIGN

The examples of Exercise 9.4 provides some test data. The design should be tested when the pattern is not there and when it is the null string.

The procedure *delete*

UNDERSTAND THE PROBLEM

It is probably easier to copy the characters which are not to be deleted to temporary string variables from which the final value of *anystring* can be constructed. Example 9.2 can be used to determine the formulae for the parameter values required by *copy*. The call was *delete*(*title*, 4, 6) with *title* initialized to 'The▽first▽amendments'. Write down calls to *copy* which will yield the undeleted strings 'The' and '▽amendments'.

temp1 := *copy*(*title*, 1, 3)
temp2 := *copy*(*title*, 10, 11)
This example now needs to be generalized.

DEVISE A SOLUTION

A final design is:

---

delete

---

anystring, index, span

1.1	if (*index* > 0) and (*span* > 0) and (*index* + *span* − 1 <= *length*(*anystring*)) then
2.1	*temp1* := *copy*(*anystring*, 1, *index* − 1)
2.2	*temp2* := *copy*(*anystring*, *index* + *span* , *length*(*anystring*) − (*index* + *span*) + 1)
2.3	*anystring* := *temp1* + *temp2*
3	ifend

---

anystring

Data table for the procedure *delete*

Identifier	Description	Type
temp1	For characters which precede those to be deleted	string variable
temp2	For characters after those to be deleted	string variable

TEST THE DESIGN

The examples of Exercise 9.2 provide some test data. The design should be tested when the whole string is deleted and when invalid values of the numeric parameters are used.

The procedure *insert*

UNDERSTAND THE PROBLEM

The design will have to check that the value of *index* does not exceed the dynamic length of *anystring* by more than one and that the strings do not have a combined length of more than 255 characters. It is probably easier to copy the characters which precede the insertion point and those which come after it to temporary string variables. The final value of *anystring* can then be constructed by concatenating the three components.

DEVISE A SOLUTION

A final design is:

insert

---

anystring, implant, index

1.1	if (*index* > 0) and (*index* <= length(*anystring*) + 1)
	and (length(*anystring*) + length(*implant*) <= 255) then
2.1	*temp1* := copy(*anystring*, 1, *index* – 1)
2.2	*temp2* := copy(*anystring*, *index*, length(*anystring*) – index + 1)
2.3	*anystring* := *temp1* + *implant* + *temp2*
3	ifend

---

anystring

Data table for the procedure *insert*

Identifier	Description	Type
temp1	For characters which precede insertion point	string variable
temp2	For characters after insertion point	string variable

TEST THE DESIGN

The examples of Exercise 9.3 provide some test data. The design should be tested when the insertion is at the beginning of *anystring* and when it is at the end of *anystring*. A test for an overlength combined string should also be carried out.

Problem 9.2

UNDERSTAND THE PROBLEM

Here, the results should not be specified using the same identifier as the procedure itself. The design will have to reflect this change in the specification.

DEVISE A SOLUTION

A specification and final design for *copy2* follows:

copy2

mainstring	The source string	string parameter
index	Index at which extracted string starts	integer parameter
span	Number of characters to extract	integer parameter
{Return to *substring* the substring of *mainstring* whose length is *span* characters starting with the character at position *index*. If *index* is larger than the dynamic length of *mainstring* or if *span* is such that the dynamic length of *mainstring* would be exceeded then return the null string.}		
substring	An extract from *mainstring*	string function value

---

copy2

---

mainstring, index, span

       {Copy a substring from *mainstring*}
1.1   *substring* := "
2.1   if (*index* > 0) and (*span* > 0) and (*index* + *span* − 1 <= length(*mainstring*)) then
3.1   loop for *j* := 0 to (*span* − 1)
3.2   *substring* := *substring* + *mainstring*[*index* + *j*]
3.3   loopend
4   ifend

---

substring

Data table for the procedure *copy2*

Identifier	Description	Type
j	Loop control variable	integer variable

TEST THE DESIGN

The data of Exercise 9.1 provides some test data to which should be added data to test invalid values of the numeric parameters.

Problem 9.3

UNDERSTAND THE PROBLEM

What would be the result of the following call to the procedure *delete2* if *word* has initial value 'Two▽words'?

delete2(word, 4, 10)

word would have value 'Two' because all the characters from the fourth onwards would be deleted. Note that here the actual parameter corresponding to *span* specifies more characters than remain starting from the fourth in the string.

DEVISE A SOLUTION

The final design is:

delete2

---

anystring, index, span

       {Delete a substring from *anystring*}
1.1   if (*index* > 0) and (*span* > 0) and (*index* <= length(*anystring*)) then
2.1   *temp1* := copy(*anystring*, 1, *index* − 1)
2.2   *temp2* := copy(*anystring*, *index* + *span* , length(*anystring*) − (*index* + *span*) + 1)
2.3   *anystring* := *temp1* + *temp2*
3   ifend

---

anystring

Data table for the procedure *delete2*

Identifier	Description	Type
temp1	For characters which precede those to be deleted	string variable
temp2	For characters after those to be deleted	string variable

TEST THE DESIGN

The design should be tested when the whole string is deleted and that the correct results are obtained when *span* specifies more characters than remain after the *index*th character.

Problem 9.4

UNDERSTAND THE PROBLEM

What would result from the call *replacechar(mystring*, 'a', 'e') if *mystring* had value 'meat'? *mystring* would have value 'meet'.

DEVISE A SOLUTION

We give a final design:

replacechar

---

givenstring, patternchar, newchar

{Replace all occurrences of *patternchar* by *newchar*}
1 loop for *i* := 1 to *length(givenstring)*
2   if *givenstring[i]* = *patternchar* then
3   *givenstring[i]* = *newchar*
4   ifend
5 loopend

---

givenstring

Data table for procedure *replacechar*

Identifier	Description	Type
i	Loop control variable	integer variable

TEST THE DESIGN

You should call this design with source data which contains the pattern character and with data which does not.

Problem 9.5

UNDERSTAND THE PROBLEM

If *long* = 'a▽few▽quite▽short▽words', what are the values of *leftpart* and *rightpart* after the call *split2(long, code, leftpart, rightpart)* for each of the following values of *code*:
(a) 'short'; (b) '▽'; (c) 'paragraph'?
They will have the following values:
(a) *leftpart* = 'a▽few▽quite▽short';   *rightpart* = '▽words'
(b) *leftpart* = 'a▽'; *rightpart* = 'few▽quite▽short▽words'
     Note that this is split at the first space character and the character itself is in the left part.
(c) *leftpart* = 'a▽few▽quite▽short▽words'; *rightpart* = ''

Here the pattern is not in the source string, so leftpart is assigned the whole of the source string. Splitting *subject* can be designed using the function *copy* in much the same way as was done for the procedure *split*.

DEVISE A SOLUTION

A final design for the procedure *split2* is:

split2
subject, pattern

	{Split *subject* at *pattern*}
1.1	{Nothing to initialize}
2.1	if *pos(pattern, subject)* = 0 then
3	*left* := *subject*
4	*right* := null
5	else
6.1	*leftstart* = 1
6.2	*leftlength* = *pos(pattern, subject)* + *length(pattern)* − 1
6.3	*rightstart* = *leftlength* + 1
6.4	*rightlength* = *length(subject)* − *leftlength*
6.5	*left* := *copy(subject, leftstart, leftlength)*
6.6	*right* := *copy(subject, rightstart, rightlength)*
7	ifend

left, right

Data table for procedure *split2*

Identifier	Description	Type
leftstart	Index of start of left substring	integer variable
leftlength	Length of left substring	integer variable
rightstart	Index of start of right substring	integer variable
rightlength	Length of right substring	integer variable

TEST THE DESIGN

The text above provides some test data. You should supplement this by data in which the pattern is not there and in which the pattern is null. It is also possible for *subject* to be null and your procedure needs to be tested when this is the case.

Problem 9.6

The procedure *menu*

UNDERSTAND THE PROBLEM

What is the major construct of this procedure?
A loop which executes until such time that the user wishes to quit.

DEVISE A SOLUTION

The design is very straightforward and a final design only is given below.
As this design does not use any local variables a procedure data table is not required.

TEST THE DESIGN

All inputs other than 1 to 6 must be ignored and so you should test your design to ensure that this is the case.

menu

{Write out menu and read in *choice*}
1   clear screen
2   repeat
3   write out ' MAIN MENU'
4   write out
5   write out '1 Enter'
6   write out '2 Display'
7   write out '3 Change'
8   write out '4 Delete'
9   write out '5 Justify'
10   write out '6 Quit'
11   write 'Enter your choice '
12   read in *choice*
13   until *choice* in ['1'..'6']

---

choice

The procedure *enter*

UNDERSTAND THE PROBLEM

When should the input of text terminate?
The user can terminate input before *maxlines* lines of text have been entered, but once this number of lines has been entered control should return to the main menu without further input from the user.

DEVISE A SOLUTION

A final design is:

enter

{Enter text from the keyboard into *prose*}
1   clear screen
2.1   write out 'Enter text one line at a time up to a maximum of ', *maxlines*, ' lines.'
2.2   write out 'Only ', *stringsize*, ' characters are permitted per line.'
2.3   write out 'No single word should have more than 20 characters.'
2.4   write out 'Terminate input by typing <ret> twice'
2.5   *linesinput* := 0
3   repeat
4.1   *GetString(temp)*
5.1   if *temp* <> *null* then
6   increment *linesinput*
7.1   *prose[linesinput]* := *temp*
8   ifend
9.1   until (*temp* = *null*) or (*linesinput* = *maxlines*)

---

prose, *linesinput*

Data table for procedure *enter*

Identifier	Description	Type
null	The null string	constant value "
temp	Text entered by the user	*sentence* variable

TEST THE DESIGN

The data given in Figure 9.2 should be included in your test data. You should also check that input is terminated on behalf of the user as soon as *maxlines* of text have been entered. If entry is terminated before this then the null string which is then generated should not be assigned to *prose* nor should the value of *linesinput* be incremented.

The procedure *display*

UNDERSTAND THE PROBLEM

The output from this procedure is either a message to say that no text has been input or is a display of the elements of *prose*. What is the major construct for this procedure design?
An *if* statement corresponding to the two possibilities.

DEVISE A SOLUTION

Again we give a final design only:

display

prose , *linesinput*

```
        {Display the contents of the array prose}
1   if linesinput = 0 then
2       write out 'No text has been entered'
3   else
4       loop for i := 1 to linesinput
5           write out i, ' ', prose[i]
6       loopend
7   ifend
```

Data table for the procedure *display*

Identifier	Description	Type
i	Loop control variable	*linetype* variable

TEST THE DESIGN

You should check that the format of the output is correct and that all the lines of text are written out.

The procedure *change*

UNDERSTAND THE PROBLEM

What is the subject string in the call to *replace*?
It is the appropriate element of the array *prose* and is given by *prose[linenumber]*.

DEVISE A SOLUTION

We give only a final design:

change

---

prose , *linesinput*

{Change some text in a given line from *prose*}

1.1   clear screen
2.1   if *linesinput* = 0 then
3.1   write out
3.2   write out 'You must Enter text before you can Change it'
3.3   write out
3.4   write out 'Press any key to continue '
3.5   read in *ch*
4   else
5.1   *display(prose , linesinput)*
5.2   write out 'Lines 1 – ', *linesinput*, ' contain text and may be Changed '
5.3   *GetLineNumber(linesinput , linenumber)*
6   if *linenumber* <> 0 then   {Note 0 exits without further display}
7.1   write 'Enter pattern: '
7.2   *GetString(pattern)*
7.3   write 'Enter object: '
7.4   *GetString(object)*
7.5   *replace(prose[linenumber], pattern , object)*
8.1   write out 'New line ', *linenumber*, ' is: ', *prose[linenumber]*
8.2   write out
8.3   write out 'Press any key to continue '
8.4   read in *ch*
9   ifend
10   ifend

---

prose , *linesinput*

Data table for procedure *change*

Identifier	Description	Type
linenumber	Number of lines to be changed	*linetype* variable
pattern	String to be replaced	*sentence* variable
object	Replacement string	*sentence* variable
ch	Any character continues	char variable

TEST THE DESIGN

All the data of Figures 9.4 and 9.5 should be used to test the design, as should data for the pattern and subject strings which do not result in changes being made.

The procedure *deleteline*

UNDERSTAND THE PROBLEM

What has to be done to *prose* and *linesinput* in order to delete a line?
The elements of *prose* have to be 'moved up' so that the line to be deleted is overwritten. The value of *linesinput* must then be decremented because the text is then shorter by one line.
There are two circumstances when a deletion will not take place. What are they?
One is when there is no text in *prose* as indicated by *linesinput* having value 0; the other is when the user selects line 0 for deletion which indicates that no deletion should take place.

DEVISE A SOLUTION

A final design is:

deleteline

---

prose , *linesinput*

      {Delete a line from *prose*}
1.1   clear screen
1.2   *display(prose, linesinput)*
2.1   if *linesinput* = 0 then
3.1   write out
3.2   write out 'You must Enter text before you can Delete it'
3.3   write out
3.4   write out 'Press any key to continue '
3.5   read in *ch*
4   else
5.1   write out 'Lines 1 – ', *linesinput*, ' contain text and may be Deleted'
5.2   *GetLineNumber(linesinput, linenumber)*
6   if *linenumber* <> 0 then   {Note 0 exits without further display}
7.1   loop for *i* := *linenumber* to *linesinput* – 1
7.2   *prose*[*i*] := *prose*[*i* + 1]
7.3   loopend
7.4   decrement *linesinput*
8.1   *display(prose, linesinput)*
8.2   write out
8.3   write out 'Press any key to continue '
8.4   read in *ch*
9   ifend
10   ifend

---

prose , *linesinput*

Data table for procedure *deleteline*

Identifier	Description	Type
linenumber	The line number to be deleted	*linetype* variable
i	Loop control variable	*linetype* variable
ch	Any character continues	char variable

TEST THE DESIGN

You should include a check that the procedure handles the case when no text has been entered and the situation when the user wishes to exit the option without first deleting a line.

Problem 9.7

UNDERSTAND THE PROBLEM

The source parameters will be used in the prompt and to validate the input. Why would the following design not satisfy the specification?

```
repeat
    write out prompt
    read in line
until line is valid
```

Because the same prompt would be written out after an invalid entry. A modified prompt is required in this eventuality.

DEVISE A SOLUTION

We give only a final design:

GetLineNumber

---

linesinput

    {Read in a valid line number}
1 write 'Enter number in this range or 0 to return to main menu '
2 read in *linenumber*
3 loop while not *linenumber* in [0..*linesinput*]
4   write 'Number must be in range 0 – ', *linesinput*, '. Re-enter? '
5   read in *linenumber*
6 loopend

---

linenumber

As there are no local variables used the procedure does not need a data table.

TEST THE DESIGN

That the correct prompts occur for invalid data needs to be checked.

Problem 9.8

UNDERSTAND THE PROBLEM

How can we avoid getting an overlength string error if a user enters more than *stringsize* characters when entering a line of text?

The input can initially be assigned to a string variable of static length 255 and after it has been truncated to 40 characters it can be re-assigned to the output parameter which is of type *sentence* and therefore is of static length 40.

DEVISE A SOLUTION

We give a final design:

GetString

    {Get a string from the keyboard, cut to 40 characters if necessary}
1   read in *temp*
2   if *length(temp)* > *stringsize* then
3.1   write out 'Your input is too long and has been cut to 40 characters, namely '
3.2   *temp* := *copy(temp, 1, stringsize)*
3.3   write out *temp*
4   ifend
5   *instring* := *temp*

---

instring

Data table for procedure *GetString*

Identifier	Description	Type
temp	Temporary variable for input	string variable

TEST THE DESIGN

This design needs to be tested with input strings having fewer than 40 characters, exactly 40 characters and more than 40 characters.

Problem 10.1

Times can be added together, so an operation of *addition* will be required. An example of such an addition is 3:45 + 2:17.5 = 6:02.5 Similarly there would need to be an operation of *subtraction*. Times are never multiplied together but they can be multiplied by real numbers. For example, recipe books often give the cooking for meat as so many minutes per pound or kilogram. To work out the time required for say, 2.5 pounds of meat, requires the cooking time to be multiplied by 2.5. By the same token division of time by a real number might also be required. Two lengths of time can be divided in order to determine the proportion one is of the other and so an operation of time division might be required. Note that dividing a time by a real number is not the same as dividing one time by another.

Problem 10.2

UNDERSTAND THE PROBLEM

What needs to be done?
The procedures must be designed and a data table provided for the module.
Describe the record type *timetype*.
The seconds field should be declared as integer subrange 0..59 since only these values are permitted in the given format. By the same token the integer subrange 0..9 can be used for the decimal parts of seconds. No restriction is placed upon the minutes and so they can be defined as integer.
The procedure *readin* will have to read in a time. What variable type could be used for this input?
A string variable is probably the easiest. Since the specification says that data is input exactly in the correct format the string can be processed using the characters ':' and '.' as delimiters between the various components.
Describe how can the character '2' be converted to the integer 2?
The *ord* function can be used to convert '2' to the integer 50. From this should be subtracted *ord*('0').
The output format for the time 2.5 seconds is specifically mentioned in the specification for *writeout*. What problems can you foresee in writing out this time as 0:02.5?
The 02 for the seconds value will require special attention.

DEVISE A SOLUTION

We give the data tables the final designs for the procedures:

Data table for *readin*

Identifier	Description	Type
input	Time entered as a string	string variable
i	Loop control variable	integer variable

Data table for module *timemodule*

Identifier	Description	Type
	PUBLIC	
timetype	Type definition representing time	private
readin	(*time*)	procedure(*timetype*)
writeout	(*time*)	procedure(*timetype*)
add	(*a, b, result*)	procedure(*timetype, timetype, timetype*)
	PRIVATE	
timetype	Record type definition	
	minutes {Minutes}	integer variable
	seconds {Seconds}	0..59 variable
	decimalpart {Decimal seconds}	0..9 variable
	recordend	

readin

time

```
1    read in input
2    with time do
3       minutes := 0
4       seconds := 0
5       decimalpart := 0
6       i := 1
7       loop while input[i] <> ':'
8          minutes := 10*minutes + ord(input[i])
              − ord('0')
9          i := i + 1
10      loopend
11      i := i + 1
12      loop while input[i] <> '.'
13         seconds := 10*seconds
              + ord(input[i]) − ord('0')
14         i := i + 1
15      loopend
16      i := i + 1
17      decimalpart := ord(input[i]) − ord('0')
18   withend
```

time

writeout

time

```
1    with time do
2       if minutes > 0 then
3          write minutes, ':'
4       else
5          write '0:'
6       ifend
7       if seconds = 0 then
8          write out '00.'
9       else
10         if seconds < 10 then
11            write '0', seconds, '.'
12         else
13            write seconds, '.'
14         ifend
15      ifend
16      write decimalpart
17   withend
```

add

a, b

```
1    total := a.decimalpart + b.decimalpart
2    result.decimalpart := total MOD 10
3    carry := total DIV 10
4    total := a.seconds + b.seconds + carry
5    result.seconds := total MOD 60
6    carry := total DIV 60
7    result.minutes := a.minutes
              + b.minutes + carry
```

result

Data table for *add*

Identifier	Description	Type
total	Sum of components	integer variable
carry	Carry resulting from addition	0..1 variable

TEST THE DESIGN

In order to test the design of an abstract data type, each of the procedures which implement the operations should be tested individually. They should be checked to ensure they have correct parameters, corresponding to the source data and results and that they perform the task in the specification. The data table for the module should be checked to see that the abstract data type is hidden from the user but that all the operations have corresponding procedures listed in the public declarations. In this problem careful testing is required on the procedures for reading in and writing out. Test data for these routines should include times such as: 2 seconds, 2.0 seconds, 59.9 seconds, 1 minute, 1 minute .5 seconds, 1 minute 9.9 seconds, 1 minute 10 seconds, 1 minute 30.5 seconds. These examples include values which require to be output in uniform format. They could also be used to test the procedure *add*, but an important part of that test is to check that times like 2:30.5 and 3:29.5 get correctly summed to 6:00.0.

Problem 10.3

Clearly quantities of money have to be added together so an operation *add* would need to be defined. By the same token an operation *subtract* would be required. Amounts of money are never multiplied together but in things like interest calculations amounts of money are often multiplied by real numbers. So this rather special form of multiplication would be required. Money may also have to be divided, for example when working out monthly repayments of a loan. This is a rather special division because a loan of say 2.45 repaid in two *equal* instalments would require repayments of 1.22 one month and 1.23 the next (or vice versa). Since money is not to be represented using a standard data type, an operation to read in an amount of money will be required. Similarly, an operation to write out an amount will also be required. Other operations you may have considered are negation, changing the sign of a money value; a zero operation which would initialize a variable to represent the value 0.00; a percent operation which expresses one amount of money as a percentage of another amount and so on. You will probably have come to a different list from the one given here. The major point of this problem is that familiar operations like addition, subtraction may need special attention when dealing with abstract data types.

Problem 10.4

UNDERSTAND THE PROBLEM

The procedure *writeout* will require integer values to be converted to dollars and cents. Which integer operators might be helpful in this design?
The operators DIV and MOD, because they will enable the number of dollars and cents to be evaluated directly. However, negative amounts of money are possible but the implementation of these integer operators in programming languages is not always the same for negative operands. This is particularly the case for the operator MOD. Our solution will therefore avoid using DIV and MOD with negative operands. You may find it easier to do likewise.

We give a data table for the module together with final designs for all the procedures:

Data table for the module *moneymodule*

Identifier	Description	Type
	PUBLIC	
moneytype	Type definition for money	private
readin	(*amount*)	procedure(*moneytype*)
writeout	(*amount*)	procedure(*moneytype*)
add	(*a, b, result*)	procedure(*moneytype, moneytype, moneytype*)
subtract	(*a, b, result*)	procedure(*moneytype, moneytype, moneytype*)
	PRIVATE	
moneytype	Type definition for money	integer

writeout

amount

1	if *amount* >= 0 then
2.1	write '$', *amount* DIV 100, '.'
2.2	if *amount* MOD 100 < 10 then
2.3	write '0', *amount* MOD 100
2.4	else
2.5	write *amount* MOD 100
2.6	ifend
3	else
4.1	write '−$', (−*amount*) DIV 100, '.'
4.2	if (−*amount*) MOD 100 < 10 then
4.3	write '0', (−*amount*) MOD 100
4.4	else
4.5	write (−*amount*) MOD 100
4.6	ifend
5	ifend

readin

1	read in *amount*
2	*amount* := round(100*amount*)

amount

add

a, b

1	*result* := *a* + *b*

result

subtract

a, b

1	*add*(*a*, −*b*, *result*)

result

TEST THE DESIGN

The procedure *writeout* requires most testing here. Test data should include amounts like 5 cents, 10 cents, 1 dollar, 1 dollar 5 cents, 1 dollar 50 cents, so that all combinations of outputs are tested.

This implementation would not be a good one in terms of information hiding because *moneytype* is compatible with integer type. This means that normal integer operators can be applied to variables of type *moneytype*. So, if the user inadvertently writes out a *moneytype* variable, without using the provided procedure for this purpose, an error will not be detected, an integer will be written out and the method of implementation will become apparent. Problem 10.5 shows how these implementation details could be hidden from the user.

Problem 10.5

UNDERSTAND THE PROBLEM

What needs to be altered?

All references to *moneytype* parameters have to be altered to references to the field of the record which now represents *moneytype*.

DEVISE A SOLUTION

Replace every occurrence of *amount* within each of the bodies of the procedures *readin* and *writeout* by *amount.cents*. Within the bodies of the procedures *add* and *subtract* replace every occurrence of *a* by *a.cents* and *b* by *b.cents*.
The data table is the same as before, other than the definition of *moneytype*.

TEST THE DESIGN

The same test data can be used as in Problem 10.4.

Problem 10.6

UNDERSTAND THE PROBLEM

Describe the tasks to be done.
The procedures have to be designed using this representation. A new module data table will also be required.
The module *readin* asks the user for a money value as a real. Which standard functions might be useful in order to extract the dollars and cents in the required format?
The function *trunc* can be used to extract the whole number of dollars. The function *round* will be required to get the number of cents as an integer.
The user enters 3.45 for the amount $3.45. How can these functions recover the two field values 3 and 45 from this real number?
trunc(3.45) has value 3. To get the cents evaluate *round*(100*3.45 – 100*3).
Does this work for negative amounts?
The procedure *add* is not so straightforward as in the other representations. To see why, consider the sum of the amounts $2.60 and $3.57 whose representation will give rise to field values 2, 60 and 3, 57 respectively. The corresponding field values cannot simply be added together to give 5, 117 because the cents field must always have a value in the range –99..99. The values required are 6, 17. How can this be done?
A carry digit would have to be kept, so that 60 + 57 = 117 which is 17 carry 1. The carry is then added to the sum of the dollar fields.
Negative amounts of money are also allowed. How can the sum of the amounts –$2.60 and –$3.57 be calculated?
Their corresponding field values are –2, –60 and –3, – 57. Adding the corresponding fields gives –5, –117. The value –117 is then translated into –17 with a carry of –1 which then gets added to –5.
Try adding the amounts $2.45 and –$3.32 in a similar way. The answer should be –$0.87. How does this come about?
The field values are 2, 45 and –3, –32. Adding the corresponding field values gives – 1, 13. But the representation does not allow the dollars field to have a different sign from the cents field. So, the –1 gets converted into –100 cents and this gets added to the cents figure of 13.
The amounts $5.20 and –$2.30 also give rise to field values which have different signs, but not in quite the same way as we have just seen. This case will also need to be dealt with.

DEVISE A SOLUTION

We give a module data table and final designs for the procedures:

Data table for *readin*

Identifier	Description	Type
moneyin	A sum of money	real variable

Data table for *add*

Identifier	Description	Type
pence	Used in cent calculation	−198..198 variable
carry	Carry from addition	−1..1 variable

add

a, b

1	*pence* := *a.cents* + *b.cents*
2.1	if *pence* >= 100 then
2.2	*carry* := 1
2.3	*pence* := *pence* − 100
2.4	else
2.5	if *pence* <= −100 then
2.6	*carry* := −1
2.7	*pence* := *pence* + 100
2.8	else
2.9	*carry* := 0
2.10	ifend
2.11	ifend
3.1	with *result* do
3.2	*cents* := *pence*
3.3	*dollars* := *a.dollars* + *b.dollars* + *carry*
3.3	if (*dollars* < 0) and (*cents* > 0) then
	{make both the same sign}
3.4	*dollars* := *dollars* + 1
3.5	*cents* := *cents* − 100
3.6	else
3.7	if (*dollars* > 0) and (*cents* < 0) then
	{make both the same sign}
3.8	*dollars* := *dollars* − 1
3.9	*cents* := *cents* + 100
3.10	ifend
3.12	ifend
3.13	withend

result

readin

1	read in *moneyin*
2	with *amount* do
3	*dollars* := *trunc*(*moneyin*)
4	*cents* := *round*(100*moneyin − 100*dollars)
5	withend

amount

writeout

amount

1	with *amount* do
2	if (*dollars* >= 0) and (*cents* >= 0) then
3	write '\$', *dollars*, '.'
4	else
5	write '−\$', *abs*(*dollars*), '.'
6	ifend
7	if *abs*(*cents*) < 10 then
8	write '0'
9	ifend
10	write *abs*(*cents*)
11	withend

subtract

a, b

1	*b.dollars* := −*b.dollars*
2	*a.cents* := −*a.cents*
3	*add*(*a, b, result*)

result

The data table for the module is the same as that for Problem 10.4 except for the definition of *moneytype* itself.

TEST THE DESIGN

The same test data can be used as in Problem 10.4.

Problem 11.1

UNDERSTAND THE PROBLEM

What index values are used to write out the stack and in what order are they used?
Writing out begins at the top of the stack and so the first index used is *stacktop*. Index values down to 1 are then used in turn.

DEVISE A SOLUTION

A final design for *print* is:

print
stack

```
1   with stack do
2       loop for i := stacktop downto 1
3           write out stackarray[i]
4       loopend
5   withend
```

Data table

Identifier	Description	Type
i	Loop control	1..*maxsize* variable

TEST THE DESIGN

The specification does not require the procedure to cater for an empty stack. Test data should include a stack of one item and a stack with several items.

Problem 11.2

UNDERSTAND THE PROBLEM

What index values are used to write out the stack and in what order are they used?
Writing out begins at the bottom of the stack and so the first index used is 1. Index values from 1 to *stacktop* are then used in turn.

DEVISE A SOLUTION

A final design for *revprint* is:

revprint
stack

```
1   with stack do
2       loop for i := 1 to stacktop
3           write out stackarray[i]
4       loopend
5   withend
```

Data table

Identifier	Description	Type
i	Loop control variable	1..*maxsize* variable

TEST THE DESIGN

The specification does not require the procedure to cater for an empty stack. Test data should include a stack of one item and a stack with several items.

Problem 11.3

UNDERSTAND THE PROBLEM

In what way does this specification of *pop* differ from that given in the text?
The item popped from the stack is not returned and so is lost.

DEVISE A SOLUTION

We have chosen not to use a with statement in the following designs.

pop	
stack	
1	if *stack.stacktop* = 0 then
2	write out 'stack underflow'
3	else
4	decrement *stack.stacktop*
5	ifend
stack	

top	
stack	
1	if *stack.stacktop* = 0 then
2	write out 'stack underflow'
3	else
4	*item* := *stack.stack*[*stacktop*]
5	ifend
item	

TEST THE DESIGN

Your test data should include the possibility that the stack is empty. It also should test that *top* leaves the stack unaltered but that *pop* removes the top item and so updates it.

Problem 11.4

UNDERSTAND THE PROBLEM

What operations should define the stack here?
Precisely those used in the text, except that *item* will be of type char and the stack will be a stack of char.
What should happen if the first scanned character is a closing parenthesis?
The expression should be reported as not being well formed. Since a stack is being used to store opening parentheses, this possibility will have to take care that it does not attempt to pop an empty stack.
What happens if the stack is not empty after all the characters in the expression have been scanned?

This would indicate that there are more opening parentheses than closing ones and so the expression is not well formed.

DEVISE A SOLUTION

The first task is to agree a specification for the stack. The same operations with the same specifications as used above can be used, but with the minor modification that the elements to be held on the stack will be of type *char*. The identifier *charstack* will be used for the stack type. The module which implements the stack will be called *charstackmodule*. An array will be used to hold the stack elements but here they will be of type character.

Data table for the module *charstackmodule*

Identifier	Description	Type
	PUBLIC	
charstack	Type definition representing a stack of character	private
push	(*stack, item*)	procedure(*charstack, char*)
pop	(*stack, item*)	procedure(*charstack, char*)
isempty	(*stack*)	boolean function(*charstack*)
create	(*stack*)	procedure(*charstack*)
	PRIVATE	
maxsize	Maximum stack size	integer constant
charstack	Record type definition	
	stackarray	array[1..*maxsize*] of char variable
	stacktop	char variable
	recordend	

The design of *push, pop, isempty* and *create* is essentially the same as that given in the text and so will not be repeated here. A top level design for the main program is:

```
    {Parentheses checking program}
1   initialize variables
2   loop while there are no errors found and there are characters to process
3       select case depending on current character
4           parenthesis : process parenthesis
5       selectend
6       move to next character
7   loopend
8   report result
```

Step 4 must either push the current character onto the stack or it must compare the current character with the character at the top of the stack. The comparison will be carried out by a function *match* specified below:

match

open	An opening bracket	char parameter
closed	A closing bracket	char parameter
{If *open* and *closed* are a matching opening and closing pair of brackets from the collection {, [, (then return the value true, otherwise return false.}		
match	True for matching brackets	boolean function value

The comparison can be made only provided the stack is not empty. If it is empty that signifies an error. The final design is:

{Parentheses checking program}

1.1	*create*(*bracketstack*)
1.2	*valid* := true
1.3	write 'Enter an arithmetic expression '
1.4	read in *expression*
1.5	*index* := 1
2.1	loop while valid and *index* <= *length*(*expression*)
3.1	select case depending on *expression*[*index*]
4.1	'(', '{', '[' : *push*(*bracketstack*, *expression*[*index*])
4.2	')', '}', ']' : if *isempty*(*bracketstack*) then
4.3	*valid* := false
4.4	else
4.5	*pop*(*bracketstack*, *lastopener*)
4.6	*valid* := *match*(*lastopener*, *expression*[*index*])
4.7	ifend
5	selectend
6.1	*index* := *index* + 1
7	loopend
8.1	if not *isempty*(*bracketstack*) then
8.2	*valid* := false
8.3	ifend
8.4	if *valid* then
8.5	write out 'Expression is valid'
8.6	else
8.7	write out 'Expression is not well formed'
8.8	ifend

Data table for main program

Identifier	Description	Type
bracketstack	Representation of char stack	variable of *charstack* from module *charstackmodule*
match	(*open*, *closed*)	boolean function(char, char)
valid	Flag denoting well-formed expression	boolean variable
expression	Input arithmetic expression	string variable
index	Index to current character	integer variable
lastopener	Character on top of stack	char variable

A final design for *match* is:

match
open, *closed*
1 *match* := (*open* = '(' and *closed* = ')') or (*open* = '{' and *closed* = '}')   or (*open* = '[' and *closed* = ']')
match

TEST THE DESIGN

The abstract data type design will need to be tested independently of the main program. The same sort of test should be applied as to the integer stack. The main program will need to consider expressions which have no brackets as well as examples like those in the question.

Problem 11.5

UNDERSTAND THE PROBLEM

The operation must not alter the stack so *pop* cannot be used. The stack must be traversed and as each item is encountered it is to be written out. How can this be achieved?

A local variable will be required which is of type *integerstack* and which can hold the record containing the item to be printed out.

DEVISE A SOLUTION

A final design is:

print
stack
1   *current := stack*
2   loop while *current* <> nil
3   write out *current^.stackitem*
4   *current := current^.link*
5   loopend

Data table

Identifier	Description	Type
current	Current record of stack sequence	*integerstack* variable

TEST THE DESIGN

This should be tested against the guidelines *empty, full, first* and *last*. The specification of *print* excludes the possibility that the stack is empty. The stack is also assumed never to be full. Again, printing the first and last elements is not meaningful given this specification of *print*.

Problem 11.6

UNDERSTAND THE PROBLEM

A design which resembles that used in Problem 11.5 can be used here.

DEVISE A SOLUTION

A final design is:

count
stack
1   *current := stack*
2   *i := 0*
3   loop while *current* <> nil
4   increment *i*
5   *current := current^.link*
6   loopend
7   *count := i*
count

Data table

Identifier	Description	Type
current	Current record of stack sequence	*integerstack* variable
i	Local counting variable	integer variable

TEST THE DESIGN

This should be tested against the guidelines *empty, full, first* and *last*. If the stack is empty then *count* returns the value 0 as it should. The stack is assumed never to be full. Counting the first and last elements is not meaningful for this operation.

Problem 11.7

UNDERSTAND THE PROBLEM

This is more difficult than the array version. This is because there is not a variable which points to the bottom of the stack. (For the array version the index 1 always 'points to' the bottom of the stack provided the stack is not empty.) Even if there was one it would not help because then we would need a pointer to its predecessor and so on to the top of the stack. The only way to overcome this is to go to the bottom of the stack, write out the element, then go to the penultimate item and write it, then to the item two from the bottom, write it out and so on. What do we need to know in order to, say, access the third item from the bottom of the stack? We need to know how many items are in the stack. The function *count* can be used to determine this. We shall assume that this function is declared in the module *stackmodule* and is available for use here.

DEVISE A SOLUTION

A final design for *revprint* is:

revprint
_____
stack
_____

```
1   noitems := count(stack)
2       loop for i := 1 to noitems
3           current := stack
4           loop for j := 1 to noitems − i
5               current := current^.link
6           loopend
7           write out stack.stackitem
8       loopend
```
_____

Data table

Identifier	Description	Type
current	Current record of stack sequence	*integerstack* variable
noitems	Number of items on the stack	integer variable
i	Loop control variable	integer variable
j	Loop control variable	integer variable

TEST THE DESIGN

This specification removes the necessity to test the design on an empty sequence. The tests for *full*, *first* and *last* are not applicable here.

Problem 11.8

UNDERSTAND THE PROBLEM

Remember that the item popped from the stack is not returned. How do you know if the stack is empty?

There are two ways: one is that *stack* has value zero and the other is to call the function *isempty*. We have chosen the latter in the solution.

DEVISE A SOLUTION

Designs for each operation are:

pop
stack
1   if *isempty(stack)* then
2   write out 'stack underflow'
3   else
4   stack := stack^.link
5   ifend
stack

top
stack
1   if *isempty(stack)* then
2   write out 'stack underflow'
3   else
4   item := stack^.stackitem
5   ifend
item

TEST THE DESIGN

Your test data should include the possibility that the stack is empty. It also should test that *top* leaves the stack unaltered but that *pop* removes the top item and so updates it.

Problem 11.9

The design of *push*, *pop*, *isempty* and *create* is exactly the same as that given in the text and Exercise 11.6 except that *item* is of type char here.

The data table below gives the details of the pointer-based representation:

Data table for the module *charstackmodule*

Identifier	Description	Type
	PUBLIC	
charstack	Type definition representing a stack of character	private
push	(*stack, item*)	procedure(*charstack, char*)
pop	(*stack, item*)	procedure(*charstack, char*)
isempty	(*stack*)	boolean function(*charstack*)
create	(*stack*)	procedure(*charstack*)
	PRIVATE	
charstack	Type definition	pointer to *stackrecord*
stackrecord	Record type definition	
	stackitem	char variable
	link	*charstack* variable
	recordend	

Problem 12.1

We give only a final design in which *current* is of type *PtrToQueueRec*.

print

queue

```
 1   if isempty(queue) then
 2       write out 'The queue is empty'
 3   else
 4       with queue do
 5           current = head^.link    {skip dummy item}
 6           loop while current <> nil
 7               write out current^.queueitem
 8               current := current^.link
 9           loopend
10       withend
11   ifend
```

Problem 12.2

Since there are either 31 or 32 cards in the stock at any given time an array could be used, indexed 1..32, of base type suitable to represent a pack of playing cards. Index 1 could then represent the top of the stock. Index 32 would represent the bottom of the stock before a card is drawn. If the drawn card was taken from the top of the stock then all subsequent elements would have to be moved up the array so that the card which was at index 2 now becomes the new top card. This would then mean that the bottom card would have index 31. The player then discards and this card would be assigned to the element at index 32. Moving the array elements can be avoided by using variables to denote the index of the current top and bottom of the stock. This is analogous to the way the top of the array representation of a stack was recorded. However, this situation is a little more complicated. Drawing from the bottom of the stock would not require the movement of the other array elements, as the draw and subsequent discard only involve the element with index 32.

An alternative representation would be to use a pointer-based system, similar to that of Figure 12.2, using a sequence of linked records with the data field representing a playing card. The same strategy to identify the top and bottom of the stock could be adopted as was used in Figure 12.3.

Problem 12.3

The reason for using a dummy item for the queue was to overcome the difficulty of inserting an item into a queue which was empty. Here, the stock will be initialized with 32 values and the operation *replace* is not required to insert a card into an empty stock. This might suggest that a dummy item will not be of benefit here.

To remove a card from the bottom of the stock, knowledge of the location of both the bottom and penultimate records is required. This is because knowledge of the location of the bottom record will enable it to be removed but after the removal the penultimate record becomes the bottom of the stock and its location must therefore be known. This location will be used to link in the subsequent discard from the player. As only one item is removed from the bottom and this is followed by an insertion of the discard, the location of records preceding the penultimate record is not required.

Problem 12.4

Data table for module *stockmodule*

Identifier	Description	Type
	PUBLIC	
suittype	Enumerated type definition	(*spades, hearts, diamonds, clubs*)
cardtype	Record type definition	
	suit {Suit of the card}	*suittype* variable
	face {Ace = 1, Jack= 11 etc}	1..13 variable
	recordend	
stocktype	Type definition representing the stock	private
makestock	(*stock*)	procedure(*stocktype*)
showbottom	(*stock*)	procedure(*stocktype*)
drawtop	(*stock, draw*)	procedure(*stocktype, cardtype*)
drawbottom	(*stock, draw*)	procedure(*stocktype, cardtype*)
replace	(*stock, discard*)	procedure(*stocktype, cardtype*)
	PRIVATE	
stockitemptr	Pointer type definition	pointer to *stockitem*
stocktype	Record type definition	
	top {Top of stock}	*stockitemptr* variable
	penultimate {Penultimate card}	*stockitemptr* variable
	bottom {Bottom of stock}	*stockitemptr* variable
	recordend	
stockitem	Record type definition	
	card	*cardtype* variable
	link	*stockitemptr* variable
	recordend	

Problem 12.5

We give final designs only. When a card is drawn from the bottom of the stock, *bottom* assumes the value of *penultimate*. We have assigned *penultimate* the value nil in this situation. The variable *temp* in the procedure *replace* is of type *stockitemptr*.

drawtop
stock
1   with *stock* do
2   *draw* := *top^.card*
3   *top* := *top^.link*
4   withend
stock, draw

drawbottom
stock
1   with *stock* do
2   *draw* := *bottom^.card*
3   *penultimate^.link* := nil
4   *bottom* := *penultimate*
5   *penultimate* := nil
6   *showbottom*(*stock*)
7   withend
stock, draw

replace
stock, discard
1   new(*temp*)
2   *temp^.card* := *discard*
3   *temp^.link* := nil
4   *bottom^.link* := *temp*
5   *penultimate* := *bottom*
6   *bottom* := temp
stock

Problem 13.1

Defining the module data table

UNDERSTAND THE PROBLEM

The operations *insert* and *remove* are both going to involve searching. Should a dummy item be included in the linked representation?

The text would suggest that this might be helpful and that problems with inserting into an empty pile might also be made easier.

Both *insert* and *remove* will have to search *pile*. If the searches are developed as routines the experience gained from the text can be exploited here. Will the same search routine do for both *insert* and *remove*?

No – the search routine for *insert* will have to find the location of the *last* existing memo from the originator of the new memo because the new one will be inserted after this last one. In contrast the routine *remove* is required to delete the *first* of the originator's list of memos.

Does this suggest that the search routines should be declared in the data table for the module, or as local routines to their respective operations?

They should be declared locally.

DEVISE A SOLUTION

Data table for module *MemosModule*

Identifier	Description	Type
	PUBLIC	
pileofmemo	A representation of the intray	private
insert	(*pile, originator, giveninfo*)	procedure(*pileofmemo*, integer, string)
isempty	(*pile*)	boolean function(*pileofmemo*)
remove	(*pile, originator, item*)	procedure(*pileofmemo*, integer, string)
create	(*pile*)	procedure(*pileofmemo*)
print	(*pile*)	procedure(*pileofmemo*)
	PRIVATE	
pileofmemo	Pointer type definition	pointer to *pilerec*
pilerec	Record type definition	
from	{Originator's number}	integer variable
info	{Text of memo}	string variable
link	{Link to next record}	*pileofmemo* variable
	recordend	

The procedure *insert*

UNDERSTAND THE PROBLEM

The design of this routine assumes the use of a dummy record and so the design can be based upon that in the text. The major problem then is specifying and designing an appropriate search routine. Should the result of the search point to the location at which the insertion is to take place or to its predecessor?

It should point to its predecessor because the previous record has to have its link field updated to point to the new item. So access to the previous record is required. We leave you to write a specification for this procedure.

An originator may or may not already have memos stored in the pile. Describe the major constructs of the search routine which will cater for both eventualities.

Essentially two loops are required. The first loop searches as far as the beginning of the originator's memos and the second then searches within them to their end.

This second search will not always have to take place. When should it not be carried out?

When the originator does not have any memos in the pile already.

DEVISE A SOLUTION

We shall not provide a solution for *insert*, as it is very similar to that in the text. Instead we give a solution to the design of the search routine which we have called *inwhere*. Note that the data table for *insert* would need to declare *inwhere*.

Data table for the procedure *inwhere*

Identifier	Description	Type
lead	Pointer to a memo record	*pileofmemo* variable
lag	Pointer lagging one record behind *lead*	*pileofmemo* variable

inwhere

---

pile, originator

1.1	*pile^.from := originator*
1.2	*lag := pile*
1.3	*lead := pile^.link*
2	loop while *lead^.from < originator*
3.1	*lag := lead*
3.2	*lead := lead^.link*
4	loopend
	{*lag* now points to the predecessor of sequence of originator memos or to the predecessor of the insertion point}
5	if (*lead^.from = originator*) and (*lead <> pile*) then
	{Find the end of the originators sequence of memos}
	{Following search must stop prior to the dummy item}
6.1	loop while (*lead^.from = originator*) and (*lead <> pile*)
6.2	*lag := lead*
6.3	*lead := lead^.link*
6.4	loopend
7	ifend
8	*location := lag*

---

location

TEST THE DESIGN

There is much to test here and the abstract data type test guidelines can help to formulate questions which in turn can generate suitable test data. The questions include the following:

Does the procedure work for an empty pile? What value of *location* should be returned in this case?

If an originator does not have any records in the current pile does this routine work? There are three situations to consider in this event – the insert goes immediately after the dummy, the insert is not at either end of the current pile, the insert should follow the last existing item.

If the originator already has memos in the pile then test data needs to be generated so that the existing memos are at the beginning of the pile, then in the middle of the pile and finally when they are at the end of the pile.

The procedure *remove*

UNDERSTAND THE PROBLEM

To remove a memo the user must choose an originator. The pile will then have to be searched for the first record with this originator. A similar routine to *flightsearch* could be specified for the search routine here but we shall consider a routine called *outwhere*, which will have only one results parameter. To which record should this result point?

If the originator number exists in the pile then the result must point to the predecessor of the record to be removed. That is because the predecessor's link field has to be updated in order to carry out the deletion.

Can the pointer value *pile* be used to denote that a memo for the originator does not exist?

No, because the search must return this value when the first record in the pile has to be deleted. We leave you to write a specification for this procedure.

DEVISE A SOLUTION

We shall give a design for *outwhere* and leave the details of the design for *remove* to you:

outwhere
pile, originator

1.1	*pile^.from := originator*
1.2	*lag := pile*
1.3	*lead := pile^.link*
2	loop while *lead^.from < originator*
3.1	*lag := lead*
3.2	*lead := lead^.link*
4	loopend
	{*lead* now points to either the first originator memo or to *pile*}
5.1	if (*lead^.from = originator*) and (*lead <> pile*) then
5.2	location := lag
5.3	else
5.4	location := nil
5.6	ifend

location

The same data table applies here as to *inwhere*.

TEST THE DESIGN

The guidelines would suggest the following questions:
Does the routine work when the pile is empty and to what should *location* point in this case?
Does *location* have the correct value when the first record is to be deleted?
Does *location* have the correct value when the last record is to be deleted?

Problem 14.1

An array could be used but there would be difficulties over determining a suitable index range because there is no mention of the maximum number of words which the concordance is to hold. A linear search would have to be used to find the frequency of occurrence of words and this might be slow if the concordance contained a large number of words. In order for the concordance to be printed out the array elements would have to be sorted into alphabetical order.

A binary search tree is an obvious choice here. It overcomes the problem of not knowing in advance how many words will be in the concordance. Searching a binary tree is also very fast and an inorder tree traversal will enable the words to be written out in alphabetical order.

Problem 14.2

Data table for the module *concordmodule*

Identifier	Description	Type
	PUBLIC	
indextype	Type definition representing concordance	private
create	(*concordance*)	procedure(*indextype*)
findwhere	(*concordance, inword, location, exists*)	private procedure(*indextype*, string, *indextype*, boolean)
insert	(*concordance, inword*)	procedure(*indextype*, string)
howmany	(*concordance, inword*)	integer function(*indextype*, string)
	PRIVATE	
indextype	Type definition	pointer to *nodetype*
nodetype	Record type definition	
	left {Pointer to left subtree}	*nodetype* variable
	word {Word data}	string variable
	count {Frequency of word}	integer variable
	right {Pointer to right subtree}	*nodetype* variable
	recordend	

Problem 14.3

findwhere

---

concordance, inword

1.1	*exists* := false
1.2	*lead* := *concordance*
1.3	*lag* := nil
2	loop while *lead* <> nil
3.1	*lag* := *lead*
3.2	if *inword* < *lead^.word* then
3.3	lead := lead^.left
3.4	else
3.5	if *inword* > *lead^.word* then
3.6	*lead* := *lead^.right*
3.7	else
3.8	*lead* := nil
3.9	*exists* := true
3.10	ifend
3.11	ifend
4	loopend
5	*location* := *lag*

---

location, exists

Problem 14.4

Data table for function *howmany*

Identifier	Description	Type
location	Pointer to node location	*nodetype* variable
exists	Flag denoting existence of word	boolean variable

insert	
concordance , inword	
1	if *isempty*(*concordance*) then
2.1	new(*concordance*)
2.2	*concordance* ^.*word* := *inword*
2.3	*concordance* ^.*count* := 1
2.4	*concordance* ^.*left* := nil
2.5	*concordance* ^.*right* := nil
3	else
4	*findwhere*(*concordance* , *inword*, *location*, *exists*)
5	if *exists* then
6	*location*^.*count* := *location*^.*count* + 1
7	else
8.1	new(*temp*)
8.2	*temp* ^.*word* := *inword*
8.3	*temp* ^.*count* := 1
8.4	*temp* ^.*left* := nil
8.5	*temp* ^.*right* := nil
8.6	if *inword* < *location*^.*word* then
8.7	*location*^.*left* := *temp*
8.8	else
8.9	*location*^.*right* := *temp*
8.10	ifend
9	ifend
10	ifend
concordance	

create	
1	*concordance* := nil
concordance	

howmany	
concordance , *inword*	
1	*findwhere*(*concordance* , *inword*, *location*, *exists*)
2.1	if *exists* then
2.2	*howmany* := *location*^.*count*
2.3	else
2.4	*howmany* := 0
2.5	ifend
howmany	

Data table for procedure *insert*

Identifier	Description	Type
temp	Pointer to new node	*nodetype* variable
location	Pointer to insertion point	*nodetype* variable
exists	Flag denoting existence of word	boolean variable

Problem 15.1

UNDERSTAND THE PROBLEM

What is the binary equivalent of decimal 6?

The binary number 110.

How can the binary number 110 be generated from the decimal number 6 using DIV and MOD?

6 MOD 2 equals 0 and this is the rightmost digit of 110. 6 DIV 2 equals 3 and so 3 must now be converted to decimal. 3 MOD 2 equals 1 and this gives the next digit from the right. 3 DIV 2 equals 1 and this is now the digit furthest from the right. Try this method with some values of your own before continuing.

What are the roles of *entity*, *article* and *subarticle* here and what does it mean to say that the *article* is trivial?

The *article* is the decimal number and the *subarticle* is the result of the integer division. The *entity* is the digit corresponding to the remainder obtained by the MOD operator. The *article* being trivial corresponds to the number being 0 or 1.

Given that output is from left to right should the *entity* be written out before the recursive call or after it?

The recursive call must precede the writing out.

DEVISE A SOLUTION

A design for *binary* is:

binary

---

number

```
1   if (number = 0) or (number = 1) then
2       write number
3   else
4       binary(number DIV 2)
5       write number MOD 2
6   ifend
```

TEST THE DESIGN

We shall test the design with the decimal value 6:

binary(6)

```
1   if (6 = 0) or (6 = 1) then
4       binary(3)

        1   if (3 = 0) or (3 = 1) then
        4       binary(3 DIV 2)          {3 DIV 2 = 1}

                1   if (1 = 0) or (1 = 1) then
                2       write out 1
                6   ifend

        5       write out 3 MOD 2        {3 MOD 2 = 1}
        6   ifend

5       write out 6 MOD 2        {6 MOD 2 = 0}
6   ifend
```

Notice the order in which the digits are written out here. The first digit output is 1, followed by 1 and finally 0. Thus what appears on the screen is 110, just as we wanted.

Problem 15.2

UNDERSTAND THE PROBLEM

What strategy should be adopted here?

The strategy here is very similar to that of Problem 15.1. We successively use integer division to divide the given number by 16 and use the MOD function to find the remainder of this division. The complication here is that the remainder is not necessarily a digit. The remainders 10 to 15 will have to be converted to their hexadecimal digit equivalents. You will have to consider whether or not the recursive call should precede the writing out of the digits.

DEVISE A SOLUTION

A top level design for *hex* is:

hex
number

1	if (*number* >= 0) and (*number* <= 15) then
2	write hex digit for *number*
3	else
4	*hex*(*number* DIV 16)
5	*remainder* := *number* MOD 2
6	write out hex digit for *remainder*
7	ifend

This may be refined to:

hex
number

1	if (*number* >= 0) and (*number* <= 15) then
2.1	if *number* <= 9 then
2.2	write *number*
2.3	else
2.4	select case depending on *number*
2.5	'10' : write 'A'
2.6	'11' : write 'B'
2.7	'12' : write 'C'
2.8	'13' : write 'D'
2.9	'14' : write 'E'
2.10	'15' : write 'F'
2.11	selectend
2.12	ifend
3	else
4	*hex*(*number* DIV 16)
5	*remainder* := *number* MOD 16
6.1	if *remainder* <= 9 then
6.2	write *remainder*
6.3	else
6.4	select case depending on *remainder*
6.5	'10' : write 'A'
6.6	'11' : write 'B'
6.7	'12' : write 'C'
6.8	'13' : write 'D'
6.9	'14' : write 'E'
6.10	'15' : write 'F'
6.11	selectend
6.12	ifend
7	ifend

Data table

Identifier	Description	Type
remainder	Remainder from integer division	0..15 variable

TEST THE DESIGN

We shall trace through this design using the value 559 as actual parameter:

hex(559)

1	if (559 >= 0) and (559 <= 15) then
4	*hex*(559 DIV 16) {559 DIV 16 = 34}

> | | |
> |---|---|
> | 1 | if (34 >= 0) and (34 <= 15) then |
> | 4 | *hex*(34 DIV 16)   {34 DIV 16 = 2} |
>
> > | | |
> > |---|---|
> > | 1 | if (2 >= 0) and (2 <= 15) then |
> > | 2.1 | if 2 <= 9 then |
> > | 2.2 | write out 2 |
> > | 2.12 | ifend |
> > | 7 | ifend |
>
> | | |
> |---|---|
> | 5 | *remainder* := 34 MOD 16 {34 MOD 16 = 2} |
> | 6.1 | if 2 <= 9 then |
> | 6.2 | write 2 |
> | 6.12 | ifend |
> | 7 | ifend |

5	*remainder* := 559 MOD 16 {559 MOD 16 = 15}
6.1	if 15 <= 9 then
6.4	select case depending on 15
6.10	write 'F'
6.11	selectend
6.12	ifend
7	ifend

Like the previous problem you should note the order in which the digits are written out. Here the order is 2, then 2, then F, corresponding to the hexadecimal number 22FH.

Problem 15.3

UNDERSTAND THE PROBLEM

What are the roles of *article*, *subarticle* and *entity* here and what corresponds to the *article* being trivial?

The strategy will be to examine the current node and go to the left or right subtree in exactly the same way as was done for the routine *insert*. Thus *entity* will be the current node, *article* the tree and *subarticle* its left and right subtrees. The *trivial* situation is where the tree is empty.

DEVISE A SOLUTION

The design for *isthere* assumes that the function *isempty* is available:

Data table

Identifier	Description	Type
found	Flag to denote item found	boolean variable

isthere

---

tree, item

```
 1   if isempty(tree) then
 2       found := false
 3   else
 4       if item < tree^.data then
 5           found := isthere(tree^.left, item)
 6       else
 7           if item > tree^.data then
 8               found := isthere(tree^.right, item)
 9           else
10               found := true
11           ifend
12       ifend
13   ifend
14   isthere := found
```

---

isthere

TEST THE DESIGN

We shall use the tree of Figure 14.5 and search for Denver. The statements labelled * record the value of the returned parameter after the call.

isthere (#10, Denver)

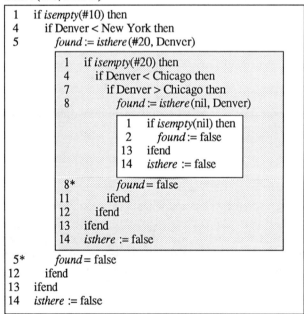

```
 1      if isempty(#10) then
 4          if Denver < New York then
 5              found := isthere (#20, Denver)

                    1      if isempty(#20) then
                    4          if Denver < Chicago then
                    7              if Denver > Chicago then
                    8                  found := isthere (nil, Denver)

                                         1   if isempty(nil) then
                                         2       found := false
                                        13   ifend
                                        14   isthere := false

                    8*         found = false
                   11              ifend
                   12          ifend
                   13      ifend
                   14      isthere := false

 5*         found = false
12          ifend
13      ifend
14      isthere := false
```

Problem 15.4

UNDERSTAND THE PROBLEM

The difficulty here is getting the recursive calls and the write statement in the correct order.

DEVISE A SOLUTION

The design is given below:

postorder

tree

```
1  if tree = nil then
2      do nothing
3  else
4      postorder(tree^.left)
5      postorder(tree^.right)
6      write out tree^.data
7  ifend
```

TEST THE DESIGN

You should test this design along the same lines as the solution to Exercise 15.5.

Problem 15.5

UNDERSTAND THE PROBLEM

The only difficulty here is getting the recursive calls and the write out statement in the correct order.

DEVISE A SOLUTION

The design is given below:

preorder

tree

```
1  if tree = nil then
2      do nothing
3  else
4      write out tree^.data
5      preorder(tree^.left)
6      preorder(tree^.right)
7  ifend
```

TEST THE DESIGN

You should test this design along the same lines as the solution to Exercise 15.5.

Problem 15.6

UNDERSTAND THE PROBLEM

What are the roles of *article*, *subarticle* and *entity* here and what corresponds to the *article* being trivial?

The total number of nodes is the number in the left subtree plus the number in the right subtree plus the current node. Thus *entity* will be the current node, *article* the tree and *subarticle* its left and right subtrees. The *trivial* situation is where the tree is empty.

DEVISE A SOLUTION

A design is:

countnodes
tree

```
1   if isempty(tree) then
2       count := 0
3   else
4       countnodes(tree^.left, leftcount)
5       countnodes(tree^.right, rightcount)
6       count := leftcount + rightcount + 1
7   ifend
```

count

Data table

Identifier	Description	Type
leftcount	Number of nodes in left subtree	integer variable
rightcount	Number of nodes in right subtree	integer variable

TEST THE DESIGN

On page 432 there is a test of this design using the data in Figure 14.5. The statements labelled * record the value of the returned parameter after the call.

Problem 15.7

UNDERSTAND THE PROBLEM

What difference is there in this specification from that of *insert*?
Here we do not have to filter out possible duplicate entries. Essentially the same design will be used with the modification that the *if* statement which dealt with duplicates is now not needed.

DEVISE A SOLUTION

The data table follows and the design is given opposite:

Data table for procedure *duplicates*

Identifier	Description	Type
temp	Pointer to current node	*stringtree* variable

TEST THE DESIGN

The design should be tested on an empty tree as well as one with data in it. The data used in Figure 15.3 would do for the latter.

duplicates

tree, item

1	if *isempty* (*tree*) then
2.1	*new*(*temp*)
2.2	*temp^.left* := nil
2.3	*temp^.right* := nil
2.4	*temp^.data* := *item*
2.5	*tree* := *temp*
3	else
4.1	if *item* < *tree^.data* then
4.2	*duplicates*(*tree^. left, item*)
4.3	else
4.4	*duplicates*(*tree^. right, item*)
4.5	ifend
5	ifend

tree

Problem 15.8

This problem is similar to the problem of counting all the nodes in a tree except that a node is included in the count only if its data matches that of the source parameter. We give only a final design:

howmany

tree, item

1	if *isempty* (*tree*) then
2	*count* := 0
3	else
4	*howmany*(*tree^. left, item, leftcount*)
5	*howmany*(*tree^. right, item, rightcount*)
6	if *tree^.data* = *item* then
7	*count* := *leftcount* + *rightcount* + 1
8	else
9	*count* := *leftcount* + *rightcount*
10	ifend
11	ifend

count

Data table

Identifier	Description	Type
leftcount	Number of matches in left subtree	integer variable
rightcount	Number of matches in right subtree	integer variable

Design test for *countnodes* (Problem 15.6)

countnodes(#10)

```
1    if isempty(#10) then
4        countnodes(#10^left, leftcount)        {#10^.left = #20, left subtree of New York}

         1    if isempty(#20) then
         4        countnodes(#20^left, leftcount)     {#20^.left = nil}

                  1    if isempty(nil) then
                  2        count = 0
                  7    ifend

         4*       leftcount = 0
         5        countnodes(#20^right, rightcount)      {#20^.right = nil}

                  1    if isempty(nil) then
                  2        count = 0
                  7    ifend

         5*       rightcount = 0
         6        count = 0 + 0 + 1
         7    ifend

4*       leftcount = 1
5        countnodes(#10^right, rightcount)        {#10^.right = #40, right subtree of New York}

         1    if isempty(#40) then
         4        countnodes(#40^left, leftcount)      {#40^.left = nil}

                  1    if isempty(nil) then
                  2        count = 0
                  7    ifend

         4*       leftcount = 0
         5        countnodes(#40^right, rightcount)   {#40^.right = nil}

                  1    if isempty(nil) then
                  2        count = 0
                  7    ifend

         5*       rightcount = 0
         6        count = 0 + 0 + 1
         7    ifend

5*       rightcount = 1
6        count = 1 + 1 + 1
7    ifend
```

APPENDIX: DESIGN LANGUAGE DESCRIPTION

This appendix gives an informal account of the design language used in this book. It includes the conventions used for declaring variables in data tables and the method by which design steps are expressed.

A.1 DATA TABLES

All variables which are used in a design must be declared in a data table. The one below illustrates the declaration of identifiers of standard types. Note that constants and variables are distinguished. The description column is intended to give the reader an idea of the purpose of the identifier. The descriptions here are hypothetical.

Identifier	Description	Type
maxsize	Constant definition	integer constant
message	String constant 'This is a message'	string constant
number	A user input value	integer variable
average	Average of user inputs	real variable
choice	User choice	char variable
surname	A surname	string variable
flag	Flag denoting input done	boolean variable

Variables of structured type are often declared using constant and type definitions. The definitions of constant and type identifiers must precede their reference. Identifiers are declared in the following order: constant declarations, type definitions and then variable declarations. The following example shows how subranges, strings, enumerated types, arrays and records may be declared. Notice how the field identifiers for a record are declared in the description column with the field type being given in the type column.

Identifier	Description	Type
maxsize	Constant definition	integer constant
indexrange	Subrange type definition	1..*maxsize*
nametype	String type definition	string[20]
monthtype	Enumerated type definition	(*dec, jan, feb, mar*)
recordtype	Record type definition	
	authorname {Name of author}	string variable
	title {Title of book}	string variable
	recordend	
namearray	An array of surnames	array[1..40] of *nametype* variable
numberarray	An array of reals	array[*indexrange*] of real variable
month	A month of the year	*monthtype* variable
author	Author details	*recordtype* variable

A.2 PROCEDURE AND FUNCTION SPECIFICATIONS

A routine, that is a procedure or function, consists of four parts: the identifier of routine, its source data, the process which transforms the source data into results and the results. The style of presentation is illustrated below. A routine which is to be designed as a function will have a single result, having the same identifier as the routine itself, and which will be of type integer, real, char or boolean (or a subrange of these types). Source data and results, which are of structured type, are declared using type identifiers as illustrated below.

minimax

first	An integer	*indexrange* parameter
second	An integer	*indexrange* parameter
third	An integer	*indexrange* parameter
{Return to *smallest* the smallest of the three source parameters and to *largest* the largest of the three source parameters.}		
smallest	Smallest of the inputs	*indexrange* parameter
largest	Largest of the inputs	*indexrange* parameter

A routine must be declared in the data table of the program which calls it. The declaration comes after the type definitions and precedes variable declarations. To declare a *procedure* its identifier is listed in the identifier column and its formal parameters are listed, enclosed in brackets, in the description column. In the type column the word *procedure* precedes the list of parameter types which must match, in order and number, the formal parameters already mentioned. The declaration of a *function* is similar except that the type column specifies the type of function result and uses the word *function* instead of procedure. Parameters which are both source data and results are declared only once in the data table. Programs which call many routines must declare them one after the other. The order in which they are declared will affect their referencing environments. The declaration for the procedure specification above is:

Identifier	Description	Type
maxsize	Constant definition	integer constant
indexrange	Subrange type definition	1..*maxsize*
minimax	(*first, second, third, smallest, largest*)	procedure(*indexrange, indexrange, indexrange, indexrange, indexrange*)

Abstract data types may be designed so that the details of the representation are hidden from the user. The term module is used for the design corresponding to an abstract data type and its data table has two parts; a public part and a private part. Typically, module data tables declaring an abstract data type will include pointer variables. The type to which a pointer variable points appears after the definition of the pointer itself. Private procedures which are required in the design of the public routines should be declared to be private, as illustrated below for the module *adtmodule*. In this illustration, *find* can be called by *operation* (because its declaration precedes that of *operation*) but *find* may not be called by the user of the module because it is declared to be private.

Identifier	Description	Type
	PUBLIC	
adttype	Type definition representing ADT	private
create	(*adtobject*)	procedure(*adttype*)
find	(*adtobject*, *search*)	private procedure(*adttype*, string)
operation	(*adtobject*, *adtobject*)	procedure(*adttype*, *adttype*)
	PRIVATE	
adttype	Type definition	pointer to *nodetype*
nodetype	Record type definition	
	word {Data}	string variable
	link {Pointer to next item}	*nodetype* variable
	recordend	

A.3 DESIGN STATEMENTS

This section gives an informal account of the design statements which appear in the book. The design fragments which appear are for illustration and so do not form a coherent piece of design. Identifiers used in designs are italicized, whereas all other design words are not.

A.3.1 Sequence

Steps in a design are successively refined as shown below:

```
1   step 1
2   step 2
3   step 3
```

```
1     step 1
2.1   first step in refinement of step 2
2.2   second step in refinement of step 2
2.3   third step in refinement of step 2
3     step 3
```

```
1.1     first step in refinement of step 1
2.1     first step in refinement of step 2
2.2.1   first step in refinement of step 2.2
2.2.2   second step in refinement of step 2.2
2.2.3   third step in refinement of step 2.2
2.3     third step in refinement of step 2
3       step 3
```

A step may be a comment, in which case it is enclosed in braces and does not have a step number. Other basic steps are illustrated below:

1	write out 'Enter a number'	{Text output is enclosed in single quotes}
2	write *number* '	{Does not go to a new line after the output of *number*}
3	read in *number*	
4	increment *number*	{This means by 1 unless stated otherwise}
5	decrement *number*	{This means by 1}
6	increment *number* by 2	
8	write out 'Your input was ', *number*	{Variables are not in quotes in write out steps}
9	update *number*	{A high level statement – will need refinement}
10	*number* := 10	{Assign 10 to number}
11	do nothing	{A dummy statement}

A.3.2 Conditional statements

The *if* statement

```
1  if condition then
2      steps
3  else
4      steps
5  ifend
```

The steps which occur in step 2 (and its subsequent refinements) are collectively referred to as the *then* clause. Those which form step 4 are called the *else* clause. If step 4 is *do nothing* then steps 3 and 4 may be omitted. A collection of *if* statements may be nested to any level but each one must have an *ifend*.

The *case* statement

This enables a choice to be made from several possibilities. The case statement executes the statement prefixed by the case label, or case range, which is equal to the value of the selector. If no such match exists and the default statement is present, the statement following the default is executed. Case selectors must be of enumerated type. In the example below *ch* is a char variable which is used as a selector.

```
1  select case depending on ch
2      'A'    : write out 'Letter is upper-case A'
3    'B'..'D' : write out 'Letter is upper-case and lies between B and D inclusive'
4      'E'    : write out 'Letter is upper-case E'
5    default  : write out 'Letter is none of A to E'
6  selectend
```

A.3.3 The *with* statement

The *with* statement is shorthand for referencing fields of a record. Within a *with* statement, the fields of one or more specific record variables can be referenced using their field identifiers only.

```
1  with author do
2      authorname := 'Sargent'
3      title := 'An Introduction to Program Design'
4  withend
```

A.3.4 Repetitive statements

There are three kinds of design loops:

The *for* loop

```
1  loop for i := 1 to 20
2      step(s) within loop body
3  loopend
```

A *for* loop is executed a predetermined number of times and the loop control variable, i in the example above, must not be updated within the body of the loop. Variables referenced in the loop must be initialized outside it.

The *while* loop

```
1  initialize variables
2  loop while expression
3      step(s) within loop body
4  loopend
```

The *expression* controlling the repetition must be of type boolean. The body of the loop must contain a statement which enables the value of the expression to be updated in order to ensure the loop eventually ceases execution. Variables which appear in the expression must be initialized prior to the loop statement.

The *repeat* loop

```
1  repeat
2      step(s) within loop body
3  until expression
```

The *expression* controlling the repetition must be of type boolean. The body of the loop must contain a statement which enables the value of the expression to be updated in order to ensure the loop eventually ceases execution. A *repeat* loop is always executed at least once.

A.3.5 Design indentation

The steps occuring between any of the following matching pairs should be indented:

```
loop – loopend
repeat – until
select – selectend
with – withend
```

The steps in the *then* and *else* clauses of an *if* statement should be indented.

A.4 PROCEDURE DESIGNS

Procedure designs are presented in a similar way to their specification except that the process part is replaced by a design showing *how* the results are to be obtained from the source data. The format of the design is the same as that for a program. The source data are listed one after the other as a formal parameter list. The type of each parameter is as given in the specification of the routine. Results are listed in a similar way.

minimax

---

first, second, third

1.1	*largest := first*
1.2	*smallest := first*
2.1	if *second > largest* then
2.2	*largest := second*
2.3	ifend
3.1	if *third > largest* then
3.2	*largest := third*
3.3	ifend
4.1	if *second < smallest* then
4.2	*smallest := second*
4.3	ifend
5.1	if *third < smallest* then
5.2	*smallest := third*
5.3	ifend

---

largest, smallest

A.5 PROCEDURE CALLS

The general form of a procedure call is illustrated by

1 *minimax(initial, middle, last, max, min)*

where *initial, middle* and *last* are actual parameters corresponding to the formal source data parameters and *max, min* are the actual parameters corresponding to the results. The actual parameters would have to be declared in the data table of the calling program.

A.6 FUNCTION DESIGNS

The same design notation is used as for procedures but a function result always has the same identifier as the function.

A.7 FUNCTION CALLS

Functions are always called in expressions. For example, if *name* is a string variable:

    loop for i := 1 to length(name);
    if length(name) > 10 then

A.8 STANDARD FUNCTIONS

abs, chr, copy, length, odd, ord, pos, pred, round, succ, trunc
Reference to their defintions can be found in the index.

A.9 STANDARD PROCEDURES

delete, insert
Reference to their defintions can be found in the index.

A.10 ASCII CODES

The following values are the ASCII codes for the alphanumeric keys on a keyboard:

32	space	51	3	70	F	89	Y	108	l
33	!	52	4	71	G	90	Z	109	m
34	"	53	5	72	H	91	[	110	n
35	#	54	6	73	I	92	\	111	o
36	$	55	7	74	J	93	]	112	p
37	%	56	8	75	K	94	^	113	q
38	&	57	9	76	L	95	_	114	r
39	'	58	:	77	M	96		115	s
40	(	59	;	78	N	97	a	116	t
41	)	60	<	79	O	98	b	117	u
42	*	61	=	80	P	99	c	118	v
43	+	62	>	81	Q	100	d	119	w
44	,	63	?	82	R	101	e	120	x
45	-	64	@	83	S	102	f	121	y
46	.	65	A	84	T	103	g	122	z
47	/	66	B	85	U	104	h	123	{
48	0	67	C	86	V	105	i	124		
49	1	68	D	87	W	106	j	125	}
50	2	69	E	88	X	107	k	126	~

Related titles are available in McGraw-Hill's International Software Quality Assurance Series